The Global Brewery Industry

NEW HORIZONS IN INTERNATIONAL BUSINESS

Series Editor: Peter J. Buckley, Centre for International Business, University of Leeds (CIBUL), UK

The New Horizons in International Business series has established itself as the world's leading forum for the presentation of new ideas in international business research. It offers pre-eminent contributions in the areas of multinational enterprise – including foreign direct investment, business strategy and corporate alliances, global competitive strategies, and entrepreneurship. In short, this series constitutes essential reading for academics, business strategists and policy makers alike.

Titles in the series include:

The Global Brewery Industry

Markets, Strategies, and Rivalries

Edited by

Jens Gammelgaard

Copenhagen Business School, Denmark

Christoph Dörrenbächer

Berlin School of Economics and Law, Germany

NEW HORIZONS IN INTERNATIONAL BUSINESS

Edward Elgar

Cheltenham, UK • Northampton, MA, USA

Published by
Edward Elgar Publishing Limited
The Lypiatts
15 Lansdown Road
Cheltenham
Glos GL50 2JA
UK

Edward Elgar Publishing, Inc.
William Pratt House
9 Dewey Court
Northampton
Massachusetts 01060
USA

A catalogue record for this book
is available from the British Library

Library of Congress Control Number: 2013932068

This book is available electronically in the ElgarOnline.com
Business Subject Collection, E-ISBN 978 1 78100 635 1

ISBN 978 1 78100 634 4

Typeset by Servis Filmsetting Ltd, Stockport, Cheshire
Printed and bound in Great Britain by T.J. International Ltd, Padstow

Contents

Contributors

Magnus Andersson is an assistant professor at the Department of Human Geography, Lund University. He is also affiliated with the Centre for East and South-East Asian Studies. His current research focuses on socio-economic development in emerging markets in East and South-East Asia.

Christoph Dörrenbächer is a professor of organizational design and behaviour in international business at the Berlin School of Economics and Law, Germany. His current research focus is on subsidiary role development, headquarters–subsidiary relationships and careers in multinational corporations.

Jens Gammelgaard is Associate Professor at the Copenhagen Business School in Denmark. His main research interests are the strategic development of subsidiaries, as well as mergers and acquisitions, and strategic alliances. Furthermore he researches the brewery sector.

Mike Geppert is Professor of Comparative International Management and Organization Studies at the Surrey Business School, UK. His research focus is on cross-national comparisons of management and organizations, and on sociopolitical issues in multinational corporations.

Mélanie Gilles is a recent graduate from the MSc programme in International Business, HEC Paris School of Management, France.

Michael W. Hansen is Associate Professor at the Center for Business and Development Studies at the Copenhagen Business School in Denmark. His main research interests are strategies of multinational corporations (MNCs) and developing countries and emerging markets (focus on Asia and India), linkages between MNCs and local firms in developing countries, outward foreign direct investment from developing countries, and foreign direct investment and the environment.

Bersant Hobdari is Associate Professor at the Copenhagen Business School in Denmark. His main research interests are the governance relations between headquarters and subsidiaries, as well as location decisions of multinational enterprises.

Anne K. Hoenen is a PhD candidate at the Institute for International Business at the WU Wien, Vienna University of Economics and Business, Austria. Before joining academia, she gained professional experience in the airline and fast-moving consumer goods industry working in Germany, France, Switzerland, Singapore and Denmark. Her research focuses on the organization and strategy of multinational corporations from an agency theory perspective, internationalization and strategy making processes.

Graham Hollinshead is Reader in International and Comparative Human Resource Management at the Hertfordshire Business School, University of Hertfordshire, UK. His research interests include organizational transition in Central and Eastern Europe, international sourcing of business services, critical international management studies and employment practices in multinational corporations.

Kristian Jakobsen is Assistant Professor at the Copenhagen Business School in Denmark. His main research interests relate to the timing and performance of foreign market entry by multinational enterprises. Furthermore, his research interests encompass mergers and acquisitions, foreign direct investment (FDI) in emerging markets and the brewing industry.

Ari Kokko is a professor of international business at Copenhagen Business School. His current research focuses in particular on the role of trade and foreign direct investment in the development process.

Andres Kuusik (PhD) is Senior Lecturer of Marketing at the University of Tartu, Estonia. His research interests are related to customer loyalty, destination marketing and with psycho physiological measurements in product development.

Jorma Larimo is Professor of International Marketing at the University of Vaasa, Finland. He also holds a part-time Professorship of International Marketing at the University of Tartu, Estonia. His current research interests focus on international acquisition and joint venture strategies, subsidiary survival and divestments and foreign market and marketing strategies by small- to medium-sized enterprises (SMEs).

Lars Lund-Thomsen is Research Librarian at the AU Library, part of business and social sciences at the University of Aarhus, Denmark. He specializes in searches on business information.

Mairi Maclean is Professor of International Management and Organisation Studies at the University of Exeter Business School, UK. Her research interests include international business elites and elite power, storytelling, philanthropy, history and strategy, and comparative organization studies.

Erik S. Madsen is Associate Professor at the Department of Economics at the University of Aarhus, Denmark. Research interests include industrial economics and international economics.

Ana María Munar is Associate Professor at the Department of International Economics and Management, Copenhagen Business School, Denmark. Her research interests are in tourism and information and communication technologies, globalization processes, destination branding and policy and trends in tourism education.

Kurt Pedersen is Associate Professor at the Department of Business Administration at the University of Aarhus, Denmark. Research interests include the history of economic theory and business history.

Nicolai Pogrebnyakov is an assistant professor at Copenhagen Business School, Denmark. His research focuses on international business strategy, cross-border issues in the technology industry and technology strategy.

Caroline Ruhe is an MSc student in finance and banking as well as international management at the University of Cologne in Germany. Her main focus of study and interests are corporate finance, banking and strategic development.

Janne Smith is a recent graduate from the MSc programme in Business Administration and Economics, Norwegian School of Economics (NHH).

Seijiro Takeshita, PhD, is Director of Mizuho International plc in London, UK. His current research interests are transformation of business systems and diverging styles of governance under competing forms of capitalism.

Ian M. Taplin is Professor of Sociology and International Studies in the Department of Sociology, Wake Forest University, North Carolina, USA and Visiting Research Professor at Bordeaux Ecole de Management. His current research focuses upon the wine industry in California and North Carolina, looking specifically at the role of networks in cluster development and knowledge sharing.

Svenja Troll is a recent graduate at Copenhagen Business School in Denmark from the MSc programme in International Marketing and Management. Her main research interests are internationalization and expansion strategies of multinational corporations.

Urmas Varblane is Professor of International Business at the University of Tartu, Estonia. His current research interests focus on the

internationalization of firms, spillover effects of foreign direct investment, and innovation behaviour of firms.

Christopher Williams, PhD, is Assistant Professor of International
Business and Walter A. Thompson Faculty Fellow at the Richard Ivey
School of Business in Canada. His research interests include innovation in
multinational enterprises, knowledge creation and transfer, and offshore
outsourcing.

Andreas Zaby is a professor at the Berlin School of Economics and Law.
His work focuses on international management and entrepreneurial
finance topics, particularly in the context of high-technology industries.

Foreword

There are far too few global industry studies in international business research. There is much current attention paid to context in terms of host country and source country conditions, but there has been a decline in research on the industry context. In the modern world economy, global industry context is extremely important as it determines the parameters of competition and constrains the feasible strategic choices of firms in that industry. The evolving technology at industry level is also a crucial determinant of developments at both firm and intra-firm levels of analysis. Bringing the industry back in is, therefore, vital for an understanding of global developments. There are far too many atomised studies of individual firms which abstract from the industry context. I am, therefore, delighted to write the foreword for this book on the global brewery industry because it pays full attention to the industry context when examining the strategies of individual firms. The industry context helps us to understand restructuring by mergers and acquisitions, the interaction of supply and demand factors and the development of the structures of multinational brewing companies. The authors of the various chapters show great awareness of the context in which their analyses are conducted and this gives a fully rounded approach to global strategy in the brewing industry. The authors and editors are to be congratulated on their in-depth understanding of the industry and the companies within it. This gives a satisfying unity to the book and allows the reader to emerge with a fully contextualised understanding of the global brewing industry.

Peter J. Buckley
Professor of International Business
Centre for International Business, University of Leeds (CIBUL)
December 2012

Acknowledgements

The volume represents the collective efforts of the contributing authors. While about one-third of the authors are affiliated with Copenhagen Business School, this book unites authors from many European countries, and from North America and Asia. First drafts of the contributions were presented and discussed at an international workshop hosted by the Copenhagen Business School in the autumn of 2011. The workshop was funded by the Department of International Economics and Management, and was strongly supported by the Head of Department, Niels Mygind. Revised chapters were submitted in the summer of 2012, and each submission was reviewed by two peers. Final papers were submitted in December 2012. The Berlin School of Economics and Law, Germany, kindly supported technical manuscript preparation and indexing of the volume.

Introduction

Jens Gammelgaard and Christoph Dörrenbächer

This volume focuses on the challenges brewery companies face as they operate in globalized markets. We intend to discuss various international business themes and to present new data on the developments in this industry. We offer new insights into relevant market developments, both globally and in specific markets. In addition, we analyse some of the major players in the industry through longitudinal studies. Finally, on the basis of conceptualizations in the international business literature, we discuss various reasons for these developments.

The brewery industry has specific characteristics that make it worthy of a detailed analysis. It is an industry that: (a) has adopted similar technologies globally, (b) offers a homogeneous product (although differentiated by brand), (c) is dominated by a few large multinational corporations (MNCs) and (d) is highly internationalized. This 'alignment' across nations and firms makes the brewery industry a fruitful context for the analysis of economic, organizational and strategic effects. However, the industry also encompasses substantial cross-country differences, especially institutional differences with regard to sector-specific regulations and subsidy levels (or tax concessions) on the one hand, and societal concerns about alcohol abuse on the other. Furthermore, formerly important West European markets show a pattern of decreasing consumption, whereas emerging markets are experiencing the opposite. In addition, MNCs from what can be characterized as small- or medium-sized countries, such as Heineken (Netherlands), Carlsberg (Denmark), Interbrew (Belgium; now known as AB InBev) and SAB (South Africa, now known as SABMiller), have adopted successful merger and acquisition (M&A) strategies, whereas important players from large countries, such as Anheuser-Busch and Miller in the US and Scottish & Newcastle in the UK, have become takeover targets.

Another interesting feature of the brewery industry is the specific internationalization path taken by its major players. The industry has a long history of internationalization, with Heineken and Carlsberg being pioneers. However, the activities of many other brewers were typically local and, therefore, internationally fragmented until the 1960s, with most focused on expansion within domestic markets. In the 1980s, the industry entered a transitional period, as firms learned to deal with more diverse economic, political, institutional and cultural environments. It was only in the 1990s that the industry became highly concentrated and truly global. Consequently, instead of focusing on small takeover targets, which have already been acquired by the big players in many markets, the focus since the beginning of this century has been on the acquisition of large MNCs.

This shift, in turn, reflects a change in entry mode decisions. In the early and transitional stages of the internationalization process, breweries concentrated on less risky export strategies, and they often liaised with local agents and distributors. International joint ventures with local breweries also began to play a significant role in the transitional period. In the past decade, however, international acquisitions and the number of large, wholly owned subsidiaries in the brewery industry have increased significantly. Given the need for a greater commitment and the amount of resources involved, the establishment of a wholly owned subsidiary through an acquisition carries a higher risk – both financially and politically – than other entry modes. However, these risks seem to pay off, at least for some players. M&As offer MNCs quick access to new markets and, more importantly, to the brands owned by target firms. Simultaneously, they enhance the possibility for global brand utilization.

The aim of this book is to shed more light on some of these processes and to discuss different international business themes in relation to this particular industry. The various market developments and the strategic decisions made by brewery companies in global markets are analysed in the context of the MNC. To frame and introduce the different chapters in this volume, this introductory chapter first provides a historical overview of the industry, and then looks at contemporary industry characteristics, market trends and internationalization patterns. It concludes with a presentation of the main findings of the individual chapters.

HISTORICAL OVERVIEW

Most brewing historians agree that the brewing of beer started in the ancient urban civilization of Mesopotamia, most likely around 6000 BC, although brewing may have originated in an ancient civilization in China even earlier (Hornsby 2003; Poelmans and Swinnen 2011). Beer was later brewed in the outer areas of the Roman Empire, where wine was scarce. In general, the Romans usually drank only wine and considered beer drinkers to be 'barbarians' (Poelmans and Swinnen 2011).

In the Middle Ages, brewing beer gradually became a commercial activity as brewers moved from a focus on family-related self-supply to brewing as a craft. At that time, beer was produced in monasteries. Beer was used as a supplement for water, which often was polluted, and it was also utilized for spiritual, medicinal and nutritional purposes. German monks began adding extracts of the hop plant for preservation and taste purposes. However, over time, monasteries lost their market dominance because of the Reformation and, later, the French Revolution. Furthermore, local policy makers supported private breweries, which could be taxed (Poelmans and Swinnen 2011). Simultaneously, demand in Europe was increasing, partly because water was polluted in many city areas. In Denmark, for example, adults consumed an average of four to six litres of beer per day (Kjersgaard 1976).

The nineteenth century was an important epoch for the brewery industry, as a number of radical product innovations took place, while external developments also significantly affected the sector. The diffusion of innovations that stabilized beer's production process – such as the thermometer, the hydrometer and Pasteur's discovery of the role of yeast in fermentation – paved the way for the industrialization of beer production (Cornell 2003). Furthermore, the development of trains and steamboats facilitated export opportunities. Simultaneously, the glass bottle (and, later, the metal can) and new methods of sealing bottles were invented (Poelmans and Swinnen 2011). Notably, many of today's large players entered the scene during this century: Denmark's Carlsberg was founded in 1847, Heineken of Amsterdam was established in 1864, Anheuser-Busch from the US was established in 1860 and South African Breweries was founded in 1895.

The post-World War II history of the brewery industry is, to a large extent, a story of the growing impact of the companies just mentioned, initially on their own national markets, then on selected foreign markets and, recently, on a global basis. Until the 1960s, the production and sale of beer was mainly a local business for several reasons, including the product's short storage life and the difficulty of transporting it over greater distances (Benson-Armer et al. 1999). From the 1960s onwards, technological innovations, such as the more effective (and, later, computer-aided) control of the brewing process, allowed for the production of longer-life beers. Moreover, faster process throughput, improved packaging (mainly in terms of bottling and canning) and the availability of more sophisticated road infrastructure facilitated the mass production and nationwide distribution of beer.

In the wake of these changes, national brewery industries experienced remarkable horizontal and vertical integration from the 1970s onwards, which in turn led to a highly concentrated industry (Gourvish 1998). By the end of the 1990s, most national beer markets (with the notable exceptions of China and Germany) were dominated by two or three players, most of which were national champions, who shared more than 80 per cent of the market (Benson-Armer et al. 1999). This dominance, combined with the high costs associated with trading beer over long distances and the persistence of national differences in consumer preferences, beer types, drinking habits, taxation and regulation allowed for only limited integration across national markets. This was reflected in the low concentration of global beer production around the turn of the millennium. In 1998, for example, the five largest breweries in the world only accounted for 25 per cent of global beer output.

However, recent years have brought a dramatic catch-up process in terms of the global concentration and internationalization of the brewery industry, with the top five players in the global beer market accounting for almost half of global beer production in 2010 (Euromonitor International 2010). As a result, the brewery industry, once an archetype of a 'multinational industry' with significant pressure for local manufacturing and products adapted to local tastes, has gradually become a 'global industry' (Bartlett and Ghoshal 1998) in which companies seek to realize cross-border standardization advantages, mainly by introducing global brands and by capitalizing on synergies in marketing and distribution.

INDUSTRY CHARACTERISTICS AND MARKET TRENDS

Beer is 'an alcoholic beverage usually made from malted cereal grain (as barley), flavoured with hops, and brewed by slow fermentation' (Merriam-Webster 2011). Today, there are about 150 different styles of beer sold in the world, most of which originate from Germany, the UK, Ireland, France, Belgium and North America (Brewers Association 2011). All styles of beer can be grouped into three broad categories: ale, lager and hybrid/mixed. Ales and lagers have distinct production processes and use specific types of yeast. They have different tastes – lager is typically characterized as 'smoother, crisper, and more subtle in taste and aroma' and should be drunk cold, whereas ale is known as 'strong, assertive, and more robust in taste' and is typically drunk at cellar temperature (Dietz 2007). Pale lager (such as pilsner) is by far the most commonly produced and consumed type of beer in the world, with all of the industry's top players focusing on this type of beer. Hybrid/mixed beers do not fit into either the ale or the lager category. The difference lies in the unique way in which these beers are brewed. For example, ale and lager production techniques are often combined, or special ingredients are added in the production process, such as fruit, rice, vegetables or spices (Eddings 2011).

As with many other consumer goods, beer is increasingly facing price-based market segmentation. Consumption of both low-price beers and premium beers is growing at above-average rates in most regions of the world. In particular, the trend towards 'premiumization' has been picked up and advanced by the major brewers. Given their command of distribution channels and their marketing expertise, these brewers are particularly well suited to capitalize on the fact that production costs for premium beer are only slightly higher than the production costs for discount beer (Madsen et al. 2011).

The general trend towards decreasing on-premise and increasing off-premise consumption of beer is also a challenge for breweries. On-premise consumption of beer refers to consumption at the site of sale, typically in restaurants, cafes, pubs and bars. Off-premise consumption takes place at home to a large extent. In such cases, the beer is typically bought in supermarkets, petrol stations or alcohol stores (WHO 2004). Currently, about 75 per cent of all beer consumed in Europe and the US is consumed off-premise (Brewers of Europe 2011; Goldammer 2008). This trend towards off-premise consumption has three important implications. First, breweries have less control over their distribution channels, as they must deal with the strong bargaining power typically held by the highly concentrated retail sector (*Economist* 2011). Second, the purchase of beer from retail outlets leads to significant changes in the brands chosen. Third, the increased off-premise consumption of beer not only results in higher packaging expenses but also requires a strong emphasis on brand packaging, which plays a critical role in consumers' purchasing decisions (Datamonitor 2011).

Marketing and its various components, such as branding, are of vital importance in the brewery industry (Lopez 2007), especially because the comparatively few technological achievements in the industry in the last century have either been of a non-proprietary nature or did not have long-term effects on the competitiveness of first-movers. In addition, real product differences among particular styles of beer are minimal (Madsen et al. 2011). In fact, older studies using blind taste tests indicate that most people have no (Allison and Uhl 1964; McConnell 1968), or only a very limited, ability to distinguish among beers of the same style in terms of aroma or taste (Jacoby et al. 1971). Consequently, competitiveness depends on brand values and efficient, distinctive marketing strategies. In general, marketing and sales expenses are high at the large breweries, with the leading breweries investing as much as 11 per cent to 13 per cent of their annual turnover in marketing and sales (SABMiller 2010; Heineken 2010, AB InBev 2010). This ratio is expected to increase to 15 per cent in the near future, which would put it at a level similar to those seen among global consumer goods companies, such as Unilever and Procter & Gamble (*Economist* 2011).

MNC breweries are also challenged by global market developments. Sales have been affected by the stagnation in almost all traditional high-volume markets in the developed world (Colen and Swinnen 2011), with beer consumption declining recently in many of these markets (for example, in Germany, the UK and Japan; Credit Suisse 2010). Notable growth in demand is evident in emerging economies, such as China, Russia and Brazil (Colen and Swinnen 2011), but profit margins are considerably lower in these countries. Global breweries need to invest heavily in order to access distribution channels and to make their brands known in these regions, while average purchasing power (measured in gross domestic product (GDP) per capita) remains relatively low. Market forecasts corroborate these trends. Canadean, a leading business intelligence firm focused on the beverage industry, expects an overwhelming majority of all growth in beer consumption between 2010 and 2016 to occur in Asia, Latin America, Eastern Europe and Africa. The US market, which has experienced modest growth over the last 30 years, is expected to remain stable, while a significant downturn in the West European markets is likely (Canadean 2011).

Other challenges lie in the dramatic changes that are underway in the brewery industry's institutional environment. One example is the opening up of Eastern Europe, where the hops and malting industry was strongly regulated and monopolized during the communist era. When these countries became independent, producers were freed from state control. However, production fell as the inefficiently run businesses were unable to handle the transition. This enabled foreign breweries to enter the market, where they either made direct investments in the value chain to secure the supply and ensure the quality of hops and malt, or they built close relationships with local suppliers by offering technical assistance and credit. Later, another institutional change – the 'EU-nization' of the market – improved conditions for independent producers through, for example, subsidies. As a result, the foreign breweries decreased their commitment to these suppliers (Swinnen and Van Herck 2011).

Another well-known example of an institutional change is the German purity law, which was introduced in 1516 and remained in place until 1987, when the European Community forced its repeal. The law obliged breweries to only use barley, malt, hops, yeast and water when brewing beer. This law affected intra-regional trade within Germany and it restricted imports, thereby preventing the development of large breweries that could become MNCs. Even today, the German brewery industry is characterized by the presence of many (approximately 1300) small breweries, and most local customers still prefer local varieties (Tongeren 2011). Moreover, German beer is still primarily sold in bottles, which again attests to the low level of integration and the lack of focus on exports (George 2011).

Yet another example of a strong institutional impact in the brewery industry is found in the US. The nationwide prohibition of alcohol from 1919–33, in combination with the economic crisis of 1929, resulted in the closure of half of the breweries in the US (Poelmans and Swinnen 2011). After the repeal of Prohibition, a three-tier system of distribution was introduced, such that brewers could not distribute their products directly to customers, on-trade businesses or retailers (Adams 2006). In addition, the Twenty-First Amendment to the United States Constitution, which was imposed by the federal government when legalizing the production and consumption of beer in 1933, turned complete control of the industry over to the individual states. Today, the diffusion of control is reflected in the different regulations across the states. In the state of Delaware, for instance, persons under the age of 21 are not allowed to enter premises selling or serving alcohol, whereas in Wisconsin one can drink at the age of 18 (Division of Alcohol and Tobacco Enforcement 2012; Kamstrup et al. 2012).

A final example of institutional impact is evident in the tight regulation of the Indian brewery industry, which was a strong deterrent to foreign direct investment (FDI) throughout the 1990s. However, the recent loosening of the restrictions immediately led many foreign breweries to invest (Arora et al. 2011; Hoenen and Hansen, Chapter 6, this volume).

INTERNATIONALIZATION

Internationalization processes in the brewery industry can be traced back to medieval times. Hopped beer was shipped from the Netherlands to England as early as the year 1300 (Unger 2004). Furthermore, some of today's major players – especially those from small home countries – internationalized their businesses soon after their foundation. Heineken, for instance, was founded in 1863 and almost immediately began to export beer to neighbouring European countries (especially France) and to the Dutch East Indies (now Indonesia). The same is true for Carlsberg, which was founded in 1847. By 1868, the company was exporting beer to Scotland.

Despite this early international trade, the overall trade of beer has never reached the levels evident among many other finished goods. Today, only about 5 per cent of global beer production is traded across national borders. This is because beer is a voluminous product that mostly consists of water, which makes its transport over large distances costly (Colen and Swinnen 2011). However, the low tradability of beer has been offset by licensing agreements and, increasingly, FDI. Over the last three decades, the number of breweries operated by the top players in the industry has increased dramatically. Currently, Heineken operates 140 breweries throughout the world, while AB InBev has 121, SABMiller has 96, and Carlsberg has 80 (Heineken 2010; AB InBev 2010; Carlsberg 2010; SABMiller 2010).

What motivated brewery groups to build up and acquire an increasing number of breweries abroad given the limited benefits associated with the cross-border integration of production? First, internationalizing companies aimed to gain footholds in those regions of the world where beer consumption was rising fast. While the 1990s and early 2000s brought significant investments in Central and Eastern Europe, the years since the new millennium have been characterized by huge investments in the Chinese market and in larger Latin American markets, such as Mexico and Brazil. Second, large brewery groups aimed to increase their initial positions in foreign markets to become dominant players in order to reap the maximum benefits of integrating nationally confined activities, such as management, distribution and production. Finally, with more globally minded consumer groups on the rise in many countries, large brewery groups aimed to benefit from the application of globally uniform marketing campaigns, which were developed at headquarters, across a larger number of local markets. Examples of such global marketing campaigns and associated slogans are 'That calls for a Carlsberg', 'This Bud is for you' (AB InBev) and 'Heineken refreshes the parts other beers cannot reach' (*Economist* 2011). Such global marketing campaigns are particularly lucrative, as expenses for brands are fixed costs that are generally independent of sales volumes (Madsen et al. 2011, p. 11). However, the centrally branded beers (such as Heineken, Budweiser, Stella Artois and Carlsberg) are produced locally, often at the expense of locally branded beers (Dieng et al. 2009).

As previously mentioned, most international growth in the industry has been driven by M&A activity. As in many industries (Wortmann 2008; UNCTAD 2010), organic growth through greenfield investments, which played a role in the early days of the industry's internationalization, is of no or very little importance today. Strikingly, however, one type of firm seems to be particularly successful in the brewery industry's acquisition merry-go-round. A comparative study by Geppert et al. (forthcoming) shows that family-owned firms from small, coordinated market economies (such as Heineken from the Netherlands, Carlsberg of Denmark and Interbrew of Belgium), which are backed by comparatively long traditions of international activities, show less risky and more sustainable international growth than publicly-owned firms from large home markets. The latter firms, which by nature of their large home markets often lack international experience, have engaged in precipitous catch-up internationalization strategies in response to pressure from the stock markets (as Taplin et al. (Chapter 10) and Dörrenbächer and Zaby (Chapter 8) demonstrate for Anheuser-Busch and Scottish & Newcastle, this volume).

Furthermore, the brewery industry has experienced numerous small- and medium-sized cross-border acquisitions in recent decades (Ebneth and Theuvsen 2007). Heineken, the most active company in this respect (Madsen et al. 2011), acquired no fewer than 35 smaller breweries around the world between 1990 and 2008 (Dieng et al. 2009; for more information, see Dörrenbächer and Zaby, Chapter 8, this volume). Often, these acquisitions involve partial shareholdings. Partial shareholdings offer the MNC a 'foot in the door' in areas where a 'big bang' market entry is not feasible due to market and ownership structures. Alternatively, such shareholdings may enable the MNC to enlarge its influence in a given country by gaining access to more firms in the local market (Meyer and Tran 2006). Dominant motives for acquisitions in the brewery industry include the desire to capitalize on synergy effects gained through upgrades of plant technology and management, cost efficiencies through layoffs and rationalization, and control over value chains and distribution channels (Dörrenbächer and Zaby (Chapter 8); Gammelgaard and Hobdari (Chapter 7), this volume).

Furthermore, M&A in the brewery industry is often a consequence of multi-point competition (Chen 1996). In this regard, a foreign brewery's market entrance can result in counter-attacks from other international players, as this volume documents for India (Hoenen and Hansen, Chapter 6, this volume) and Estonia (Larimo et al., Chapter 5, this volume). This trend has also been evident elsewhere, such as in China (Bai et al. 2011) and Russia (Deconinck and Swinnen 2011). In some contexts, these attacks are not restricted to the host countries but are extended to the main competitors' home countries. One example is Heineken, which, via its ownership of Alken-Mae, holds around 14 per cent of the Belgium market, home to its archrival AB Interbrew (Persyn et al. 2011).

As these insights indicate, MNC breweries operate in a global market that is consolidated and highly competitive. The overall aims of this book, therefore, are to analyse the dynamics of these markets and to illustrate how brewery firms act strategically in this environment.

AIM, OUTLINE AND CONTRIBUTIONS OF THIS BOOK

The short introduction above points to international business as a relevant discipline when studying the brewery industry and its main players. Most books on international business choose a specific theme, such as entry mode or headquarters–subsidiary relationships, and then survey that theme in different contexts. This book approaches its subject from the other direction – it starts with a particular industry and then looks for relevant international business themes. A careful reading of the individual contributions of this volume highlights six overarching themes: (1) international market developments and firm performance, (2) host country institutional effects, (3) multi-point competition and rivalries, (4) cross-border M&A integration and subsidiary development, (5) leadership and internationalization, and (6) boundless customer interfaces through such elements as social media and tourism. These themes serve as the structure for this volume.

Part 1, 'International market developments and firm performance', consists of a chapter by Pedersen, Madsen and Lund-Thomsen, which investigates how M&As have led to restructurings in the international brewery industry. It is followed by Jakobsen's more detailed survey of East European markets.

Pedersen et al. find that the top four breweries (AB InBev, SABMiller, Heineken and Carlsberg) have *not* performed better than a control group of 200 large breweries. This puts the rationale for the substantial numbers of M&As evident in the contemporary brewery industry into question, as the authors find no proof that efficiency gains or improved market power enhance performance. This is a key finding in relation to the international business literature, which the authors suggest only guides us in how to handle internationalization (for example, it provides advice on when to engage in FDI), but fails to tell us whether a decision was the best strategy in retrospect.

Jakobsen, who follows up on these issues in Chapter 2, concludes that the large international players have started to withdraw from Eastern Europe, and that those who stay face declining markets due to unfavourable changes in demographics. Furthermore, brewing companies are challenged by increasing regulation in this region. Despite these negative developments, Jakobsen suggests that foreign breweries are gaining from their FDI into this region. However, their success depends on first-mover advantages and/or the achievement of a leading position in the market.

In Part 2, 'Host country institutional effects', Hollinshead and Maclean (Chapter 3), as well as Andersson and Kokko (Chapter 4) investigate institutional effects in countries that are rarely studied, that is, Serbia and Lao PDR. Together, the studies illustrate that an MNC that wishes to operate in either country would face significant institutional challenges, which would require a differentiated approach to such activities such as the development of an entry strategy and subsidiary management.

Hollinshead and Maclean provide an overview of the political changes that have taken place in Serbia following the civil war, and they connect those changes with privatization and FDI. They study institutional effects through a case study of a Turkish brewery that has acquired a Serbian brewery. In focusing on micro-political issues and, especially, on the conflicts between the expatriated foreign management and the local work force, the chapter illustrates the discrepancies arising from the differences of a Turkish headquarters following West European standards, and the logic of internationalization in the brewery industry, which is based on rationalization on the one hand and a shared ethos based on worker solidarity and principles of self-management on the other. The authors also investigate the destiny of the subsidiary, which was eventually closed. In contrast, most surveys in international business analyse only successful 'centre of excellence' subsidiaries.

Andersson and Kokko take a look into the brewery industry in Lao PDR. Previously, sector regulations ensured that only one type of beer was offered. Furthermore, all beer was produced at a single location but offered across the country. Lao PDR therefore offers a perfect setup for an investigation of price determination. The chapter adds yet another element that seems to be neglected in most international business surveys – the impact of transportation-related costs and infrastructure. As Lao PDR is a developing country, the transportation of beer by lorry was impossible in some cases, leading to higher prices. Subsequent improvements in the infrastructure, however, led to substantial price reductions.

Part 3 investigates 'Multi-point competition and rivalries'. In this regard, Larimo, Kuusik and Varblane (Chapter 5) investigate the strategic attacks and counter-attacks of foreign breweries in the Estonian market. Hoenen and Hansen (Chapter 6) analyse 'follow-the-leader' market entrances in the Indian brewery industry.

Larimo et al. study the three leading Estonian breweries, all of which were acquired by Nordic breweries after the fall of the Iron Curtain. For an extended period of time, Saku was the market leader, but the second largest Estonian brewery, A.LeCoq, has managed to challenge this position by increasing its market share from 10 per cent to 30 per cent over the span of a few years. Interestingly, the market appears to be settled in an almost collusive agreement. When questioned, neither of the two leading market players indicate that they intend to acquire the third largest player,

Viru. Instead, the companies compete through product launches and TV commercials.

Like the Estonian market, the Indian beer market has an oligopolistic structure. Hoenen and Hansen claim that international business studies have apparently forgotten Hymer's (1976) seminal notion on FDI in relation to competitive industry structure dynamics, where FDI is a consequence of the imperfections of such markets and where firms can utilize their firm-specific advantages. In their investigation, Hoenen and Hansen look at 'follow-the-leader' behaviour. India, an emerging country, is a market with a very low average consumption of beer per inhabitant. Therefore, this market is highly competitive and FDI is likely to lead to overcapacity. In such markets, it is of the utmost importance to become the market leader or to capture first-mover advantages (see Jakobsen, Chapter 2, this volume). On the basis of Carlsberg's activities in the country, Hoenen and Hansen demonstrate that massive follow-the-leader investments in the Indian brewery markets were unleashed after Heineken's initial investment. Only 14 months after Heineken's initial move, the other four breweries among the global top five had entered the market. Carlsberg was basically forced into this game, given its small size relative to the other actors.

In Part 4, 'Cross-border M&A integration and subsidiary development', the focus is on the 'destiny' of acquired breweries. Gammelgaard and Hobdari (Chapter 7) investigate six of Carlsberg's subsidiaries and their development over the years, while Dörrenbächer and Zaby (Chapter 8) examine Heineken's two largest takeovers: Scottish & Newcastle and FEMSA.

Gammelgaard and Hobdari show that Carlsberg's takeovers typically led to a modernization process that involved rationalization and investment in technology at the newly acquired subsidiaries. Therefore, the development of these subsidiaries in terms of strategic mandates and autonomy is highly ambiguous. Apparently, these subsidiaries win and lose mandates simultaneously. This trajectory fits Carlsberg's newly implemented GloCal strategy, which seeks to balance global integration with local responsiveness. This chapter offers an alternative view to that offered in much of the headquarters–subsidiary relationship literature, which suggests either a positive or a negative development.

Dörrenbächer and Zaby investigate the integration of newly acquired subsidiaries from the viewpoint of headquarters. Referring to a previous study on Heineken's small- and medium-sized acquisitions (Dieng et al. 2009), which found that target firms are generally absorbed by Heineken (referred to as 'Heinekenization'), Dörrenbächer and Zaby investigate the likelihood of best practices being transferred from large acquisition targets to Heineken as the acquiring firm. The study finds little evidence of such transfers, even though the targets are resource rich, and even though Heineken has substantial experience in internationalization processes and acquisition integration.

While Parts 1 through 3 provide analyses on the market level and Part 4 offers investigations at the company level, Part 5, 'Leadership and internationalization', moves our focus to the level of individual actors by investigating managerial decision-making and its effects on internationalization. Williams, Takeshita, Gilles, Ruhe, Smith and Troll (Chapter 9) investigate the case of Japan's Asahi Breweries. Taplin, Gammelgaard, Dörrenbächer and Geppert (Chapter 10) examine the US-American brewer Anheuser-Busch. In both cases, leadership is found to have a huge impact on the company's internationalization, with Asahi's internationalization a success and the internationalization of Anheuser-Busch ending in a fiasco. The latter contributed to the company being taken over by Belgian Inbev in 2008 in the largest acquisition in brewery history up to that point.

Williams et al. investigate the strategic decisions underling Asahi's internationalization. By focusing on the impact of leadership succession on internationalization, they address an issue previously neglected in the international business literature. On the basis of their in-depth case study, Williams et al. show that although some leaders 'prepared' their organization for internationalization through their strategizing, a successor chief executive officer (CEO) was needed for the internationalization to be successful. They also demonstrate that these various phases go hand-in-hand with different leadership styles. In the preparation and start-up phases a transformational leadership style is required, while the actual move abroad demands a transactional leadership style in which leaders set clear performance standards.

The impact of leadership on internationalization is also the topic of the chapter by Taplin et al. In their study of the internationalization of Anheuser-Busch, they address a different kind of case. The CEO, overly concerned with increasing competition on the US home market, failed to initiate sound preparations for a move abroad. As a result, the company undertook a number of high-risk foreign investments within a short period of time, which finally resulted in a loss of independence. In contrast to more experienced players in the industry, such as Heineken or Carlsberg (see Dörrenbächer and Zaby, Chapter 8, this volume), Anheuser-Busch and its CEO encountered serious problems related to liabilities of foreignness and liabilities of outsidership (see also Johanson and Vahlne 2009).

Finally, in Part 6, 'Boundless customer interfaces: social media and tourism', we take the customer perspective on board. Pogrebnyakov (Chapter 11) analyses the role of social media (especially Facebook) in the

US microbrewing industry, whereas Munar (Chapter 12) looks at tourism und tourists' drinking behaviour at a particular location in Majorca

Pogrebnyakov's empirical study finds that US microbreweries typically have Facebook pages that are strongly localized to the sites in which their beers are consumed. They are therefore able to engage local customers in discussions related to the brewery and its products, and on issues such as social events like sporting tournaments. Given the fact that, as Pogrebnyakov points out, location strongly matters in social media, large MNC brewery companies wishing to follow this trend would need to tailor their social media profiles to fit individual countries or even individual locations. Language specificity is one reason for doing so and the establishment of a link to local cultural events might be another.

On-site consumption of beer at a particular location is the concern of Munar's chapter. She investigates how the German beer culture produces extreme and novel forms of consumption on the 'Bierstrasse' (Beer Road) on the Spanish island of Majorca. German tourists travel to Bierstrasse to engage in outrageous behaviour based on heavy beer drinking. The restaurants on the Bierstrasse deliberately attract German tourists by imitating German restaurant styles and by advertising their focus on partying. Referring to Kostova and Zaheer's (1999) framework on the legitimacy problems faced by MNCs, Munar reflects on the negative spillovers that this particular consumption pattern might have on the reputation of those German breweries supplying beer to the Bierstrasse.

In summary, this edited volume on the brewery industry and its operations in the global market offers readers an opportunity to investigate various aspects of company strategies, market developments and rivalries. In addition, it offers empirical inroads into different international business themes. Many major MNC breweries are investigated in detail, including Carlsberg, Heineken, Anheuser-Busch and SABMiller, and medium-sized players are also analysed, such as Scottish & Newcastle, Asahi, FEMSA, Baltika, Tetley and Kronenbourg. Furthermore, small players are considered, such as Okocim, Holsten, Feldschlösschen, Pancevo, Saku, A.LeCoq, Carib Beer, Brooklyn Brewery, Sprecher Brewery, Krombacher, Veltins and Oberbayern. Likewise, a number of markets are covered, including the US, China, India, Serbia, Japan, Estonia, Lao PDR and Spain, whereas other chapters investigate entire regions (such as Europe) or the global market. Finally, a wide variety of core international business themes is touched upon, including internationalization strategies, foreign entry modes, cross-border M&A activities, multi-point competition, liabilities of foreignness, headquarters–subsidiary relationships and international marketing.

We hope you will enjoy the manifold aspects of this book, which are based on new data and findings, and we hope it will offer you new insights into the global brewery industry.

REFERENCES

AB InBev (2010), *Anheuser-Bush Inbev Annual Report 2010*, Brussels: AB InBev.

Adams, W.J. (2006), 'Markets: beer in Germany and the United States', *Journal of Economic Perspectives*, **20** (1), 189–205.

Allison, R. and K.P. Uhl (1964), 'Influences of beer brand identification on taste perception', *Journal of Marketing Research*, **1** (August), 36–9.

Arora, A., A. Bhaskar, B. Minten and A. Vandeplas (2011), 'Opening the beer gates: how liberalization caused growth in India's beer market', in J.F.M. Swinnen (ed.), *The Economics of Beer*, Oxford: Oxford University Press, pp. 308–34.

Bai, J., J. Huang, S. Rozelle and M. Boswell (2011), 'Beer battles in China: the struggle over the world's largest beer market', in J.F.M. Swinnen (ed.), *The Economics of Beer*, Oxford: Oxford University Press, pp. 267–86.

Bartlett, C.A. and S. Ghoshal (1998), *Managing across Borders. The Transnational Solution*. Boston, MA: HBS Press.

Benson-Armer, R., J. Leibowitz and D. Ramachandran (1999), 'Global beer: what's on tap?', *McKinsey Quarterly*, February, 111–21.

Brewers Association (2011), *Brewers Association Beer Style Guidelines*, accessed 18 October 2011 at www.brewersassociation.org/pages/publications/beer-style-guidelines.

Brewers of Europe (2011), 'The contribution made by beer to the European economy', mimeo, Amsterdam: Brewers of Europe.

Canadean (2011), 'The global beer market – green shoots of recovery?', News from Canadean, 24 October, accessed 30 October 2011 at www.canadean.com/News/Canadean_News/ItemId/2275.aspx.

Carlsberg (2010), *Carlsberg A/S Annual Report 2010*, Copenhagen V: Carlsberg.

Chen, M. (1996), 'Competitor analysis and interfirm rivalry: toward a theoretical integration', *Academy of Management Review*, **21** (1), 100–34.

Colen, L. and J. Swinnen (2011), 'Beer drinking nations. The determinants of global beer consumption', Working Paper No. 79, mimeo, American Association of Wine Economists (AAWE).

Cornell, M. (2003), *Beer: The Story of the Pint*, London: Headline.

Credit Suisse (2010), 'Global map of beer', accessed 31 October 2011 at http://wpc.186f.edgecastcdn.net/00186F/mps/Equity_Research_Test_Account/11/257/Global_Beer_Map_2010.pdf.

Datamonitor (2011), 'Beer industry profile: China', Industry Profile, New York: Datamonitor Plc.

Deconinck, K. and J.F.M. Swinnen (2011), 'From vodka to Baltika: a perfect storm in the Russian beer market', in J.F.M. Swinnen (ed.), *The Economics of Beer*, Oxford: Oxford University Press, pp. 287–307.

Dieng, S., C. Dörrenbächer and J. Gammelgaard (2009), 'Subsidiary brands as a resource and the redistribution of decision making authority following acquisitions', in S. Finkelstein and C. Cooper (eds), *Advances in Mergers and Acquisitions*, Vol. 8, Bingley: Emerald Group Publishing Limited, pp. 141–60.

Dietz, R. (2007), 'What is the difference between an ale and a lager?', www.beer-faq.com, accessed 25 October 2011 at www.beer-faq.com/difference-ale-lager/

Division of Alcohol and Tobacco Enforcement (2012), *Educational Resources – Server Training Booklet*, accessed 15 May 2012 at http://date.delaware.gov/dabcpublic/program_outline.jsp.

Ebneth, O. and L. Theuvsen (2007), 'Large mergers and acquisitions of European brewing groups – event study evidence on value creation', *Agribusiness*, **23** (3), 377–406.

Economist (2011), 'Sell foam like soap. The global beer industry', *Economist*, 5 May.

Eddings, B. (2011), 'Hybrid beer styles. Neither ale nor lager', Beer.about.com Guide, accessed 25 October 2011 at http://beer.about.com/od/hybridstyles/a/HybridStyles.htm.

Euromonitor International (2010), 'Strategies for growth in an increasingly consolidated global beer market', www.euromonitor.com/strategies-for-gro wth-in-an-increasingly-consolidated-global-beer-market/report.

George, L.M. (2011), 'The growth of television and the decline of local beer', in J.F.M. Swinnen (ed.), *The Economics of Beer*, Oxford: Oxford University Press, pp. 213–26.

Geppert, M., C. Dörrenbächer, J. Gammelgaard and I. Taplin (forthcoming), 'Managerial risk-taking in international acquisitions in the brewery industry: institutional and ownership influences compared', *British Journal of Management*.

Goldammer, T. (2008), *The Brewer's Handbook. The Complete Book to Brewing Beer*, 2nd ed., Centreville: Apex Publishers.

Gourvish, T.R. (1998), 'Concentration, diversity and firm strategy in European brewing, 1945–90', in R.G. Wilson and T.R. Gourvish (eds), *The Dynamics of the Modern Brewing Industry*, New York: Routledge, pp. 80–92.

Heineken (2010), *Heineken NV Annual Report 2010*, Amsterdam: Heineken.

Hornsby, I.S. (2003), *The History of Beer and Brewing*, Cambridge: Royal Society of Chemistry.

Hymer, S.H. (1976), 'The international operations of national firms: a study of direct foreign investment', MIT Monographs in Economics 14, Cambridge, MA: MIT Press.

Jacoby, J., J.C. Olson and R.A. Haddock (1971), 'Price, brand name, and product composition characteristics as determinants of perceived quality', *Journal of Applied Psychology*, **55** (6), 570–9.

Johanson, J. and J-E. Vahlne (2009), 'The Uppsala internationalization process model revisited: from liability of foreignness to liability of outsidership', *Journal of International Business Studies*, **40** (9), 1411–31.

Kamstrup, F., K.K. Laursen, M. Thorup and S.L. Hermansen (2012), 'The beer industry in China and the US', unpublished manuscript.

Kjersgaard, E. (1976), *Mad og Øl i Danmarks Middelalder*, Copenhagen: Nationalmuseet (Danish National Museum).

Kostova, T. and S. Zaheer (1999), 'Organizational legitimacy under conditions of complexity: the case of the multinational enterprise', *Academy of Management Review*, **24** (1), 64–81.

Lopez, T. (2007), *Global Brands. The Evolution of Multinationals in Alcoholic Beverages*, Cambridge: Cambridge University Press.

Madsen, E.S., K. Pedersen and L. Lund-Thomsen (2011), 'M&A as a driver of global competition in the brewing industry', Working Paper 11–10, mimeo, Aarhus University, Department of Economics and Business.

McConnell, J.D. (1968), 'Effects of pricing on perceptions of product quality', *Journal of Marketing Research*, **5** (August), 300–3.

Merriam-Webster (2011), 'Beer', accessed 18 October 2011 at www.merriam-webster.com.

Meyer, K. and Y.T.T. Tran (2006), 'Market penetration and acquisition strategies for emerging economies', *Long Range Planning*, **39** (2), pp. 177–97.

Persyn, D., J.F.M. Swinnen and S. Vanormelingen (2011), 'Belgian beers: where history meets globalization', in J.F.M. Swinnen (ed.), *The Economics of Beer*, Oxford: Oxford University Press, pp. 79–106.

Poelmans, E. and J.F.M. Swinnen (2011), 'A brief economic history of beer', in J.F.M. Swinnen (ed.), *The Economics of Beer*, Oxford: Oxford University Press, pp. 3–28.

SABMiller (2010), *SAB Miller Plc Annual Report 2010*, London: SABMiller.

Swinnen, J.F.M. and K.V. Herck (2011), 'How the east was won: the foreign takeover of the Eastern European brewing industry', in J.F.M. Swinnen (ed.), *The Economics of Beer*, Oxford: Oxford University Press, pp. 247–66.

Tongeren, F.V. (2011), 'Standards and international trade integration: a historical review of the German "Reinheitsgebot"', in J.F.M. Swinnen (ed.), *The Economics of Beer*, Oxford: Oxford University Press, pp. 51–61.

UNCTAD (2010), *World Investment Report*, Geneva and New York: UN.

Unger, R.W. (2004), *Beer in the Middle Ages and the Renaissance*, Philadelphia: University of Pennsylvania Press.

WHO (2004), *Global Status Report: Alcohol Policy*, Geneva: World Health Organization.

Wortmann, M. (2008), *Komplex und Global. Strategien und Strukturen Multinationaler Unternehmen*, Wiesbaden: VS-Verlag.

PART I

International market developments and firm performance

1. How mergers and acquisitions restructured the international brewery industry 2000–10 – and why

Kurt Pedersen, Erik S. Madsen and Lars Lund-Thomsen

INTRODUCTION

Global beer consumption ran into 185 bn liters in 2009. Wine (27 bn liters) and spirits (19 bn liters) trailed beer consumption, while powerful premixes (4.6 bn liters) and cider (1.5 bn liters) were much smaller in quantity. Beers therefore constitute the largest market for alcoholic drinks measured in quantities, and the last decade has seen a considerable concentration in the industry where the top four brewery groups account for more than 40 percent of the production. The increasing concentration has been caused by mergers and acquisitions (M&As) rather than by organic growth, and consolidation is likely to continue, albeit at a somewhat lower speed.

The industry structure has been changed by the aggressive policies of the top-ranking breweries, and, by acquiring Anheuser-Busch, Interbrew assumed a dominating role with close to 20 percent global market share. In 2000 Anheuser-Busch had a global market share (in volume) of 8.8 percent and Interbrew of 4.0 percent. In 2009 this combined 12.8 percent share of the world market had grown to 19.5 percent. Similarly, Miller Brewing and South African Breweries commanded 3.6 percent and 3.3 percent, respectively, with a combined market share of 6.9 percent in 2000. Nine years later the combined share had grown to a respectable 9.5 percent. Heineken and Carlsberg had grown from 4.3 percent to 6.9 percent and from 1.7 percent to 5.9 percent over the same period.

The pattern is not restricted to the top breweries. While Chinese breweries were absent on the top ten lists in 2000, they now take places five, six and nine. The two Japanese brewers, Asahi and Kirin, have dropped out of the list. The three Chinese fast movers are China Resources (4.5 percent), Tsingtao (3.1 percent) and Beijing Yanjing (2.5 percent). A more

Table 1.1   Concentration rates CR5 and CR10 in the global brewery
            industry (by volume)

Year	CR5	CR10
2000	25.4%	37.3%
2004	36.2%	48.0%
2009	46.3%	59.3%

Note: The two concentration measures indicate the market share of the five or ten largest companies in the worldwide industry.

Source: Various sources.

complete picture is given by the concentration figures for the years 2000, 2004 and 2009 in Table 1.1.

The unquestionable industry leader was established by the Anheuser-Busch/Inbrew merger in 2008. Even the briefest inspection reveals that the combination now covers all significant markets in the world. In 2000 Anheuser-Busch was market leader in the USA and Mexico, while Inbrew had a strong presence in Europe. In contrast, since the 2002 merger SABMiller has acquired a number of local breweries around the globe and has this way strengthened its global reach. One such example is SABMiller's stake in China's leading brewery, China Resources. SABMiller is a large player in many smaller markets – including growth markets in Africa and China, while AB InBev is now in control of a number of large markets.

Numbers 3 and 4, Heineken and Carlsberg, accomplished the other major acquisition in 2008 by jointly taking over Scottish & Newcastle in the UK and dividing its businesses between them. Heineken got increased access to the British market and India, while Carlsberg expanded in Eastern Europe and in China. Of the two, Heineken is more global, while Carlsberg does not include Africa or the Americas in its strategy. In the second tier of competitors, a declining trend in Japanese beer consumption has driven the local firms towards a more global positioning. For instance, in 2009 Asahi acquired a 20 percent equity stake in China's number two, Tsingtao, from AB InBev, while Kirin and Suntory at the same time merged into a highly diversified conglomerate with a market presence in Western Europe.

Section two of this chapter provides an overview of the recent globalization of the industry with a focus on the M&A wave, 2000–09, and the geographical configuration of M&As. Based on this background a rationale will be derived in section three which applies international business (IB) theory to the M&A strategies. We show how a combination of positioning for market shares, entry mode and resource dependency theories suffices to define the rationale of globalization by way of M&A. The section can be seen also as an attempt to bridge international business and industrial economics.

Section four evaluates the performance of the four leading brewing groups. It is obvious that M&A strategies have paved the way to dominant worldwide positions, but the mix of M&A and organic growth differs across the leading players. It is further shown that the four groups differ in terms of financial performance and that an extreme M&A-based expansion strategy seems not to benefit the owners of the acquiring firms.

Industrial organization literature operates with two standard motivations for horizontal M&A: the efficiency hypothesis and the market power hypothesis. The research offers only limited support to either motivation. Section five, the conclusion, presents and qualifies the findings.

STRATEGY AND GEOGRAPHY – AN OVERVIEW

It appears from the above that 'globalization' – which followed upon the opening up of several major markets like China, Russia, Eastern Europe and India – has greatly impacted the international beer industry. While in 2000 most breweries were focused on the home market and a limited number of neighboring countries, there has been a race among industry leaders for global reach. The following section will put this into a business theory context, while the basic figures are produced here.

Table 1.2 shows a matrix of the leading brewing companies in 2000 and 2009 with regional market shares above 5 percent. In the table all cases are indicated in which a brewery has a 5 percent or higher share of the regional beer market. The table shows how fragmented the world market for beers was in the year 2000, with only local market leaders and no global leaders. Of the ten largest breweries observed in 2000, only two were present in more than one of the six regional markets: Heineken in three regions and Inbrew in two. All eight remaining companies were limited to having significant presence in only one region.

The last four rows of the table show how a decade with aggressive M&A strategies has changed the global picture radically. The four leading breweries have picked a strategy of going global and are now present in several regional markets. AB InBev is the leading global player and is present in five of the six regional markets. SABMiller is present in four regional markets, Heineken in three and Carlsberg in two. To some extent the number of regional markets that the four largest breweries have challenged also reflects the current size of the companies. While in 2000 only

Table 1.2   *Bottles indicate market share above 5 percent in 2000 and 2009*

	Asia	Eastern Europe	Middle East/Africa	Western Europe	Latin America	North America	Globalization index
Ten leading breweries in 2000							
Anh-Busch						🍾	🍾
Amr. Bevr.					🍾		🍾
Heineken		🍾	🍾	🍾			🍾🍾🍾
Inbrew		🍾		🍾			🍾🍾
Miller						🍾	🍾🍾
S. African		🍾	🍾			🍾	🍾🍾
Coors							🍾
Modelo					🍾		🍾
Asahi	🍾						🍾
Kirin	🍾						🍾
Four leading breweries in 2009							
AB InBev	🍾	🍾		🍾	🍾	🍾	🍾🍾🍾🍾🍾
SABMiller		🍾	🍾	🍾	🍾	🍾	🍾🍾🍾🍾
Heineken		🍾	🍾	🍾			🍾🍾🍾
Carlsberg		🍾		🍾			🍾🍾

Note: One bottle for a market share above 5 percent in the regional market.

Source: Various sources.

24

Anheuser-Busch had a *global* market share in excess of 5 percent, now all of the four leading companies command above 5 percent of the world market. This globalization is reflected in tough regional competitions where Eastern Europe has become oligopolistic, and Western Europe is much more concentrated than previously, with CR3 moving from 0.25 to 0.40.[1]

Acquisition of equity shares in other breweries has been much less important than M&A. Among the four leading breweries emphasis on this expansion path differs greatly. SABMiller, with an 18 percent share of equity volume, has been the most active player, while AB InBev and Heineken hold equity shares of about 8 percent of the total production (Euromonitor 2010, p. 35). Carlsberg has proved least active in this field. It should be noted that all four leaders have taken to this model in the Chinese/Far East market. AB InBev has a 28.5 percent share in Zhujiang (but maybe more importantly a +50 percent share in Modelo), SABMiller has a 49 percent interest in China Resources, and Carlsberg a 29.7 percent share in Chongqing.

The industry has seen only a limited number of joint ventures; generally the joint ventures are based on the two parties' existing brewing facilities in a given country and have increased efficiency (and possibly protection towards hostile acquisitions) as their main purpose. The largest of them is MillerCoors, which was established between the second and third largest (Miller and Coors) companies in the USA.

Table 1.3 takes a closer look at the acquisition strategy of the four leading breweries since 1995 using the Orbis[2] database of mergers and takeovers. In the period since 1997 the four companies have made a total of 58 acquisitions, amounting to €90 billion. AB InBev has dominated with 21 acquisitions amounting to €56 billion, SABMiller and Heineken have made 15 acquisitions each amounting to €10 and 15 billion and Carlsberg only executed seven acquisitions amounting to €9 billion in the period.

Of the 58 acquisitions only a small number have had a major strategic impact. Inbrew's takeover of Anheuser-Busch in 2008 accounts for almost half of the total deal value and makes AB InBev the undisputed industry leader. SABMiller's takeover of Bavaria in 2005, Carlsberg and Heineken's takeover of Scottish & Newcastle in 2008 and Heineken's acquisition of FEMSA in 2010 were much smaller, but significant in shaping the industry. An important precondition for any large acquisition is the ability to raise capital to finance it. Heineken and Carlsberg have been constrained in this respect and this may partly explain why they ended up losing ground. Carlsberg is owned by a foundation which until 2008 had to have a controlling share in the company, but this requirement

*Table 1.3   Acquisitions of the four leading breweries by year and region
            (million €)*

	AB InBev	SABMiller	Heineken	Carlsberg	Total
Acquiring year					
1997				152	152
1998			119		119
1999			877		877
2000	2915			563	3479
2001	3810		169		3979
2002	491	223	1164		1878
2003	1210	350	1541		3101
2004	4301	814		510	5624
2005	1827	6262	567		8656
2006	575	262			837
2007		529			529
2008	41173	816	5898	6986	54873
2009		837			837
2010			4434	292	4726
Acquiring regions					
Asia	786	199		397	1382
M. East		718	228		947
EEU	1861	837	1879	5361	9938
WEU	7614	1543	7544	2745	19446
Latin A.	4867	6628	4881		16377
North A.	41174	167	237		41578
Total	56303	10094	14769	8503	89668

Notes:
The figures are all deal value in million €. Only deals above half a million € are included.
Heineken's share of the Scottish & Newcastle deal is allocated to WEU (Western Europe),
while Carlsberg's is allocated to WEU and EEU (Eastern Europe) with 78 percent and 22
percent respectively.

Source: The Orbis company database covering more than 8000 breweries worldwide.

was changed so that today the foundation has to control the company
through preference shares. Heineken is family owned and its acquisition
of FEMSA in 2010 reduced the family's ownership in the group to just the
controlling share.[3]

It can also be seen from Table 1.3 that Carlsberg and Heineken were the
first movers in this takeover strategy with minor acquisitions, but Inbrew
quickly caught up with larger acquisitions in the following years. The
largest number of deals took place in North America, followed by Western

Europe, Latin America and Eastern Europe. The four leading breweries are all based in Western Europe, from where they have globalized through the acquisitions. AB InBev misses the Middle East, Heineken misses Asia and Carlsberg misses the Middle East and the Americas. Carlsberg is therefore less global but probably well positioned for future growth, as will be explored in the last section.

APPLYING IB THEORIES TO THE BREWING INDUSTRY

A Survey of IB Theories

Business managers could throughout the 1990s and 2000s draw on a wide range of IB theories to support internationalization strategies. In the wake of US cross-border foreign direct investment (FDI) in the early post-World War II period, Raymon Vernon produced his famed theory on international investments seen in the light of the product life cycle (Vernon 1966). Along the cycle, production was moved from higher developed to less developed nations. While Vernon took a macroeconomic approach, his contemporary, Stephen Hymer, took industrial economics as his point of departure (Hymer 1976). In his view, a foreign entrant into a market faced obstacles which he termed *liabilities of foreignness*. In order to overcome such obstacles, the invading company must possess some advantages, termed *firm specific advantages (FSA)*. Hymer's work, originally a PhD thesis from 1960, was published only in 1976. It combined the Harvard school of industrial economics with a Marxist exploitation assumption: the driving force in Hymer's perspective was market power and FSA was expressed in terms of the product offered in new markets.

In the mid 1970s John Dunning initiated his efforts to develop the 'eclectic paradigm', or the OLI framework, which incorporated Hymer's FSA in the 'O' – ownership variables. While originally an attempt to explain patterns of international production, the paradigm developed into a framework for assessing the necessary (but not the sufficient) conditions for FDI to take place. Besides the multinational corporation (MNC) ownership advantages, the location (L) conditions should be attractive, and internalization (I) of operations should be advantageous. The eclectic approach has triggered numerous publications and continued to expand over time. Dunning (1988) presented the theory on the eve of globalization, while Dunning and Lundan (2008) have presented a recent and expanded statement of the paradigm.

In Harvard the industrial economics tradition received a twist in 1980 when Michael Porter (1980) included a chapter on global industries. It was followed up in 1986 with an analysis of internationalization in the cross field of (geographic) configuration and (strategic) control of value-creating activities (Porter 1986).

From his colleagues in Reading, Peter Buckley and Mark Casson, Dunning imported the concept of internalization. Internalization of activities in the MNC was seen as a consequence of imperfect markets – it minimized transaction costs (Buckley and Casson 1985). Further internalization played an essential role in transaction cost economics (TCE), which developed rapidly after the publication of Williamson's *Markets and Hierarchies* (1975). The title of his work immediately reveals what it is about; there is a thread back to Coase (1937) and the discussion of the 'boundaries of the firm'. A specific application of transaction cost economics to IB was given by Anderson and Gatignon (1986).

Starting with Penrose (1959) – or for that matter David Ricardo – the resource-based view (RBV) was developed on the basic assumption that (internal) expansion must be based on resources (or capabilities, or competences, or core competences) internal to the firm. This 'inside-out' view is contradictory to the Hymer/Porter tradition in Harvard.[4] Wernerfelt (1984) and Barney (1991) were proponents of the RBV, the latter adding his 'VRIO' model in order to operationalize the theory. Finally, Teece et al. (1997) added dynamics to the resource-based approach, bordering on a new strand of theory – the 'knowledge driven' multinationals.

Across the board it was assumed more (RBV) or less (TCE) explicitly that international expansion had to be driven by firm-controlled resources, or ownership advantages in Dunning's terminology. If a crucial resource is missing, it must be circumvented, built or acquired. Pfeffer and Salancik (1978) addressed this case in what came to be known as resource dependence theory. More recently, network theory has taken a similar position – resources as well as markets are sourced through the network (Håkansson 1982). In this perspective, focus to some extent migrates to subsidiaries and the mandates or roles given to subsidiaries (Nohria and Ghoshal 1997).

Finally, the so-called Uppsala model conceives of internationalization as a gradual process, by which the international firm takes on markets of increasing psychic distance, and with increasing commitment. Manufacturing FDI in distant countries is the ultimate sign of internationalization (Johanson and Vahlne 1977). An Uppsala model mark II was launched 30 years later, emphasizing the network aspects rather than the development of an internal knowledge base (Johanson and Vahlne 2009). Liability of foreignness was substituted by liability of outsidership.

Even based on this brief survey, it is abundantly clear that the theories would provide us with a broad range of rationales for the internationalization of the brewing industry over the period observed. The rapidity of change and the massive use of high-commitment entry modes will leave out the Uppsala model and, largely, the network theories. Since the strategic drive was much more one of grabbing strategic opportunities than one of transaction cost minimizing, TCE must be discarded. The Harvard approach of Hymer and Porter appears appropriate, as there was a competitive race for market shares and competitive positions region by region. In combination with resource-based theory, the eclectic paradigm is useful in indicating firm-specific advantages, relative attractiveness of national markets and benefits of internalization of operations. Since the acquired firms around the world possessed valuable, rare and not easily imitable competences – notably in downstream activities – use of resource dependency thinking is another option.

Forsgren (2008) provides a categorization of MNCs. He shows how six different 'tales' of the MNC can be based on IB schools of thought, relating theory to corporate strategy. The key words of the six groups of MNC are 'market power', 'cost efficiency', 'organizational capability', 'strategic fit', 'relations' and 'political legitimacy'. We believe that the leading international brewery groups were driven, most importantly, by the market power motive. This is what we focus on in this chapter. In the process towards globalization other perspectives were obvious, not least the strategic fit as expressed by roles and mandates of subsidiaries. Whether cost efficiency or market power was the predominant motive will be revealed by the econometric analysis.

One final possible explanation of the rush for M&As could be simple herd behavior – tumultuous internationalization. Knickerbocker (1973) has presented this as a likely conduct in global oligopolies: FDI is induced mostly by *competitors'* FDI. This explanation assumes relevance particularly if no clear performance evidence can be demonstrated from the M&A strategies.

Positioning in a Globalizing Environment

Following the structure, conduct, performance paradigm (Bain 1956), the *performance* of the brewery industry is determined by *structural* conditions, such as economies of scale in production, the characteristics of the product, market size, barriers to entry, and so on, as well as by the *conduct* of the firms in the industry. This section will discuss some of the main changes in the basic conditions which have promoted the globalization of the industry and influenced the conduct of breweries.

The most obvious changes in the structure of the global brewery

industry were political, when China and India opened their doors and
the Iron Curtain fell in Europe and enlarged the beer market into a real
world market.[5] These events opened new *emerging growth markets* which
differed from mature markets in a number of ways, and there was a rush
to capture lucrative parts of the new markets among traditional industry
leaders.

In addition, it should be mentioned that in the period of globalization,
that is, post-1990, the traditional factors that tend to impede globalization have been rather weak in the brewing industry. Transportation and
transaction costs are declining at the same time as bureaucratic obstacles
to trade have diminished (tariffs, corruption, local content requirements,
and so on). Consumer tastes across the globe seem to dovetail, and local
producers have been unable to defend their local distribution chains.[6]

A global industry may be defined as one where the global firm's position
in one particular market is affected by its overall global position (Porter
1986). Headquarters and subsidiaries develop skills and knowledge that
can be applied across products or markets. Such skills may refer to any
value-creating activity (production, logistics, marketing, organization,
research and development, and so on). Competing on a (more-or-less)
worldwide scale will bring economies of scale and scope and give significant strategic advantages from these activities. The terminology of
Bartlett and Ghoshal (1989) defines a set of variations of multinational
corporations that may be instructive: companies may act as global firms
with integrated value activities and some national responsiveness towards
customers; or as multinational firms with dispersed value activities and
thorough segmentation of customers; or as transnational firms with highly
integrated value activities and a limited responsiveness towards national
customer groups.

This approach was incidentally present in Porter (1986), where global
industries are defined with respect to (1) products, (2) customers and
(3) competitors. The criteria that should be met for an industry to be
'global' are that the product is well-defined, that the customers have
roughly the same needs, and that the same competitors are active in (all)
major markets. Otherwise, in Porter's terminology, the market will be
'multi-domestic'. It seems fair to say that international brewing is still predominantly multi-domestic (or multi-regional), but it has moved towards
globalization. Therefore, to understand the path of globalization in the
brewing industry and why it emerged, it is useful to take a closer look at
the attributes of the products.[7]

First of all, beer is not a weightless good and it takes up a large space
in the retailing sector compared to other consumer goods. Distribution is
therefore costly and a separate distribution channel for beer has evolved

over time, often run by the breweries themselves and with point deliveries at restaurants, pubs and retail outlets. Further, as transportation is expensive, it is more efficient to produce beer close to the marketplace. Transportation of beers to countries far away is close to non-existent so very low shares of production cross national borders.[8] The distribution mode of beers therefore works as an entry barrier for foreign breweries and the first mode chosen for penetrating a foreign market is often to have the brand distributed by a local brewery, which sometimes produces on license. Entry modes largely exclude greenfield FDI, as acquisition of a local brewery is a more attractive pathway to the consumers.

Second, beer is a homogeneous but branded good. The product has not changed in living man's memory and involves only three raw materials: barley, hops and water. There is some vertical differentiation in beer due to different qualities of barley and different ways to handle the brewing process, but typically these differences are minor among mass-produced beers and the production costs of a premium brand are only slightly above the production costs of a discount brand. Of course, automation of the brewing process has taken place over the years and the production has become more capital-intensive; that, however, has not added much to product quality.

However, there is some horizontal product differentiation with variation in flavor and bitterness due to differences in the malting process of the barley, types of hops and the mix of malt and hops in the brewing process. Still, most people cannot distinguish one beer from another when they face a blind test, or identify different brands within the same category of beer, like lager or pilsner. Real differences are quite small, both with respect to vertical and horizontal product quality, and the product therefore fulfills Porter's condition for a global market. For another view on the degree of product differentiation in the beer market, see Persyn et al. (2010).

While the real product differences are apparently limited, the perceived differences by the consumers in beer quality between brands are, on the other hand, very large. This reveals incomplete information among the consumers regarding beer quality and a kind of non-rational behavior due to the branding effect in the market. McConnell (1968) made an illustrative, controlled experiment of this branding effect. He made 24 home deliveries of six-packs of beer over two months to a large sample of beer drinkers. All the beer was identical, so there were absolutely no quality differences. The consumers did not know this as the regular labels were removed and new labels were added with three different prices corresponding to the average price of a popular, premium and super-premium beer on the American market at that time. When assessing the quality of the beers, the respondent rated the high-priced beer higher in quality than the other two beers with a wide margin. One drinker even said of the brand he thought was cheap, 'I could never finish a bottle'.

Naturally breweries then started to advertise some of their brands as premium beers. This became a real money machine. By increasing the price and branding Budweiser as a premium beer, Anheuser-Busch increased their market share from 4 percent in 1950 to over 45 percent in 1990 (see Greer 1993). While the price difference between discount and premium beer is large, production costs are about the same; advertising thus assumes increasing importance. As expenses for branding to a large degree are fixed costs and independent of the production scale, the larger brands earned a competitive advantage in the branding game. This was a main reason for the restructuring of the industry and the emergence of national brands in the years after World War II when national broadcasting took off. For a discussion of the main drivers behind the emergence of these large regional breweries, see Adams (2006).

The political changes that opened up the possibilities of going global may at the same time have released some advantages related to economies of scale for a global competitor. While production largely remains local, there are still economies of scale to be reaped in management, technology and global branding. The increase in tourism and information sharing between regions through the internet and broadcasting has also raised the profit potential from a globally promoted brand. Further, the main segment of the beer market is young males, and branding often relates to sports activities. As major sports activities like world championships or the Olympic Games have become world events, the breweries can capitalize on their brand by moving into other regional markets, and this may be a reason for the large number of cross-border acquisitions that have taken place in the last decade. But countervailing forces are in play as well. Public regulations against beer pull towards a multi-domestic industry – in the USA there are differences between states in respect to advertising, minimum age for beer customers, and so on.

As pointed out above, the main markets for beers in the West have become mature and highly competitive and breweries have to look at the emerging new economies in the East for further growth. Product life cycle (PLC) management thinking assumes that products pass through a number of stages, each stage calling for a specific strategy. As conditions change, so does the marketing strategy. In Western Europe and North America the product has without question reached the *maturity stage*, with slow growth at best and tough competition for market share. The competitive battlefield changes towards greater emphasis on costs and service as price competition has squeezed profit.

The mature, or maturing, industry is thus exposed to changing mobility barriers and this will probably increase rivalry. The slow growth in demand forces companies to plan and implement strategies with more care as failures may become even more costly than before. In particular, cost control assumes importance, including decisions on product mix and pricing. In the mature industry, price as a means of cross-subsidization may become more important. Often process innovation becomes more important than product innovation as a key to keep costs low. Equally, vertical and horizontal integration become increasingly important as competitive measures in a mature industry. Finally, companies that originate in competitive markets will often be tempted by internationalization into less sophisticated markets in order to exploit their superior technology, management and marketing skills.

Following the PLC's theoretical considerations we can, with some confidence, conclude that the international beer market consists of somewhat heterogeneous countries at different levels of development. While beer functionally fulfills the same set of needs in all markets, there may be local differences in the use of the product. The West European markets are all mature with a slight decline in beer consumption, and the dominating international breweries all originate here. The Americas trail Europe, while markets in the Far East and Eastern Europe can be described as emerging growth markets. Historically, of course, beer has been well-known and the Czech Republic was one of Europe's dominating beer nations around 1900, both in production quantity, product quality and beer consumption. Soviet dominance after World War II restricted innovation and restructuring in Eastern Europe, and post-1990 internationalization has opened these markets to the now dominating Western European breweries.

As a consequence of globalization, beer is at various stages of the product life cycle across the markets – in the growth phase in Eastern Europe and the Far East and in maturity or even decline in North America and Western Europe. An international or global company cannot count on automatically gaining from a sweeping homogeneous strategy. It would be helpful, once more, to consult Porter (1980, Ch. 13) in order to outline sources of competitive advantage in markets under globalization:

(1) Comparative advantage in production factors (cheap labor, water quality, etc.).
(2) Economies of scale in production lead to cost advantage.
(3) Economies of scale in marketing; distributing costs across labels and nations.
(4) Cross-market exchange of experience.
(5) Product differentiation, for instance a mix of local and globally advertised brands.
(6) Set up entry barriers for local potential entrants.

Handling Globalization Challenges

Porter's six sources of competitive advantage include some owner-ship advantages (scale and differentiation), some location advantages (local markets and factor supply) as well as internalization advantages (cross-market knowledge transfer) which immediately links the *why* of global positioning to the *how* of market operations. In the framework of the eclectic paradigm there are sufficient observations to argue in favor of FDI as the preferred entry mode. The very nature of the product further excludes export as a dominating operational mode.

Alternatives to either export or fully owned subsidiaries would be some contractual form, such as international joint ventures. Heineken used this form in its recent expansion, and Carlsberg has to some extent used it in all of its international expansion efforts since the 1960s. Similarly, minority holdings have been widely used, for instance in the Chinese market, maybe due to Chinese industrial policy restrictions, while equity restrictions have motivated Heineken and Carlsberg to use this entry mode.

The reason why breweries are eager to secure control is given in the above subsection: increasingly beer is a branded product and this calls for full control of not only the taste and quality of the product, but virtually the whole value chain from raw materials procurement to positioning in stores, bars and restaurants. As has been abundantly illustrated in industrial economics literature, investment in branding makes poor business sense if product quality does not meet customer expectations.[9]

Observing Porter's value chain (1985), some value functions tend to be more crucial to control than others in a global industrial regime. We believe that challenges from globalization pose major challenges to *corporate infrastructure*. This implies the question of expansion into new markets at optimal speed and in a profitable geographical sequence, as well as the organization and management of a multinational enterprise spanning a scattered configuration of numerous functions. One clue may be the framework consisting of carefully orchestrated degrees of central-ization, formalization and socialization across subsidiaries, as presented in, for example, Nohria and Ghoshal (1997).

One important element of international management and strategy obvi-ously will be the increased emphasis on *human resource management*. The necessity to brew close to the market, the different roles of subsidiaries and the cultures that a major brewing company spans call for knowledge exchange and carefully tailored roles for subsidiaries and employees.

As standardized, branded goods require quality uniformity over time, both *procurement and distribution functions* assume increased importance.

Large brewers can no longer afford not to extend firm control to major suppliers of, for instance, hops – which are produced in a few dominating areas of the world – and water sources, which are by nature local.

Beer production has scale advantages in the brewing process, even if we show later that they may have been fully reaped by larger brewers, and qualitatively the processes are still under development. But it is in *marketing* that the real scale advantages are to be found, with the emergence of dozens of globally advertised brands.

We see these five value functions as the major challenges that global brewing companies must face up to at the corporate level by optimal integration and coordination of subsidiaries. We also find that the eclectic paradigm offers a relevant frame of reference for interpreting the FDI wave in international brewing, as O-variables, L-variables and I-variables have been identified as essential components of international positioning. All of the leading brewing groups command substantial ownership advantages in the value functions that we find crucial to international competitiveness.

However, we are still left with the question why international expansion has been dominated by M&As rather than greenfield operations. Here, the eclectic paradigm is of limited use. The final step of the interpretation of globalization by IB theories – why M&A? – will be a combination of positioning theory and resource dependence theory. The reason is that the eclectic paradigm does not raise the question 'how much O advantage is enough?', that is whether existing O-advantages are *sufficient* for FDI to take place. And the paradigm in consequence neglects the question of missing O-advantages as a driver of international direct investments.

The Rationale of M&A

This subsection offers a strategic rationale for M&As as the dominating entry mode in emerging beer markets. We find that resource dependence theory, as introduced by Pfeffer and Salancik (1978), provides a convincing argument, taking as its starting point that all organizations depend on outside resources and according to circumstances are under pressure to acquire or otherwise control them.

If outside resources are critical for the organization in order to realize its strategic goals – for instance increased market share – or if the resources are available with a limited number of outside organizations, the quest for controlling them will increase. The firm will be more vulnerable the more critical the external resource is for its business, and the more concentrated the possession of it is.

During the 1990s and 2000s international breweries operated in a
strategic window that added a narrow time restriction to the absence of
resources critical to the players. The leading groups virtually raced to
acquire access to emerging markets. Access meant access to customers and
distribution channels, and the fastest way to obtain access – and control
of critical external resources – was M&As with qualified local breweries.
A late case in point is Heineken's takeover of FEMSA in 2010; this acquisition changed the Latin American environment and closed the last gate
into it for, for example, Carlsberg (even if there may still be doors left for
entry).

One side aspect is brand management. By M&A the leading brewery
groups acquire an increasing number of local brands. While acquisitions
open new markets for the groups' own brands to a wider audience, they
also give rise to considerations concerning which ones among the acquired
brands may qualify as new global brands.

Internalizing critical resources is the safest way to obtain control and is
superior to other mechanisms such as contractual relationships and international joint ventures. It is argued that discrete power over resources is
a measure of the firm's independence of the environment. At the core is
avoidance of uncertainty. From a resource dependency view, the argument
runs as follows:

> An industry's concentration and the munificence of resources determine
> the conflict level of the industry, while the degree of interconnectedness and
> resource munificence determines the degree of interdependence which again
> impacts the level of conflict. Uncertainty, finally, is decided by the degree of
> conflict and the degree of interdependence. (Pfeffer and Salancik 1978, p. 68)

Expanding the firm and its market share by M&A is one way of extending
control to vital functions controlled by other organizations, and in consequence reducing dependency and commercial uncertainty. M&A tends
to indicate a corporate growth strategy aiming at increased stability and
predictability in the industry, not least by its focus on interdependence:

> We argue that merger is a mechanism used to restructure environmental inter-
> dependence in order to stabilize critical exchanges. (Pfeffer and Salancik 1978,
> p. 115)

There is some evidence that uncertainty is inverse-U shaped in relation to
industrial concentration. As concentration moves towards a few dominating large firms and becomes oligopolistic, uncertainty begins to drop
and mutual stable expectations (may) develop concerning competitive
behavior:

The greatest uncertainty arises where there are enough large firms to have major impact on each other but too many separate organizations to be tacitly coordinated. (Pfeffer and Salancik 1978, p. 125)

Pfeffer and Salancik found that uncertainty and merger activity would be at a maximum when CR4 – the combined market share of the four leading players – was around 40 percent; which was the case in the global brewing industry in the late 2000s.

If growth is a consequence of human decisions, the M&A wave must be interpreted as an expression of explicit strategic plans, because M&As were seen as superior to other methods of market expansion in order to achieve the growth objective – market share. The main restriction was that only a comparatively few breweries were candidates for takeover, which added the temporal impetus to the competitive M&A race in the industry.

Even if the wave of M&As in the international beer industry has not fully globalized the industry, at least it has been moving in that direction. The following section presents a description of recent developments focusing in particular on the performance of the leading breweries and attempts to assess whether the M&A strategy has paid off.

PERFORMANCE OF THE FOUR LEADING BREWERIES

IB theories have focused on different advantages for the companies in their internationalization processes, where some economy of scale or scope could be reaped by serving several foreign markets at the same time. The expectation of higher efficiency could therefore be the leading motive behind the M&A strategy of the individual brewery, and the M&A wave may have changed the performance of the breweries depending on their adoption of this strategy.

Table 1.4 shows the growth and size of the M&A activities of the current four leading breweries, which were about the same size in 2000. The acquisition period dramatically changed the situation; AB InBev became the market leader with the combined size of SABMiller and Heineken in turnover and growth of more than 300 percent over the period. Also SABMiller experienced a very fast growth, but from a lower level in 2000, whereas Heineken and Carlsberg have had more moderate growth rates.

The last two columns list the size of the acquisitions made by the four breweries in the period since 1997 and relate the total bill for acquisitions to turnover in 2000. AB InBev stands out, while the other three groups have comparable ratios in spite of widely differing growth rates. The M&A

Table 1.4   Growth and M&A strategies of the four leading breweries

	Turnover (billion €)		Growth in turnover	Acquisitions (billion €)	Ratio of acquisitions to turnover in 2000
	2000	2009	2000–09	1997–2010	
AB InBev	5.9	26.0	323%	56.3	9.54
SABMiller	3.4	14.7	300%	10.1	2.97
Heineken	7.0	13.6	110%	14.8	2.11
Carlsberg	4.8	8.0	67%	8.5	1.77

Source: The Orbis company database covering more than 8000 breweries worldwide.

Table 1.5   Growth by M&A strategies or an organic strategy?

	Growth factor 2000–09	Ratio of M&A to turnover in 2000	M&A expenditure per growth factor 2000–09	Share of M&A in emerging markets 2000–09
AB InBev	3.23	9.54	2.95	13.3
SABMiller	3.00	2.97	0.99	83.0
Heineken	1.10	2.11	1.92	47.3
Carlsberg	0.67	1.77	2.64	67.8

Source: The Orbis company database covering more than 8000 breweries worldwide.

strategy apparently has not been equally efficient across the four breweries, and to analyse this further Table 1.5 lists the M&A expenditures per growth factor for the four leading breweries. Comparing AB InBev and SABMiller, they hold about the same growth factor over the period, but SABMiller's accumulated deal value of acquisitions is only one-third of AB InBev's when measured relative to turnover in 2000. Therefore, SABMiller has a much lower M&A expenditure per growth factor of 0.99 compared with 2.95 for AB InBev. The better M&A performance for SABMiller in this period can either be the result of more successful M&A investment deals or a higher organic growth compared to AB InBev.

Also, Heineken has a relatively high M&A expenditure per growth factor. As mentioned, the higher M&A growth performance could be a result of higher organic growth for SABMiller and Heineken due to their strategic positions in regions with higher growth in beer consumption, but it could just as well be a result of a more efficient production and market management. To further explore this question, the last column

Table 1.6   Performance of the four leading breweries, 2000–09

	EBIT margin	Return on total assets	Return on shareholder funds	Total assets 2009	Per employee growth 2000–09
AB InBev	19.3	6.9	17.4	670	118%
SABMiller	12.9	11.6	32.8	365	123%
Heineken	17.4	9.4	19.7	327	106%
Carlsberg	10.7	5.1	19.4	415	107%
Very large breweries*	12.6	7.6	18.5	308	8%

Notes: * The largest 200 breweries excluding the four largest in 2009.

Source: The Orbis company database covering more than 8000 breweries worldwide.

in Table 1.5 lists the share of their M&A investments going into emerging markets. It is clear from the figures that SABMiller, Heineken and Carlsberg have improved their positions in high growth markets to a much larger extent than AB InBev, and this can partly explain AB InBev's inferior performance.

The four leading breweries have played a major role in the restructuring of the global brewing industry, but has this acquisition and growth strategy also paid off for the shareholders of these companies? To illustrate this question, Table 1.6 takes a look at some of the key financial results for the four companies in the acquisitions period from 2000–09. The figures are compared to the average for the very large breweries in the Orbis database – about 200 breweries worldwide and most regional breweries.

Measuring the profitability as earnings before interest and taxes (EBIT), AB InBev and Heineken performed better than the large regional breweries, SABMiller did only marginally better and Carlsberg had lower earnings. However, concerning the return on total assets and the return on shareholder funds, SABMiller outperforms the other three while Heineken still earns a higher return than the very large breweries on average.

The fact that the company that has the highest growth through acquisitions, AB InBev, also presents a low return on assets poses some questions for the acquisition strategy. An acquisition strategy may be a fast, but also expensive, road to growth. If market shares are bought at a high price the strategy will put a lot of goodwill on their books and thereby reduce the return on assets and the return on shareholder funds. The last two columns of Table 1.6 verify that this could be the case for AB InBev as its book value of assets per employee was exceptionally high in 2009. One interpretation of the low return is that the local shareholder has reaped most of the benefits from the synergies emerging from the acquisitions only leaving a normal return for the acquirer. An alternative interpretation could be that it may take some time to reap the benefits of the globalization strategy and it will pay off in the future.

These results for the brewery industry are in line with the general empirical evidence of the performance of acquiring firms post-acquisition. In a large event study of more than 937 acquisitions of listed firms in the US, Agrawal et al. (1992) found that the acquiring firms on average suffered a wealth loss of about 10 percent when corrected for firm size bias. Roler et al. (2001) surveyed a large number of studies and found an average gain for the acquired firm of 30 percent, whereas the acquiring firms on average just broke even. This verifies that the owners of the acquired firms on average walked away with most or all of the net benefits of the merger.

Beside cost savings, mergers may also increase market prices through a reduction in the number of competitors; a number of studies have examined this market power hypothesis. Gugler et al. (2003) found some evidence by studying 15000 mergers worldwide from 1981–99, where half of the cases experienced rising profits and falling sales consistent with the market power hypothesis. However, Weinberg (2007) surveyed nine studies, testing for pre- and post-merger prices, and found that only a minority of mergers resulted in higher prices.

Mergers can also be a result of failing firms preferring merger to the alternative of a bankruptcy process which involves large legal costs. Tremblay and Tremblay (1988) studied the performance of acquiring and acquired breweries in the US from 1950–84 and found the growth rate to be significantly lower in the acquired breweries. Greer (1993) further found that the acquiring breweries in the US had not performed very well and had lost market share to Anheuser-Busch, which had relied exclusively on organic growth. The failing market hypothesis therefore seems to explain the restructuring of the national brewing industries immediately after World War II.

To further highlight the market power hypothesis, Figure 1.1 compares EBIT and return on shareholder funds for the four largest breweries, with a control group of about 200 of the largest breweries during the M&A wave minus the top four. It appears that EBIT is higher for the four largest breweries during the whole period and it has been rising. However, EBIT has not been rising to the same extent for the other breweries, which should be expected if increasing concentration in the industry had raised beer prices. The main reason for the rise in EBIT for the four largest breweries is therefore probably an increase in efficiency due to economies of scale due to their investment in M&A.

Figure 1.1 also verifies that the return on shareholder funds has decreased for the four largest breweries whereas it has been rather stable

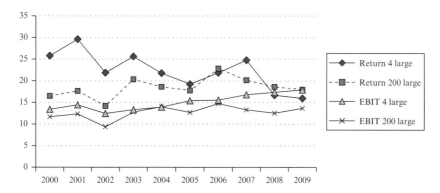

Notes: The largest 200 breweries exclude the top four largest at the end of the period in 2009.

Source: The Orbis company database covering more than 8000 breweries worldwide.

Figure 1.1   Performance of the four largest breweries compared with 200 large breweries

for the control group of 200 large breweries. This indicates that the large M&A investments have increased the EBIT margin through economies of scale but not enough to cover their normal return on new investment. As a result, the return on shareholder funds has decreased in the period.

To further study the differences in productivity between the breweries the total factor productivity is calculated using a CobbDouglas formulation of the production function:

$$Y = A \, C^\alpha \, L^{1-\alpha} \tag{1}$$

Where Y is the total turnover, A the total factor productivity, C the total assets, L the number of employees and α is the output elasticity for capital. Dividing through by L gives the following expression for output per labor:

$$Y/L = A \, (C/L)^\alpha \tag{2}$$

The log of equation (2) gives our estimation equation (3) where D_j is an individual dummy for brewery j and has been added to pick up differences in total labor productivity.

$$Log(Y/L) = Const + \alpha \log(C/L) + D_j \tag{3}$$

The database used in the estimation of equation (3) is Orbis which holds information of more than 8000 breweries worldwide. The estimation

Table 1.7 Estimates of production efficiency of the four leading breweries, 2000–09

	Whole period 2000–09	First period 2000–04	Last period 2005–09
Intercept	3.153	−0.015	3.807*
	(0.509)	(1.154)	(0.678)
Capital labor	0.385*	0.956*	0.268*
ratio (log)	(0.090)	(0.207)	(0.120)
AB InBev	−0.300*	−0.293*	−0.335*
	(0.073)	(0.088)	(0.099)
SABMiller	0.047	0.283*	0.029
	(0.075)	(0.122)	(0.092)
Heineken	−0.178*	−0.211*	−0.006
	(0.074)	(0.086)	(0.105)
Carlsberg	−0.126	0.025	−0.157
	(0.070)	(0.093)	(0.089)
R-square	0.338	0.556	0.346
Observations	48	25	23

Notes:
* Significant at least at the 5 percent level.
All coefficients are OLS estimates.

Source: The Orbis company database covering more than 8000 breweries worldwide.

covers the period from 2000–09 and includes the four largest breweries as well as the averages for the 200 largest breweries excluding the four largest. This gives a total of 50 observations, but figures for total labor employed were not available for Heineken in the Orbis database for the last two years, so only 48 observations are used. Table 1.7 lists the results of the estimation and this simple formulation of the production technology is able to explain about one-third of the variation in turnover per employee in the period. Also the estimated output elasticity is highly significant but the size decreases dramatically in the period. This decline in the productivity of capital over the period could be a consequence of the low return to M&A investment found above, as this estimation of the coefficients is dominated by the four largest breweries (only the averages are used for the control group of the 200 largest breweries).

For AB InBev and Heineken the estimated total factor productivity is significantly below the total factor productivity in the control group of 200 large breweries over the whole period, while it is not significantly different for Carlsberg and SABMiller. However, looking at the development in total factor productivity from the first period to the last period a different picture develops. AB InBev is consistently about 30 percent less efficient in both periods, but Heineken is only significantly less efficient in the first period and has improved its total factor productivity to be in line with the control group for the last period. Both SABMiller and Carlsberg saw a decrease in their total factor productivity over the period. SABMiller moved from being 29 percent more efficient than the control groups to just matching their productivity and Carlsberg suffered a considerable, but statistically insignificant, drop.

It must be admitted that the estimation of labor productivity above uses total turnover for the breweries and therefore includes price changes. A change in their product portfolios to more valuable and expensive beers would be measured as an increase in productivity. As the four largest breweries have introduced their own high-priced labels in the new markets the estimated total factor productivity is biased upwards.

CONCLUSIONS

From an internationalization perspective, as well as from an industrial organization view, the recent concentration in the brewing industry invites some conclusions.

The rather abrupt opening up during the 1990s of a global market for beer started a *positioning race* between some of the leading breweries, mainly located in Western Europe. Competitors have weighted M&A and organic growth differently. It is still too early to draw firm conclusions on the relative merits of the two strategies, but SABMiller which has emphasized organic growth has so far performed more convincingly than its competitors.

Performance measures do not indicate that the four top breweries have done significantly better than a control group of 200 large breweries. This finding can be interpreted as an indication that scale advantages are meaningless at smaller capacities than those commanded by the top brewing groups. Still, figures of increasing concentration at least indicate that first-movers in the industry gained advantages by spotting and exploiting new business opportunities in the two decades of globalization. Considering the relative performance of the second and third tiers of breweries, it is far from certain that the concentration drive will continue.

Industrial organization advances an old discussion regarding whether structure determines behavior or vice versa. The brewing case demonstrates that changes in the environment may spark hefty strategic moves (behavior) with significant effects on industry structure, a view predominantly held by the Chicago school of industrial organization.

Relating to this question, the research attempted to investigate the two main drivers of M&A, viz. the efficiency hypothesis and the market power hypothesis. Neither of the two hypotheses was vindicated by figures. Scale apparently does not lead to significantly better performance in terms of labor productivity (that is, efficiency), nor has the M&A wave improved the performance of the control group as the market power hypothesis would predict.

Finally, the complex of IB theories gives support for interpreting and understanding the M&A strategies. While positioning theory explains the drive for change in a newly opened international market, the eclectic paradigm provides the arguments for the FDI entry mode, and the resource dependency philosophy gives the rationale for choosing the M&A form of FDI. In short, IB theory works as a guide for how to handle internationalization (doing things right), while it remains to be seen if internationalization was the best strategy (doing the right things).

We find that our conclusions are fairly robust and in a meaningful way tie recent historical development to IB theory and empirical investigations. The industry in fact reacted as one might have forecasted: first-movers conquered large market shares, even if financial results materialized only hesitantly. The case certainly illustrates how the changing rules of an industry can cause radical structural changes over a short span of years.

NOTES

1. CR expresses the concentration ratio in an industry. CR3 measures the share of the industry's three largest firms in (some measure of) total industry size. For a more detailed analysis of the foreign takeover of the Eastern Europe brewing industry, see Swinnen and Herck (2010).
2. Orbis is a large company database product including data from various sources.
3. Concerning ownership issues, see Geppert et al. (forthcoming).
4. Porter (1985) introduced the value chain concept which was indeed internal, but distinguished it from the RBV by emphasizing activities (flow) rather than assets (stock). Porter (1991) attempts to further bridge the internal and the external views.
5. For more about this topic see Swinnen (2011, part IV).
6. For a systematic elaboration of obstacles to globalization, see, for instance, Ghemawat (2001).
7. Adams (2006) provides a brilliant discussion of global versus multi-domestic markets by comparing a broad set of differences between the American and German beer markets.
8. Average export shares of about 4 percent retrieved from the Orbis database of breweries. Curiously enough, *consumers* are often willing to transport beer over considerable distances across borders in order to exploit price and taxation differences – arbitrage opportunities which are not available to the breweries.
9. The discussion goes back to Akerlof (1970), but the signal value of brands in the case of repeated purchases was first handled by Milgrom and Roberts (1986).

REFERENCES

Adams, William J. (2006), 'Beer in Germany and the United States', *Journal of Economic Perspectives*, **20**, 189–205.

Agrawal, A., J.F. Jaffe and G.N. Mandelker (1992), 'The post-merger performance of acquiring firms: a re-examination of anomaly', *The Journal of Finance*, **47**, 1605–21.

Akerlof, G.A. (1970), 'The market for lemons: quality uncertainty and the market mechanisms', *Quarterly Journal of Economics*, **84**, 489–500.

Anderson, E. and H. Gatignon (1986), 'Modes of foreign entry: a transaction cost analysis and propositions', *Journal of International Business Studies*, **17**, 1–26.

Barney, J. (1991), 'Firm resources and sustained competitive advantage', *Journal of Management*, **17**, 99–120.

Bartlett, Christopher A. and Sumantra Ghoshal (1989), *Managing across Borders – The Transnational Solution*, Boston, MA: Harvard Business School Press.

Buckley, P. and M. Casson (1985), *The Economic Theory of the Multinational Enterprise*, London: Macmillan.

Coase, R.H. (1937), 'The nature of the firm', *Economica*, **1**, 386–405.

Dunning, J. (1988), *Explaining International Production*, London: Unwin Hyman.

Dunning, J. and S. Lundan (2008), *Multinational Enterprises and the Global Economy*, Cheltenham, UK and Northampton, MA, USA: Edward Elgar.

Euromonitor International (2010), *Strategies for Growth in an Increasingly Consolidated Global Beer Market*, Euromonitor International.

Forsgren, M. (2008), *Theories of the Multinational Firm*, Cheltenham, UK and Northampton, MA, USA: Edward Elgar.

Geppert, M., C. Dörrenbächer, J. Gammelgaard and I.M. Taplin (forthcoming), 'Managerial risk-taking in international acquisitions in the brewery industry: institutional and ownership influences compared', *British Journal of Management*.

Ghemawat, P. (2001), 'Distance still matters', *Harvard Business Review*, **79**, 137–47.

Greer, Douglas F. (1993), 'Beer: causes of structural change', in Larry L. Duetsch (ed.), *Industry Studies*, New York: Prentice-Hall, pp. 85–115.

Gugler, K., D.C. Muller, B.B. Yurtoglu and C. Zulehner (2003), 'The effects of merger: an international comparison', *International Journal of Industrial Organization*, **21**, 625–53.

Håkansson, H. (ed.) (1982), *International Marketing and Purchase of Industrial Goods*, Chichester: John Wiley & Sons.

Hymer, S. (1976), *The International Operations of National Firms*, Cambridge, MA: MIT Press.

Johanson, J. and J.-E. Vahlne (1977), 'The internationalization process of firms', *Journal of International Business Studies*, **1**, 23–32.

Johanson, J. and J.-E. Vahlne (2009), 'The Uppsala internationalization model revisited: from liability of foreignness to liability of outsidership', *Journal of International Business Studies*, **33**, 1–21.

Knickerbocker, F.T. (1973), *Oligopolistic Reactions and Multinational Enterprises*, Cambridge, MA: Harvard University Press.

McConnell, J.D. (1968), 'The price-quality relationship in an experimental setting', *Journal of Marketing Research*, **5**, 300–3.

Milgrom, P. and J. Roberts (1986), 'Price and advertising signals of product quality', *Journal of Political Economy*, **94**, 796–821.

Nohria, N. and S. Ghoshal (1997), *The Differentiated Network. Organizing Multinational Corporations and Value Creation*, San Francisco: Jossey-Bass.

Penrose, E. (1959), *The Theory of the Growth of the Firm*, Oxford: Basil Blackwell.

Persyn, D., J.F.M. Swinnen and S. Vanormelingen (2010), 'Belgian beers: where history meets globalization', LICOS Discussion Paper 271/2010, Katholieke Universiteit Leuven.

Pfeffer, J. and G. Salancik (1978), *The External Control of Organizations. A Resource Dependence Perspective*, New York: Harper & Row.

Porter, Michael E. (1980), *Competitive Strategies: Techniques for Analyzing Industries and Competitors*, New York: The Free Press.

Porter, Michael E. (1985), *Competitive Advantage: Creating and Sustaining Superior Performance*, New York: The Free Press.

Porter, Michael E. (ed.) (1986), *Competition in Global Industries*, Boston, MA: Harvard Business School Press.

Porter, Michael E. (1991), 'Towards a dynamic theory of strategy', *Strategic Management Journal*, **12**, 95–117.

Roler, L., J. Stennek and F. Verboven (2001), 'Efficiency gains from mergers', report for EC, London: Center for Economic Policy Research.

Swinnen, Johan F.M. (ed.) (2011), *The Economics of Beer*, Oxford: Oxford University Press.

Swinnen, J.F.M. and K.V. Herck (2010), 'How the east was won: the foreign take-over of the Eastern European brewing industry', LICOS Discussion Paper 268/2010, Katholieke Universiteit Leuven.

Teece, D., G. Pisano and A. Shuen (1997), 'Dynamic capabilities and strategic management', *Strategic Management Journal*, **18**, 509–33.

Tremblay, V.J. and C.H. Tremblay (1988), 'The determinants of horizontal acquisitions: evidence from the US brewing industry', *Journal of Industrial Economics*, **37**, 21–45.

Vernon, R. (1966), 'International investment and international trade in the product cycle', *Quarterly Journal of Economics*, **80**, 190–207.

Weinberg, Matthew (2007), 'The price effects of horizontal mergers', *Journal of Competition Law & Economics*, **3**, 433–47.

Wernerfelt, B. (1984), 'A resource-based view of the firm', *Strategic Management Journal*, **5** (2), 171–80.

Williamson, Oliver (1975), *Markets and Hierarchies*, New York: The Free Press.

2. Market leadership, firm performance and consolidation in the Central and Eastern European brewing sector

Kristian Jakobsen

INTRODUCTION

In this chapter I provide an analysis of the financial performance of foreign-owned subsidiaries in the brewing industry in Central and Eastern Europe (CEE). The chapter also provides a description of market entry behavior, industry concentration and branding strategy. Long-term organic growth prospects are explored based on market penetration levels and projected future population developments in CEE. Finally, the chapter concludes with a discussion of the structural and managerial implications of the findings.

Over the last two decades the brewing industry has experienced a rapid process of global consolidation, primarily led by four international brewers: Anheuser-Busch InBev (AB InBev), SABMiller, Heineken and Carlsberg. Combined, these four brewers account for more than 40 percent of the world market (Pedersen, Madsen and Thomsen, Chapter 1, this volume). An interesting aspect of the global consolidation of the brewing industry has been a strong emphasis on investment in emerging and transition economies.

> We were one of the first brewers, for example, to see value in emerging markets. While others were reluctant to take the risk, we pioneered the buying of emerging-market businesses and were able to build leading positions. (SABMiller 2007, p. 7)

With local brewing assets made accessible through the privatization processes in the former Eastern bloc countries, all the leading international brewers and many regional brewers have pursued growth opportunities in CEE. As a result, foreign-owned brewers control the lion's share of sales in nearly every national market in the region. Growing demand has also elevated CEE's relative importance as a regional beer market. While CEE accounted for 9 percent of world consumption in 1993 this share had grown to 15 percent by 2008. For some brewers that has turned CEE into a major source of revenues and profits. In 2009 the Carlsberg-owned Baltica group alone generated just short of US$1000 million in operating profits. On the other hand, many foreign brewers have exited CEE either through divestment or simply by being acquired. In spite of attractive past growth rates and the relative size of the regional market, even large international brewers have started to withdraw from the region. To shore up its balance sheet, AB InBev withdrew from most of CEE in late 2009 by divesting its assets to a private equity firm. Though it initially retained a buyback option, AB InBev has since opted not to exercise it. Similarly, SABMiller withdrew from Russia and Ukraine in 2011 through an asset for shares swap with Turkish Anadolu Efes.

This raises some central questions about the internationalization of the brewing industry. Which firms are ultimately able to operate profitably and what level of competition can a national or regional market sustain? To answer these questions I analyse the performance of foreign-owned subsidiaries in CEE and the regional prospects for future growth.

In the following section I provide an overview of the data sources and methods employed in this study. This is followed by an analysis of the financial performance of foreign brewers in CEE. While Pedersen, Madsen and Thomsen (Chapter 1) examine the performance effect of the increasing globalization of the brewing industry at the aggregate level of the industry's emergent global leaders, this section examines the financial performance of foreign-owned subsidiaries at the level of the national market. Based on accounting data for large foreign-owned subsidiaries, the study provides evidence that market leaders tend to outperform market challengers by a substantial margin. This is followed by a discussion of the key features of the brewing industry in CEE, including the typical mode of market entry and the branding strategies of the international brewers. It is found that acquisition has been the typical mode of market entry employed by international brewers. Moreover, international brewers have relied mainly on local brands to serve markets in CEE. However, with the current level of industry concentration the potential for further growth through the acquisition of local brewers is limited in most countries in CEE. I then proceed to the analysis of the development of beer consumption in CEE and the future organic growth prospects for the region. While current economic woes brought on by the financial crisis have stifled demand growth, the question remains whether the region still offers significant long-term growth potential. This issue is explored by analysing the evolution in per capita consumption as well as the demographic outlook for the region. The analysis indicates a strong convergence of beer consumption across the region with the peak level probably close to current levels. This in turn suggests limited potential for growth through increasing market penetration. This problem is further compounded by exceedingly poor demographic prospects for the region with populations expected to face long-term decline.

Finally, I discuss the results of the study and propose managerial implications. In the absence of viable local acquisition or organic growth options I argue that strong market leadership advantages are likely to prompt further consolidation, probably through divestment of activities, leading to an increasing division of markets between the international brewers. In turn, international brewers are likely to become increasingly regional rather than global in scope.

METHODS AND DATA SOURCES

Geographical Definitions

This study utilizes firm and country level data from 15 different countries which I define as being in the geographical region of Central and Eastern Europe (CEE). Furthermore, I use the following terms to represent geographical sub-regions within CEE: South Eastern Europe (SEE): Bulgaria, Croatia, Romania and Serbia; Central Europe (CE): Czech Republic, Hungary, Slovakia and Slovenia; North Eastern Europe (NEE): Estonia, Latvia, Lithuania and Poland; The Commonwealth of Independent States (CIS): Belarus, Russia and Ukraine.

Market Entry Identification

The data used in this study were obtained from several different data sources. Most market entries and acquisitions were identified though either the database Zephyr or were derived from Larimo et al. (2006). In a few cases, typically due to incomplete or mis-specified industry code, market entries were uncovered through the annual accounts of foreign firms operating in CEE or from local company websites. In total, 74 foreign market entries[1] were identified between 1991 and 2009[2] and these were carried out by 24 different foreign firms or groups of firms. By 2009, 13 of these were still active in the region and between them controlled a total of 50 country level operations.

Firm Performance

To analyse subsidiary performance, accounting data on firm size, sales and operating profits were obtained through the firm database Orbis for the period 2005–09. Frequently a foreign parent company has multiple local subsidiaries in a host market and as the study is concerned with the overall market position of the foreign owner, subsidiary data were aggregated on a national level. This was done through a simple dollar for dollar consolidation among horizontally related subsidiaries that are directly held by the same foreign owner. However no attempt was made to consolidate subsidiary accounts for vertically related subsidiaries. Hence for the remainder of this study a subsidiary is taken to mean all the legal entities and assets held in a country by the same foreign parent company.

Due to missing values and qualitative issues with the accounting data, both Belarus and Slovakia had to be excluded from the analysis of subsidiary performance. Moreover, because no foreign brewer operated in Slovenia through FDI during the period 2005–09, Slovenia was not relevant for the subsidiary performance analysis. This left 12 countries that had at least three active foreign-owned brewers in each accounting year between 2005 and 2009.

To measure subsidiary performance I use earnings before interest and tax (EBIT). The main advantage of using EBIT is that it neutralizes the effect of capital structure on performance and it eliminates potentially distorting non-recurring income and expenses. I calculate two commonly used measures of operational performance ROA and ROS. EBIT relative to total assets (ROA) provides a measure for how effectively firms utilize their assets, while EBIT relative to sales (ROS) measures the firm's ability to convert sales into profits. Both measures are included because goodwill or large new investments in physical assets can affect the relative relationship between these measures, in the short run.

Industry Structure and Brands

For country level comparisons I use market share for firms and beer brands obtained from Euromonitor. These are calculated based on the volume traded by the retail sector, commonly referred to as off-site consumption. Most beer consumption in CEE tends to occur off-site and this is particularly the case in the high growth markets in CIS and NEE. In Russia, the largest and fastest growing market in the region, off-site consumption accounts for roughly 90 percent of total consumption. Nonetheless, since on-site consumption choices may differ from off-site consumption choices this is a potential bias and limitation of the present study.

For the purpose of analysing the relationship between market position and subsidiary performance I use the reported sales revenues of the largest brewers instead. The main advantage of a revenue-based market share measure is that it also captures potential differences in the composition of low- versus high-margin products between firms. Furthermore, with three-firm concentration ratios (CR3) between 65 and 90 percent among foreign firms (Table 2.1), most competitive dynamics are likely to play out between the largest two or three firms.

I use two measures to proxy the structure of competition in a market. *Market share* is used to capture a subsidiary's relative positioning advantage and is calculated by dividing subsidiary sales by the aggregated sales of the three largest firms in the country. In addition I use a derivation of the *Hirfindahl Hirschman Index (HHI)* to capture the degree of competitive asymmetry in a market. This measure was calculated as the sum of the squared market shares of the three largest foreign-owned subsidiaries in a market.

Consumption and Demographics

The data for beer and alcohol consumption were obtained from the statistical source of the United Nations Food and Agricultural Organization, FAOstat. The data on demographics were obtained from the statistical data source of the International Labor Organization.

To calculate per capita consumption I use a subset of the population, the adult working age population (15–64), rather than the full population. This is done because beer consumption is not expected to be evenly distributed over all age groups but rather is expected to fall sharply at the lower age range and again at the higher age range. Under conditions where demographics are changing over time this should provide a more accurate estimate of the actual market penetration of beer.

MARKET POSITION AND SUBSIDIARY PERFORMANCE IN THE BREWING INDUSTRY

The brewing industry is undergoing a process of consolidation both domestically (Gourvish 1994) and, more recently, internationally. However, the importance of scale as a rationale for the rapidly increasing consolidation of the brewing industry has been subject to some debate.

Operating Scale in the Brewing Industry

At the level of the brewing plant, the minimum efficient scale (MES) for beer production has been estimated to be quite substantial, even to the point that Gourvish (1994) found that very few brewers had achieved efficient production output at the time of his study. Even in the comparatively concentrated US market, Tremblay and Tremblay (1988) estimated that as much as 92 percent of all brewers operated inefficiently in 1978. Internationally, the constraint of domestic demand, in the presence of production related scale economies, can have provided a strong impetus for internationalization (Hennart 2007), which may explain why many leading international brewers originate from comparatively small home markets. Even so, the desire to exploit home-based scale advantages in production has not been an important feature in the recent internationalization of the brewing industry. For example, while Carlsberg's foreign sales have increased more than tenfold from 12.5 million hl in 1990 to 137 million hl in 2009 the combined Danish exports of beer have increased roughly 23 percent for the corresponding period, from 2.3 million hl to 2.8 million hl. Rather, the growth in foreign sales of the leading international brewers has been facilitated almost exclusively through FDI.

Despite the increasing globalization of the brewing industry, imported beer still accounts for a very limited share of beer consumption. In 2009 roughly 6 percent of world consumption was supplied by imports. However, trade patterns in CEE exhibit a clear link between market size and the propensity to import, pointing towards some, albeit limited, exploitation of production scale advantages on a regional level. While imported beer accounts for a negligible share of consumption in the larger markets in CEE, the share of imported beer has increased considerably between 1993 and 2009 in the smaller CEE markets (Figure 2.1). Most of this increase in trade has occurred with neighboring countries.

There are clear similarities between the recent internationalization of the brewing industry and the preceding domestic consolidation processes. Studying the historical development of the brewing industry in Germany, the UK and the US, Gourvish (1994) found that the average plant size markedly differed between countries and these differences had been persistent over time. Moreover, despite average plant sizes being well below estimated MES, the average number of production plants per brewer had grown over time. This led Gourvish to conclude that the cost advantages of consolidating production on fewer, more efficient production plants were offset by strong localization advantages. Taste preferences, brand loyalty and logistical concerns might all provide reasons to maintain a close proximity to the end consumers, thereby serving to keep brewing

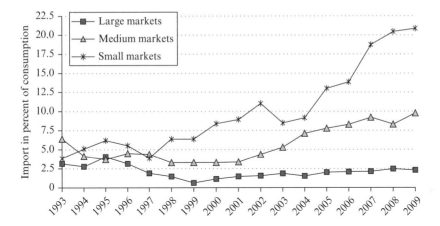

Notes: The 15 Central and Eastern European countries are divided into three groups of five countries based on the relative market size in 1993.

Source: Calculated based on FAOstat data.

Figure 2.1   *The share of imported beer as a percentage of total beer consumption in Central and Eastern Europe between 1993 and 2009*

plants small. This in turn suggests that firm level scale advantages could be the driving force behind increasing consolidation. Unsurprisingly, international brewers are optimistic about the firm level scale advantages that internationalization can deliver. For instance, SABMiller emphasizes international cross-selling, cost savings through global joint purchasing and the ability to exploit technological inventions and best practices across its global network as key firm level advantages of scale (SABMiller 2007, pp. 16–17). Though some of these perceived synergies may have been more difficult to realize, reports produced on behalf of the Brewers of Europe (Brewers of Europe 2006, 2011) find that sourcing and procurement needs are often covered locally in the respective host country.

International trade in malt, a key ingredient in beer, provides an example of some of the locational dynamics in the value chain. Swinnen and Herck (2011) found that the poor quality of locally produced malt initially compelled international brewers to import malt to support local production. But the brewers simultaneously made investments in developing local quality and capacity. Figure 2.2 illustrates how the increasing presence of international brewers in CEE prompted a large increase in the import of malt during the 1990s, only to decrease again as locally produced malt could gradually substitute imported malt. The development of

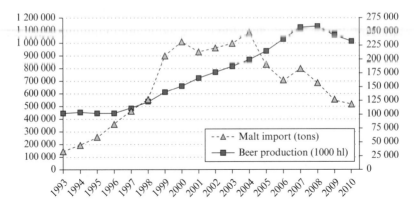

Notes: Notes: Beer production (right axis); malt import (left axis).

Source: Calculated based on FAOstat data.

Figure 2.2   *Beer production and malt import by Central and Eastern*
European countries; including intra-regional trade

local malting industries has also created supply sources closer to the destination countries and as such intra-regional trade accounts for a growing share of malt imports.

Internationalization and Firm Performance

In a meta-analysis of the determinants of financial performance Capon et al. (1990) made the observation that having a high market share was associated with superior performance but that it was unclear whether trying to gain market share was a good idea. Fundamentally this also appears to be the key question for the brewing industry. Two recent studies have explored the link between the increasing internationalization of the brewing industry and firm performance and both studies question whether the process of gaining market share has indeed been cost effective. In this volume Pedersen, Madsen and Thomsen (Chapter 1) examine the question by comparing the financial performance of the four leading international brewers against a control group of 200 other large brewers. Ebneth and Theuvsen (2007) have also examined the performance implications of the increasing internationalization of the brewing industry. They noted that past studies have frequently found that acquisition driven growth tends to be value destroying for the shareholders of the acquirer and to test if that has also been the case for the brewing industry they used an event study methodology on a sample of large international mergers and acquisitions within the industry. Their results did not indicate that international mergers and acquisitions had been value destroying per se, but, on the other hand, they did not find that mergers and acquisitions had been value creating either. In a second test they examined the relationship between the degree of internationalization and the performance of 18 large brewing groups, but they found no positive relationship.

Host Market Position and Firm Performance

While growing international scale does not appear to have strongly influenced firm performance, local market position may be a major determinant of firm performance in the brewing industry. Ebneth and Theuvsen (2007) found that a strong market position in the home market was positively associated with group performance. Anecdotal evidence from CEE also suggests that there is a positive relationship between host market position and firm performance. For instance, Carlsberg enjoys strong operational performance in Russia where its subsidiary Baltica holds a leading position. On the other hand, in Poland, where Carlsberg holds position number three, its performance is correspondingly poor.

High industry concentration is also indicative of a positive market position – firm performance relationship and the brewing industry in CEE is clearly concentrated. With the exception of Slovenia, the three-firm concentration ratios (foreign CR3) of foreign brewers vary between 64 percent and 90 percent of sales, measured by volume (Table 2.1). The

Table 2.1   Market concentration of the brewing industry in Central and Eastern Europe for 2011

	Belarus	Bulgaria	Croatia	Czech Rep.	Estonia	Hungary	Latvia	Lithuania
CR5	86.3	91.8	80.9	82.0	91.4	82.9	83.9	74.8
Foreign CR3	63.9	76.7	68.2	71.9	90.0	73.3	76.2	69.2

	Poland	Romania	Russia	Serbia	Slovakia	Slovenia	Ukraine
CR5	90.2	86.6	82.2	96.3	88.2	90.0	96.5
Foreign CR3	84.7	71.2	65.2	86.2	80.3	8.6	68.9

Notes: CR5 includes both foreign and domestically owned brewers whereas foreign CR3 includes only foreign-owned brewers.

Source: Calculated based on Euromonitor data.

entry and exit behavior of international brewers in CEE further suggests
that market level factors have strongly influenced firm performance.
Roughly half the foreign entrants into CEE have either divested their
assets in the region or been acquired. Even among foreign brewers still
active in CEE many have relinquished activities in some markets, suggesting that the industry is characterized by a positional struggle at the level
of the national markets.

In this respect Central and Eastern Europe provide a particularly suit-
able testing ground to examine the relationship between host market position and performance for the international brewers. Foreign investment
activity in CEE has been sufficiently great that there are multiple foreign
brewers in most host countries and all of the four leading international
brewing groups have had activities spanning multiple countries in CEE.

Table 2.2 presents the results of a stepwise ordinary least squares (OLS)
regression on subsidiary performance, which is a useful technique to assess
the relative importance of multiple explanatory variables. For comparative
purposes Models I–III use ROA as the dependent variable, whereas Models
IV–VI use ROS as the proxy for subsidiary performance. The relative
market share is found to be positively associated with subsidiary performance and is highly significant at the 0.10 percent level for both ROA in
Model I and for ROS in Model IV. Relative *market share* is able to explain
approximately 38 percent for ROA and 30 percent for ROS of the variance
in subsidiary performance between the leading foreign brewers. *Firm size*,
measured by the natural logarithm of sales, is also found to be positively
associated with firm performance and statistically significant at the 1
percent level for both ROA in Model II and ROS in Model V. Though, with
roughly 3 percent of the variance in firm performance explained by *firm
size*, the relative explanatory power of *firm size* is considerably smaller than
that of *market share*. Finally the HHI included in Model III and Model VI
was not found to be significant; consequently an asymmetrical competitive
structure does not appear to affect average subsidiary performance.[3]

The performance effect of market position can clearly be observed in
Table 2.3. On average a foreign-owned market leader could expect an
annual ROA as high as 22.2 percent and roughly twice (10.3 percent) what
the second largest foreign-owned brewer could expect. In turn, the third
largest foreign-owned brewer could on average only expect a ROA of 2.8
percent. The results are largely similar for ROS. Firm size, in this case controlled for by weighting ROA and ROS with total assets and sales respectively, has a small positive effect on overall performance but does not
fundamentally change the relative performance between market leaders
and market contenders. If the market position–performance relationship
was caused by an MES-type effect we would have expected that larger

Table 2.2 *Stepwise OLS regression on subsidiary performance*

	ROA			ROS		
	I	II	III	IV	V	VI
Constant	11.884***	11.884***	11.884***	9.513***	9.513***	9.513***
	(0.789)	(0.771)	(0.774)	(0.838)	(0.816)	(0.819)
Market share	8.017***	6.729***	6.719***	7.137***	5.671***	5.683***
	(0.792)	(0.890)	(0.893)	(0.841)	(0.942)	(0.945)
Firm size		2.604**	2.656**		2.963**	2.901**
		(0.890)	(0.903)		(0.942)	(0.960)
HHI			-0.254			0.300
			(0.790)			(0.836)
F	102.584***	57.948***	38.453***	72.016***	42.914***	28.498***
R square	0.382	0.410	0.407	0.302	0.338	0.335
R square change	–	0.028	-0.003	–	0.036	-0.003
N	165	165	165	165	165	165

Notes:
All explanatory variables have been standardized so the beta value reflects the percentage change in the depended variable resulting from a one standard deviation change in the explanatory variable.
*** Significant at p < 0.001
** Significant at p < 0.01.

Source: Calculated based on Orbis data.

Table 2.3   *Financial performance of foreign-owned subsidiaries in Eastern*
             Europe between 2005 and 2009

	Market leader		Second largest		Third largest	
	ROA	ROS	ROA	ROS	ROA	ROS
Mean	22.2 (26.3)	17.5 (21.9)	10.3 (12.6)	10.1 (12.2)	2.8 (4.0)	0.6 (3.9)
Median	22.8	18.1	9.5	9.3	3.7	3.0
SD	11.7	9.3	8.1	7.4	11.8	15.5
N	59	59	60	60	57	57

Notes: Weighted mean in brackets.

Source: Calculated based on Orbis data.

market contestants, in absolute terms, would more easily reach production scales that were large enough for them to compete effectively. As it happens, scale effects in the brewing industry appear to mainly derive from national level effects, such as, for instance, the ability to efficiently exploit distribution networks or gain cost advantages in national branding.

These results suggest that room for profitable market participation, in a given national market, is only available to very few international brewers. This is less surprising given that mature markets, even large markets such as the US, also tend to be dominated by one or a small number of competitors. What is perhaps more surprising is that these structures and the associated market leadership advantages have developed over a relatively short period of time in a highly competitive environment. Global advantages related to skills, scale or scope have clearly not been sufficient to overcome a disadvantageous local market position.

The practical implication that can be drawn in terms of the internationalization–performance relationship is that it is better to be big in a few markets than small in many, all else being equal. Even so, I shall venture to suggest that the present study may still show the relative performance of the international brewing groups in a slightly more favorable light. All else being equal, an internationally diversified large brewer may, on average, hold a greater share of underperforming market positions than a large domestic or regional brewer. In the long run these underperforming market positions can potentially be improved through growth or acquisitions, or they can be divested. In the following sections I look closer at the prospects for improving a market position in CEE. First, I do so by examining the root causes of the industry's acquisition driven growth pattern and the current scope for acquisitions in the region. Second, I examine the organic growth prospect for CEE.

MARKET STRATEGY AND INDUSTRY CONCENTRATION IN CENTRAL AND EASTERN EUROPE

Acquisition and Industry Concentration

Acquisition has emerged as the leading mode of foreign expansion for the industry, both in CEE and globally. The leaders in this consolidation process have been the four large international brewery groups AB InBev, Carlsberg, Heineken and SABMiller, which have all acquired and established activities broadly throughout the region. A second tier of regional brewers still active in CEE includes Danish Unibrew, Finnish Olvi OYJ and Turkish Anadolu Efes. These groups have typically favored target markets in close geographical proximity to their respective home markets.

While the intensity, speed of commitment and subsequent investment strategies have varied, practically all market entries in the region have occurred through acquisition. In some cases the investing foreign brewer entered through a partial acquisition and then gradually acquired the remaining outstanding shares. In other cases foreign entrants have made strong immediate commitments. For example, when Carlsberg, a relative latecomer to the Bulgarian market, entered Bulgaria in 2002, it did so by fully acquiring two regional brewers nearly simultaneously. Most frequently, entry has occurred through the acquisition of state-owned or freshly privatized local brewers made available by the ongoing privatization processes (Larimo et al. 2006). But in some cases market entries have also occurred through the direct or indirect consolidation of the foreign market participants themselves. The acquisition of the brewing assets of Bass by Interbrew, BBAG by Heineken and Orkla and later Scottish & Newcastle by Carlsberg are examples of such acquisitions that brought with them assets in Central and Eastern Europe.

This is a trend that appears common not only for the brewing industry (Larimo et al. 2006) but also for a broader range of food and drink industries (Lynch 2006). Hennart (2009) attributes the prevalence of acquisition as a means to enter into new foreign markets, within food and drink industries, to the modularity of the acquired assets, arguing that the multinational enterprise is typically able to superimpose superior skills on the existing local production facilities and brand assets.

Brands and Branding Strategy in the Brewing Industry

In the brewing industry control over local brands appears to be particularly essential to successful market entry. In contrast to the concentration

*Table 2.4   The brand structure of Central and Eastern European beer
markets in 2011.*

Country	Largest brand	Top 5 brand share	Foreign brands included in top 5
Belarus	17.6	67.4	Baltica(Ru)
Bulgaria	15.4	61.0	
Croatia	34.0	66.8	Tuborg(Dk); Löwenbräu(De)
Czech Republic	17.6	52.3	
Estonia	31.2	60.6	Carlsberg(Dk)
Hungary	18.1	50.7	
Latvia	8.7	36.9	
Lithuania	19.2	47.5	
Poland	12.5	45.0	
Romania	14.3	48.2	
Russia	16.3	33.7	
Serbia	31.9	75.8	
Slovakia	10.8	39.0	Starobrno(Cz)
Slovenia	32.9	80.4	
Ukraine	22.6	66.9	

Source: Calculated based on Euromonitor data.

of the industry itself, the brand structure tends to be more heterogeneous in the region. Table 2.4 presents details on the brand structure in CEE, with the first column presenting the market share of the leading brand and the second column presenting the combined market share of the five largest brands in the respective countries.[4]

While larger markets are usually expected to be able to support greater diversity of choice (Krugman et al. 2012, p. 194), this does not fully explain the structural heterogeneity between CEE markets. Russia, the largest market in the region, does have the highest apparent brand diversity, with the five leading brands accounting for just 34 percent of the total sales volume. However some small markets in the region, such as Latvia and Slovakia, also boast comparatively high brand diversity, with the combined share of the five leading brands accounting for 37 percent and 39 percent of total sales respectively.

Rather, persistent local consumer preferences have played an important role in shaping the structure of the markets. In a study of Interbrew's entry into CEE, Marinov and Marinova (1998) noted that despite serious quality challenges consumers tended to be conservative and had remained loyal to local tastes and brands.

In contrast, foreign brands tend to have played a more marginal role and have rarely achieved substantial local market shares (Table 2.4). Part of the explanation is naturally that foreign brands are often placed in the premium segment. However, rather than just pushing a slate of existing global premium brands on top of a portfolio of economy or standard priced local brands, the industry has typically also differentiated existing local brands. SABMiller describes this as a differentiation process not just between local and international brands but also as a process of reshaping and differentiating existing local brands.

> What we often find in new markets is that some consumer needs are ignored while others are over-served by too many undifferentiated brands. We then begin the process of adjusting the portfolio to span the market. This may mean refreshing and repositioning our brands, importing brands from elsewhere, adding innovation to existing brands or creating new brands altogether. (SABMiller 2007, p. 12)

Carlsberg's entry into Bulgaria provides an example of this type of local differentiating strategy. With the acquisition of the Bulgarian brewers Pirinsko and Shumensko, the respective brands were positioned to capture different segments of the local beer market. The Pirinsko brand was shaped to target the standard segment, while the Shumensko brand was aimed at the local premium segment.

> Applying a portfolio approach to brand rationalization has resulted in specific roles with a long-term perspective for brands and packs. Shumensko brand architecture, positioning and marketing mix have been updated to place the brand in the mainstream plus segment and local premium segments. (Carlsberg 2003, p. 59)

Through this process the leading international brewers have essentially become managers of vast portfolios of predominantly local brands.

Local Consumer Preferences

The importance of branding and consumer loyalty within the brewing industry is historically well established. In a study utilizing a blind test methodology, Allison and Uhl (1964) found that participants largely appeared unable to discern taste differences between beer brands. However, when faced with labeled versions of the same beer brands, the test results revealed that the participants rated the perceived quality significantly higher. Moreover, the individual preferences of the participants, established before the tests, were also clearly manifested. Accordingly,

Table 2.5   The labeling of leading brands in selected Central and Eastern European countries

Bulgaria	Czech Republic	Poland
Kamenitza (1881)	Gambrinus (1869)	Tyskie (1629)
Shumensko (1882)	Radegast	Zubr (1768)
Ariana	Velkopopovicky Kozel (1874)	Zywiec (1856)
Zagorka (1902)	Staropramen (1869)	Lech
Bolyarka (1892)	Pilsner Urquell (1842)	Tatra

Source: The author's own data collection.

labeling and brand association emerges as a critically important means of product differentiation for the brewing industry. Often the historical heritage and regional origin of a brewery is emphasized as part of the brand identity. Notable international examples include the Carlsberg-owned super premium brand Kronenbourg 1664 and AB InBev's Stella Artois, which features 'anno 1366' on its label.

Similar branding and labeling practices are used in CEE, where international entrants have often preserved and emphasized the historical heritage of the acquired local breweries. Table 2.5 presents an overview of the leading brands in Bulgaria, the Czech Republic and Poland and whether the brand label features the local brewery's historical heritage. Alpert and Kamins (1995) found that consumers tend to be favorably disposed towards brands perceived to be pioneers within their market, which helps explain the attractiveness of this labeling practice. From a resource-based perspective (Barney 1991), this form of brand identity is also inherently difficult to imitate and can provide an explanation both for the continued resilience of local brands and the prevalence of acquisition as a means to enter and consolidate new markets.

Consumer loyalties grounded in national or within country regional ethnocentric attitudes provide another explanation for the overall success of local brands. Many international brewers find it strategically important to be perceived as locally embedded. The vision of the Olvi group is perhaps one of the strongest testaments to the perceived importance of local embeddedness (Figure 2.3).

In an interview-based study on consumer attitudes and preferences among young Polish consumers Siemieniako et al. (2011) observed strong tendencies towards national and regional ethnocentric attitudes in beer preferences. These tendencies are also recognized and even exploited by international brewers. SABMiller has had tremendous success in Poland with its local economy brand Zubr (Polish for bison). Acquired

OLVI GROUP'S VISION

| The most attractive and respected | Finnish Estonian Latvian Lithuanian Belarusian | beverage company. |

Source: OlviOyj (2011, p. 9).

Figure 2.3   The Olvi Group's vision

and relaunched in 2003, the Zubr brand has gone from being a virtually unknown regional brand to the bestselling brand in Poland, commanding a 12.5 percent market share in 2011. Siemieniako et al. (2011) attribute the success of the Zubr brand to a very regionally oriented brand identity, with advertising images, messages and sponsoring activities designed to align the brand with an iconic regional symbol.

Acquisition is clearly the dominant mode of international expansion in the brewing industry. Part of the explanation for this is connected to the intrinsic consumer loyalty that local brand assets can command, though, as the Zubr case shows, the value of a local brand does not necessarily depend wholly on existing sales. Rather, a local brand can provide a form of legitimacy or authenticity that can be leveraged by the foreign owner. Nonetheless, with most brewing assets in the region already in foreign hands, the opportunity for further acquisition-driven expansion is largely exhausted. Looking forward, additional consolidation in CEE must occur at the level of the international or regional brewers themselves. Here the ability to gain ownership control over existing local assets is likely to be one of the main obstacles to further consolidation. Slovenia, as the only Eastern European country where the brewing industry still remains in domestic hands, offers an interesting case. Originally Interbrew entered the Slovenian market in 2001 through the acquisition of a minority stake in the second largest local brewer Pivovarna Union. However Pivovarna Lasko – Slovenia's largest brewer – responded to the perceived threat by acquiring a stake of its own in Pivovarna Union. What followed was a series of attempts by both sides to gain a controlling stake. Interbrew even resorted to filing an antitrust lawsuit against Pivovarna Lasko. When this too proved unsuccessful Interbrew/InBev finally conceded defeat and sold its own stake to Pivovarna Lasko in 2005. A more common control issue arises from the concentration of ownership and voting rights in the hands of foundations or families. Carlsberg experienced such problems in South Korea, where the unwillingness of the local partner to sell out prompted

Carlsberg to divest its own stake in Hite breweries. Restrictive ownership structures are a common feature among the remaining international
brewers in CEE. Carlsberg, Heineken and Olvi OYJ are all controlled by
foundations, whereas Anadolu Efes and the latest international entrant,
Molson Coors, have founder or family ownership, which may also prove
a challenge.

ORGANIC GROWTH PROSPECTS IN THE CENTRAL AND EASTERN EUROPEAN BEER MARKETS

Taken together, CEE has been a major growth area for the international
brewing industry. In 1993 CEE accounted for 9 percent of worldwide beer
consumption, with regional consumption amounting to 102 million hl. By
2008 regional beer consumption had peaked at 259 million hl corresponding to 15 percent of worldwide consumption. However, in the aftermath
of the financial crisis growth in regional beer consumption has been
depressed. While the crisis may have been at the heart of the stagnation it
remains to be seen whether growth will return to pre-crisis levels. In the
following section this question is explored further by examining the level
of market saturation and the demographic outlook for the region.

Market Penetration of Beer

Table 2.6 presents the evolution of per capita beer consumption in CEE
between 1993 and 2009. Initial consumption levels and subsequent growth
rates have varied considerably across the region, tending to follow sub-
regional characteristics. Consumption in the traditional beer drinking
countries in Central Europe has largely remained stable, with a slightly
negative tendency throughout the period. The Czech Republic in particular is notable for its traditionally exceptionally high beer consumption.
In turn, the main growth markets have been in NEE and the three CIS
countries, which have all experienced high growth rates, although from
substantially lower 1993 levels. Over this time period Russia has been one
of the fastest growing beer markets in the world, quadrupling per capita
consumption. Overall, the development over the time period has shown a
strong trend towards converging demand levels across national markets.
At the end of the time period, CEE clearly appears a much more homogeneous regional market than it did at the beginning. Furthermore, with
a tendency towards declining consumption levels in the mature Western
markets, the consumption gap between East and West has also narrowed
substantially.

Table 2.6   Annual beer consumption in liters per working age individual (15–64) between 1993 and 2009

	1993	1994	1995	1996	1997	1998	1999	2000	2001	2002	2003	2004	2005	2006	2007	2008	2009
Major traditional western beer drinking countries																	
Germany	190	**193**	190	184	182	177	179	183	179	171	163	158	154	165	160	155	152
UK	158	**162**	159	162	163	155	157	147	152	152	157	154	152	142	137	132	118
USA	**144**	142	138	138	137	136	136	136	135	135	131	131	130	131	131	128	125
North Eastern Europe																	
Baltic states	43	48	48	48	56	65	79	84	89	105	106	109	118	123	**124**	123	116
Poland	50	56	59	65	75	81	90	97	97	103	108	112	117	126	**129**	127	113
The Commonwealth of Independent States																	
Belarus	33	23	21	26	31	32	33	28	28	26	27	33	46	59	70	**73**	67
Russia	27	23	24	22	27	34	44	51	63	69	74	82	89	99	**113**	112	108
Ukraine	27	27	20	18	19	20	25	31	37	42	48	59	67	74	87	**88**	82
Central Europe																	
Czech Rep.	222	**236**	230	228	234	233	233	228	223	224	225	226	228	228	206	220	211
Slovakia	120	143	124	126	**154**	120	121	122	126	132	128	116	112	113	114	111	112
Slovenia	122	128	**129**	126	118	109	120	90	92	97	93	113	129	117	119	119	119
Hungary	123	**125**	110	104	101	100	100	105	104	104	110	107	104	101	103	105	107
South Eastern Europe																	
Bulgaria	76	84	75	73	53	67	73	74	76	74	82	74	78	93	104	**105**	98
Romania	65	62	58	53	50	65	73	81	81	82	88	103	99	112	131	**133**	126
Croatia	78	98	99	102	108	108	111	127	**129**	123	127	121	118	119	126	124	117
Serbia	76	98	109	109	114	121	**136**	132	117	115	117	110	98	115	112	108	87

Notes: Numbers highlighted in bold represent peak consumption levels.

Source: Calculated based on FAOstat data and ILO population data.

A main factor explaining the convergence of demand within CEE is probably economic conditions, with rising disposable income affecting the demand for beer proportionally more in countries with relatively low incomes and beer consumption. Reviewing the literature on the income elasticity of demand for beer, Colen and Swinnen (2011) noted that the majority of studies have found a positive relationship between income and beer consumption, and the stagnating or falling demand in CEE, in response to current economic hardship, tends to confirm that beer consumption in the region behaves in a normal pro-cyclical manner.

Even so, demand heterogeneity between markets has historically been quite persistent. A root cause for the increasing demand convergence may be endogenous to the industry itself. The tendency towards demand convergence coincides with a massive internationalization of the brewing industry in the region. It is very likely that increasingly standardized marketing techniques and practices have shaped local consumption patterns and reduced some of the traditional heterogeneity between countries. The growth in beer consumption has occurred mainly in the off-site segment, possibly suggesting the emergence of new drinking patterns rather than a fundamental switch in existing drinking patterns.

In a study of the relationship between trade integration and alcohol consumption in 38 countries, Aizenman and Brooks (2008) found that increasing trade integration had led to converging alcohol consumption patterns. A similar tendency is observable for the CEE countries in this study. Both beer and wine consumption show evidence of convergence over the time period 1993–2009 (Table 2.7). Although, relative to beer consumption, regional heterogeneity in wine consumption does remain larger, and consumption of spirits does not show any signs of convergence. Arguably, the brewing industry in the region has experienced a very high degree of internationalization, so the dissimilarities in the convergence patterns between the different alcoholic drinks could be explained by differences in the level of foreign involvement in the respective industries.

The convergence in beer consumption across the region may also reflect governmental attempts to control and curb alcohol abuse. All countries employ instruments aimed at curbing demand or restricting access to alcohol. Typically these include excise taxes, a minimum legal drinking age and restrictions on advertising and distribution. Public policy initiatives based on health concerns may act as a countervailing power, inversely proportional to the level of consumption. Russia, a key market for the Carlsberg group, provides a telling recent case of governmental intervention. While originally perceived as a healthier alternative to vodka, the tremendous growth success of the brewing industry in Russia has given rise to a sharp public policy backslash (BBC 2011a). A wide range of measures

Table 2.7   Regional heterogeneity and convergence in alcohol consumption in Central and Eastern Europe

	1993	1995	1997	1999	2001	2003	2005	2007	2009
Average beer consumption	75.3	78.6	81.8	91.3	94.0	100.7	107.7	117.6	111.5
Standard deviation	(53.1)	(55.0)	(56.3)	(49.4)	(45.5)	(43.8)	(42.2)	(32.0)	(34.2)
Average spirits consumption	11.2	10.1	10.5	9.3	8.5	9.4	9.9	11.2	11.4
Standard deviation	(5.9)	(4.6)	(5.0)	(5.0)	(3.7)	(4.5)	(4.7)	(5.5)	(6.9)
Average wine consumption	19.5	19.1	21.0	17.1	17.2	17.9	17.0	17.0	16.7
Standard deviation	(23.3)	(19.2)	(22.0)	(18.1)	(17.7)	(16.1)	(13.1)	(12.7)	(10.9)

Notes: Annual consumption measured in liters per working age individual (15–64).

Source: Calculated based on FAOstat data and ILO population data.

has been implemented to curb the growing beer consumption and more are expected to follow. Excise taxes have been substantially and repeatedly increased and restrictions on advertising have been implemented. Beer has even been reclassified as an alcoholic substance on a par with wine and spirits (BBC 2011b), which, in turn, also affects the availability of distribution channels. Similarly, with eight substantial excise tax increases between 2003 and 2010, Turkey provides another example of active governmental pressure on the brewing industry (Brewers of Europe 2010). The constant increases in excise taxes contributed to Carlsberg's decision to divest its Turkish subsidiary, Türk Tuborg, in 2008.

An interesting element in both the Russian and Turkish case is that the initial policy decision appears to have created a momentum leading to rapidly increasing regulatory pressure on the beer and alcoholic drink industries. The policy makers appear to have acted on the basis of perceived acceptable consumption thresholds. These perceptions in turn have clearly been affected by tradition, culture or religious factors. In Turkey the annual beer consumption had been as low as 15–20 liters per working age individual.

Demographic Market Prospects

Demographics are an important determinant of alcohol and beer consumption, which in turn make the brewing industry susceptible to demographic

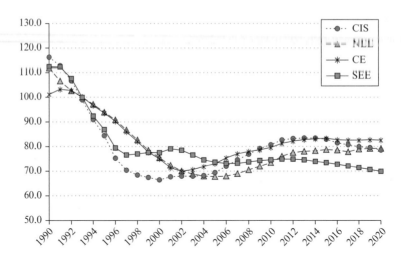

Notes: Males aged 0–4; index 1993 = 100.

Source: Calculated based on ILO population data.

Figure 2.4 The actual and projected infant population by sub-region for the period 1990–2020

changes. In a European study on drinking behavior, which also included the Czech Republic and Hungary, Mäkelä et al. (2006) found that men are (1) generally more likely to drink, (2) drink more often, (3) drink greater quantities and (4) have a markedly higher propensity to drink beer than women. Siemieniako et al. (2011) also note that studies on beer consumption in Poland suggest that the average beer consumer is young and male. The typical advertising and sponsoring behavior of brewers also indicates that young males are perceived to be the primary target group.

A major social and economic problem that CEE is facing is the prospect of declining and aging future populations. Figure 2.4 shows the past and the projected future development in the number of male children[5] between zero and four years of age for the period 1990–2020. As can be observed, the system change in CEE has resulted in a substantial and lasting fertility reduction throughout CEE. The long-term implications of reduced fertility will be gradually aging and decreasing populations, which in turn means smaller prospective markets. In practice these long-term prospects have not yet materially affected the potential markets for beer. By and large the male working age segment has been relatively stable or even growing over the period 1993–2009. In fact, Poland and most of Central Europe have experienced favorable growth in the working age population over the period.

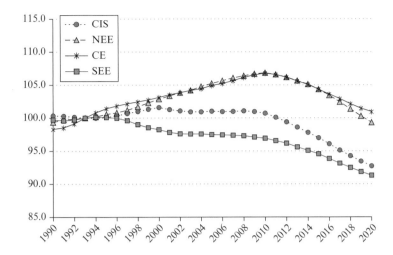

Notes: Males aged 15–64; index 1993 = 100.

Source: Calculated based on ILO population data.

Figure 2.5   *The actual and projected working age population by sub-region for the period 1990–2020*

However this trend is expected to change as the smaller post-system change generations start to enter the workforce (Figure 2.5). In particular, the primary growth regions for beer in CIS and NEE are faced with near-term declining populations with the aggregated male working age population projected to drop by 8 percent and 7 percent respectively between 2010 and 2020.

The comparatively strong projected reversal for CIS and NEE is attributable to a relatively sharp decrease in new entrants into the workforce. Figure 2.6 presents the past and projected development in the number of young adult males aged 15–24. As can be observed, this age group has been steadily declining in Central and South-Eastern Europe since the mid 1990s and is projected to continue falling in the near future. On the other hand, the growth markets in CIS and NEE have largely experienced favorable development in this segment up to the early-mid 2000s but are faced with a much sharper reversal. While the CIS countries represented a combined market potential of 17 million young male consumers aged 15–24 in 2005, the corresponding figure for 2020 is projected to be less than 10 million.

Hence there are strong reasons to expect that the beer markets in CEE have little prospect for future growth. In part this is due to the past success the brewing industry has enjoyed in the region. Per capita consumption

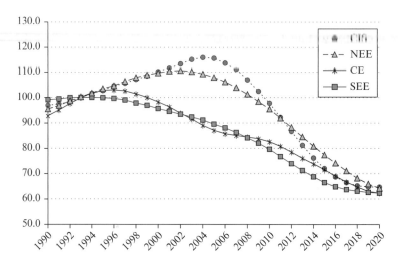

Notes: Males aged 15–24; index 1993 = 100.

Source: Calculated based on ILO population data.

*Figure 2.6   The actual and projected young adult population by sub-region
for the period 1990–2020*

has increased tremendously in the traditionally spirits-oriented countries
in CIS and NEE. In some of these countries beer consumption has reached
or even eclipsed the consumption levels of some of the traditional beer
drinking countries in Central Europe. Generally, per capita consumption levels within the region have converged markedly since the early
1990s. This in turn raises doubt as to whether there is significant scope
for growth through increased market penetration. The past success of
the brewing industry may also mean that it must contend with tougher
regulatory environments in the future. Especially in Russia, the brewing
industry has enjoyed very lenient regulatory conditions, mainly because
beer was considered the lesser evil in the traditionally vodka drinking
country. But as beer consumption has grown, that lenience has vanished.
Continued growth in beer consumption in CEE will almost certainly invite
future policy interventions, because curbing alcohol abuse is a legitimate
public policy aim and therefore provides an easily justifiable *casus belli*,
often with the added benefit of providing additional tax revenues (*The
Economist* 2009), but also because the emerging international structure of
the brewing industry lacks natural defenses against policy interventions.
In practice the international brewers tend to be more dependent on the

host countries for market access than the host countries are dependent on the international brewers. While the industry contributes to the local economy through tax revenues and job creation, particularly indirect job creation, it lacks more pressing motives for public policy lenience, such as the generation of export revenues. With brewers increasingly owned by foreign firms, the local political clout the industry can muster is also likely to diminish.

A problem that has the potential to be much worse is that populations in the region are projected to face long-term decline. This is, of course, a serious social and economic challenge, but it will also impact CEE as a market. And this impact will probably affect the global brewing industry earlier and harder than many other industries partly because of the relatively young demographic profile of beer drinkers and partly because of the very large investments made by the industry in the region.

DISCUSSION AND CONCLUSION

For the brewing industry, CEE has been one of the most dynamic world regions over the last two decades. Beer consumption in the region has expanded considerably and extensive FDI means that nearly all markets are effectively controlled by international brewers.

However, CEE lacks prospects for continued growth. Strongly converging consumption levels across the region point to an emerging equilibrium close to current levels. There are also signs that the brewing industry may face increasing regulatory pressure, which could further hamper growth. Russia provides a strong case that countries in the region can and will respond very decisively to levels of beer and alcohol consumption that are perceived to be undesirable, though the most pressing long-term growth challenge is undoubtedly the negative demographic outlook for the region. Birth rates are markedly lower than the level necessary to maintain current populations. In a sense the brewing industry in CEE might be about to face two of mankind's most enduring constants, death and taxes.

Studies of the internationalization of the brewing industry have found little evidence that brewers gain from international growth per se. However the results of the current study show that international brewers clearly gain from having a strong host market position. Market leaders tend to substantially outperform market challengers in terms of operational performance, suggesting the existence of very strong national level scale or scope advantages. It is possible that these advantages are linked to first-mover advantages. The typical international brewer in CEE has a broad portfolio of brands, with local brands accounting for most of the sales. Boulding and Christen (2009) found that early product market entry in combination with a broad product line can be performance enhancing. When the product line itself comprises mainly assets (local brands) that can be pre-empted (Lieberman and Montgomery 1988) through acquisition that would be a very reasonable explanation.

Managerial Implications

What are the managerial implications of this study? Unless there are important strategic reasons, it will only pay to operate in a foreign market if a position as market leader, or at least number two in the market, is achievable. In most countries in CEE there are too few independent brewers left for local acquisitions to materially influence current market positions. Furthermore, the absence of organic growth prospects may also prove particularly problematic for market challengers. A declining consumer base, especially of new drinkers, possibly even coupled with increasing restrictions on advertising, will probably increase the cost and difficulty of changing brand preferences. All else being equal, rigid brand structures favor the established market leaders.

Consequently, the positioning struggle in CEE may have reached the endgame, where the international brewers will want to deal with markets in which they do not hold leading positions. This in turn will require consolidation of activities between the international brewers themselves. In theory this can of course be achieved through consolidation among the top end direct competitors themselves. This would arguably be the fastest and most direct approach, though in practice the ownership structure of many of the remaining international brewers in the region tends to be unaccommodating for mergers.

A more likely scenario is that the brewers will simply divest assets in unpromising markets and divert the resources to more promising markets. The configuration of the international brewers' activities has remained largely local in nature, which in turn makes the assets of the international brewers relatively modular and correspondingly easy to transfer between firms. There is already some evidence of such a process. The world's largest brewer, AB InBev, has been actively divesting assets in both CEE and Asia while strengthening its position in other markets through, for example, the buyout of the Mexican Modelo group.

In the US market, SABMiller and Molson Coors chose to combine their operations in a joint venture in order to strengthen their position. A similar strategy might also be advantageous in CEE. In this respect the strategic initiative could be in the hands of SABMiller. Having recently traded its assets in Russia and Ukraine for a minority stake in Anadolu

Efes, it remains to be seen if this is a precursor for a full exit or for a future takeover of Anadolu Efes. The acquisition of Starbev, the former CEE assets of AB InBev, by Molson Coors may also offer strategic opportunities for SABMiller, since the two firms already serve the US market together. Combining parts or all of the CEE assets of SABMiller and Molson Coors would decidedly change the competitive landscape in CEE. Among the more regional brewers, Unibrew and the Olvi group share some market overlap in the Baltic countries that could form the basis for cooperation.

Are the dynamics of the brewing industry local or global? The evidence from this study suggests that the performance dynamics of the brewing industry are mainly local. There is some evidence of emerging regional trade dynamics in beer and raw materials, though these still appear too limited to suggest that a regionalization could directly enhance performance (Rugman and Oh 2010). Even so, there are behavioral indications pointing towards increasing regional focus among the international brewers. Some international brewers, such as Carlsberg, have already declared their intent to focus on specific regions. The AB InBev divestment was clearly also regionally motivated as there were very successful national operations among the divested assets. For competitive reasons it may simply be expedient to concentrate activities geographically. Since national markets are unable to support a great many brewers, a more narrowly defined geographical scope can be a useful signal in a positioning struggle. Hence, while the leading international brewers have expanded their global reach dramatically over the last two decades, we may see a process of de-globalization in the future, with brewers refocusing and concentrating resources and efforts on fewer regional markets. Because of the inherently local competitive dynamics of the brewing industry it is unlikely that we will see the emergence of truly global brewers as defined by Rugman and Verbeke (2009). Similarly, what might be required for a truly global beer brand to emerge is a resurgence of a niche market focus through, for example, the licensing of premium brands. But the increasing scarcity of independent brewers will probably make such alternative modes of operation problematic. Moreover, while increasing premiumization might change the dynamics of local markets in favor of high margin products, the widespread cultivation of local premium brands means that it is far from certain that international brands will be the main beneficiaries.

NOTES

1. A foreign market entry is considered on a one firm or group/one country basis. As such, a foreign market entry is considered to have occurred when a foreign-owned firm or con-

sortium of firms establishes or acquires brewing activities in a country in which the firm or consortium had no prior foreign direct investment (FDI) activities. An acquisition in which the acquirer gains brewery activities in multiple national markets, typically an indirect acquisition, can correspond to multiple market entries. On the other hand, the simultaneous or sequential acquisition of multiple local breweries in the same national market, a common occurrence, is not treated as additional foreign market entry. Firms owned by foreign legal entities whose ownership could be traced back to nationals or legal entities of the host country are not treated as foreign market entry either.

2. Since then the former assets of AB InBev have passed to the private equity firm CVC Partners and subsequently to the Canadian/US beer group Molson Coors. Meanwhile, SABMiller has divested its assets in Russia and Ukraine to the Turkish Anadolu group, and the Danish brewer Unibrew has sold its Polish activities to Polish Van Pur. These changes are not included in the figures.

3. In a separate test (not reported) HHI was found to be positively and significantly associated with aggregated industry performance. In other words, an industry structure with one large and two small firms would generate larger combined profits than an industry structure with three equally sized competitors. However the gains fall entirely to the market leader, which means that a simple average is unable to capture this effect.

4. The figures include all direct brand extensions such as light, dark, original, special or premium.

5. The analysis focuses on male consumers as these are expected to represent the main target group for brewers. However, the demographic trends are broadly similar for women. Significant gender discrepancies only appear at higher ages due to a general tendency for women to live longer.

REFERENCES

Aizenman, J. and E. Brooks (2008), 'Globalization and taste convergence: the cases of wine and beer', *Review of International Economics*, **16** (2), 217–33.

Allison, R.I. and K.P. Uhl (1964), 'Influence of beer brand identification on taste perception', *Journal of Marketing Research*, August, 36–9.

Alpert, F.H. and M.A. Kamins (1995), 'An empirical investigation of consumer memory, attitude and perception toward pioneer and follower brands', *Journal of Marketing*, **59**, 34–45.

Barney, J. (1991), 'Firm resources and sustained competitive advantage', *Journal of Management*, **17**, 99–120.

BBC (2011a), 'Russia beer sales suffering tax hike', BBC, 31 May, accessed 16 November 2012 at www.bbc.co.uk/news/business-13604311.

BBC (2011b), 'Russia classifies beer as alcoholic', BBC, 21 July, accessed 16 November 2012 at www.bbc.co.uk/news/world-europe-14232970.

Boulding, W. and M. Christen (2009), 'Pioneering plus a broad product line strategy: higher profits or deeper losses?', *Management Science*, **55** (6), 958–67.

Brewers of Europe (2006), 'The contribution made by beer to the European economy', The Brewers of Europe, Amsterdam, January, accessed 16 November 2012 at www.brewersofeurope.org/docs/publications/Country%20chapters%20Economic%20impact%20of%20beer.pdf.

Brewers of Europe (2010), 'Turkey: excise duty increased twice in 10 months. 55% of consumer price is tax', Brewers of Europe, 8 November, accessed 16 November 2012 at www2.brewersofeurope.org/asp/newsroom/l1.asp?doc_id=220.

Brewers of Europe (2011), 'The contribution made by beer to the European economy', The Brewers of Europe, Amsterdam, September, accessed 16 November 2012 at www.brewersofeurope.org/docs/flipping_books/contribu tion_report_2011/index.html.

Capon, N., J.U. Farley and S. Hoenig (1990), 'Determinants of financial perform- ance: a meta-analysis', *Management Science*, **36** (10), 1143–59.

Carlsberg (2003), 'Annual report 2003', Carlsberg, accessed 16 November 2012 at www.carlsberggroup.com/investor/downloadcentre/Pages/AnnualReport 2003new.aspx.

Colen, L. and J. Swinnen (2011), 'Beer drinking nations. The determinants of global beer consumption', Working Paper No. 79, April, American Association of Wine Economists, 1–39.

Ebneth, O. and L. Theuvsen (2007), 'Large mergers and acquisitions of European brewing groups, event study evidence of value creation', *Agribusiness*, **23** (3), 377–406.

Gourvish, T.R. (1994), 'Economics of brewing, theory and practice: concentra- tion and technological change in the USA, UK and West Germany since 1945', *Business and Economic History*, **23** (1), 253–61.

Hennart, J.-F. (2007), 'The theoretical rational for a multinationality-performance relationship', *Management International Review*, **47**, 423–52.

Hennart, J.-F. (2009), 'Down with MNE-centric theories! Market entry and expansion as the bundling of MNE and local assets', *Journal of International Business Studies*, **40**, 1432–54.

Krugman, P.R., M. Obstfeld and M.J. Melitz (2012), *International Economics, Theory and Policy*, 9th ed., Boston, MA: Pearson.

Larimo, J., M. Marinov and S. Marinova (2006), 'The Central and Eastern European brewing industry since 1990', *British Food Journal*, **108** (5), 371–84.

Lieberman, M.B. and D.B. Montgomery (1988), 'First-mover advantages', *Strategic Management Journal*, **19** (2), 41–58.

Lynch, R. (2006), 'International acquisitions and other growth strategies: some lessons from the food and drink industry', *Thunderbird International Business Review*, **48** (5), 605–22.

Mäkelä, P., G. Gmel, U. Grittner, H. Kuendig, S. Kuntsche, K. Blomfield and R. Room (2006), 'Drinking patterns and their gender differences in Europe', *Alcohol & Alcoholism*, **41**, i8–i18.

Marinov, M. and S. Marinova (1998), 'Investor strategy development and adapta- tion: the case of Interbrew', *European Management Journal*, **16** (4), 400–10.

OlviOyj (2011), 'Annual report 2011', OlviOyj, accessed 16 November 2012 at www.olvi.fi/c/document_library/get_file?folderId=202211&name=DLFE- 11514.pdf.

Rugman, A.M. and C.H. Oh (2010), 'Does the regional nature of multinationals affect the multinationality and performance relationship', *International Business Review*, **19**, 479–88.

Rugman, A.M. and A. Verbeke (2009), 'The regional dimension of multinationals and the end of "varieties of capitalism"', in Simon Collinson and Glenn Morgan (eds), *Images of the Multinational Firm*, Chichester: Wiley, pp. 23–44.

SABMiller (2007), 'Annual report 2007', SABMiller, accessed 16 November 2012 at www.sabmiller.com/files/reports/ar2007/.

Siemieniako, D., K. Kubacki, E. Glinska and K. Krot (2011), 'National and regional ethnocentrism: a case study of beer', *British Food Journal*, **113** (3), 404–18.

Swinnen, J.F.M. and K.V. Herck (2011), 'How the East was won: the foreign takeover of the Eastern European brewing industry', in J.F.M. Swinnen (ed.), *The Economics of Beer*, Oxford: Oxford University Press, pp. 247–64.

The Economist (2009), 'Sin-tax error; public health trumps brewing, but not distilling', *The Economist*, 22 October.

Tremblay, V.J. and C.H. Tremblay (1988), 'The determinants of horizontal acquisitions: evidence from the US brewing industry', *The Journal of Industrial Economics*, **37** (1), 21–45.

PART II

Host country institutional effects

3. Reaching distant parts? The internationalization of brewing and local organizational embeddedness

Graham Hollinshead and Mairi Maclean

INTRODUCTION

The brewing industry has been subject to the forces of internationalization and structural change over the past decade. As Chapter 1 by Pedersen, Madsen and Lund-Thomsen contained in this volume suggests, the industry possessed a highly localized and fragmented character in 2000, with only local market leaders being evident. By 2012, through an aggressive programme of mergers and acquisitions (M&As), the four leading global brewers – namely Heineken, Carlsberg, AB InBev and SABMiller – were present across a number of local markets. Major drivers of the internationalization of the brewing industry have been the momentous geopolitical developments which have rendered China, India, Russia and Central and Eastern Europe 'open for business' for producers. Despite recent economic downturns, emerging growth markets have presented tantalizing opportunities for international breweries to tap into a growing taste for beer in those localities and, as Pedersen, Madsen and Lund-Thomsen point out, there has been a rush to be the first-mover in these newly liberalized trade regions.

The structural features of the nascent international brewing industry remain under-researched, yet it is clear that they are highly distinctive due to the nature of the product under consideration. Of great significance is the physical heaviness of this ancient alcoholic beverage, which renders its transportation across geographical space both costly and unwieldy. In consequence, a compelling operational logic dictates that beer should be produced close to its potential consumers. Also, as is highlighted by various contributors to the present volume, the composition of the product itself is relatively crude, comprising only barley, hops and water. Therefore, the processes of beer manufacture are arguably less amenable to vertical and spatial disaggregation, as increasingly manifested in global production chains in lighter and higher-tech industries. Rather, dispersed productive facilities can be characterized by relative homogeneity in processes and technology, with market differentiation being achieved by assiduous and creative branding (Pedersen, Madsen and Lund-Thomsen, Chapter 1).

Given new trends towards the globalization of beer production and consumption, and the competitive advantages accruing to first-movers, it is perhaps of little surprise that target breweries in the recent wave of M&A activity have tended to have been situated in transitional economies. We focus in this chapter on the study of such an acquisition in the highly transitional, and volatile, political setting of the Republic of Serbia. As an antidote to studies in international management which are prone to envisage multinational linkages in primarily operational or transactional terms, we follow a body of literature in political economy, organizational institutionalism and comparative historical institutionalism (see, for example, Kostova and Roth 2002; Hall and Soskice 2001; Morgan and Kristensen 2006; Dörrenbächer and Geppert 2011), to commence with the premise that M&A targets are distinctively *embedded* in specific institutional and cultural contexts in the host country (Bouquet and Birkinshaw 2008; Harzing and Sorge 2003). Accordingly, the human actors who are responsible for managing and working in subsidiary breweries are profoundly subject to the local sociopolitical influences being exerted upon them, as well as to the 'pull of history' in their region. In placing a recently acquired Serbian subsidiary of a Turkish-owned international brewer 'centre stage' in our study, we aim to bring to the fore the organizational and strategic complexities and challenges being experienced at company level in the new era of globalization of brewing, with reference to the local context of the brewery in question. A central theme which emerges from our case study analysis relates to the tensions experienced as headquarters-based and local level managers seek to implement and negotiate their respective mandates in a profoundly asymmetrical power relationship (Bouquet and Birkinshaw 2008).

THE SERBIAN CONTEXT

History

In the following section, since we are concerned to *contextualize* the position of the brewery forming the focal point of our study, we provide an overview of the Serbian sociopolitical environment. In the early part of the new millennium, the Republic of Serbia found itself in a state of social and economic devastation, seriously lagging behind neighbouring Central and Eastern European states which were advancing in the transition from socialism to capitalism, many of which were achieving rehabilitation in the economic and political structures of an enlarged European Union (EU). Although the relative disadvantages confronting Serbia were manifold, the following are indicative of the damning legacies of the 1990s: (1) serious damage to the national infrastructure, including transport, as a result of NATO (North Atlantic Treaty Organization) bombardments; (2) a loss of 60 per cent of gross domestic product (GDP) in the decade from 1989–99; (3) the haemorrhaging of around 300 000 people to the West between the summers of 1991 and 1992 at the outbreak of hostilities, including many educated people (Collin 2001); (4) approximately one million refugees (around 10 per cent of the population), placing an extra burden on drained social services; (5) and last but not least, a deficit in educational and technological advancement as a legacy of economic sanctions and isolation.

Moreover, it can be observed that fragility and impermanence has characterized much institutional life during the new millennium. As Hollinshead (2006) has observed, despite a broad political drive towards reform and democratization, the forces of the status quo continue to be evident in all walks of Serbian life, threatening a return to state socialism combined with militant nationalism. A series of governmental coalitions over the past ten years have uneasily combined reformist with retrogressive party interests, the latter arguably reflecting the mood of the rural, non-cosmopolitan tranche of the Serbian populace which is influenced by Russian religious orthodoxy, and which is prone towards deference to a single source of authority as opposed to acceptance of the legitimacy of multiple sources (Upchurch and Cicmil 2004). Pejovich (2004) has argued that the values of collectivism and egalitarianism remain strong and that, among the older and poorly educated segments of the population, anti-free-market sentiment is powerful, accompanied by ethno-nationalism and xenophobia (Hollinshead and Maclean 2007). The challenge to reformist political and economic development was most starkly and brutally demonstrated through the assassination of pragmatic and pro-Western Prime Minister Zoran Djindjić in March 2003.

Serbia has unfortunately been tarnished with the status of a 'pariah state' within European and international trading blocs for much of the past two decades, largely due to its culpability in 'ethnic cleansing' in Bosnia and Croatia during the Yugoslav civil wars, and to its failure to endorse the declaration of independence of the southern province of Kosovo as an independent state in February 2008 (Obradovic-Wochnik 2009). Kosovo represents an 'ancestral' and spiritual 'birthplace' to many Serbians, particularly those of a nationalistic persuasion; yet it is, in

reality, home to a majority Albanian population. Inter-ethnic tensions in
Kosovo have persisted for centuries, the region straddling the ideological
fault line between Western and Eastern traditions. Indeed, matters came
to a head in March 1999, following NATO bombardments of Kosovo,
when Serbian nationals in the province were forced to flee as Albanian
interests threatened reprisals for previous ethnic atrocities.

In recent years, there have been welcome signs of growth in the Serbian
economy, coupled with gestures of reconciliation at the national political
level with the former adversarial states of Bosnia, Croatia and Kosovo.
The EU, in a landmark decision in October 2011, offered Serbia EU candidate country status on condition that the Republic normalized relations
with Kosovo. This followed the handing over of suspected war criminals
Radovan Karadzić (2008), Radko Mladić and Goran Hadzić (2011) to the
international tribunal in The Hague, as demanded by the United Nations
(UN). Despite building bridges within the EU, and more generally in the
West, Serbia retains strong dependency on Russia, which gained control
of the Republic's oil distribution in 2008 and which provided a €1 bn loan
in 2009 to alleviate economic difficulties, buttressed by a further €3 bn
loan in the same year from the International Monetary Fund (IMF).

In 2012, the nationalist politician Tomislav Nikolić confounded expectations by unseating Liberal Democrat, and pro-Western incumbent, Boris
Tadić, from the position of prime minister. Mr Nikolić's political career
was founded in the ultra nationalist Serbian Radical Party, although he
now espouses more 'progressive' and pro-European policies, supporting EU membership as well as retaining strong links with Russia. At the
time of writing, prospects for Serbia are still unclear, yet it benefits from
a highly skilled workforce, and occupies a geopolitical 'bridge' between
East and West, and a central position in the Central Europe Free Trade
Agreement (CEFTA). On the negative side, the fundamental institutions
for market democracy have yet to be truly established, while corruption,
organized crime, tax evasion and financial fraud have remained commonplace, although the Serbian government approved the establishment of an
anti-corruption agency (ACA) in 2008. In light of these factors, the World
Bank ranks Serbia in 92nd position out of a total of 183 countries as a
good place in which to do business (2012).

The Serbian Approach to Privatization

Although enterprise privatization in Serbia commenced in 1990, its
progress was retarded during the period of war and sanctions in the decade
that followed. The post-Milosević era has witnessed a 'shock-therapy'
approach (Ristić 2004), catalysed by a new law effective from 1 June 2001.

The former Yugoslavia, since the Tito era, had diluted central planning in favour of decentralized economic management, this being associated with a comparatively high number of small businesses, including shops and restaurants. Many enterprises still remain technically in the control of employees and management committees acting on their behalf. The new law on privatization represented a fundamental challenge to Yugoslavian economic and social traditions by stipulating that the privatization of socially-owned enterprises was mandatory, effectively transferring enterprise ownership from workers, via the state, to external stakeholders (Đuričin 2000). Under the 2001 law, 70 per cent of a privatized company was to be sold to Serbian and foreign investors, with 15 per cent of equity remaining for workers and 15 per cent for citizens. This abolished the 1997 Privatization Law, introduced under the Milosević government, which allocated 60 per cent of shares to workers. The privatization of socially-owned enterprises, in sectors such as light engineering, banking and insurance, hotels and restaurants, occurred alongside the transfer of ownership of state-owned enterprises into private hands, such as electricity and telecommunications. As international trade union interests point out (UNISON 2002–05), the legacy of social ownership means that many employees resent the denationalization (especially in the case of mass voucher schemes) of companies they felt they already owned. Many of the larger enterprises have been effectively bankrupt since the collapse of the former Yugoslavia, having been dependent upon the internal Yugoslav market. However, they were kept open, often with a largely passive workforce, as a means of maintaining social peace. Socially-owned enterprises also operated an extensive system of subsidies for housing, public utilities and basic foods, all of which are being removed through the privatization agenda. As Hollinshead and Maclean (2007) argue, as foreign interests gained a foothold in the Serbian economy, and patterns of industrial ownership became more diffuse, so Serbian workers were exposed to the ravaging effects of capitalist modernization programmes. However, the combined effects of political oppression and international isolation have created a syndrome of impotence at workplace level. In cases of privatization, worker representatives have become resigned to taking rearguard action, negotiating severance packages only retrospectively (UNISON 2002–05). Stanojević (2003) asserts that Serbian trade unions constitute a special case, being severely disadvantaged by outright government rejection of market-related reforms in the late 1980s and 1990s, and the use of nationalism as an instrument of labour pacification. The ability of unions, untrained in negotiation, to represent effectively the interests of their (falling) memberships is open to question (Maclean and Hollinshead 2011). In the face of new management practices imported from the West,

Serbian workers remain disorganized and beyond the regulative scope of formal institutions (Hollinshead and Maclean 2007)

Foreign Direct Investment and Brewing

Prospects of economic growth and regeneration in Serbia, and hopes for the Republic's rehabilitation within international trading structures have tended to rest on its potential to attract foreign direct investment (FDI). The Serbian government has therefore offered some of the lowest business taxation rates in Europe, alongside various subsidiaries, to encourage inward investors into the Republic. However, the legal and institutional infrastructure relating to FDI is in need of rationalization and modernization, currently consisting of a set of rather piecemeal laws, in conjunction with the Constitution of the Republic of Serbia, and the Privatization Law (Petrović and Čerović 2011). As a consequence, over much of the first decade of the 2000s, FDI inflow has been lower than anticipated. From 2000–05 FDI rose from approximately €40 m to €122 m. In 2006 the figure peaked at €3.380 m (Petrović and Čerović 2011) with the sale of Mobtel Telecommunications to the controversial Austrian entrepreneur Martin Schlaff, and subsequently to Norwegian Telecom. The Serbian Chamber of Commerce reported that approximately €1550 m of FDI was received in 2011. Over this period the most significant FDI has been in the areas of financial mediation, manufacturing and telecommunications. In 2011, notable investors were Delhaize (Belgium), Bosch (Germany), Benetton (Italy), Cooper Tires (US) and Swarovski (Italy). According to statistics recording gross FDI income in the region, Serbia remains in fourth place, marginally behind Romania, Bulgaria and Croatia (The International Business Sector in Serbia Conference 2010).

For the first quarter of 2010, in the food and drinks sector Serbia slipped from ninth to twelfth position in the emerging market matrix (*South East European Industrial Market* 2010). From an industry perspective, as expressed by *South East European Industrial Market* (2010), Serbia remains a less viable target locality for food and drinks companies than the Baltic states, as the economic situation in the latter improves. The widespread grey economy, high unemployment, unresolved political issues and the downward pressure on the food and drinks process are cited as deterrents to FDI in the short term. However, in the longer term, there is optimism in the industry that prospects in Serbia will become brighter as per capita consumption of food and drinks is buoyant.

In general, investors into the sector have originated from Europe, most notably with the French company Groupe Danone complementing investments in Bulgaria and Romania with acquisitions of dairy facilities in Serbia.

However, it is larger players based in other former Yugoslavian territories which have demonstrated the least reluctance to invest in the Republic, for example the Slovenian-owned mass grocery retailer Mercator has invested extensively in Serbia (*South East European Industrial Market* 2010).

Turning more specifically to brewing, conditions have generally deteriorated across the Central and Eastern European (CEE) countries since early 2009, as the recession has impacted negatively on the consumption of non-essential beverages. Moreover, the stagnant demographics associated with the region do not favour brewers, particularly those which are not market leaders (*South East European Industrial Market* 2010). In Serbia, the brewing industry has been subject to significant M&A activity in recent years. Key players include the following:

- Carlsberg Serbia/Pivaro Celarevo, now called Carlsberg Srbija, became part of the Carlsberg Group in 2003. The acquisition has been heralded as one of the most successful privatizations in Serbia, as it involved the relaunching of the local LAV brand as well as the timely launching of Tuborg in Serbia.
- Apatinska Pivara was originally built in 1756, and is now the largest brewery in Serbia. Its major products are Jelen Pivo and Pils Light. The brewery possesses some of the most advanced technologies in Europe due to German involvement, and is operational for 24 hours a day, seven days a week. In October 2009, private equity fund CVC Capital Partners bought the majority stakes previously held by the US/Brazilian/Belgian-owned group Anheuser-Busch InBev in the entire CEE region, including Apatinska Pivara.
- Novosadski Pivara (Novi Sad brewery) is the youngest brewery, having started production in 2003. Through an aggressive marketing campaign, which included local celebrity endorsement and sponsorship of basketball team KK Partizan, it quickly established its MB Pivo brand. Heineken International acquired the brewery in February 2008, at which time the company changed its name to Brauerei MB. The company merged with Efes Srbija in October 2008 to form a new entity Ujedinjenesrpskapivare (United Breweries of Serbia). The three market leaders in Serbia are currently United Breweries of Serbia, Apatinska Pivara and Carlsberg Serbia (*South East European Industrial Market* 2010).

Serbian Epochs and the Case Study Brewery

Pančevo was the oldest brewery in the Balkans, having been established on 22 May 1722. Since that time it continued to operate for nearly three centuries, gradually developing its technological capacity. A critical stage in its development occurred at the end of the nineteenth and beginning of the twentieth century when the German family Weise[1] took charge and developed the first steam brewery. The brewery's international connections were useful in learning brewing techniques from abroad, particularly from Austria and Germany.

During the Tito era, Pančevo was nationalized, family ownership giving way to the socialistic organizational form of 'social ownership'. Accordingly, the brewery was owned by the workers themselves and managed by their representatives. In 1970, the brewery became a subsidiary entity within the PIK Tamiš holding company, which also possessed interests in agriculture and other sectors. In the 1980s Pančevo enjoyed rapid development and increased capacity, serving markets in Serbia, Montenegro, Macedonia and Croatia through the establishment of distribution centres in these regions. In June 1989, Pančevo became a legal entity through the provisions of the first law on companies.

During the 1990s, in common with other Yugoslav enterprises, Pančevo suffered as a result of war and sanctions. Indeed, the Pančevo community was particularly badly affected by NATO bombings. In addition to losing valuable markets as the former Yugoslavia disintegrated, the brewery was unable to attract new investment from government or to import new technology and equipment. Nevertheless, there remained a sustained demand for beer throughout the period of civil conflict, and local producers retained a stranglehold over the market. In 1991, the brewery became one of the first privatizing organizations in Serbia, with shareholders acquiring 60 per cent of socially-owned capital. This figure rose to 90 per cent in 1998 as a result of the new privatization and transformation law. Accordingly, although the general assembly overseeing the company comprised appointed individuals, the general manager operated in an independent capacity, with a primarily professional, as opposed to political, orientation (Maclean and Hollinshead 2011).

INSTITUTIONAL AND MICRO-POLITICAL ISSUES IN THE MNC

In recent years, there has been growing recognition amongst scholars that institutional theory might be used to greater effect to comprehend the complexities of organization in multinational corporations (MNCs). As Morgan and Kristensen (2006, p. 1468) observe, 'Only recently, however, have institutionalists begun to explore the consequences of the pluralistic nature of social embeddedness processes in multinationals.' These writers assert that such a development is welcome as it represents 'a significant corrective to rational and economistic models of the multinational' (2006, p. 1468). Underlying such institutional theorization is the recognition, as articulated in a seminal fashion by Meyer and Rowan (1977), that organizations are concerned to acquire legitimacy within the rationalized and institutionalized norms and expectations emanating from their environment (Geppert et al. 2006). *Organizational institutionalism* holds that organizational actors are powerfully influenced by regulative and cognitive frames in their immediate surroundings (Powell and DiMaggio 1991; Scott 2001). Accordingly, MNCs are likely to manifest various 'social spaces', headquarters being embedded in the institutional milieu of their home locality, while subsidiaries will tend to internalize the prevalent sociopolitical and related configurations of their situated geographical positions (Harzing and Sorge 2003). In keeping with this trajectory, Kostova (1999) asserts that MNC subsidiaries frequently find themselves in a situation of *institutional duality*, on the one hand being subjected to powerful regulatory and normative influences emanating from corporate headquarters, while, on the other, being pressured to adopt practices consistent with host country convention (see also Kostova and Roth 2002; Kostova and Zaheer 1999; Morgan and Kristensen 2006). *Comparative and historical institutionalism* (Morgan and Kristensen 2006) is more concerned with the macro-level effects of institutional arrangements in societies, and is closely associated with the established literature on business systems (Whitley 1999) and varieties of capitalism (Hall and Soskice 2001). The central thrust of such theorization is that the nature of the business system in the country of origin of the MNC, including means of ownership, degrees of competition or collaboration between industrial and commercial concerns, and the quality of relationship between management and worker/trade unions (Whitley 1999) will fundamentally determine the structural and cultural characteristics of the outwardly expanding international concern. Accordingly, 'policies, practices, national templates and routines of control' (Morgan and Kristensen 2006, p. 1471) emanating from the home country will tend to be subject to diffusion and replication amongst subsidiaries.

Drawing upon these strands of institutional theorization as they impact the MNC, yet stressing the significance of social agency and power relationships in defining 'social spaces' in MNCs in a dynamic and negotiated, rather than purely structural, fashion, Dörrenbächer and Geppert (2011, p. 27) argue that 'power relations are context specific (institutional and culturally shaped but not determined) and actively and discursively constituted by actors with specific identities and interests (subjectivity)'. In framing their research-based volume *Politics and Power in the*

Multinational Corporation (2011), which advocates that a 'bottom-up' view of MNC organization is necessary to understand its reality. Dörrenbächer and Geppert (2011) postulate three assertions, which have direct relevance for the current study as follows:

(1) Formal authority and power structures in MNCs should be regarded as fragmented, combining domains of knowledge and expertise emanating from various host contexts, in effect representing a 'federation of national companies' (Morgan and Kristensen 2006). Even highly globalized corporations cannot assume that they assert hierarchical control and standardized practice and processes across subsidiaries. The notion of the 'multinational federation' has particular validity in cases of international M&As.

(2) Local resource building activities are of critical significance in understanding how managers (and workers) in the subsidiary environment seek to mobilize and negotiate mandates emanating from headquarters (HQ) and elsewhere. Some local actors are more adept at resisting the transfer of strategies and practices from extraneous sources within the MNC than others, depending upon their political adroitness (Bélanger et al. 2003) and ability to utilize local institutionally-based reserves.

(3) Micro-political 'game playing' represents a crucial dynamic within the sociopolitical fabric of the MNC. Typically involving key actors from HQ and subsidiary, such political contestation may relate to budget allocation, mandate change, relocation decisions, benchmarking systems and coercive comparisons between subsidiaries by HQ (Becker-Ritterspach and Dörrenbächer 2009; Dörrenbächer and Geppert 2009; Kristensen and Zeitlin 2001; 2005; Morgan and Kristensen 2006). According to Morgan and Kristensen (2006), subsidiaries may opt to adopt relatively passive 'boy scout' or more aggressive 'subversive' tactics in countering attempted impositions from HQ. In the specific context of CEE, Clark and Geppert (2006) reveal that key subsidiary actors may assume 'cosmopolitan' or 'local patriotic' strategic identities. Depending upon the quality and form of 'political sensemaking' arrived at by major stakeholders in HQ and subsidiaries, MNCs in post-communist countries could potentially either nurture transnational social spaces unified by shared identities or create a climate of instability and disorder.

Clearly, the ability of local managers and workers in the subsidiary environment to deploy inimitable reserves of knowledge and skill at their disposal in a tactical fashion will be critical in their defending of a social space within the MNC, or even in surviving. In a specific study of MNC strategies in CEE, Manea and Pearce (2004) assert that the *creative contribution* made by the subsidiary to the inward-investing MNC is a vital factor in determining the destiny of the former. Such creative activity may occur in relation to three broad strategic areas of intent, as follows:

(1) *Market-Seeking* represents the extension of an MNC's production and distribution activity into a new country or region. This has the primary motive of securing an effective development of the local market for the most successful of the group's existing products. The objective in the opening up and marketization of CEE economies is thus to be locally responsive in terms of adapting products and/or processes to local circumstances and generally securing early mover experience of the conditions in these new market spaces.

(2) *Efficiency-Seeking* involves the relocation of the production of established goods to CEE economies to improve *network* supply effectiveness. This seeks to improve the cost-efficiency of supply, with the goods then being (mainly) exported back to the markets where they have an already established high level of demand that is, however, perceived as now needing to be actively defended.

(3) *Knowledge-Seeking* (KS) involves the pursuit by MNCs of new technological capabilities, scientific capabilities (research facilities) and creative expertise (for example, dimensions of tacit knowledge) from *particular* host countries, in order to extend the *overall* competences (product range and core technology) of the group. In the context of early MNC involvement with the transition economies, KS is treated as manifest in localized product development. Two forms of KS are identified as follows. KS1 involves developing products in a particular CEE subsidiary to target the market of that host country and other CEE markets. Thus, KS1 represents a logical extension and deepening of the market-seeking role, building on, and formalizing, the value of locally responsive learning processes. KS2 essentially refers to the extension of the MNC's product range in a distinctive fashion in CEE through the discovery of new capabilities or product characteristics in the CEE context.

In now turning our attention to the organization which constitutes the focal point of our study, we wish to highlight the critical role of subsidiary level managers as 'keepers of the gate' between the spheres of vested interests deriving from HQ and local constituencies. These individuals occupy a precarious 'fault line' in international management engagement, and are concerned to deploy the resources they have at their disposal to protect the 'frontier of control' encircling the subsidiary (Taylor and Bain 2001). We will hear, first hand, their stories concerning the functional and strategic contributions they are making to the newly merged organizational entity. As Geppert et al. (2006) point out, the role of such individuals in the international enterprise is potentially complex and ambiguous, as they are required to interpret, edit, translate (Czarniawska and Jeorges 1996) or transpose (Boxenbaum and Battilana 2005) ideas and practices as they travel across boundaries.

THE SERBIA BREWERY CASE

Eden Ark (EA) is the holding company of the Eden Beverage Group's (EBG) businesses, as well as an operating company under which the Turkish beer operations are managed. EA is listed on the Istanbul Stock Exchange. The EBG, as an 85 per cent subsidiary of EA, is a system of companies producing and marketing beer, malt and soft drinks across a territory ranging from the Adriatic to China, consisting of 14 breweries, four malteries and nine Coca-Cola bottling facilities in ten countries. To date, EBG has possessed a pronounced strategic orientation towards CEE, its field of operations concentrating upon Russia, Ukraine, Kazakhstan, Romania, Moldova as well as Serbia. State of the art brewing facilities in Moscow were developed with the assistance of the European Bank for Reconstruction and Development (EBRD) that contributed a loan of €20m in 2001. The group is amongst the ten largest European brewers by sales volume. Insight into the international strategic intentions of EBG can be gained from an interview with the EA Marketing Director in Paris in October 2002. According to him:

> We are the major player in Turkey, but that will not be enough in the future. Especially when Turkey eventually becomes part of the EU and we will not have the protection of the monopoly system. We already produce Becks and Miller beer under license in Turkey, as one means of avoiding too many competition concerns when Turkey joins the EU, but we need to do more to ensure that our business continues to thrive after that date.

> We have focused on Eastern Europe for one main reason – money invested there goes a lot further than it does in the west. Of course, Turkey has also had traditional links with that part of Europe as well, so it makes it the ideal place to start expanding sales of Eden. (Food and Drink. Com 2004)

The following quotation by a senior executive at EA indicates that perceived *cultural consonance* between Turkey and the host country of Serbia

(Serbia having previously been a vassal state prior to becoming part of the Ottoman Empire, resulting in cultural affinities between the two countries) strongly impacted on investment decisions:

> An environment which might seem impossible to a Luxembourg company is business as usual to us. (EA CEO cited in Barrett 2002, p. 21)

Research Process

Data collection was carried out by one of the authors of this chapter, with the assistance of a Serbian academic, in the course of three separate visits to Serbia in 2004–05, during which three sets of semi-structured interviews were obtained. These included, first, five in-depth, semi-structured interviews in Belgrade with government officials, designed to shed light on the privatization process; second, interviews with senior managers, including the human resource (HR) manager, company lawyer, production manager and the sales manager, who served as 'guides to insider understandings' (Lofland and Lofland 1995, p. 61, cited in Soulsby 2004, p. 50); and finally, interviews with six lay representatives of the trade union Nezavisnost, which represented most of the workers, in a rare opportunity for direct access to low-power actors in an MNC in a post-socialist transitional setting (Bouquet and Birkinshaw 2008). The first set of interviews were carried out in the Serbian capital, Belgrade, while the latter two sets of interviews took place at the brewery: those with management were conducted in a smart office suite, the worker representatives being interviewed conversely as a group in a committee room within the brewery, a strong smell of malt and tobacco pervading the atmosphere. Interviews with government officials and managers were conducted in English, whereas those with worker representatives were in Serbian, with the Serbian academic assuming the role of interpreter, and providing simultaneous translation.

New Management at Pančevo

Following the above analysis of the effects of privatization on ownership structures, the effects of moving from 'insider' to 'outsider' systems of ownership have had dramatic effects of the characteristics of management in recent years. As Eden Weise (EW) became the new company name, the protocol for merging was formulated and a 'transition team' of senior managers from EBG and Pančevo was appointed to steer the process of organizational integration. This team included the former general manager at Pančevo, as well as legal, sales, technical and finance managers. It was joined, on a project-by-project basis, by temporary expatriate experts offering assistance and advice on matters such as information technology and quality control.

At the time of our first visit, approximately 18 months after the takeover, a new team of managers was in place at EW. Although the general manager, appointed immediately after the establishment of the joint venture, was of Belgian nationality, having been recruited from the senior ranks of the Belgian-owned multinational giant Interbrew, the majority of the senior management team at EW was of Serbian origin. All three of the four top managers we interviewed (excepting the company lawyer who was a time-served employee at Pančevo) were relatively young (maximum 35 years old) and were business graduates of Serbian higher educational institutions. All three had 'worked their way up' in other multinational drinks producers based in Serbia, one (the HR manager) at Coca-Cola and two (the plant manager and sales manager) at Interbrew. The plant manager had also gained significant international managerial experience in the sector, having worked for some time for Interbrew in Montenegro and the UK. All three also possessed considerable fluency in the English language. In classifying the new cadre of managers at Pančevo, it would be possible to describe them as professional and specialist practitioners, who, while possessing Serbian nationality, had acquired considerable internationally acquired know-how in their functional areas.

Perceived Parent–Subsidiary Relations

As our study was situated in Pančevo, our primary focus was on managerial perceptions of the degree of control exerted by parent on subsidiary. All our management interviewees were asked about the frequency and form of contact they experienced with representatives of the parent in Istanbul. The production manager, who was also responsible for coordinating the financial investment from EA, contrasted the rigorous system of international control he had experienced whilst working at Interbrew with the greater room for flexibility and independence permitted by EA. This related not only to the respective size of each parent (Interbrew owning 300 breweries compared with 14 in the EA portfolio), but also the cultural empathy possessed by EA towards Serbia, resulting from its CEE origins and domain of operations. According to this manager, a 'positive' form of monitoring by the parent was apparent, whereby they always 'kept an eye on you'. This was understandable as Pančevo had now become the property of EA, although it was observed by the interviewee that the parent had confidence in the work of local managers, was prepared to delegate to them and appreciated their work. The production manager explained that he had frequent conversations with 'Mr Miller', the chief executive officer

(CEO) of EA, which were typically cordial, covering subjects such as the weather in Serbia and Istanbul, but which were also greatly concerned with the meeting of pre-set targets and deadlines:

> We are talking about the same things. They really appreciate my work, and I really have a lot of confidence. I chat to these people from time to time in phone calls: and how is life there, how is the weather there? Is everything okay, how was your holiday? . . . We are at the same level. (Production Manager)

On the issue of prescribed targets, however, the production manager stated:

> I have a list of KPIs [key performance indicators], and every month we are discussing about them. We are comparing ourselves with the previous year to see where we are. But there is no signing with the blood! But in a positive way I am pushing my people to achieve it. (Production Manager)

Despite the Pančevo team being able to develop plans and policies 'in a personal way', the group sales manager at EA monitored results rigorously, expecting reports on sales volumes on a daily basis. Nevertheless, the guiding ethos, according to the sales manager, was overwhelmingly, 'let local people be creative'. In the ensuing sections we examine this proposition more closely.

Creative Contributions

All interviewees were asked to reflect upon the personal 'value' they added to the new venture, on the basis of their accumulated professional and educational expertise. Responses may be divided into three main functional areas (sales, production and human resources), corresponding to the specialist areas of the managers interviewed. We would point out that the HR manager and company lawyer were interviewed together, this possibly reflecting the legalistic nature of the employment relationship in Serbia, so we shall aggregate this data. Managers' views are subsequently contrasted with those expressed by worker representatives.

Sales and Marketing

The overall task with which the sales manager was entrusted was 'to recover the brand in the market'. He maintained it was necessary for him to convey to his team that the Serbian market was different from the rest of the world. Macroeconomic and political volatility created an environment which was highly unpredictable and rapidly changing, at constant risk of inflation and/or devaluation: 'the Serbian market is really unstable, changing month to month'. Furthermore, it needed to be understood that business dealings were not always conducted with propriety. Cash flow issues loomed large, a major problem relating to delays in payment for delivered items, despite having to pay value added tax (VAT) and excise duties 'up front'. Since his appointment in 2003, the sales manager had devoted his time to building up the sales profile of EW from a very low base, the Serbian brewery having been indebted, and having failed to invest in branding and marketing. In conjunction with the previous HR manager, the sales manager had recruited a sales force from scratch by 2004, covering all major Serbian regions and sub-regions, and embracing Bosnia, Montenegro and Macedonia. Members of the sales force were typically inhabitants of major Serbian cities, who had developed a good track record in sales. Lacking direct distribution links, they were charged with forming a 'chain' between EW and customers in a very direct and personal fashion. One activity, for example, was to visit stores to observe and negotiate the position of Weise beers on shelves. In gradually building the market in a predominantly wine-growing area, it was also necessary for the EW sales team to be acutely aware of distinctive Serbian tastes in beer, which could be discovered through market research and 'blind' tasting, beer containing more sweetness in Serbia in contrast to Russian preferences for more bitter-tasting beer. According to the sales manager, 'You have to adapt to what the market wants if you want to survive. Otherwise you will die in two months.' Indeed, in achieving a 100 per cent increase in sales from 2003 to 2004, the manager stated that a critical aptitude displayed on his behalf was 'adaptability'.

Production

The plant manager pointed out that when he joined, approximately three months before our visit in February 2005, having spent eight years working for the Belgian company Interbrew, he was viewed by the workforce with deep suspicion, being regarded 'as a Belgian spy' despite what he saw as his good intentions:

> It was really hard for me, because all the people accept me as a Belgian spy. I was rejected all the time, but I was really pushing to collect some information. I am leading my people in a professional way. . . . I was a Belgian spy because I was trying to introduce some things, and it was rejected [by the workforce]. (Plant Manager)

The sentiments expressed here strike a chord with Ferner's (2000, p. 534) observation that managers brought in to effect subsidiary change are often perceived as 'double agents', trusted neither by the local labour force, since they are seen as a creature of the centre, nor by headquarters, for fear that he or she may have been 'co-opted by the local culture'.

At the time of the plant manager's arrival at the brewery, EW had already modernized its production process through the introduction of new technology to enhance quantity and, vitally, quality of production. On arrival, his critical contribution was to generate a 'new style of working' at the brewery, by coaching supervisory staff in a direct and interactive fashion, instructing them specifically on the following:

> To be more patient, cost oriented, company loyal oriented, transferring international practices on to the domestic mentality, like polyvalence. I am trying to point the organization in that direction . . . People are scared. If you want to implement something new, they have to change, in a normal and reasonable way, I am trying to tell them that they must . . . Some don't have the background, but they're willing to work. Step by step. Anyhow, they have to see that at the end of the day it's a new philosophy. (Plant Manager)

Elaborating on the need to inculcate this 'new philosophy', the plant manager cited the example of the introduction of a new labelling machine which required multiple skills on the part of the affected workers. Despite initial resistance to change on the part of the worker in question, based on him appearing to be 'totally lost', eventually he adapted to the new way of working through appropriate training and by 'talking problems through' with the plant manager himself and with his direct supervisor. According to the plant manager, the new production culture at the brewery was based on the notion, 'make mistakes but don't repeat them. From A to B we're expecting a lot of mistakes, but learn from them'. Signs of organizational learning were already discernible: 'People are ready to learn, the most important thing, and to work very hard.' As a result, production at the brewery had more than doubled from just 170 000 hl prior to the joint venture to 310 000 hl afterwards, reaching 400 000 hl at the time of our visits.

Human Resource Management

The HR manager and the company lawyer had been primarily involved in introducing the programme of employment changes at EW following the takeover by EA. The single most significant development had been the technological surplus agreement which involved a workforce reduction of over one-third. This agreement had been implemented with adherence to Serbian employment law and established collective agreements, which require consultation on matters such as redundancy and levels of redundancy payment, as well as providing for the redeployment of redundant workers where possible for a period of three years. Thus, a number of redundant workers had retained their association with the brewery, including former drivers who had purchased trucks with their severance pay, and who were now operating at the brewery on a self-employed basis, a legacy of the collective ethos which had previously prevailed at the brewery.

Thus, a vital strategic contribution of the HR team had been to ensure that Serbian employment law had been applied in change programmes, the law remaining the primary determinant of the substance of the employment relationship. Accompanying the administration of the more technical aspects of change, the newly established HR department devoted considerable attention to communicating and explaining new policies to workplace representatives. Reflecting upon the technological surplus agreement, the HR manager stated that 'breaching the employment relationship is like breaching any relationship; it needs to be explained sensitively to affected parties'. The HR department was now spearheading a broader cultural change programme across EW, epitomized by the incorporation of 'performance-related' elements into formerly standard rates across all job categories. The HR team had also been instrumental in moulding new management structures at Pančevo. Accordingly, over the past few years, new departments had been established in marketing, quality assurance and logistics, and certain managerial functions, for example in HR itself, had been outsourced.

Workers' Views

In our visit in May 2005 our interviews with lay representatives of the recognized trade union, Nezavisnost, provided an alternative and less positive view of organizational developments since the EA takeover, insisting: 'what you heard as a positive story, we can't agree with them [senior managers]'. Taking issue with management's perspective on the takeover, it was stated that a climate of secrecy had prevailed at Pančevo, with little information having been forthcoming on specific work changes or the future direction of the business. Indeed, it was alleged that important financial data had been manipulated to bolster the interests of the incoming management. The lay officials asserted that the original value of the Pančevo brewery had been understated to lessen its purchase price:

> Before privatization, they do everything to make the value of the company less . . . The workers have to accept everything or they'll be locked out of the factory. We were told, there is only EA that wants to buy, and this is your last

chance. They wanted to lower the value of the factory, and reduced the quality of the beer. (Worker Representative)

This also served to reduce the value of payments due to workers according to their status as 'social owners'. Furthermore, it was alleged that the profitability of the enterprise, which was now highly productive, was being constantly downplayed in order to justify low average pay for workers (approximately €100 per month compared to €1000 for managers): 'The factory could not have any loss, because they're selling so much beer . . . Production is going up. They say there is no money, but there is money.'

Turning to the technological surplus agreement, the worker representatives disputed its very existence: 'There was no technological surplus. They could move some people to admin, or re-educate them, but they didn't want to do that.' Although severance pay had been relatively high by Serbian standards (€330 per year of service), the process of selection had been far from scrupulous. According to these representatives, 'psychological pressure' had been brought to bear on employees over the age of 35, predominantly student workers having been recruited by an outside agency to replace their relatively costly in-house predecessors, who had also possessed greater legal and social protection at work:

> They employ students . . . For example, they work in one shift, two full-time people and two students. You pay them only when there is work to be done, and you don't pay them money for pensions. The company has nothing to do with them. A third party organizes this, an agency. They take the students on temporarily. They don't have any rights. They are not in the union. They don't have a pension or insurance. No one knows what is the difference between part-time workers and students. These students are working for €150 a month. (Worker Representative)

'New' machinery that had been installed was in fact, in their view, second hand:

> Almost everything which is coming is used machinery, it's not new. It's imported from Germany or somewhere . . . The plastic bottle machine is new, everything else is used, ten years old. It's all used. They bought new equipment, but it was not used. They know nothing. (Worker Representative)

Moreover, the poorly trained temporary workers who supplanted more skilled, time-served employees were ill-equipped to use this machinery, creating inefficiencies and hazardous working conditions.

The worker representatives reported that, in fact, their own jobs had changed very little since the takeover, and certainly there was no evidence of enrichment or upgrading of their status or activity: 'the way of production is the same as before'. Turning to broader observations concerning organizational culture, the worker representatives referred to the higher, managerial stratum of the brewery as 'EA', confirming their perceived status as 'double agents' (Ferner 2000), despite the predominantly Serbian nationality of the latter. If the new and youthful management grouping were offending a workforce steeped in the principles of self-management, this was exacerbated by the withdrawal of social benefits enjoyed prior to the takeover, resulting in a tangible downgrading of quality of life. According to the worker representatives: 'We were promised everything before they came, now nothing's happened. We had sport activities, paid for by the company. That's all stopped.'

MAKING SENSE OF MARKET-ORIENTED INSTITUTIONAL LOGICS

Returning to the declared strategic intent underlying EA's investment in Serbia and other regions in Eastern Europe, it may be deduced that key considerations are: (1) the need for international market diversification in the context of the corporation's monopoly in Turkey; (2) the attraction of low-cost production in the CEE region; and (3) traditional links between this relatively small, Eastern-orientated international player and other CEE countries. Additional strategic benefits include the proximity of the city of Belgrade as a primary market, the adjacent River Danube as a key artery for transportation purposes, and the possibility of sourcing raw materials from local agricultural regions. To make sense of developments, we apply the theoretical contribution of Manea and Pearce (2004) to the Pančevo case.

Market-Seeking

Undoubtedly, EA was attracted by Serbian market opportunities, which offer considerable growth potential. Departing, however, from the strategic trajectory predicted by Manea and Pearce (2004), EA did not seek to secure effective development of the local market for the most successful of the group's existing products. Instead, the *existing* lines at Pančevo (Weise and Standard) were rebranded, repackaged and subject to quality upgrading through enhanced technology. A remaining research question is whether such a strategy of international product diversification, which promotes local products for indigenous tastes in CEE and beyond, is sector specific.

Efficiency-Seeking

The level of productivity in relation to costs has been a vital consideration since the inception of EW. The introduction of the technological surplus agreement represented at once a significant cost-saving measure, and also a watershed in working arrangements at Pančevo. It is undeniably at workplace level that efficiency measures were most assiduously implemented, demanding high levels of productivity for extremely poor rates of pay by Western standards, terminating social benefits associated with longstanding principles of self-management. Again, in contention with Manea and Pearce's (2004) typology, there was no obvious strategic intent to use Pančevo to enhance network supply effectiveness. In other words, productivity improvements occurred to enhance product flow into domestic Serbian markets, not to serve Turkish or Western markets.

Knowledge-Seeking

Occurring concurrently with market- and efficiency-seeking behaviours in the Serbian environment, the critical organizational drive to 'unlock' Pančevo centred on the newly appointed managerial team at the brewery. It is clear that the parent had vested a high level of trust in these individuals, who acted as mediators in the combination of international and local domains of managerial know-how, as 'cultural go-betweens' and 'interpreters' of the local context (Ferner 2000, p. 530). This trust was nevertheless bounded by the need for the management team to demonstrate results on a day-to-day basis. All members of the new management team had experience in larger international breweries, such as Interbrew and Coca-Cola, English-language proficiency being critical in facilitating such international awareness. Accordingly, they were able to import 'state of the art' ideas and techniques into their specialist areas of activity. However, it may be asserted that a vital area of 'creativity' that each brought to the new enterprise was intuitive and informed know-how concerning the Serbian social environment. Thus the new managerial cadre, who were predominantly Serbian nationals, were able to 'make sense' of the highly distinctive way of organizing production and sales in Serbia (Weick 2001). Creative contributions therefore referred to factors such as awareness of the volatile, turbulent climate for business dealings; insight into the reality of business transactions where corrupt practice had been rife; first-hand knowledge of local tastes; or detailed technical knowledge of Serbian labour law. Perhaps transcending all other factors was their preparedness and ability to engage in direct personal interaction with important actors inside and outside the organization, thus establishing 'chains' between the organization and customers, or connecting production workers with the 'new philosophy' through exhortation

DISCUSSION AND CONCLUSION

Our case study depicts an international M&A marked from its inception by considerable asymmetry in the power relationship between major actors in the HQ and subsidiary. While the rhetoric emanating from EA at the time of the international acquisition heralded factors such as equity, synergy and cultural consonance, which bound the partners, in reality institutional forms emanating from a more advanced economic setting were being imposed upon the subsidiary site located in a fragile, yet apparently amenable, host environment. While the imposition of 'alien' institutional structures by an inward investor may be associated with organized forms of resistance in certain regional settings (see, for example, Lane 2001; Geppert et al. 2003; Morgan and Kristensen 2006), in the fractured, post-war, sociopolitical climate of Serbia, and following our analysis above on privatization, it tended to be associated with disorganization, disenfranchisement and 'exit'. Our reporting of case study findings has implied a separation of status between managers and workers at the Pančevo site, yet, in a sense, they may be regarded as combined into closely overlapping social spaces, perhaps manifesting a legacy of social ownership and worker self-management traditions in the contemporary era. This was physically manifested, at the time of our visit, by the presence of a long-serving member of the brewery 'house' union conversing informally (in Serbian) and taking biscuits and coffee with the newly appointed, Serbian national, HR manager. Our discussion with the manager in question revealed she was at pains to manage rationalization in a manner which was in keeping with Serbian employment legislation, traditions and customs and local sensibilities. Moreover, as a result of the coercive comparisons being exerted on Pančevo by its Turkish-headquartered parent, these also impinging on a 'sister' brewery in Serbia, as well as on subsidiaries more widely dispersed across the Balkan region, the fates of all parties at the site were undoubtedly shared. Nevertheless, in keeping with the aforementioned assertions by Dörrenbächer and Geppert (2011) concerning political interplays and social spaces in the MNC, it was clear that the newly appointed management team at Pančevo were mobilizing the various resources at their disposal to keep at bay the worst potential incursions of the HQ 'confederation'. Such resources included the ability to 'work' local networks, whether in the workplace or in chains of supply and demand, where language proficiency is at a premium as well as tacit knowledge regarding the ways of doing business in a volatile, undoubtedly corrupt environment. Various other aspects of 'creativity' helped to sustain the position of management, and the workers for whom they were responsible, at least in the short term, including knowledge of Serbian employment customs and law as well as distinctive attributes of the local beer market. There was also evidence of micro-political 'game playing' by these managers, as they toed the line in the implementation of HQ-imposed rationalization programmes, whilst seeking to keep the faith amongst their worker compatriots at the site. Game playing was apparent in the day-to-day cordial telephone conversations they enjoyed with senior managers at HQ, whilst knowing that coercive comparisons were being made with a sister site, this being a game that the Pančevo managers ultimately lost.

The ending of our story of the Pančevo brewery is ultimately not a happy one. In 2008, Pančevo and its sister brewery at Zaječar were taken over by an inward-investing large multinational entity. As a result, the Pančevo brewery closed down later that year, its remaining employees, just 30 of whom, less than 10 per cent of an original workforce of 350, remained in post at the time of closure, being transferred to EA's more productive and profitable sister subsidiary at Zaječar. At the time of writing, the brewery at Zaječar continues to operate. Clearly there are issues here to do with subsidiary management by parent companies where there is international competition amongst subsidiaries for parent company resources (Birkinshaw and Hood 1998; Boddewyn 1979, 1983; Delany 1998; Dörrenbächer 2007; Morgan and Kristensen 2006; Mueller 1996), which we have reflected on elsewhere (see Maclean and Hollinshead 2011). Important as these issues are, our purpose is not to return to them here. Our focus in this chapter is on internationalization and institutionalism, our premise being the distinctive local embeddedness of M&A targets in the international brewing industry in specific institutional and cultural host-country contexts, such that indigenous actors assigned responsibility for managing and operating subsidiary breweries are themselves subject to often strong sociopolitical and historical influences exerted upon them by the local region (Harzing and Sorge 2003). In this sense, we follow Mueller (1996, p. 441) in regarding organizations as 'social entities integrated into the institutional and value structures', which together comprise the societal fabric in which such actors operate, and within which they are embedded.

In the case of Pančevo, both conflicting and more consonant institutional logics may be discerned at the brewery (Seo and Creed 2002; Thornton 2002; Thornton and Ocasio 1999). Despite the Turkish origin and CEE orientation of the MNC in question, initially reassuring to managers and employees at the target subsidiary, the new market-oriented logics emanating from the West which EA sought to introduce (para-doxically, given the location of the MNC's headquarters in Istanbul, but understandable at the same time since the corporation was subject to pervasive Western influence in its system of governance) were clearly at odds with the more traditional, societal logic which prevailed at the Pančevo brewery. Such Western market-oriented institutional logics were apparent in the 'new philosophy' which managers sought to instil, exem-plified by their adoption of 'KPIs' or of a new manner of working based on 'polyvalence', and evident in the establishment of new departments in the brewery, including marketing, quality assurance and human resource management. At the same time, the logic of internationalization, which effected a root-and-branch transformation of both state structures and working conditions during the lifetime of this project, characterized by 'a hollowing out of democratic institutions and a privatisation of the public sphere' (Bauman 2004, p. 5), was on a collision course with the longstand-ing societal logic emanating from a shared ethos based on worker solidar-ity and the principles of self-management.

As transnational social space becomes more of a reality for individual managers (Dörrenbächer and Geppert 2006; Dörrenbächer 2007), a social space in which actors seek to articulate, contest and advance their positions (Morgan and Kristensen 2006), the Turkish MNC ulti-mately proved to be like many others in terms of the apparent concern it displayed towards subsidiary employees, emerging in this sense in their eyes as placeless, stateless and essentially footloose (Ohmae 1995). Information flows from MNCs become more opaque when traversing national cultural borders (Ferner 2000). The faceless nature of HQ man-agers, in marked contrast to the previously strong, paternalistic attach-ment of the brewery to the sociopolitical fabric of the locality in which it was embedded, is indicative of the 'institutional distance' between the two entities (Kostova and Roth 2002; Morgan and Kristensen 2006). Despite the workers equating the new management at Pančevo with EA, it is clear that this young management team were low-power actors in their own right, with limited ability to negotiate and contest their social space. As Bouquet and Birkinshaw (2008, p. 480) contend, subsidiaries often lose their capacity to influence outcomes because 'the environments in which they are located are distant, complex, and fragmented', a description which effectively encapsulates the Serbian context. Ultimately, actors lacking centrality are also likely to lack the power to build coalitions or co-opt the resources of other actors in order to influence MNC deci-sions in their favour (Bouquet and Birkinshaw 2008; Dörrenbächer and Geppert 2006).

The Pančevo brewery finally turned off its machines and closed its doors in October 2008, concluding our story. Except to say, by way of a coda, that as 'overt', engaged researchers of post-socialist CEE organizational transition, motivated by the desire to understand (*Verstehen*) and to empathize with research subjects and interviewees, we are left with an unanswered question: What happened to all those lost souls?

NOTE

1. Company and personal names are given as pseudonyms in order to protect anonymity and confidentiality of participants.

REFERENCES

Barrett, L. (2002), *Business in the Balkans: The Case of Cross-Border Cooperation*. London: Centre for European Reform.

Bauman, Z. (2004), *Identity: Conversations with Benedetto Vecchi*, Cambridge: Polity Press.

Becker-Ritterspach, F. and C. Dörrenbächer (2009), 'Intra-firm competition in multinational corporations: towards a political framework', *Competition and Change*, **13**, 199–213.

Bélanger, J., A. Giles and J.-N. Grenier (2003), 'Patterns of corporate influence in the host country: a study of ABB in Canada', *International Journal of Human Resource Management*, **12**, 469–85.

Birkinshaw, J. and N. Hood (1998), 'Multinational subsidiary evolution: capability and charter change in foreign-owned subsidiary companies', *Academy of Management Review*, **23**, 773–95.

Boddewyn, J. (1979), 'Foreign divestment: magnitude and factors', *Journal of International Business Studies*, **10**, 21–6.

Boddewyn, J. (1983), 'Foreign and domestic divestment and investment decisions: like or unlike?', *Journal of International Business Studies*, **14**, 23–35.

Bouquet, C. and J. Birkinshaw (2008), 'Managing power in the multinational corporation: how low-power actors gain influence', *Journal of Management*, **34**, 477–508.

Boxenbaum, E. and J. Battilana (2005), 'Importation as innovation: transposing managerial practices across field', *Strategic Organization*, **3** (4), 355–83.

Clark, E. and M. Geppert (2006), 'Socio-political processes in international management in post-socialist contexts: knowledge, learning and transnational institution building', *Journal of International Management*, **12**, 340–57.

Collin, M. (2001), *This is Serbia Calling: Rock'n Roll Radio and Belgrade's Underground Resistance*, London: Serpent's Tail.

Czarniawska, B. and B. Jeorges (1996), 'Travel of ideas', in Barbara Czarniawska and Guje Sevón (eds), *Translating Organizational Change*, Berlin: De Gruyter, pp. 13–48.

Delany, Ed (1998), 'Strategic development of multinational subsidiaries in Ireland', in Julian Birkinshaw and Neil Hood (eds), *Multinational Corporate Evolution and Subsidiary Development*, London: Macmillan, pp. 239–67.

Dörrenbächer, C. (2007), 'Inside the transnational social space: cross-border management and owner relationship in a German subsidiary in Hungary', *Journal of East European Management Studies*, 4, 318–39.

Dörrenbächer, C. and M. Geppert (2006), 'Micro-politics and conflicts in multinational corporations: current debates, reframing, and contributions of this special issue', *Journal of International Management*, 12, 251–65.

Dörrenbächer, C. and M. Geppert (2009), 'Micro-political games in the multinational enterprise: the case of mandate change', *Management Revue*, 20, 373–91.

Dörrenbächer, C. and M. Geppert (2011), 'Introduction', in Christoph Dörrenbächer and Mike Geppert (eds), *Politics and Power in the Multinational Corporation*, Cambridge: Cambridge University Press, pp. 3–38.

Đuričin. S. (2000), *Pre/posleprivatizacioniprocesi u preduzećima in Transfornacijap rduzecaifinansijsksatržišta*, Belgrade: University of Belgrade.

Ferner, A. (2000), 'The underpinnings of "bureaucratic" control systems: HRM in European multinationals', *Journal of Management Studies*, 37, 521–39.

Food and Drink. Com (2004). Accessed 18 August 2012 at www.foodanddrink. com.

Geppert, M., D. Matten and P. Walgenbach (2006), 'Transnational institutional building and the multinational corporation: an emerging field of research', *Human Relations*, 59 (11), 1451–65.

Geppert, M., D. Matten and K. Williams (2003), 'Change management in MNCs: how global convergence intertwines with national diversities', *Human Relations*, 56 (7), 807–38.

Hall, P.A. and D. Soskice (eds) (2001), *Varieties of Capitalism, the Institutional Foundations of Comparative Advantages*, Oxford: Oxford University Press.

Harzing, A.-W. and A. Sorge (2003), 'The relative impact of country of origin and universal contingencies on internationalization strategies and corporate control in multinational enterprises: worldwide and European perspectives', *Organization Studies*, 24, 187–214.

Hollinshead, G. (2006), 'Educating educators in a volatile climate: the challenge of modernising higher business schools in Serbia and Montenegro', *European Journal of Education*, 41 (4), 131–49.

Hollinshead, G. and M. Maclean (2007), 'Transition and organizational dissonance in Serbia', *Human Relations*, 60 (10), 1551–74.

International Business Sector in Serbia Conference (2010), Hyatt Regency Hotel, Belgrade.

Kostova, T. (1999), 'Transnational transfer of strategic organizational practices: a contextual perspective', *Academy of Management Review*, 24, 308–24.

Kostova, T. and K. Roth (2002), 'Adoption of organizational practice by subsidiaries of multinational corporations: institutions and relational effects', *Academy of Management Journal*, 45, 215–33.

Kostova, T. and S. Zaheer (1999), 'Organizational legitimacy under conditions of complexity: the case of the multinational enterprise', *Academy of Management Review*, 24, 64–81.

Kristensen, Peer Hull and Jonathan Zeitlin (2001), 'The making of a global firm: local pathways to multinational enterprise', in Glenn Morgan, Peer Hull Kristensen and Richard Whitley (eds), *The Multinational Firm*, Oxford: Oxford University Press, pp. 172–95.

Kristensen, Peer Hull and Jonathan Zeitlin (2005), *Local Players in Global Games*, Oxford: Oxford University Press.

Lane, C. (2001), 'The emergence of German transnational companies: a theoretical analysis an empirical study of the Globalization process', in Glenn Morgan, Peer Hull Kristensen and Richard Whitley (eds), *The Multinational Firm*, Oxford: Oxford University Press, pp. 69–96.

Maclean, M. and G. Hollinshead (2011), 'Contesting social space in the Balkan region: the social dimensions of a "red" joint venture', in Christoph Dörrenbächer and Mike Geppert (eds), *Politics and Power in the Multinational Corporation*, Cambridge: Cambridge University Press, pp. 380–411.

Manea, J. and R. Pearce (2004), *Multinationals and Transition: Business Strategies, Technology and Transformation in Central and Eastern Europe*, Basingstoke: Palgrave Macmillan.

Meyer, J.W. and B. Rowan (1977), 'Institutionalized organizations: formal structure as myth and ceremony', *American Journal of Sociology*, **83**, 340–63.

Morgan, G. and P.H. Kristensen (2006), 'The contested space of multinationals: varieties of institutionalism, varieties of capitalism', *Human Relations*, **59** (11), 1467–90.

Mueller, F. (1996), 'National stakeholders in the global context for corporate investment', *European Journal of Industrial Relations*, **2**, 345–68.

Obradovic-Wochnik, J. (2009), 'Knowledge, acknowledgement and denial in Serbia's responses to the Srebrenica massacre', *Journal of Contemporary European Studies*, **17**, 61–74.

Ohmae, K. (1995), *The End of the Nation State*, London: Harper Collins.

Pejovich, S. (2004), 'The uneven results of institutional change in Central and Eastern Europe: the role of culture', conference proceedings, Justice and Global Politics, Bowling Green University, 21–24 October.

Petrović, P. and S. Čerović (2011), 'The characteristics of foreign direct investments in Serbia', *Journal of Knowledge Management, Economics and Information Technology, Scientific Papers*, www.scientificpapers.org, **6** (October).

Powell, W.W. and P.J. DiMaggio (eds) (1991), *The New Institutionalism in Organizational Analysis*, Chicago, IL: University of Chicago Press.

Ristić, Z. (2004), 'Privatisation and foreign direct investment in Serbia', *South East Europe Review*, **2**, 121–36.

Scott, William R. (2001), *Institutions and Organizations*, 2nd ed., Thousand Oaks, CA: Sage.

Seo, M.-G. and W.E.D. Creed (2002), 'Institutional contradictions, praxis, and institutional change: a dialectical perspective', *Academy of Management Review*, **27** (2), 222–47.

Soulsby, Anna (2004), 'Who is observing whom? Fieldwork roles and ambiguities in organizational case study research', in Ed Clark and Snejina Michailova (eds), *Fieldwork in Transforming Societies*, Basingstoke, Hampshire: Palgrave MacMillan, pp. 29–56.

South East European Industrial Market (2010), The Industrial Magazine of the SEE region, **1**, Sofia: Bulgarian Publishing House for Professional Technical Periodicals.

Stanojević, M. (2003), 'Workers' power in transition economies: the cases of Serbia and Slovenia', *European Journal of Industrial Relations*, **9** (3), 183–301.

Taylor, P. and P. Bain (2001), 'Trade unions, workers' rights and the frontier of control in UK call centres', *Economic and Industrial Democracy*, **22** (1), 39–66.

Thornton, P.H. (2002), 'The rise of the corporation in a craft industry: conflict and conformity in institutional logics', *Academy of Management Journal*, **45** (1), 81–101.

Thornton, P.H. and W. Ocasio (1999), 'Institutional logics and the historical contingency of power in organizations', *American Journal of Sociology*, **105** (3), 801–44.

UNISON International Europe (2002–05), *Trade Unions in Serbia and Montenegro*, London: UNISON International Europe.

Upchurch, M. and S. Cicmil (2004), 'The political economy of management knowledge transfer: some insights from experience in Serbia and Montenegro', *South East Europe Review*, **7**, 101–20.

Weick, K.E. (2001), *Making Sense of the Organization*, Cambridge, MA: Blackwell.

Whitley, R. (1999), *Divergent Capitalisms. The Social Structuring and Change of Business Systems*, Oxford: Oxford University Press.

World Bank (2012), *Doing Business, 2011*, Washington, DC: World Bank.

4. Market integration and transportation: beer in Lao PDR

Magnus Andersson and Ari Kokko

INTRODUCTION

To study the process of domestic market integration in Lao People's Democratic Republic (hereafter Lao PDR), this chapter explores the spatial variation in beer prices and its relationship with transport costs and various local market characteristics. More specifically, we study how the price of a 640 ml bottle of Beer Lao varies across the country. In a well-integrated market, we expect the law of one price to hold. Controlling for transaction costs, a homogeneous product should have the same price throughout the market. Sellers trying to charge a higher price will find that potential buyers turn to competing suppliers. Those starting out with a lower price will meet high demand and realize that they can maximize their profit by raising their price. Well-integrated markets where price signals are rapidly transmitted across space are more efficient, since both consumers and producers are better able to adjust to changes in supply and demand conditions.

In reality, however, markets are not perfectly integrated. Natural or man-made obstacles to economic interaction, such as lack of transport routes, excessive transport costs, or formal trade barriers, may block information flows and arbitrage. In some locations, monopolies and other market imperfections may restrict competition and keep prices excessively high (Christaller 1933; Badiane and Shively 1998). Differences in tastes and preferences across consumer groups can also result in price differences. While it may be difficult to argue that some preferences are better than others, there are strong reasons to identify and remove impediments to market integration – fragmented markets make up a serious development obstacle, often forcing poor people to pay too much for their purchases and leaving them with too little in compensation for their work effort.

The purpose of this chapter is therefore to explore the market integration in the Lao market by mapping the spatial variation in beer prices and to explore why price differences persist, that is, why markets remain fragmented. In particular, we will focus on the role of transport infrastructure and market conditions. Although the focus is on market integration at the macro level, the chapter will also be interesting from the perspective of the beer industry. Given the fragmented nature and the low level of development of the Lao market, it is clear that the future growth of the country's beer industry will mainly occur as a result of market integration – consumption of beer will rise when peripheral parts of the country become more integrated with the national market, resulting in price reductions for beer and other manufactured products, and when the incomes of consumers in peripheral parts of the country increase as market efficiency improves.

The beer market in Lao PDR in the early 2000s provided a unique opportunity to examine the relationship between prices and market conditions. At that time, Beer Lao was a homogeneous retail product manufactured in one single location in Lao PDR but available throughout the country. Only one type of bottled Beer Lao was available in the country, a lager beer sold in 640 ml glass bottles. Beer Lao did not market any other beers, and imports were prohibited (but rare exceptions were made when local production fell short of demand). This makes it possible to control for various supply side factors to a much better extent than what is possible in most other cases. For example, the pricing of locally produced agricultural goods sold in local markets depends on a variety of local factors such as fertility of land, climate, access to irrigation, usage of pesticides and fertilizers, and the quality of products (Deaton 1988). In the beer case, we are able to disregard the supply side determinants and concentrate on the role of transaction costs and market conditions for market integration. Moreover, foreign analyses of the Lao beer market in the 1990s suggested that beer was the preferred drink of Lao consumers, who were also satisfied with the taste and quality of their national beer (Annez et al. 2001). Given the fact that Beer Lao was consumed widely across the country and marketed even in small villages without road access, we assume that there were no marked differences in preferences for beer between geographical areas (although the quantity of sales would of course vary depending on prices, consumer incomes and other determinants of demand). This means that we also assume that differences in beer prices between geographical locations were not caused by differences in production costs or preferences, but rather by transport costs and market conditions.[1]

The analysis focuses on the early 2000s, because the degree of product differentiation in the Lao beer market has increased notably since that time. At the time of writing, in 2012, Beer Lao remains the dominant brand, but in addition to the lager beer referred to in our analysis the company has started to produce a dark beer as well as a light (low alcohol) beer – both of these, as well as the original Beer Lao, are available in cans and bottles of different sizes. A second Beer Lao factory was established in Champasak in southern Lao PDR in 2008 and several imported brands entered the market after 2008, as a result of the country's membership in the Association of Southeast Asian Nations (ASEAN) Free Trade Area. Beer is no longer a homogeneous product, and supply side factors vary depending on product variety and producer.

The remainder of this chapter will be structured as follows. The next section will discuss the link between infrastructure and market integration, and outline some of the factors that contribute to market fragmentation in Lao PDR. Section three introduces our empirical material, with some further comments on markets and road access in Lao PDR. Section four provides a brief description of the Lao beer market and discusses pricing patterns and how they relate to market characteristics, while section five summarizes the main findings.

INFRASTRUCTURE AND MARKET INTEGRATION

In an integrated market, prices of homogeneous goods will tend to converge: competition will tend to drive down consumer prices to production cost plus necessary transport costs. Transport costs, together with costs for retrieving information about prices and market conditions, are at the center of any discussion about market integration. Geographical factors such as location, distance to markets and transport linkages naturally have a significant impact on these costs. High transport costs will lead to market fragmentation and limited competition at the local level. Policies for market integration typically strive to minimize transaction costs, for example through investments in infrastructure, information diffusion and measures to reduce man-made barriers to entry and competition.

Investments in infrastructure and transport services can raise productivity and incomes by raising the production potential of an economy or region (Aschauer 1989; Munnel 1992). The traditional theoretical view suggests that a transport improvement that reduces transport costs (through shorter transport times and lower vehicle operating costs) enables firms to sell their products at lower prices. This stimulates greater demand, providing enhanced economies of scale and initiating a process of cost reductions and sales growth as the market area expands. In addition, the reduction in transport costs lowers barriers to entry in sales and distribution, which tends to raise the number of market actors, raising competition and lowering mark-ups, with further reductions in consumer prices as a result.

Market integration is particularly important in developing countries where a large share of the population is involved in agriculture. Access to well-functioning markets is crucial for farmers' opportunities to increase household income by participating in the market economy by selling their output. At the same time, well-functioning markets are also important for providing the incentive goods that encourage farmers to specialize and shift from a subsistence economy into a market-based economy.

Lao PDR: A Fragmented Market

Lao PDR faces a number of serious challenges when it comes to market integration and economic development. In 1975, after the American exodus from Indochina, the country was taken over by a communist government that attempted to introduce a socialist command economy. The attempt was not successful, and market economic reforms were initiated in 1986 when the new economic mechanism (NEM) was introduced as a first step in the transition towards a market economy. Under the NEM, the Lao government announced a variety of measures to promote the development of a private sector, including deregulation of price and production controls, and to give managerial and financial autonomy to state-owned enterprises. The reform measures were intended to contribute to domestic market integration as well as internationalization of the Lao market. On the domestic side, the most important reforms were broad price liberalization, agricultural reform (including the abolitition of the state monopoly for rice marketing), and privatization of selected state enterprises. In the international arena, the key measures were trade liberalization and unification of the multiple exchange rate system, as well as reforms aiming to attract foreign direct investment (FDI) (Andersson et al. 2007). Together with applications for membership in AFTA (ASEAN Free Trade Area) and World Trade Organization (WTO) membership, these reforms created a much less complicated environment for export and import activities (Bourdet 2000) and improved the possibilities for Lao firms to become active participants in the world market.

The economic reforms since the late 1980s have strengthened the country, but the Lao economy remains weak and fragmented. It is heavily dependent on agriculture, which employs three-quarters of the population. The government has tried to upgrade the sector with special emphasis on production technology, infrastructure and human resources development, but the majority of households rely on simple agricultural activities with low productivity and value added, and many parts of the country remain weakly integrated with the national market, let alone the regional or global market. Despite rapid growth during the past decade, fueled mainly by inflows of FDI and increased revenues from mining and hydroelectric power, Lao PDR remains one of the poorest countries in the world, with the nominal gross domestic product (GDP) per capita at about US$1281 in 2011 (Bird and Hill 2011).

There are four key elements that affect market integration in Lao PDR: landlockedness creating a dependency on transit routes through neighboring countries; a small population of five million people scattered over a land area of nearly 240000 square kilometers, much of which is mountainous; high dependence on subsistence agriculture; and an insufficient transport infrastructure impeding integration of scattered local and provincial markets. Large investments in transport infrastructure have been carried out to alleviate the negative impact of these characteristics on economic development, but the market remains fragmented (Warr 2010).[2]

The Importance of Market Integration

The efficiency of the market system is important for sales of industrial goods, but also for sales of handicrafts produced by local households and for the ability of households to access consumer products at local markets (Sadoulet and de Janvry 1995). Access to infrastructure in the form of transportation and markets is therefore a crucial part in the process where households start to interact with emerging local and regional markets, exchanging handicrafts and agricultural goods for manufactured products. Efficient distribution systems with low transaction costs are expected to transfer goods produced elsewhere to the local consumer at a competitive price, at the same time as local producers can get a competitive price for their commodities (Carter and Ferrin 1995; Pelton et al. 2002). Geographical factors such as location, distance to markets and road accessibility naturally have a significant impact on the costs of intermediate and final goods (Christaller 1933; Hoover 1948; Berry 1967; Gramlich 1994). This means that transaction costs – including transport costs and costs for retrieving information about prices and market conditions – can have a direct effect on households' opportunities to increase their income by participating in the market economy (Arrow 1969; Gannon and Liu 1997; Banister and Berechman 2001).

This is of special relevance in countries where large parts of the population are involved in agricultural production based on self-sufficiency and where production within individual households determines the levels of consumption (Ali and Pernia 2003; Deaton 1997). Self-sufficiency and isolation are seldom voluntary phenomena, but rather consequences of poor transportation infrastructures and high transport costs (Ahmed and Rustagi 1984). An improved market situation reduces the width of price bands (Sadoulet and de Janvry 1995; Badiane and Shively 1998) and households are able to increase the diversification of income-earning activities and interact at markets in order to sell oversupply and access necessary input goods.

Several earlier studies have examined market integration in Lao PDR. For instance, Andersson et al. (2005) study the Lao rice market using provincial production data and farm gate prices collected from the Third Lao Expenditure and Consumption Survey (LECS 3), and find that farm gate prices of glutinous paddy rice follow yield patterns, with high prices in the northern parts of the country and in Vientiane Municipality. The lowest prices are found in the more productive central and southern parts of the country with access to the Mekong River, relatively developed road networks and relatively easy access to markets in Thailand. Furthermore, the pattern of prices and yield on rice clearly indicate fragmented markets even at the provincial level. Similarly, Richter et al. (2005) analyse prices of four agricultural commodities – rice, vegetables, meat and fish – using prices from LECS 3, and find large spatial price variation across the country. Urban areas enjoy higher levels of market integration, giving lower transaction costs in terms of lower transportation costs and higher competition between traders, resulting in lower prices. Rural villages typically exhibit higher prices, although the price variations are large even between villages that are located relatively close to each other. There are also differences between products for the degree of spatial price variation, presumably related to storability, transport costs and supply conditions.

Andersson et al. (2005) point to some other geographically determined differences in the consumption possibilities of rural households. The spatial distribution of fertile land is uneven, which has strong implications for households dependent on agricultural production. Access to foreign markets is also uneven. Owning a household business seems to contribute most to household consumption in the South. A higher reliance on cash crops as well as better access to the Thai market may improve opportunities for various kinds of business operations.

Similar findings apply for many other developing countries. For instance, Minten and Kyle (1999) demonstrate the effect of distance and road quality on food collection and marketing margins with data from Zaire. They show that transportation costs have a major impact on regional differences in food prices and that quality of roads is an important factor in the transportation costs. Moreover, considerable attention has been focused on the relative isolation of rural markets and the implication of this isolation for agricultural producers and consumers (for example, de Janvry et al. 1991).

However, few developing country studies have explicitly linked the spatial price patterns of homogeneous retail products with village characteristics such as location, size, income level and number of competing retailers. A reasonable expectation, drawing on findings from developed countries, is that larger and more developed villages with regular marketplaces should benefit from lower prices for their imports. An often-cited example is a study by Cotterill (1986), who uses a cross-section of prices of a product basket from 35 supermarkets in rural Vermont. The findings suggest that prices are high where supermarket concentration is high. Yet, the link between regional concentration and prices does not seem to be very strong. The reason for this could be that the transport and distribution systems in rich countries are highly developed, with relatively low transport and transaction costs and good opportunities for arbitrage, which leaves little price variation between localities at any given time. However, in developing countries, where transport systems are poor and markets are not well integrated, there is reason to expect clearer spatial differences in pricing patterns (Deaton 1997).

MARKET CONDITIONS IN LAO PDR: ROAD ACCESS AND MARKET ACCESS

The empirical parts of the study are based on a micro-level data set of Lao households, the Third Lao Expenditure and Consumption Survey from 2002–03 and information from Lao Brewery. The household survey provides detailed data on the expenditure, consumption patterns of households and price information on a large number of commodities. It covers all provinces, with each provincial sample stratified into urban areas, rural villages with road access and rural villages without wet season road access. The sample consists of 8100 households selected through a two-stage sample design. A random sample of villages was selected in the first stage. The villages were stratified on 18 provinces and within provinces on urban/rural sector. The rural villages were further stratified on villages with 'access to road' and 'no access to road'. The total first-stage sample consists of 540 villages. Fifteen households were selected with systematic sampling in each village, giving a sample of 8100 households.

The number of villages (primary sampling units) in the sample is 540 with 397 villages reporting prices of a bottle of Beer Lao.[3] The analysis of prices distinguishes between several geographical areas. Three spatial levels are used: the four geographical regions (South, Central, North, and Vientiane Municipality), the interaction between the captial Vientiane and all provincial centers, and lastly the interaction between the provincial centers and villages located in the province. In addition, the data make it possible to distinguish between urban and rural prices, and take into account village characterisation such as road access, quality of road access, markets and transport services as possible determinants of price differences. We also have statistics on production and transport costs from Lao transport providers, the producer of Beer Lao and other data sources. It should be emphasized that the time period studied, 2002–03, presents a unique opportunity to explore market integration using beer prices as an instrument. Lao authorities have conducted expenditure and consumption surveys both before and after this time, in 1992–93, 1997–98 and 2007–08, but none of the other surveys can be used to replicate the results from 2002–03. The earlier surveys did not collect price data in a systematic manner, and since 2002–03 there have been notable changes in the Lao beer market, complicating the analysis. In particular, product differentiation and trade liberalization have introduced many types of beer to the Lao market, which makes it impossible to regard beer as a homogeneous consumer product.

Economic reforms in Lao PDR seem to contribute to favorable outcomes in terms of lower poverty rates and high levels of expenditure by permitting greater participation in both local markets and markets in neighboring countries. The majority of the poor in Lao PDR lives in rural areas and depends on subsistence level agriculture with limited availability of resources, agricultural land, physical productive assets, livestock, number of dependents in households and lack of access to physical and social infrastructure (Andersson et al. 2005; Richter et al. 2005).

However, Warr (2010) illustrates in his analysis of LECS 2 and LECS 3 the importance of road development, with the purpose being to provide access to markets and connectivity between provinces all year round. His results indicate that there are limited opportunities to participate in the free market without physical access to roads and markets. This seems to be of special importance during the wet season when many roads are impassable due to flooding. Geographical factors such as location, distance to markets and road accessibility naturally have a significant impact on the costs of intermediate and final goods.

Table 4.1 presents descriptive data on village access to markets at the national and regional level. Market access is one of the factors influencing price levels. Only 9.5 percent of the villages at the national level in the sample from LECS 3 report having a regular daily market in the village. The market access rises to 12.7 percent if occasional markets are included. Villages located in Vientiane Municipality are well covered by markets, which can be explained by the area's urban structure. The other regions report significantly lower coverage of daily markets. When expanding the definition of market access to also account for occasional markets, there

Table 4.1   Market access characteristics

Region	Village markets, share of villages	
	Daily	Daily or occasional
Vientiane	27.2	29.2
Central	7.3	9.6
North	8.4	12.8
South	7.4	10.2
Lao PDR	9.5	12.7

Source: Authors' calculations based on LECS data.

Table 4.2   Road access characteristics

Region	Road access, share of villages	
	Dry season	All seasons
Vientiane	100	100
Central	88.2	70.2
North	54.7	43.8
South	77.8	61.1
Lao PDR	74.5	61.1

Source: Authors' calculations based on LECS data.

is a slightly higher coverage across the board. Occasional markets seem to have a larger importance in the North than in other parts of the country.

The variability in the quality of the road infrastructure, over time and space, is an important determinant of spatial price differences as these factors influence transport costs. Poor quality and seasonal differences in road access have direct effects on transport costs and time required to reach the villages, and will therefore raise prices of retail products. The road conditions in Lao PDR differ according to seasonal changes in weather, as seen in Table 4.2. Road access during the dry season is considerably higher in all regions. At the national level, 61 percent of the villages in the studied sample have all season access to a road. Another 14 percent of villages have dry season access only. Unsurprisingly, road access is best in Vientiane Municipality and the Central region, and weakest in the North.

The regional differences between villages regarding access to roads are significantly higher than the regional differences between villages regarding access to markets. Access to markets can still be considered a rare facility in large parts of Lao PDR. Yet, it is important to note that the absence of a market does not mean a fully self sufficient livelihood, as very basic retail products are marketed by small individual village shops. The market can be seen as an agglomeration of suppliers that provides a larger variety of marketed products. The larger number of suppliers is also likely to provide competition and lower prices, since it tends to reduce the market power (and profit margins) of the individual suppliers or traders.

BEER LAO AND THE LAO BEER MARKET

Lao Brewery Co. was founded in 1973 as a joint venture between investors with links to the Lao diaspora in France and businessmen located in Lao PDR under the registered name of Lao Beer and Ice Factory. At that time the company had an annual production capacity of three million liters of beer, 1.5 million liters of carbonated drinks and a daily production capacity of 120 tonnes of ice. In December 1975, the Lao government took over the ownership of the brewery. In 1993, two firms from Thailand – Loxley Public Co. and Italian-Thai Public Co. – invested in the company, which had changed its name to Lao Brewery Co. (we will refer to the company as Beer Lao). The Thai involvement was due to stranded negotiations between the Lao government and a French company that was orginally selected to be the partner in privatization of the company.

The Thai involvement mainly consisted of capital used for expansion of the production facilities in Vientiane in order to meet the rising demand. In 2002 there was a change in foreign joint venture partners: the new owners became the Lao government (50 percent), Carlsberg Asia Co. Ltd (25 percent) and TCC International Co. Ltd (25 percent). In 2005 there was another change in ownership, with the Lao government keeping its 50 percent share and Carlsberg Breweries raising its stake to 50 percent.

Beer Lao held approximately 99 percent of the market for beer in Lao PDR in 2006, despite a very rapidly growing market. Figure 4.1 illustrates how the production of beer and bottled water increased significantly during the decade around the turn of the millennium.

The demand for beer in the Lao PDR market has occasionally exceeded supply even though production has been growing rapidly. Therefore, when it held a monopoly position, Lao Brewery intermittently imposed a quota system on the distribution of beer throughout the country. The company also imposed strict control on the marketing of beer, including price controls to ensure that shortages did not lead to price hikes – the main purpose was presumably to discourage the emergence of smuggling networks. With prices of Beer Lao held at a relatively low level, it appears

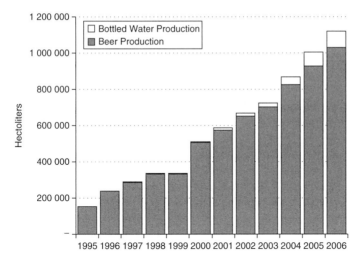

Source: Lao Brewery Ltd.

Figure 4.1   Beer and water production in Lao PDR

that the potential profits for smugglers were too low to justify the efforts involved. The two main developments in the recent past have been the expansion of capacity (a new production line at the Vientiane Brewery and a new brewery at Pakse in the southern Champsak Province) and the reduction of import restrictions in 2008, when foreign beer companies invested in Lao PDR and began to challenge the complete market dominance of Beer Lao.

The Distribution System

To examine spatial price variations, we will base our framework of analysis on Beer Lao's actual distribution system, in order to reflect the domestic value chain of the product. The distribution of Beer Lao takes place through an extensive distribution network, as shown in Figure 4.2. The beer is produced in Vientiane. In Vientiane Municipality, Lao Brewery delivers directly to retail outlets through trucks owned by the company. For distribution to other parts of the country, Lao Brewery contracts three trucking companies. The distribution is divided into three regions: Northern, Central and Southern. The trucking companies deliver to the provincial agencies who in turn distribute to the retail outlets. The company covers the transport costs for delivering the beer to the provincial wholesalers. There are always at least two provincial agencies in each

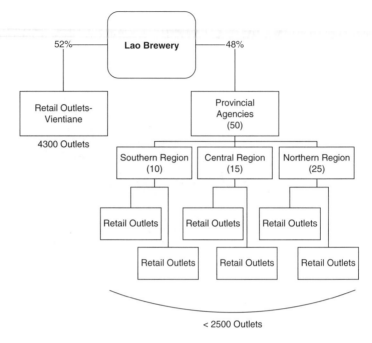

Source: Lao Brewery Ltd.

Figure 4.2   National distribution network 2007

province in order to avoid a monopoly market situation. The provincial
agencies are private companies who are contracted by Lao Brewery to sell
to the retail outlets. The price of beer is controlled and the agencies cannot
increase their prices more than 15 percent above the price charged by
Lao Brewery. However, retailers in villages are allowed to set their prices
depending on local market conditions. This system provides a rather
uniform price band at the provincial wholesale market level. The total beer
market in 2002–03 was shared approximately equally between Vientiane
and the provinces.

A summary of the outlets is provided in Table 4.3. Most of the retail
outlets are in the Vientiane area, and they are supplied directly by the
company. The outlets in the other parts of the country are supplied by the
provincial agencies.

The main types of retail outlets are entertainment venues (karaoke
bars, beer houses, night clubs, restaurants, guesthouses, sports clubs and
hotels), retailers and sundry shops, as illustrated in Figure 4.3. The sundry
shops can be described as micro-enterprises – they are family operated

Table 4.3   Lao Brewery distribution network 2007

Location	Number of agencies	Number of retailers/outlets
Vientiane	Direct distribution	4300
Northern region	25	1042
Central region	15	929
Southern region	10	562

Source: Lao Brewery Ltd.

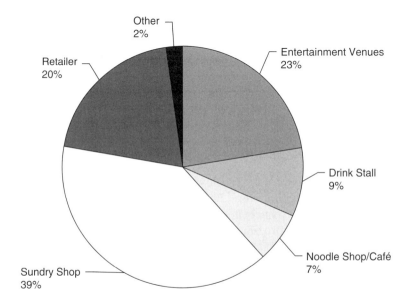

Source: Lao Brewery Ltd.

Figure 4.3   Type of supplier of beer 2007

businesses providing income for the immediate family and they rarely employ people other than family members. The entertainment venues differ in size (number of employees).

BEER LAO AND SPATIAL VARIATION IN PRICES

The first step in the analysis of the spatial variation in beer prices is to compare the retail price per bottle of Beer Lao in the provincial centers,

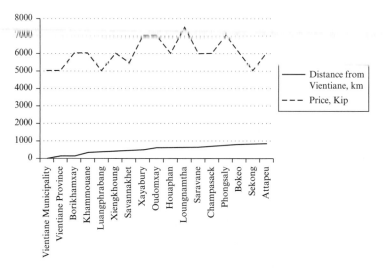

Source: National Geographic Department 2005, LECS 3 and MPWT.

Figure 4.4   *Provincial capitals: price of Beer Lao and distance from*
Vientiane 2002–03

as presented in Figure 4.4. The lowest prices are found in Vientiane
Municipality, Luangphrabang, Phongphong (which is the provincial
center of Vientiane Province) and Sekong in the South, which all exhibit
a price per bottle of approximately 5000 Kip (corresponding to US$0.70).
Loung Namtha's provincial center Namtha exhibits the highest price per
bottle at 7500 Kip. Oudomxay, Xayabury and Phongsaly, all located in
the North, far away from Vientiane, also record about 7000 Kip per bottle.

Already this very rough pattern suggests a complex relationship
between distance and beer prices. Prices tend to be higher further away
from Vientiane, but there is no linear relationship between price and distance. For example, Luangphrabang is located 397 km from Vientiane,
but the price of Beer Lao is the same as that in the two markets that
are closest to Lao Brewery, Vientiane Municipality and Phongphong in
Vientiane Province. Despite the distance, Luangphrapang dealers are
able to serve their markets with the same price as the dealers located next
to the production site in Vientiane. One reason could be the character of
Luangphrapang as an important tourist destination: the heavy competition for customers keeps prices down. The ability to adjust mark-ups suggests that the physical transportation costs to the provincial capitals are
not very large in comparison with the profit margins of retailers.

Another interesting observation is that there is a 50 percent difference

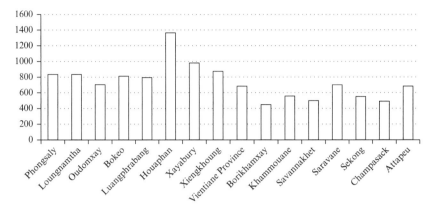

Source: Freight service operator located in Vientiane Municipality, Lao PDR.

Figure 4.5 *Freight rates from Vientiane to provincial centers (year 2006 in Kip per ton kilometer by six-wheel truck, based on a 12-ton load)*

in the average retail price per bottle between the provincial center of Xayabury and Luangaphrabang, which are located only 111 km apart. This large price gap probably reflects market conditions – lower competition in Xayabury – but it is also related to transport costs. Countries like Lao PDR, with large differences in the quality of road infrastructure and market access, exhibit a large variation in transport costs per km. These costs add substantially to the expenses of retailers in Xayabury. Luang Prabang is connected to Vientiane by Highway 13, a paved road in good condition. The transport route from Vientiane to Xayabury goes via Luang Prabang and continues on Highway 4, large sections of which are still unpaved.

To illustrate how the differences in road quality influence transport costs, Figure 4.5 reports the freight rates in Kip per ton for six-wheel truck loads to the provincial centers in Lao PDR.

As shown in Figure 4.5, the freight rates to the provinces located in the Northern Region – Phongsaly, Loungnamtha, Oudomxay, Bokeo, Luangphrabang – are roughly equal, at around 800 Kip per ton-kilometer, with Oudomxay as the cheapest destination at around 700 Kip per ton-kilometer. Oudomxay is the communication crosspoint for cargo between Vientiane and China. Houaphan is located on the north-east border to Vietnam and exhibits the highest freight rate in the country. Xayaburi, which also records a relatively high freight rate, is only accessible via Luangpraphang. The freight rates for the Southern provinces are generally at a lower level. A notable observation is that the cost per ton-kilometer to Vientiane Province is relatively high, which probably reflects a scale effect: fixed costs account for a larger share of the total freight rate for destinations that are located near Vientiane.

The information on freight rates shows that the national road transport system is relatively well integrated. However, there is a general pattern where provinces located off the large national roads at higher altitude show higher freight costs than provinces located at lower altitude.

Table 4.4 provides more detailed information on the importance of transport infrastructure, presenting data on beer prices for three types of villages in Lao PDR: urban villages (which always have access to roads), rural villages with access to roads, and rural villages without access to roads. The information is shown separately for the four major regions (Vientiane, North, Central and South) as well as for the country as a whole. Looking at the pattern at the national level, the results are as expected, with the lowest average prices in urban villages and the highest prices in rural villages without road access.

Turning to the regional level, the lowest average prices (5348 Kip per bottle) and the lowest variation (standard errors) are found in urban villages in Vientiane. Urban villages in the North record higher prices than urban villages in the South, which presumably reflects differences in transportation distance from Vientiane. Road access also has a strong impact on both the mean and the standard deviation of prices. Rural villages with access to roads (in particular, those with wet season road access) have lower average prices than rural villages without road access. The standard deviation of prices is also lower, suggesting that there are relatively few villages where traders are able to use their market power to raise prices: the access to road transportation means that the market is contestable, that is, a competitor may enter if the profit margin begins to grow. In rural villages without road access, the entry barriers made up by transport costs are higher, which presumably gives more market power to traders and contributes to wider dispersion in prices, depending on demand and other market conditions. Comparing rural villages without road access, it should be noted that the distance to the closest road varies between villages, which influences the transport cost and the final price of beer. This results in a high standard deviation of prices, since we are not controlling for the distance to the nearest road.

It can be seen that the highest average prices as well as the highest standard deviations are recorded in the Central and Southern parts of the country. This indicates either that the transportation costs to these villages are higher and vary more than in the North, or that competition is lower than in the North, or a combination of the two.

Table 4.4   Price of one 640 ml bottle Beer Lao and access to roads

Vientiane				
Urban village	Mean (in Kip)	5 348	Max. (in Kip)	6 500
	Std. Error	79.9	Min. (in Kip)	5 000
Rural village with	Mean	5 654	Max.	7 000
access to road	Std. Error	173.48	Min.	5 000
				N = 46 villages
Central				
Urban village	Mean	6 138	Max.	8 000
	Std. Error	140.1	Min.	5 000
Rural village with	Mean	6 905	Max.	10 000
access to road	Std. Error	117.6	Min.	5 000
Rural village without	Mean	8 103	Max.	12 000
access to road	Std. Error	286.6	Min.	6 000
				N = 159 villages
North				
Urban village	Mean	6 696	Max.	8 000
	Std. Error	177.1	Min.	5 000
Rural village with	Mean	7 714	Max.	12 500
access to road	Std. Error	166.0	Min.	5 000
Rural village without	Mean	7 810	Max.	10 000
access to road	Std. Error	254.1	Min.	6 000
				N = 111
South				
Urban village	Mean	6 233	Max.	8 000
	Std. Error	200.4	Min.	5 000
Rural village with	Mean	7 309	Max.	13 000
access to road	Std. Error	169.7	Min.	5 000
Rural village without	Mean	8 000	Max.	12 000
access to road	Std. Error	315.3	Min.	6 000
				N = 81
Lao PDR				
Urban village	Mean	6 020	Max.	8 000
	Std. Error	86.14	Min.	5 000
Rural village with	Mean	7 155	Max.	13 000
access to road	Std. Error	86.49	Min.	5 000
Rural village without	Mean	7 986	Max.	12 000
access to road	Std. Error	164.51	Min.	6 000
				N = 397

Source: Authors' calculations based on LECS data.

Table 4.5   Price of one 640 ml bottle Beer Lao and access to markets

Urban village	With market or	Mean (in Kip)	5990
	occasional	Std error	86.7 (n = 96)
	Without market or	Mean	6750
	occasional	Std error	478.7 (n = 4)
Rural village with	With market or	Mean	7143
access to road	occasional	Std error	87.2 (n = 212)
	Without market or	Mean	7313
	occasional	Std error	442.2 (n = 16)
Rural village without	With market or	Mean	
access to road	occasional	Std error	
	Without market or	Mean	7985
	occasional	Std error	164 (n = 69)

Notes: Total number of villages is 397.

Source: Authors' calculations based on LECS data.

Table 4.5 focuses on the importance of competition by comparing prices in villages with and without markets. The presence of a market, where several sellers are likely to compete for customers, clearly reduces both the average price and the standard deviation of prices. It was already noted that weaker competition could account for the higher prices in rural villages without road access. This is confirmed in Table 4.5, which shows that none of the sample villages without road access has a market. Market size can also be assumed to influence the price pattern. Large villages should exhibit lower prices, since they should attract a larger number of sellers. Larger villages can also provide economies of scale in the transportation of beer.

Table 4.6 shows the national price variation depending on the type and size of the village. Villages are divided into large villages, with more than 50 households, and small villages, with fewer than 50 households. The expected pattern, with a lower price in large villages, holds for urban and rural villages with road access, but not for rural villages without road access. This is very interesting, and suggests that the entry barriers for traders acting in villages without road access are quite high. The fact that larger villages without road access record higher prices indicates that they do not attract more sellers: instead, it is likely that the incumbent seller just meets more demand which allows him or her to raise prices. In these cases, improved road access would not only result in lower prices because of the reduction in transport costs, but also because of the reduction in entry barriers and the market power of traders.

Table 4.6   Price of one 640 ml bottle of Beer Lao in small and large villages

Urban village	Large village	Mean (in Kip)	5979
		Std error	86.00 (n = 96)
	Small village	Mean	7000
		Std error	408.25 (n = 4)
Rural village with access to road	Large village	Mean	7069
		Std error	92.42 (n = 190)
	Small village	Mean	7584
		Std error	226.25 (n = 38)
Rural village without access to road	Large village	Mean	8083
		Std error	208 (n = 48)
	Small village	Mean	7762
		Std error	257 (n = 21)

Notes: Total number of villages is 397.

Source: Authors' calculations based on LECS data.

The free flow of products between markets is of great importance for the functioning of any economy. An integration of markets, supported by improvements in market infrastructure and transportation systems, can reduce transaction costs and allow trade between locations, with gains from comparative advantages and specialization. The descriptive analysis of beer prices indicates that transport costs in Lao PDR are not only determined by distance. Road access and the presence of markets are important determinants of prices at the village level.

The high average prices and large price variations between villages without access to a road are likely to reflect a high variation in transportation costs and competition. The prices are high not only because it is expensive to transport Beer Lao to villages lacking road access, but also because there is not likely to be much competition between traders. Given the high entry barriers (in terms of transport costs) the markets are too small to support several traders and the incumbents can therefore charge high profit margins. New traders are discouraged from entering because they realize that the profit that can be generated from a share of the small market is not sufficient to cover the transport costs, or because they understand that prices will fall as a result of competition if they try to capture a larger share of the market, which also reduces profits. This suggests that the benefits of improvements in transport infrastructre can be very substantial, extending far beyond the cost savings related to transport costs. By making the local markets contestable, transport investments can contribute to a reduction in the cost of imported products. However, transport infrastructure alone may not bring down the observed fragmentation of prices. Minten (1999), studying Madagascar, argues that improvements in soft infrastructure are also needed to influence prices.

At the same time, it is important to note that the increased efficiency related to the inflow of goods to villages benefiting from improved transport infrastructure reflects only part of the overall increase in welfare. Stronger links to the national (and perhaps even the international) economy will not only affect the expenditures but also the earnings of local households. It is likely that the prices of the goods produced by local households will increase, since less is lost in transport costs and profit margins charged by traders with market power. Goetz (1992) and de Janvry et al. (1991) argue that due to transaction costs, a specific price band exists when following a product between its purchase and selling price – the poorer the infrastructure, the greater the size of the band. The descriptive statistics above provide evidence for the influence of transport and market infrastructures on spatial price patterns.

CONCLUSION: ASSESSING THE DETERMINANTS OF BEER RETAIL PRICES

This chapter has sought to improve our understanding of the determinants of the spatial price pattern of beer retail prices at the village level in Lao PDR. The results indicate that type of village and road access influence the retail price where urban villages and rural villages with access to roads exhibit lowest prices.

Turning to the geographical location, the lowest average prices (5348 Kip per bottle) and the lowest standard errors were not surprisingly found in urban villages in Vientiane. Urban villages in the North record higher prices than urban villages in the South, which presumably reflects differences in transportation distance from Vientiane. Road access also has a strong impact on both the mean and the standard deviation of prices. Rural villages with access to roads (in particular, those with wet season road access) have lower average prices than rural villages without road access. In rural villages without road access, the entry barriers are higher, which presumably gives more market power to traders and contributes to a larger price band, depending on demand and other market conditions. Comparing rural villages without road access, it can be seen that the highest average prices as well as the highest standard deviations are recorded in the Central and Southern parts of the country.

Market size can also be assumed to influence the price pattern of the studied product. Large villages should exhibit lower prices, since they should attract a larger number of sellers. Villages were divided into large villages, with more than 50 households, and small villages, with fewer than 50 households. The expected pattern, with a lower price in large villages, holds for urban and rural villages with road access, but not for rural villages without road access. This is very interesting, and suggests that the entry barriers for traders acting in villages without road access are quite high. The result, that larger villages without road access record higher prices, indicates that they do not attract more sellers: instead, it is likely that the incumbent seller just meets more demand, which allows him or her to raise prices. In these cases, improved road access would not only result in lower prices because of the reduction in transport costs, but also because of the reduction in entry barriers and the market power of traders.

Drawing upon the descriptive analysis presented in this chapter, it is possible to identify four principal determinants of the degree of market integration. These include (1) type of village, (2) access to road, (3) size of the market, and (4) access to a daily market.

The results from the first part of the analysis indicate that the distance between producer and consumer is not a perfect predictor of the retail price of consumer goods. A very rough price comparison between the retail price in the provincial centers suggests that it is necessary to account for differences in transport costs emanating from uneven road quality, as well as differences related to the degree of competition (or the number of traders) in each location. These results also follow studies conducted on spatial price patterns and market integration in the former Zaire and Madagascar (Minten and Kyle 1999; Minten 1999). The analysis of prices at the village level indicates that road access and the presence of markets are additional important determinants. The results show high average prices and large price variations in villages without access to a road. Prices are high not only because it is expensive to transport Beer Lao when road access is limited, but also high transport costs work as a barrier to entry: high transport costs will deter potential competitors from entering distant villages even if it is known that there are potential profits to be made.

Given the high entry barriers (in terms of transport costs) the markets are too small to support several traders, and the incumbents can therefore charge high profit margins. This suggests that the benefits of improvements in transport infrastructure can be very substantial, extending far beyond the cost savings related to transport costs. By making the local markets constestable, transport investments can contribute to a reduction in the cost of products transported to the local markets. At the same time, it is important to note that the increased efficiency related to the inflow of goods to villages benefiting from improved transport infrastructure reflects only part of the overall increase in welfare. It is likely that the prices of the goods produced by local households may increase, since less is lost in transport costs and profit margins charged by traders with market power.

A conclusion from these findings is that improvements in transport infrastructure can be expected to yield substantial benefits, both directly, through a reduction in the cost of transportation, and indirectly, through the effects on competition: villages with road access are contestable markets, in the sense that high prices will attract new sellers that put downward pressure on prices. Both of these effects will benefit local communities. Apart from giving them access to goods at lower prices, market integration will also improve their chances of selling their own products at more favorable prices.

NOTES

1. It is possible that inter-regional differences in the price and availability of substitutes (other beverages and spirits) may also influence beer prices. However, these differences will to some extent be captured by our proxies for market conditions.
2. For example, Oraboune (2008, p. 7) reports that nearly 60 percent of aggregate public investment went to the transport sector in 2000.
3. A sample of 397 villages is used for the descriptive analysis.

REFERENCES

Ahmed, R. and N. Rustagi (1984), *Agricultural Marketing and Price Incentives: A Comparative Study of African and Asian Countries*, Washington, DC: IFPRI.

Ali, I. and E.M. Pernia (2003), 'Infrastructure and poverty reduction: what is the connection?', ERD Policy Brief No 13, Manila: Asian Development Bank.

Andersson, M., A. Engvall and K. Kokko (2005), 'Determinants of poverty in LAO PDR', Country Economic Report 2005:10, Stockholm: SIDA.

Andersson, M., A. Engvall and K. Kokko (2007), 'Regional development in Lao PDR: growth patterns and market integration', EIJS Working Paper 234, Stockholm: Stockholm School of Economics.

Annez, P., S. Sarakosas and D. Vandenberghe (2001), 'Loxley: the development of the Lao Brewery Company', ASEAN Business Case Studies No 20, Antwerp: CAS, Chennai, and CIMDA.

Arrow, K.J. (1969), 'The organization of economic activity: issues pertinent to the choice of the market versus nonmarket allocation', in *The Analysis and Evaluation of Public Expenditure: The PPB System*, 1, US Joint Economic Committee, 91 Congress, 1st Session, Washington, DC: US Government Printing Office, pp. 59–73.

Aschauer, D. (1989), 'Public investment and productivity growth in the group of seven', *Economic Perspectives*, **13** (5), 17–25.

Badiane, O. and G.E. Shively (1998), 'Spatial integration, transport costs, and the response of local prices to policy changes in Ghana', *Journal of Development Economics*, **56** (2), 411–31.

Banister, D. and Y. Berechman (2001), 'Transport investment and the promotion of economic growth', *Journal of Transport Geography*, **9**, 209–18.

Berry, B.J.L. (1967), *Geography of Market Centers and Retail Distribution*, Engelwood Cliffs, NJ: Prentice-Hall.

Bird, K. and H. Hill (2010), 'Tiny, poor, landlocked, indebted, but growing: lessons for late reforming transition economies from Lao PDR', *Oxford Development Studies*, **38** (2), 117–43.

Bourdet, Y. (2000), *The Economics of Transition in Laos*, Cheltenham, UK and Northampton, MA, USA: Edward Elgar.

Carter, J.R. and B.G. Ferrin (1995), 'The impact of transportation costs on supply chain management', *Journal of Business Logistics*, **16** (1), 189–212.

Christaller, W. (1933), *Central Places in Southern Germany*, Jena: Fischer [English translation by C.W. Baskin, London: Prentice-Hall, 1966].

Cotterill, R.W. (1986), 'Market power in the retail food industry: evidence from Vermont', *Review of Economics and Statistics*, **68**, 379–86.

Deaton, A.S. (1997), *The Analysis of Household Surveys: A Microeconomic Approach to Development Policy*, Baltimore, MD: John Hopkins University Press.

Deaton, A.S. (1988), 'Quality, quantity, and spatial variation of price', *American Economic Review*, **78** (3), 418–30.

De Janvry, A., M. Fafchamps and E. Sadoulet (1991), 'Peasant household behaviour with missing markets: some paradoxes explained', *The Economic Journal*, **101**, 1400–17.

Gannon, C. and Z.A. Liu (1997), 'Poverty and transport', TWU discussion papers, TWU-30, Washington, DC: World Bank.

Goetz, S.J. (1992), 'A selectivity model of household food marketing behaviour in sub-Saharan Africa', *American Journal of Agricultural Economics*, **64**, 444–52.

Gramlich, E.M. (1994), 'Infrastructure investments: a review essay', *Journal of Economic Literature*, **32**, 1176–96.

Hoover, E.M. (1948), *The Location of Economic Activity*, New York: McGraw-Hill.

Minten, B. (1999), 'Infrastructure, market access, and agricultural prices', MTID Discussion Papers 26, International Food Policy Research Institute (IFPRI).

Minten, B. and S. Kyle (1999), 'The effect of distance and road quality on food collection, marketing margin, and traders' wages: evidence from the former Zaire', *Journal of Development Economics*, **60** (2), 467–95.

Munnell A. (1992), 'Infrastructure investment and productivity growth', *Journal of Economic Perspectives*, **6**, 1989–98.

Oraboune, S. (2008), 'Infrastructure (rural road) development and poverty alleviation in Lao PDR', IDE Discussion Paper No. 151, Chiba: Institute of Developing Economies.

Pelton, L.E., D. Strutton and J.R. Lumpkin (2002), *Marketing Channels – A Relationship Management Approach*, New York: McGraw-Hill/Irwin.

Richter, K., R. van der Weide and P. Sopuksavath (2005), 'Lao PDR Poverty Trends 1992/3–2002/3', draft report, Vientiane: Committee for Planning and Investment, National Statistical Center and World Bank.

Sadoulet, E. and A. de Janvry (1995), *Quantitative Development Policy Analysis*, Baltimore, MD: John Hopkins University Press.

Warr, P. (2010), 'Roads and poverty in rural Laos: an econometric analysis', *Pacific Economic Review*, **15** (1), 152–69.

PART III

Multi-point competition and rivalries

5. The Estonian beer market: the battle for market leadership

Jorma Larimo, Andres Kuusik and Urmas Varblane

INTRODUCTION

Over the past 20 years there have been a lot of changes in most industry sectors in Europe. Often these changes have been especially remarkable in various Central and Eastern European (CEE) countries and the Commonwealth of Independent States (CIS), where the economic systems have also been changing. In the consumer goods sector the European brewing industry is one good example of an industry that has experienced a lot of changes during the last 20 years.

In this chapter we will focus on one CEE market – Estonia – and try to review the market development during the last 20 years, focusing especially on the strategies of the key players in the market. Although the Estonian market is the smallest beer market in CEE and CIS, it is interesting because the growth of beer production and consumption was the second largest within CEE and CIS from 1992 until 2007–08 (Swinnen and Van Herck 2011) and Estonia was among the first Eastern European markets to be entered by foreign breweries through acquisitions. The current analysis is the first long-term review covering the development trends and strategies of the brewery market in Estonia in more detail. The general beer industry related data used in the chapter are obtained from different alcohol market research reviews made by the Estonian Institute of Economic Research as well as other market research companies (for example, Faktum Ariko), international business journals and brewery organizations. The company level data is based on interviews with the managing directors and one additional person in the two leading local breweries, supplemented with material published in the annual reports and web pages of the companies. Information concerning two other key Estonian breweries is based on the web page information of those companies.

The structure of this chapter is as follows: first we provide an overview of beer consumption in Estonia from the time of transition until 2011. It reveals the relative importance of beer among the other alcoholic drinks and compares Estonian beer consumption internationally. The next section is devoted to the period of opening up of the Estonian beer market in the early 1990s, when foreign breweries used the privatization process launched in Estonia to enter the market through acquisitions. The following section provides an overall view of the fight for market leadership in the Estonian beer market, concentrating on firm level strategies. It opens with an analysis of the product policies of the major breweries, including changes in product portfolio and packaging of products. It is followed by a comparison of the behaviour of key competing players in the field of product promotion policy. Additionally, pricing and distribution policies are briefly covered. The chapter ends with a summary and conclusions concerning the key development trends, events and strategic decisions made by major players in the Estonian brewery market.

DEVELOPMENT OF ESTONIAN ALCOHOL MARKETS

It is very difficult to determine the date when beer production and consumption started in Estonia. Relying on archaeological discoveries from around 1000 BC, the major crop of grain was barley and hence beer production was possible. The first written record comes from 1284, when the Bishop of Saaremaa required tax payments in beer. Between the thirteenth and nineteenth centuries German landlords played an important role, transferring knowledge about producing beer from Germany to the Baltic provinces of Russia. The industrial production of beer in Estonia started in the early nineteenth century, again on the initiative of the Baltic Germans. The Saku brewery was established in 1820 and the Tartu brewery in 1826 (A.LeCoq 2012b). Next to domestic needs they also served the demand of St Petersburg, the capital of the Russian Empire, and also parts of Moscow. After Estonia gained independence in 1918 beer production in Estonia was mainly limited to the domestic market, which caused a reduction in production levels, although production methods remained unchanged.

Important changes in beer production in Estonia occurred after World War II, when Estonia was incorporated into the Soviet Union. All beer factories were nationalized and the market-based system was replaced by a centrally planned system. This caused a fast reduction in the quality of beer produced as the competition between producers was eliminated. The production of Western European style lager or stout beer in the

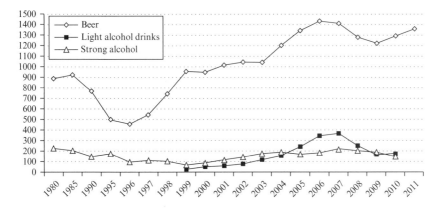

Source: Statistics Estonia (2012); Estonian Institute of Economic Research (2012); Estonian Institute of Market Research (2004, 2005, 2006, 2007, 2008, 2009, 2010a, 2010b).

Figure 5.1   Production of beer, strong alcohol and light alcohol drinks in Estonia, 1980–2011 (in thousand hl)

Baltic States or Russia was very limited. The dominating official local products, such as Žiguli eripruul (Žiguli special brew), Moskva (Moscow) and Kuldne Oder (Golden Barley), were produced by several producers following centrally fixed preparation recommendations. Even so, every producer also had its own mixture. There were four main beer producers: Saku, Tartu, Pärnu and Viru. Due to weaknesses in production technology the beer lasted for only two weeks, which seriously limited the distribution range of the breweries. Consequently, the breweries mainly served nearby regions: Saku served the capital Tallinn and its surroundings, Tartu served southern Estonia, Pärnu served western Estonia and Viru served the north-eastern region. In addition to the big breweries there were also around 25 microbreweries in operation.

The development of total production of beer from 1980 until 2010 can be seen in detail in Figure 5.1, which also shows the relative position of beer production compared to strong and light alcoholic drinks. The production of beer was 88.9 million litres in 1980 and peaked in 1985 with 92.3 million litres. The total production of beer dropped heavily in the early 1990s due to the severe economic crisis caused by the transformation from a planned to a market economy. An additional reduction in beer consumption occurred after the monetary reform in 1992 and the launching of excise tax, which heavily reduced the purchasing power of the population. Hence beer production dropped two-fold to only 40 million litres in 1992. Along with the reduction of beer production in the early 1990s, consumption shifted towards strong alcohol. The production of strong alcohol (mainly vodka) was almost 40 per cent of the total production of beer. The recovery of beer production started after the mid 1990s when Western style lager and stout beers started to dominate and the first wave of economic growth increased consumer demand. Since 1999 beer production has gradually increased and the role of strong alcohol has decreased in the structure of production. In 2010 the total production of strong alcohol made up around 12 per cent of total beer production.

Beer production reached its pre-crisis level in 1999 and continued to grow until 2007, when total production was 141 million litres. Thus, total production increased around 2.8 times between 1995 and 2007. A slight reduction in beer production occurred during the 2008–10 economic recession, which was enforced by an excise tax increase in 2008 and a value added tax increase in 2009. Still, the recovery was rather quick and preliminary production figures from the leading firms in 2011 indicated that beer production would have regained its pre-recession level.

The relative position of beer among other alcoholic drinks in the Estonian market was challenged in the late 1990s, when light alcohol drinks were introduced (see Figure 5.1). In 2003, light alcohol drink production was some 10 per cent of beer production, rapidly increasing to around 25 per cent during the economic boom between 2004 and 2007. Interestingly, after the 2008–10 economic crisis the share of light alcohol drinks decreased to 15 per cent of the level of beer production in 2010 and remained low.

International Comparison of Estonian Beer Consumption and Production

In 2009, Estonian beer consumption per capita was 85.4 litres, which is clearly above the EU27 average of 75.3 litres. Figure 5.2 provides a comparative view of the per capita consumption of beer and its dynamics in the Baltic Sea region, the UK and Germany in 2003 and 2009. Estonian beer consumption per capita increased from 71.2 to 85.4 litres during this time and almost reached the Finnish consumption level. Lithuania and Poland followed a similar beer consumption growth trend. In contrast, a declining trend in beer consumption occurred in the UK, where consumption dropped from 101.3 litres in 2003 to 75.8 litres in 2009. In the Baltic Sea region, Denmark experienced a sharp decline in per capita consumption of beer from 96.2 to 71.5 litres, while Latvia and Sweden have maintained a lower beer consumption level. According to statistics by the Food and Agriculture Organization of the United Nations (see Swinnen and Van Herck 2011, p. 249), in Estonia the growth of beer consumption, during 1992–2007, and the growth of beer production, during 1992–2008,

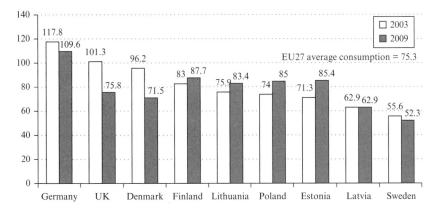

Source: Based on data from Beer Statistics (Brewers of Europe 2010 edition, p. 12).

Figure 5.2   *Beer consumption per capita in the Baltic region, UK and Germany in 2003 and 2009*

were second highest after Russia, the former growing by 160 per cent and the latter by 221 per cent. The figures clearly show the great change that has occurred in the Estonian beer market during the last 20 years.

Hence, based on the previous discussion one could conclude that Estonian beer consumption is high and growing. Until the early 1990s imports of beer to Estonia were extremely limited and domestic beer was mainly consumed. However, in the mid 1990s imports started to grow and their share gained around 10 per cent from total sales. The share of imported beer has slowly continued to grow and by 2010 it comprised 14 per cent of total sales.

Before transition exports were only marginally important due to the nature of the product (local beer lasted for only two weeks). This situation continued until the mid 1990s; for example, in 1995 the volume of exports was only 0.4 million litres. However, in the late 1990s exports started to grow, reaching 17.4 million litres in 1999. Thus, the share of exports in 1999 was already around 18 per cent of total production. The main export targets were predominantly the neighbouring countries Latvia, Lithuania and Finland, but in small quantities also to the USA and other countries. Between 1999 and 2009 exports were rather stable, with annual volumes of around 20 million litres. The new growth wave of exports started in 2010, when a record export volume of 44.8 million litres was reached (Estonian Institute of Economic Research 2012). Also, the role of exports in total production increased clearly in the 2000s and reached 34.7 per cent by 2010 – thus, the relative importance of exports doubled compared to the late 1990s. For the first time, during the period under review, exports of beer from Estonia also exceeded the volume of imports in 2010. The rapid growth of exports could be partly explained by the change in strategies of the major brewing companies. They started to rationalize their production and reduce overlaps in their portfolio (Thirst for Great 2012), leading to a concentration of production of specific beer brands in one location for the whole company. This strategic change generated a new wave of intra-firm trade; the export of beer from Estonian breweries to Finland, Latvia, Lithuania, Denmark, Belarus and so on, where the beers are sold as brands of the multinational beer corporation. On the other hand, the importation of other beer brands from the production sites of these corporations into Estonia also increased. Hence, both exports and imports increased in 2010.

Finally, it is important to mention a special feature about the Estonian beer market. A large amount of tourists, mainly from Finland, visit the country. Estonia is a very popular target for Finns to make short trips to due to extremely favourable connections. There were 19 ferry and 11 flight connections per day between Tallinn and Helsinki in summer 2012 (Port of Tallinn 2012; Tallinn Airport 2012). The estimated number of Finnish tourists in Estonia is between six and seven million per year. The travel time from Helsinki to Tallinn by ferry is between one and two hours and usually costs only €15–40 depending on the time of day and speed of the ferry. The ferry between Stockholm and Tallinn takes some 12 hours and costs somewhat more.

Market surveys by the Estonian Institute of Economic Research within the last decade have shown that the price of a typical lager beer (4.5 per cent alcohol) in Finland (Helsinki region) has steadily been around 2.8–3 times higher than in Estonia (Tallinn area) (Estonian Institute of Economic Research 2012, p. 40). This is mainly the result of the high taxation of alcohol products in Finland. The significant price differential and easy travel conditions have produced a strong interest by tourists to purchase beer and other alcoholic drinks. In addition, an important change occurred after 1 May 2004, when Estonia joined the European Union (EU). This increased the amount of beer allowed to be imported from Estonia from 16 litres to 110 litres. It was a major institutional change which forced breweries to pay more serious attention to tourists as a segment of consumers and speeded up different innovations in product packaging and distribution channels. A survey carried out in 2005 by Emor, the leading market research company in Estonia, has shown that almost 80 per cent of Finnish tourists purchased alcohol to take back with them (Emor, www.emor.ee, 30 March 2005). It also indicated that around two-thirds of the Finnish tourists visited Estonia at least twice a year.

Interestingly, several market surveys revealed that the majority of beer is bought by Finnish tourists. Tourists from other countries, for example Sweden and Russia, preferred more expensive strong alcohols (Estonian Institute of Market Research 2010c).

More recent surveys by the Estonian Institute of Market Research revealed that tourists bought approximately 15.8 million litres of beer from shops and ferries in 2010. This was approximately 21 per cent of total consumption of beer in Estonia (excluding consumption of beer in catering) (Estonian Institute of Economic Research 2012). Hence, tourists as a consumer group should also be taken into consideration, both in analysing the market trends but also evaluating the marketing strategies of main breweries. The main breweries also need to consider major trends in alcoholic beverage consumption among tourists. According to the Estonian Institute of Market Research, beer purchases by tourists have increased within recent years, but they are still below the record quantity of 29.1 million litres in 2006 (Estonian Institute of Economic Research 2012). However, during recent years there has been a rapid increase in tourists' consumption and purchase of light alcoholic beverages instead.

OPENING UP OF THE ESTONIAN BEER MARKET – THE ENTRY OF FOREIGN BREWERIES

By the end of the late 1980s about 30 breweries were active in Estonia. The two oldest and biggest breweries were Saku and Tartu and other important breweries were Karme, Nigula, Pärnu, Saare and Viru. After the occupation of Estonia by the Soviet Union in 1940 all breweries were nationalized. Therefore, already by the late 1980s Estonian economists started to work on privatization policy principles and The Act of Small Scale Privatization was passed by the Supreme Soviet (the Estonian parliament during the Soviet period) on 13 December 1990 (Terk 2000). After the collapse of the Soviet Union in 1991 the privatization of state-owned firms was a critically important issue for Estonia in order to introduce a market-based economic system. Hence, a large-scale privatization strategy was developed extremely quickly and real privatization started following the German *Treuhand* model by late 1991, which was targeted at the sale of firms for real money (not privatization vouchers like in Lithuania or the Czech Republic) to investors (Terk 2000). It generated great interest among foreign investors, first of all in neighbouring Finland and Sweden.

The brewing industry was among the first sectors to be targeted by foreign investors. This also seems to have been the situation in several other CEE markets (see, for example, Marinov and Marinova 1999, Larimo et al. 2006). In the following part of this section we will review the process of foreign entry into the Estonian brewing industry, following the timing of entry by foreign breweries. Hence, we first describe the foreign entry into Saku, then the Viru and Tartu breweries. Alongside the description of the privatization processes we also briefly reveal the major changes made by foreign investors after the acquisitions.

Saku brewery had been the leading Estonian brewery for the previous 50 years. In 1976 (during the Soviet period), Saku was given the title Experimental Brewery, which provided special preferences from the Soviet Planning Agency (GOSPLAN) towards investments. It helped Saku to invest and therefore made it the most attractive target among breweries for foreign investors. Saku succeeded in being included in the so-called pilot privatization list of firms and hence was among the first Estonian companies that were privatized after Estonia regained independence in 1991 (Terk 2000). The company had focused only on beer production and had been the biggest brewery in Estonia for a long time. A majority (60 per cent) of the shares of Saku was acquired by BBH (Baltic Beverage Holding), a company that was jointly established only somewhat earlier by two Nordic breweries – namely Pripps from Sweden and Hartwall from Finland – to establish and manage brewery operations in various CEE and CIS countries. BBH had been formed as a means of market expansion, as in the early 1990s Hartwall had a market share of around 60 per cent in Finland and Pripps was clearly the leading brewery in Sweden, and therefore growth possibilities in their domestic markets were relatively limited. The remaining shares of Saku brewery were owned by several local investors. BBH immediately started significant reconstruction and development operations in the brewery. The production of the brewery in 1992 was around 20 million litres and the company had 210 employees (Arnold et al. 2000).

In 1995 Pripps and the Norwegian brewery Ringnes merged to form Pripps Ringnes, and after some additional transactions in 1997 Pripps Ringnes was wholly owned by ORKLA – parent company of Ringnes. Thus, from 1997 the owners of BBH were Hartwall and ORKLA. In 1998 production had increased to 38 million litres and in 1999 it reached 47.5 million litres. Alongside a production growth of 150 per cent, the company's personnel increased by only 20 per cent to 260 employees in 1999. The company started exports to Finland and Sweden in 1996. In 1999, exports were some three million litres (6 per cent of total production). In addition to the above countries, exports were directed to Latvia, Lithuania, Ukraine and also, but less so, the USA. In the late 1990s, the Saku brewery also had licensing agreements with Lithuanian and Ukrainian companies for the production of Saku's luxury beers for the local markets. The company was also the official representative of the leading Finnish beer brand in the 1990s – Lapin Kulta – in Estonia. Saku had a market share of over 50 per cent during 1994–99. Thus, in the 1990s the company was the clear market leader in Estonia. In fact, the company was the biggest brewery in the whole of the Baltic states during the 1990s. Since 27 January 1998 the shares of Saku brewery have been traded on the Tallinn Stock Exchange (Arnold et al. 2000).

The Viru brewery, located in Rakvere, some 60 kilometres east of Tallinn, was also nationalized soon after Estonia regained independence. This brewery was established in 1975 by a collective farm in order to diversify its business. It was common practice for collective farms in the Soviet Union to facilitate production of consumer goods in addition to their main activities. The company originally produced only one beer brand – Žiguli beer – but also started to produce other brands during the 1980s. In 1991, the name of the brewery was changed to AS Viru Õlu. By 1992 a Danish brewery, AS Harboes Bryggeri, had already acquired a majority share in Viru Õlu. Following the strategy of BBH, Harboe also increased its ownership in the brewery to 75 per cent some years later. In contrast to BBH's Saku strategy, Harboe decided to expand Viru's product assortment and Viru also started to produce soft drinks in 1995 (Harboes Bryggeri 2012).

As in the case of Saku, the foreign owner modernized the production processes, but it took more time as the starting position differed from Saku. Hence, Viru Õlu could not benefit from the new situation (being owned by a foreign investor) as much as would have been possible. After the company started to produce a beer called 'Bear Beer' with a very strong alcohol content (7.5 per cent) under licence from the Danish parent company, Viru started to gain more market share. Although the alcohol content was high, the price of the beer was low, which together with the economic slowdown gave Viru a market share of over 10 per cent and therefore second position in the Estonian market of the late 1990s.

Tartu Õlletehas (Tartu Brewery) was not as successful in the privatization process, but was an important player in the history of Estonian beer production. In 1826 Justus Reinhold Schramm started to manufacture lager style beer in Tartu, which after 1893 was operated as the Tivoli brewery. In 1830 a tradesman, Albert L.J. Le Coq, settled down in London to expand the family wine business and to start bottling and exporting under the name Russian Imperial Stout. In 1904 A.LeCoq was transformed into a private limited company and the company's headquarters and bottling plant was moved from London to St Petersburg in 1906.

Six years later the company was granted the title of the Russian Imperial Court supplier. In the same year A.LeCoq acquired Tivoli, renaming the brewery A.LeCoq, and in 1913 the manufacturing of Imperial Extra Double Stout was started in Tartu. In 1938 the company opened a new modern bottling and beverage plant in Tallinn and in 1940 the company became other leading manufacturer of beer in Estonia after Saku. After nationalization of the breweries, the name of the company was changed to Tartu Õlletehas in 1941. The company was thoroughly reconstructed in the 1950s and early 1960s, and in 1960 the company was appointed the leading enterprise of beer and beverages. In 1968 the company became the first Estonian company to bottle mineral water.

When the company was privatized in 1992 it was expected that the Finnish brewery Sinebrychoff would be the new main owner of the company. However, there were problems in the negotiations and after two offers Sinebrychoff decided to abandon the acquisition. There were also discussions with a US-based company about their investment in the Tartu brewery, but these negotiations also failed to result in any agreement. In 1995 an Estonian holding company, Magnum Group, acquired Tartu Õlletehas. The idea was to develop the company and to resell the restructured company. The production of Tartu Õlletehas at that time was only 13.5 million litres.

By October 1996 Magnum Group had sold 15 per cent of its shares to the Finnish Olvi Corporation, which was at that time a relatively small but growing family-owned brewery in the Finnish market (Olvi Group 2012b). In 1995 the company had started sales cooperation with Tartu Õlletehas; thus acquiring a small share was quite a logical next step in trying to intensify cooperation. In addition to the share price, Olvi Corporation promised to invest 75 million Estonian kroons in the development of the company. Around one month later Olvi also bought another brewery from Magnum Group – Saare Õlu – which was the fifth biggest brewery but only had 2 per cent market share. In 1997 Olvi increased its ownership in the two breweries. As the financial resources of the company were quite limited, a temporary arrangement was agreed whereby Olvi and the Baltic Investment Bank together acquired Tartu Õlletehas. Olvi promised to invest a total of 270 million Estonian kroons for the development of the company during the following years. Large investment projects to renew the production processes and quality of the beer produced were started immediately. The facilities were ready in 1999 and in the same year the production volume reached around 30 million litres – twice as much as the production volume of Tartu Õlletehas in 1995. In order to rationalize operations production at the previously acquired Saare brewery in Saaremaa was mostly closed down and only the trademark Saare Õlu was kept. Production was transferred mainly to Tartu; only some special order beers were brewed in Saaremaa.

In 1999 a holding company, A.LeCoq, was established to control Olvi's operations in Estonia and the newly acquired subsidiaries in Latvia and Lithuania. In addition, the name of the company was changed from Tartu Õlletehas to A.LeCoq. The name A.LeCoq was strange and difficult for Estonians to pronounce but, as was discussed in subsection two, this was the name of the Tartu brewery before nationalization in 1941. The benefits of the old well-established name were regarded as greater than keeping the same name or adopting a new name. In 1999 A.LeCoq also decided to diversify alcohol production outside the beer industry and became the first Estonian company to manufacture cider. The Finnish parent company Olvi had started cider production some years earlier and the positive experiences of this diversification in Finland provided a basis for the respective diversification outside beer production in Estonia.

The third largest local brewery – Viru brewery – was acquired by the Danish company Harboes Bryggeri during the first privatization wave. However, the modernization did not proceed quickly enough and it was only at the end of the 1990s, with the launch of a strong beer produced under licence, that clear growth and a stronger market position for the company occurred. Only the fourth local brewery in the early 1990s – Pärnu brewery – could not find a foreign owner. The company kept its market position of 8–9 per cent until 1997, but after that it started to lose its market share.

In conclusion, by 1996 there was a foreign investor in all three of the main breweries. In all cases investments were in the form of partial acquisition. Acquisition was also the main form of investment in the brewery sector in the other CEE countries in the 1990s as well as outside CEE, a situation that has continued into the 2000s (see Larimo et al. 2006; Madsen et al. 2011). In 1994–98 the Saku brewery was the clear market leader in the Estonian market. The company, with its new foreign owner BBH, could use its role as pioneer very well in the changed situation and had a market share of over 50 per cent during most of the 1990s. The situation was very different at Tartu Õlletehas. There were several negotiations between Tartu Õlletehas and various foreign companies, and when the company was finally sold the new owner was a local who planned to make a moderate level of investment and then to sell the company. At the end of the 1990s ownership of the company started to stabilize when the Finnish Olvi Corporation acquired at first a minority share, later the majority share and finally the whole company. At the end of the 1990s the company regained its lost market share, based on a significant modernization project and successful launch of the old name of the brewery.

FIGHT FOR MARKET LEADERSHIP

As discussed earlier, at the end of the 1990s the Saku brewery was majority owned by BBH, which was a joint venture between the Finnish Hartwall and Norwegian Orkla. In 2000 the Danish Carlsberg brewery merged with Orkla's brewery sector and a company called Carlsberg breweries was formed. Subsequently, BBH was jointly owned by Hartwall and Carlsberg breweries. At the time of the merger, both BBH and Carlsberg had breweries in Latvia, Lithuania and Russia, whilst Carlsberg also had breweries in Poland and several additional countries.

In 2002 – only two years after the change in ownership – there was again a change in the ownership of BBH and therefore also in the ownership of Saku. Hartwall was acquired by the UK-based brewery Scottish & Newcastle. This meant that while BBH was owned by two relatively small Nordic breweries in the 1990s, the company was now owned jointly by two much larger international breweries. This period lasted some six years. In 2008 Heineken and Carlsberg jointly acquired Scottish & Newcastle. The companies decided to divide the acquired subsidiary in such a way that Carlsberg received all subsidiaries previously owned by BBH. Thus, after the deal Saku was wholly owned by Carlsberg. On 20 September 2008 the shares of Saku brewery were delisted from the Tallinn Stock Exchange. The change in ownership could be seen very quickly in the company's mission, vision, values, image and marketing strategies. Since 2008 the mission has been to offer enjoyable refreshment and new experiences with quality beverages, and the vision has been to be the market leader in every branded category in which the company chooses to compete, following the mission and vision of the parent company Carlsberg (Carlsberg Group 2012). As may be expected, Carlsberg's products have since received much more attention than they did previously. The numerous changes in the ownership of Saku had an influence on the company's production and marketing strategies, as can be seen later.

The first structural change that occurred in Tartu Õlletehas was that following its long-term plans the Finnish Olvi Corporation acquired the shares owned by Baltic Investment Bank in spring 2000 and Olvi became the sole owner of the brewery via the holding company A.LeCoq. In the early 2000s the production volume of beer almost doubled. However, at the same time A.LeCoq also decided to continue expanding outside beer production. In 2001 the company became the first in Estonia to manufacture a sport drink, and at the same time expanded production of soft drinks and cider. In 2002 the company became the leading drink producer in Estonia with a volume of 55 928 million litres. An additional significant strategic move occurred one year later when it acquired the Estonian beverage company AS Ösel Foods, which manufactured juices, mineral waters and vitamin-enriched soft drinks. In 2004 the name of the company changed from Tartu Õlletehas to A.LeCoq Tartu Õlletehas. During the same year the company became the first drink manufacturer to exceed the production margin of 100 million litres in Estonia.

In 2005, the company became the first in Estonia to produce near water, that is, water-based beverages with a light fruit content. The latest structural change occurred in late February 2012 when A.LeCoq decided to buy 49 per cent of the microbrewery Karksi Õlletehas (Karksi Brewery). The acquisition was not motivated by the beer production of the Karksi company, but by the existing conditions and means for producing apple wine that is used to make ciders and long drinks. Due to the growth of both domestic sales and exports of ciders and long drinks, A.LeCoq needed to quickly extend its capacity and Karksi provided this opportunity. Thus, at least in the short run, the partial acquisition has not greatly influenced the beer sector. The mission, vision and core values of A.LeCoq are partly similar but partly different compared to those of Saku. The mission of A.LeCoq is to create positive enjoyment, the objective is to be the most attractive and respected beverage producer in Estonia, and the core values focus on Estonianness, responsibility, positivity, customer focus and openness and development.

In the 2000s key events related to the Viru brewery have concerned the introduction of large 1.5 litre PET (plastic) bottles to the Estonian market in 2003 and later the acquisition of the HF Puls trademark and licence to produce gourmet beer for the parent company Harboes Bryggeri. The Pärnu brewery introduced a new beer brand, Puls, in 2005. Based on the success of the beer brand, the name of the company was also changed to Puls brewery in 2006. Due to decreasing sales, Viru brewery acquired the HF Puls trademark in 2008 and the production of beer was transferred in the same year from Pärnu to the Viru brewery (HF Puls 2012). Another significant strategic change happened in 2011, when the parent company Harboes Bryggeri closed down its brewery in Roskilde, Denmark, and transferred production to Viru brewery. Licensed production under the trademark Gourmet Bryggeriet is – at least at the moment – exported by the parent company to Denmark. Hence the role of Viru brewery is underestimated if we limit our analysis only to its market shares in Estonia as its role within Harboes Bryggeri has steadily risen. In fact similar trends could also be followed by Saku and A.LeCoq as they both export and import beers from their parent companies and other subsidiaries.

The development of the market shares of the leading Estonian breweries in 2000–11 are presented in Figure 5.3. As a note to the figure, it should be stated that different sources publish different figures, and, especially after

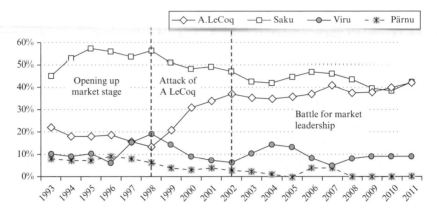

Source: Sepp (2007); Olvi Group (2012a); Kastein (2012); Noop (2012).

Figure 5.3   The development of the market shares of the leading breweries in Estonia, 1993–2011

2005, when the competition became very tight, the information is often contradictory. Saku still claims that it is the leader of the beer market, but at the same time the numbers in annual reports by Saku and Olvi indicate that this is not definite. In its last annual report Olvi noted that Saku and A.LeCoq have relatively equal market shares.

To summarize, Saku was the clear market leader during the whole of the 1990s and the early 2000s. However, Tartu Õlletehas started to gain a greater market share from the early 2000s, and in 2003 reached a market share of over 35 per cent. In 2003–05 Viru Õlu also acquired an increasing market share based mainly on its use of a new 1.5 litre PET bottle. Although Saku has still in the 2000s been the market leader in the Estonian beer market, its position as leader has not been as clear as previously. In fact, there has been very tight competition for the market leadership between Saku and A.LeCoq during the last ten years.

Related to future market development, the interviewed managers both in Saku and A.LeCoq were asked whether the company would be interested in buying any of the existing local breweries, especially the third largest company, Viru brewery. Both of the managers replied that their companies were not interested in buying any of the existing breweries. Key reasons were that both companies had already reached production capacity and that the image of the products of the potential acquisition targets did not fit very well with the image of their own companies. Another question concerned the potential acquisition of the interviewed companies by others. Again, this was considered to be very unlikely. It would demand a substantial decrease in the total sales of the subsidiaries in Estonia. Both companies have significant brewery operations in the neighbouring countries but it would be difficult to serve the Estonian market totally from subsidiaries located in neighbouring markets, and the area strategies of both companies also require the existence of a subsidiary in Estonia. Also, the ownership background of A.LeCoq – the family-owned Finnish Olvi Corporation – prevents not only the acquisition of the whole Olvi Corporation but also makes it difficult to buy any of the subsidiaries owned by the company. The resources of the Olvi Corporation would be enough to buy Saku, perhaps even to buy all of the subsidiaries of Carlsberg in the Baltic states, but not the whole Carlsberg Group. However, EU competition law prevents deals between Olvi and Carlsberg. If one of the companies would buy the subsidiary (or subsidiaries) owned by the other firm in one or more Baltic states (or in Finland), the company would be in a too dominant market position. Thus, deals between the two companies are not probable alternatives. Based on the above, it is quite evident that the battle for leadership in the Estonian beer market will continue between Saku and A.LeCoq in the future.

MARKETING STRATEGIES OF KEY PLAYERS

In this section the main marketing strategies of the key players (Saku and A.LeCoq) will be discussed. First, product, branding and packaging strategies will be analysed, then the focus will move to advertising and promotion strategies, and finally pricing and distribution issues will be considered.

Product and packaging have played a very important role in the marketing strategies of both companies (Noop 2012; Kastein 2012). There has been a huge shift in breadth and depth of product assortment in both companies. During the Soviet period they mainly offered a very similar centrally fixed assortment of products, although nowadays both breweries have developed strong and distinct leading brands which are supported by very different brands for various special customer segments. Table 5.1 reveals the main brands in the portfolios during the period 2000–12.

Table 5.1 clearly indicates that the depth of the assortment has grown in almost all segments. Both companies have increased variety in premium and mainstream segments, which is in accordance with major trends in the Western markets. The number of labels in the low segment (strong beers) has not changed and a totally new segment, light beers, has emerged. As the marketing manager of A.LeCoq commented, the demand for beer is shifting clearly in the direction of light beers (Vernik 2012). In the

Table 5.1 Beer product portfolios of Saku and A.LeCoq breweries

Segment	Saku		A.LeCoq	
	2000	2012	2000	2012
Premium	Saku Originaal	Saku Kuld	A.LeCoq Premium	A.LeCoq Special
	Sack bei Reval	Saku Originaal	A.LeCoq Porter	A.LeCoq Premium
	Saku Porter	Saku Originaal Ehe		A.LeCoq Premium Export
		Saku Porter		A.LeCoq Premium Extra
				A.LeCoq Porter
				A.LeCoq Chocolate Porter
Mainstream	Saku Rock	Saku Rock	A.LeCoq Pilsner	A.LeCoq Pilsner
	Saku Hele	Karl Friedrich	Alexander	Alexander
	Saku on Ice	Presidendi Pilsner	Saaremaa Tuulik	Alexander Suur
	Saku Pilsner	Saku Pilsner		Saaremaa Tuulik
	Saku Tume	Saku Tume		A.LeCoq Organic
		Saku Hele		Tõmmu Hiid
		Saku Manchester		A.LeCoq Maiz
		Saku Praha		A.LeCoq Pils
		Saku Dublin		A.LeCoq Disel
		Saku Stuttgart		Saaremaa Tume
		Saku Ehe		
Low segment	Saku Sarvik	Presidendi 8	Bock	Double Bock
	Saku 7.5	Taurus	Saaremaa X	Saaremaa

Light	Saku on ICE	A.LeCoq I
	Saku DLight Lemon	Beershake Tequila & Citrus
	Saku DLight Cool Mint	Beershake Cranberry & Lime
	Saku DLight Pomegranate	Beershake Grapefruit
	Saku 2.8%	Premium Extra Lemon
Non-alcohol	Saku Originaal non-alcoholic	Saku Originaal non-alcoholic
Imported	Rock zero	Heineken
	Carlsberg	Buckler
	Tuborg	Sandels
	Kronenbourg 1664	Olvi Export
	Baltika 3 Classic	Lidskoje Premium
	Baltika 7 Export	Edelweiss
	Baltika 0	
	Holsten	
	Staropramen Premium	
	Staropramen Dark	
	Koff Export	

Source: Saku (2012); A.LeCoq (2012a); Kastein (2012); Vernik (2012).

non-alcoholic segment only Saku has labels to offer, but as is revealed from the table, both breweries have started to offer a very wide range of imported beers. The key brands for Saku have been Carlsberg and more recently Baltika (and other products belonging to the Carlsberg Group). The significant growth of Baltika is not only limited to Russia; the brand has also had an increasing role in Estonia (about one-third of total beer imports to the country in 2010). Private labels (microbreweries) and seasonal beers are not included in Table 5.1. In the case of private labels it is known that their market share is growing but there is no data available about the distribution of production between breweries.

Figure 5.4 presents the timings of the different product strategy activities of the breweries, together with their market shares in Estonia. The figure reveals that product launches and several packaging decisions have had a great influence on the market shares of the companies.

The success of Saku began with the launch of Saku Originaal in 1993. Until now it has been Saku's leading brand (alcohol content 4.6 per cent). The second strong brand is Saku Rock, which was launched immediately after Saku Originaal and was targeted at younger consumers. As Saku Originaal and Saku Rock are quite masculine brands, Saku started very early on to produce special milder tasting labels for more feminine segments: in 1999 it launched Saku on Ice and in 2006 Saku DLight. In the premium segment, Saku launched Sack bei Reval for the 180th anniversary of Saku in 2000 and Saku Kuld (Saku Gold) in 2005. Other labels have not had so much influence. More recent launches have included

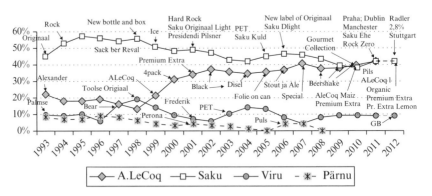

Source: Sepp (2007); Olvi Group (2012a); Kastein (2012); Noop (2012); Vernik (2012); Saku (2012); A.LeCoq (2012a); Viru Õlu Brewery (2012); Estonian Beer Guide (2012).

Figure 5.4   The market shares of the main breweries and the timing of their product strategy activities in Estonia, 1993–2012

the introduction of the Saku Gourmet collection in 2010 and a set of European beers in 2011, which included three brands of different styles of beer: Dublin (stout), Manchester (ale), and Praha (dark beer). In 2012 this European collection was complemented by Stuttgart (wheat beer). In 2011 and 2012 Saku also launched several milder (Saku Ehe), lighter (Saku 2.8 per cent and Radler) and non-alcoholic beers (Rock Zero). The Carlsberg brewery has been famous for its frequent launch of new brands (see, for example, Vrontis 1998), thus Saku's behaviour is similar to that of its parent company.

The main brand produced by Tartu Õlletehas during the whole of the 1990s was Alexander. It was launched as a response to Saku Originaal. It is interesting to note that without any special promotion Alexander is still one of the leading labels on the Estonian beer market today (Vernik 2012). As discussed earlier, in 1999 Tartu Õlletehas again adopted the old brand name A.LeCoq. In the 2000s the main brand produced by the company was A.LeCoq Premium (alcohol content 4.7 per cent). In 2011 A.LeCoq Premium represented around 35 per cent of the total beer sales of the company, followed by Alexander. A.LeCoq has supported its leading brand several times with short-run special editions: in 2001, 2010 and 2012 A.LeCoq launched different kinds of A.LeCoq Premium Extras. A.LeCoq's third strong brand is A.LeCoq Special, which is a premium beer and was launched in 2007 for the 200th anniversary of A.LeCoq. The company also tried to compete with Saku Rock and in 2002 launched a beer called Black, but this was not successful. Therefore, it was replaced with Disel in 2004. Disel is still on the market but is not as successful as Saku Rock. As A.LeCoq Premium does not have such a masculine image, A.LeCoq had no need to offer special products for more feminine segments. Only in 2008 did A.LeCoq start to offer lighter products for women – beer cocktails (Beershake Rose in 2008, Beershake Tequila & Citrus in 2009 and Beershake Cranberry & Lime and Beershake Grapefruit in 2010) and special beers (Premium Extra and Premium Extra Lemon in 2012). More recent launches of new types of beer by A.LeCoq include A.LeCoq Maiz (2010), in which 20 per cent of the malt has been replaced with corn malt, A.LeCoq Pils (2011), a Czech type beer, and A.LeCoq Organic (2012), which was the first organic beer in Estonia.

Other companies have also experienced success based on new product launches. In 1996 Viru launched Bear Beer, which increased its market share to 18 per cent in 1998. The Pärnu brewery launched Perona in 2001 and Puls in 2006. Both had an influence on the market share of the company. The brand Puls is still on the market, now owned by Viru, and as a leading brand plays the main role in keeping Viru brewery's market share at around 9 per cent.

Figure 5.4 reveals that until 2010 Saku had been more active and launched more labels targeted at various small segments compared to A.LeCoq. At the same time, A.LeCoq has behaved more like a market follower, copying (and modifying) only the best decisions of Saku. For example, Saku Originaal was followed by A.LeCoq Premium (six years later), Saku Rock was followed by Black (eight years later) and Saku Kuld was followed by A.LeCoq Special (two years later). The marketing activities of Saku have therefore been more fragmented between different niche labels at the same time, while A.LeCoq has focused more on supporting its main brands. This could be one explanation for A.LeCoq's success in catching up with Saku. Since 2010 the situation has changed. Market shares have equalized and both companies are very active and have introduced a lot of new brands, including low alcohol and speciality beer brands. The active launching of new products indicates a close following of moves by the competitor and their quick response to them.

As the focus of both key players has shifted from leading brands to new speciality niche labels this has given an opportunity to other niche players. In 2011, Viru brewery started to produce Gourmet beer under licence from its parent company Harboes Bryggeri. Harboes Bryggeri closed the production of Gourmet beer in Roskilde, Denmark, and transferred production to the Estonian subsidiary. Under the brand GB (Gourmet Bryggeriet) there are ten different types of gourmet beer, including ginger, coffee and chocolate flavoured beer. Initially, the whole production of the gourmet beer was exported to Denmark, although in spring 2012 Viru also started to sell GB products in Estonia.

Regarding brand strategies as a whole, it may be said that generally BBH applied a local brand strategy until the early 2000s, shifting towards a multi-tier strategy (a portfolio of global and local brands) in the mid 2000s. Carlsberg's brand strategy may have recently shifted again, back towards a global strategy, which was also Carlsberg's brand strategy pre-2000 (see, for example, Meyer and Tran 2006). Olvi has mainly applied a local brand strategy – in recent years some brands produced in other Olvi-owned subsidiaries have also been launched in the Estonian market, thus moving the company somewhat towards a multi-tier strategy.

Figure 5.4 also reveals that packaging has played a very important role in the marketing strategies of breweries. During the whole of the 1990s the bottle was clearly the preferred type of packaging. In 1998–99 bottled beer accounted for about 85 per cent of Estonia's beer market. The sales of draught beer were some 10 per cent of total sales and canned beer represented some 3–5 per cent of total sales. There were also attempts in the 1990s to sell beer in PET bottles, but this was not very successful.

In spring 1998 Saku brewery launched a new type of 0.5 litre bottle.

The new packaging was needed because the previous type of bottle, inherited from the Soviet period and in use ever since, had quality problems accompanied by a poor image. The new bottle, and the new more attractive boxes that contained the bottles, had a clear influence on Saku's market share in 1998. A.LeCoq has influenced the beer market several times with its packaging – in 2000 A.LeCoq launched four-packs and in 2005 covered cans with foil. Both of those innovations were very successful. In the 2000s the share of canned beer clearly increased, although the role of canned beer in Estonia is not as dominant as, for example, in the Finnish beer market. Speciality and premium beers are still mainly sold in glass bottles. More recently, A.LeCoq introduced pint-size (0.568 litre) packages. In 2009 it released a pint-size can and in 2012 A.LeCoq introduced Alexander Suur (Alexander the Great) in a pint-size bottle.

One clear difference between the Estonian and Finnish beer markets is that in Finland a large share of beer is sold in 6-packs, 12-packs and 24-packs. In Estonia 12-packs and 24-packs can be found mainly in shops close to the Tallinn harbour, where the main target consumer group is Finnish and Swedish visitors taking beer back to their home countries.

Viru brewery has also experienced success concerning its packaging decisions. In 2003 Viru launched the 1.5 litre PET bottle. Its influence was so strong that Saku brewery also reacted and invested in a PET packaging production line.

Pricing and Distribution

Until now price and distribution have not played an important role in the battles for market share. Figure 5.5 reveals that in the 1990s the average price of local beer was about €0.55 for 0.5 litres. At the same time, imported beer was about twice as expensive.

During the 2000s prices have been relatively stable and have increased mainly because of taxes. Thus, instead of price wars companies have decided to use branding and the launching of new products as their main marketing strategies. Still, Figure 5.5 reveals that the difference between prices of domestic and imported beers has vanished, which means that the competition between domestic and imported brands will increase. This is also mirrored in the change in consumer preferences towards domestic beer in Estonia. According to regular surveys, the share of consumers who always buy Estonian domestic beer has fallen from 54 per cent in 1996 to 27 per cent in 2010. The share of consumers who always or in the majority of cases buy domestic beer has fallen too – from 79 per cent in 1996 to 51 per cent in 2010 (Estonian Institute of Market Research 2011b, p. 38). The

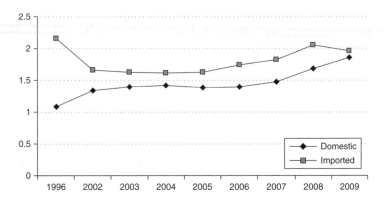

Source: Estonian Institute of Market Research (2010c).

Figure 5.5   Prices of domestic and imported beer in cans, 1996–2009 (EUR/L)

local breweries in Estonia have been prepared for that change. Instead of competing with imported brands their strategic response is to represent these on the local market (see Table 5.1).

Although Estonia is among the smallest European countries, the beer market was for a long time quite regional, even inside the country. Saku has been and is still strong in North Estonia (Tallinn area), A.LeCoq has been and is very strong in Southern Estonia (Tartu area), and Viru Õlu has been and is strong in the eastern part of Estonia and, after the acquisition of Puls, also in the Pärnu area. In the 2000s the distribution and sales of all of the main breweries covered the whole country.

A key feature of beer markets is how much of the total sales is on-trade (sales in bars, restaurants and so on) and how much is off-trade (sales taken away, for example, consumed at home). A typical feature of the Estonian beer market has been that the role of on-trade has been much smaller than the role of off-trade. In the 2000s as high a share as 90 per cent or more has been off-trade and among EU countries this figure is clearly the highest. The very low on-trade figure is typical also for Latvia and Lithuania. The other extremes in Europe have been Greece, Ireland, Portugal and Spain where on-trade sales have reached 60–70 per cent of total sales (Brewers of Europe 2010).

Advertising and Sales Promotion

Based on interview information, the breweries spent €5 million advertising beer in 2011. The largest amount of money – almost half – was spent on advertising by Saku, over one-third on advertising by A.LeCoq, and 6–7 per cent on advertising by both Heineken and Viru. The advertising of beer has concentrated clearly on television – with almost 90 per cent of all advertising investments. The share of print advertising was some 6 per cent, and outdoor and internet advertising both 3 per cent of total advertising investments in 2011. There was no radio advertising of beer in 2010–12.

Of the leading breweries, A.LeCoq's advertising has concentrated even more on television – 96 per cent. Print advertising comprises 3 per cent and internet 1 per cent. There is no outdoor advertising by A.LeCoq at all. The company believes that the only place where outdoor advertising could be used is the Tallinn area, but due to the high price and regulations concerning outdoor advertising the company has not decided to use that media (Vernik 2012). The aforementioned figures mean that although the main advertising media related to Saku is also clearly television, the advertising by Saku is not as fully concentrated on television as is the situation with A.LeCoq. For a long time there were no special regulations concerning beer advertising, but since the 2000s the rules concerning outdoor advertising prevent beer being advertised close to schools and nursery schools and advertising on television and radio was prevented before 20:00 and more recently before 21:00.

A.LeCoq launched A.LeCoq Premium with a big advertising campaign in 1999 with the slogan 'it's all about taste' (taste matters). The campaign was awarded the Marketing Act of the Year in 2000. Another larger campaign related to the beer brands was in 2007 when the company launched A.LeCoq Special beer with the slogan 'to trust your senses is to trust your taste'. Thus, in this campaign the company also continued the same type of taste-focused slogan as earlier.

The campaigns by A.LeCoq have usually not been targeted especially at men or women, although some exceptions can also be found, such as the advertising related to Disel beer which has been targeted at men. In contrast, Saku brewery has had several campaigns targeted clearly either at men or women. In most cases the advertising has been very masculine, but the campaigns for Saku Ice and Saku DLight have been clearly targeted at women. Appendix 5.1 presents some examples of the advertisements of the leading brands by Saku and A.LeCoq.

The brands of the Finnish Olvi company have not been advertised in Estonia. Instead, especially from 2008 onwards, Carlsberg has advertised its flagship lager beer in Estonia. The slogan has been the same as in other countries: 'Probably the best beer in the world'. In spring 2011 Carlsberg introduced the new slogan 'That calls for a Carlsberg' across 140 markets. The introduction of the new slogan was not possible in Estonia, however, because the local advertising law (§28.3.1) prohibits the use of messages in advertisements which call for the purchase or use of alcohol. Thus, the old slogan is still in use in Estonia.

The main forms of promotion are point of sales support to retail channels, channel campaigns and various sponsorship arrangements, mainly for music and sport events. Also, with promotional activities there are signs that A.LeCoq has behaved as a market follower. Saku was the first brewery to sponsor a basketball team (TÜ Rock) – A.LeCoq reacted very quickly, also starting to support a basketball team (TTÜ A.LeCoq). Saku invested in the Saku Big Hall arena in 2001. A.LeCoq followed suit the next year and invested in the A.LeCoq Arena. Saku was the first main sponsor of the Estonian General Singing and Dance Festival, but since 2001 A.LeCoq has been the main sponsor of the event. Only in the case of lotteries and other promotional games was A.LeCoq the introducer, in 2002. Saku followed in 2003. Both breweries have arranged several bottle cap lotteries where cars have been the main prize. In recent years the importance of lotteries has decreased tremendously because of tightened legislation restrictions. Related to promotional activities, Saku has arranged beer festivals in Tallinn and in other cities. The company has also been giving the Saku Painting Award annually and the company has been the key sponsor of the Estonian Olympic Committee, whereas A.LeCoq has sponsored scholarships to support students in the Tartu and Võru vocational education centres studying, for example, mechatronics and information technology.

SUMMARY AND OUTLOOK

This chapter analysed the development of the beer market in Estonia during the last 20 years, focusing especially on the main events and decisions related to and made by the leading Estonian breweries Saku and A.LeCoq and less so by Viru brewery. Although the beer market in Estonia is among the smallest in Europe, there has been a significant growth in the market as well as other significant changes. Over the last 20 years the growth in per capita consumption has been the second largest inside the CEE and CIS markets, with a growth rate of over 160 per cent. The total production volume increased even more, over 220 per cent in 1992–2008. The growth rates were the second highest in the area after Russia. In 2003, the average consumption was 71 litres and in 2008 over 85 litres, which was 10 litres more than the average consumption in EU countries. In the 2000s the export of beer from Estonia also grew significantly, especially to neighbouring countries.

During the last 20 years huge technological and managerial changes as well as market concentration have existed. Two foreign breweries first entered the Estonian market via acquisitions in the early 1990s and a third in the late 1990s. Thus, before the end of the 1990s the three leading local breweries – Saku, Tartu and Viru – were owned by foreign, in each case Nordic, breweries. The market development can be divided into three stages: (1) The opening up of the Estonian beer market from 1991 until 1998, during which time the Saku brewery was a clear market leader with Saku Originaal as the main brand. Tartu Õlletehas lost the second position in the market to the Viru brewery mainly because of the success of their strong Bear Beer brand. (2) The Tartu Õlletehas attack period, from 1999 to 2003. During this period Tartu Õlletehas was able to finish its large-scale renovation project, adopt first the brand name A.LeCoq and later change the name of the whole brewery to A.LeCoq – which was an old name of the brewery. Saku brewery, with Saku Originaal, was still the market leader, but the market share of A.LeCoq and the brand A.LeCoq Premium grew from 10 per cent to around 30 per cent. (3) The stabilization stage, starting from 2004 and lasting (at least) up to 2012. During this period the battle between Saku and A.LeCoq continued and the market situation was very equal between the competitors. Some additional key features in the market have been the several changes in ownership of the Saku brewery. For more than 15 years it was owned by BBH – which was a joint venture, first between two Nordic breweries and then in the 2000s between two international breweries – Scottish & Newcastle and Carlsberg. From 2008 BBH and Saku have been wholly owned by Carlsberg. Another key feature has been the heavy expansion of the A.LeCoq brewery outside the beer industry, covering soft drink, mineral water and long drink products.

Although mainstream and premium segments have been the main beer segments, the clear growth in consumption has meant more consumers with individual needs and tastes, also providing opportunities for other segments. The full owner of Saku from 2008 onwards – Carlsberg brewery – has been famous for its frequent launch of new brands and the same strategy has also been followed by Saku, especially in recent years. A.LeCoq has focused more on its main brands and acted generally as a market follower. Beer consumption in Estonia recently seems to have been less price sensitive, which has also provided more opportunities for new niche brands. Related to communication, the main form of advertising has clearly been television advertising, around 90 per cent of total advertising efforts. Earlier, advertising focused mainly on men, later there was a change, with advertising campaigns targeted mainly at women or, as with most campaigns by A.LeCoq, without any clear focus either on male or female consumers. In addition to advertising, sales support to retail channels and sponsorship have played a significant role, including sponsorship of large music and sport events and scholarships for athletes, musicians and other talented persons.

In this chapter we have concentrated the analysis mainly on the situation and strategies used by the leading brewery companies Saku and A.LeCoq in the Estonian market. Both leading companies belong to concerns owned by foreign companies – Carlsberg and Olvi – which also have subsidiaries in other Baltic states. Furthermore, Olvi also has a brewery in Belarus and Carlsberg has breweries in several other Eastern European countries such as Poland and Russia and also further afield, especially in China. Thus, one interesting way to continue the study would be to analyse the brewery markets in the other Baltic states and cooperation and integration between the Estonian located subsidiaries and especially other Baltic located subsidiaries, but also other subsidiaries in the same concern. An additional potential avenue would be to analyse the degree of standardization versus adaptation of the marketing strategies in various Baltic states and in other countries.

ACKNOWLEDGEMENTS

The authors acknowledge the support of the Estonian Science Foundation's Grant 8546 and target financing of the Estonian Ministry of Education and Research No. 0180037s08.

REFERENCES

A.LeCoq (2012a), accessed 15 November 2012 at www.alecoq.ee.
A.LeCoq (2012b), 'About the beginning of beer brewing in Tartu', accessed 22 November 2012 at www.alecoq.ee/eng/company/history/?articleID=797.
Arnold, S., J. Larimo, M. Miljan, R. Virvilaite, E. Frize, N. Starshinova and E. Tarasenko (2000), 'A comparative analysis of the beer market in selected European countries – Estonia, Finland, Lithuania, Russia and the UK', in Petr Chadraba and Reiner Springer (ed.), *Proceedings of the 8th Annual Conference on Marketing Strategies in Central and Eastern Europe*, Vienna: Wirtschaftsuniversität, 7–25.
Brewers of Europe (2010), 'Beer statistics 2010 edition', accessed 27 September 2012 at www.brewersofeurope.org/docs/flipping_books/stats_2010/index.html.
Carlsberg Group (2012), accessed 15 November 2012 at www.carlsberggroup.com.
Eesti Ekspress (2011), No. 25(1124), 22 June.
Estonian Beer Guide (2012), accessed 15 November 2012 at www.beerguide.ee.

Estonian Institute of Economic Research. National Institute for Health Development (2012), 'Alcohol market, consumption and harms in Estonia, yearbook 2011', Tallinn, accessed 22 November 2012 at www.tai.ee/terviseandmed/uuringud/download/148.

Estonian Institute of Market Research (2004), 'Eesti alkoholiturg 2003. Aastal', Tallinn, accessed 14 March 2012 at http://rahvatervis.ut.ee/bitstream/1/869/1/EKI2004_1.pdf.

Estonian Institute of Market Research (2005), 'Eesti alkoholiturg 2004. Aastal', Tallinn, accessed 14 March 2012 at www.agri.ee/public/juurkataloog/UURINGUD/eki_alkoholiuuringud/Eesti_alkoholiturg_2004_aasta.pdf.

Estonian Institute of Market Research (2006), 'Eesti alkoholiturg 2005. Aastal', Tallinn, accessed 14 March 2012 at www.agri.ee/public/juurkataloog/UURINGUD/eki_alkoholiuuringud/Eesti_alkoholiturg_2005_aastal.pdf.

Estonian Institute of Market Research (2007), 'Eesti alkoholiturg 2006. Aastal', Tallinn, accessed 15 March 2012 at www.agri.ee/public/juurkataloog/UURINGUD/eki_alkoholiuuringud/Eesti_alkoholiturg_2006_aastal.pdf.

Estonian Institute of Market Research (2008), 'Eesti alkoholiturg 2007. Aastal', Tallinn, accessed 15 March 2012 at www.agri.ee/public/juurkataloog/UURINGUD/eki_alkoholiuuringud/Eesti_alkoholiturg_2007_aastal.pdf.

Estonian Institute of Market Research (2009), 'Eesti alkoholiturg 2008. Aastal', Tallinn, accessed 17 March 2012 at www.agri.ee/public/juurkataloog/UURINGUD/eki_alkoholiuuringud/Eesti_alkoholiturg_2008._aastal.pdf.

Estonian Institute of Market Research (2010a), 'Eesti alkoholitootjate konkurentsivõime 2009', Tallinn, accessed 18 March 2012 at www.agri.ee/public/juurkataloog/UURINGUD/eki_alkoholiuuringud/Alkoholitootjate_konkurentsivoime_2009.pdf.

Estonian Institute of Market Research (2010b), 'Eesti alkoholiturg 2009. Aastal', Tallinn, accessed 17 March 2012 at www.agri.ee/public/juurkataloog/UURINGUD/eki_alkoholiuuringud/Eesti_alkoholiturg_2009._aastal.pdf.

Estonian Institute of Market Research (2010c), 'Turistide alkoholi ostumaht 2009. Aastal', Tallinn, accessed 17 March 2012 at www.agri.ee/public/juurkataloog/UURINGUD/eki_alkoholiuuringud/Turistide_alkoholi_ostud_2009.pdf.

Estonian Institute of Market Research (2011a), 'Eesti alkoholiturg 2010. Aastal', Tallin, accessed 6 May 2012 at www.agri.ee/public/juurkataloog/UURINGUD/eki_alkoholiuuringud/Eesti_alkoholiturg_2010._aastal.pdf.

Estonian Institute of Market Research (2011b), 'Elanike toitumisharjumused ja toidukaupade ostueelistused', Tallinn, accessed 15 April 2012 at www.agri.ee/public/juurkataloog/UURINGUD/eki_tarbijauuringud/EKI_Elanike_toitumisharjumused_ja_toidukaupade_ostueelistused_2010.pdf.

Harboes Bryggeri (2012), accessed 15 November 2012 at www.harboes-bryggeri.dk.

HF Puls (2012), accessed 15 November 2012 at www.hfpuls.ee.

Kastein, Margus (2012), Interview with CEO of Saku Corporation, 17 January 2012.

Larimo, J., M. Marinov and S. Marinova (2006), 'The Central and Eastern European brewing industry since 1990', *British Food Journal*, **108** (5), 371–84.

Madsen, E., K. Pedersen and L. Lund-Thomsen (2011), 'M&A as a driver of global competition in the brewing industry', working paper 11–10, Department of Economics, Copenhagen Business School.

Marinov, M. and S. Marinova (1999), 'Foreign investor strategy development in the Central and Eastern European context', *Thunderbird International Business Review*, **41** (1), 400–10.

Meyer, K. and Y.T.T. Tran (2006), 'Market penetration and acquisition strategies for emerging economies', *Long Range Planning*, **39**, 177–97.

Mikli, Inna (2012), 'Saku Õlletehas sai 70 miljoni kroonise investeeriingu', *Saku Teataja*, accessed 15 November 2012 at www.sakuvald.ee/36911.

Noop, Tarmo (2012), Interview with CEO of A.LeCoq Corporation, 17 January 2012.

Olvi Group (2012a), 'Annual reports', accessed 1 November 2012 at www.alecoq.ee/corp/majandusinfo.

Olvi Group (2012b), accessed 15 November 2012 at www.olvi.fi.

Port of Tallinn (2012), 'Passenger ship schedules', accessed 28 August 2012 at www.ts.ee/passenger_ship_schedule.php?k=3.

Saku (2012), accessed 15 November 2012 at www.saku.ee.

Sepp, A. (2007), *Õllelinn Tartu. Pühendatud A.LeCoq'i 200. Sünnipäevale*, Tartu: OÜ Greif truck.

Statistics Estonia (2012), 'Statistical database/economy/industry/foodstuff', accessed 30 October 2012 at www.stat.ee.

Swinnen, J. and K. Van Herck (2011), 'How the east was won: the foreign takeover of the Eastern European brewing industry', in Johan Swinnen (ed.), *The Economics of Beer*, Oxford: Oxford University Press, pp. 247–64.

Tallinn Airport (2012), 'Flight plan', accessed 28 August 2012 at www.tallinn-airport.ee/eng.

Terk, Erik (2000), *Privatisation in Estonia. Ideas. Process. Results*, Tallinn: Greif.

Thirst for Great (2011), Presentation by Jørn P. Jensen, Deputy CEO and CFO of Carlsberg Group in Morgan Stanley Global Consumer Conference.

Vernik, Katrin (2000), Presentation in the conference 'Password 2000', March 2000, Tartu.

Vernik, Katrin (2008), Presentation in the conference 'Password 2008', March 2008, Tartu.

Vernik, Katrin (2012), Interview with the marketing manager of A.LeCoq Corporation, 25 April 2012.

Viru Õlu Brewery (2012), accessed 15 November 2012 at www.wiru.ee.

Vrontis, D. (1998), 'Strategic assessment of branding in the European beer market', *British Food Journal*, **100** (2), 76–84.

APPENDIX

Source: Mikli 2012

Figure 5A.1   Style of Saku Originaal – choice of friends

Source: Vernik 2000

*Figure 5A.2   Outdoor visuals of A.LeCoq Premium launch campaign in
            1999 – matter of taste*

Source: Saku 2012

Figure 5A.3 Visual of Saku Kuld 2012 – top layer of the beer

Source: Vernik 2008

Figure 5A.4 Visual of A.LeCoq Special launch campaign in 2007 – to trust your mind means to trust your taste

Source: Eesti Ekspress 2011, p. 2

Figure 5A.5 Print advertisement of Saku. Message: Midsummer Eve cocktail for men. Saku Originaal. The right one

Source: Eesti Ekspress 2011, p. 26

Figure 5A.6   Print advertisement of A.LeCoq. Message: confirmation of good taste

6. Carlsberg in India: entry strategy in global oligopolistic industries

Anne K. Hoenen and Michael W. Hansen

The big multinationals like Heineken, InBev, and Carlsberg, are currently all going crazy about investing here in India. They spend tremendous amounts of money buying local competitors at ridiculously over valuated prices and building greenfield production sites at a scale that will exceed consumption levels in India for the next 20 years – even if the market does de-regulate, which actually no one knows for sure it will. For me, this is very strange. (Member of the Executive Board at United Breweries, Bangalore, India in 2007)

INTRODUCTION

Firms' internationalization behaviour and foreign market entry strategy, most notably entry mode choice, is typically studied at the firm level and/or the country level using a variety of well-established theoretical perspectives, such as transaction cost economics (Puck et al. 2009), internalization theory (Agarwal and Ramaswami 1992), internationalization process models (Johanson and Vahlne 2009) or resource- and knowledge-based perspectives (Kogut and Zander 1993; Sharma and Erramilli 2004). Scarce attention, however, is paid to the industry level perspective of foreign market entry (Buckley and Casson 1998; Graham 1992). While early foreign direct investment (FDI) literature emphasized oligopolistic industry structure and competition in the home market as a driver of internationalization (Flowers 1976; Graham 1978; Hymer 1976; Knickerbocker 1973), this notion has virtually disappeared from the contemporary international business (IB) literature. These early studies inform our extended view of foreign market entry strategy that takes global industry level characteristics into account. Understanding the industry context is important for a more insightful study of firm internationalization as global oligopolies are becoming more common (Carr and Collis 2011; Scherer and Ross 2009). They are spreading in industries such as the brewery industry, but also in media, cement, stainless steel, home appliances, pharmaceuticals and agricultural seeds. Specifically, global oligopolistic industries that are dominated by only a handful of key players worldwide are characterized by high transparency, that is to say, the key players are well known. As a result, strategic moves of one company, for instance entering a new market, likely trigger strategic responses by other key players. Thus, firm internationalization decisions are not only driven by efficiency-, resource-, asset- or market-seeking motives, but might also be affected by strategic moves of key global competitors in oligopolistic industries.

This chapter reports a longitudinal case study (Dubois and Gadde 2002; Rescher 1978; Yu 1994) to examine how industry level characteristics and strategic interaction among key players in global oligopolistic industries can explain foreign market entry strategy. Strategic interaction refers to how industry level characteristics, competitive forces and mutual inter-dependence shape the behaviour of multinational corporations (MNCs) vis-à-vis their peers in a global oligopolistic industry. The market entry into India by Carlsberg A/S, one of the largest players in the oligopolistic global brewery industry, illustrates this phenomenon. Specifically, we discuss Carlsberg's India-related moves over a period of almost two decades from the company's initial strategic interest in the early 1990s until the launch of its premium pilsner Carlsberg in late 2007. Strategic interaction and competitive dynamics are amplified in emerging markets such as India. These markets are 'critical global markets' (Hamel and Prahalad 1994) as they are the key battlegrounds in oligopolistic industries: whereas mature markets of advanced economies are mostly consolidated and offer only limited growth potential, the 'greenfield' markets of emerging econo-mies bear extraordinary opportunities (such as very high growth rates, abundant resources, and the lack of established institutions in a traditional sense enabling rapid changes in the marketplace) (Arnold and Quelch 1998; Hoskisson et al. 2000). High stakes are involved because it is possible to effectively move the market and benefit from enormous future growth.

Based on this longitudinal case study of the foreign market entry venture of Carlsberg in India, we present new insights into foreign market entry strategy that are particularly relevant in oligopolistic industries such as the global brewery industry. The chapter is organized as follows: first, a literature review discusses the early insights of oligopolistic competition in relation to more dominant explanations of foreign market entry sum-marized in a conceptual model of foreign market entry. Second, the case narrative of Carlsberg in India is presented. Third, the theoretical ideas are confronted with the case to develop more specific propositions about how oligopolistic industry structure impacts foreign market entry strategy in such global industries.

LITERATURE REVIEW

Dominant Theories vs Oligopolistic Competition Theory of FDI

The early literature on FDI departed from an explanation of it in terms of competitive industry structure dynamics (Hymer 1976). Hymer's seminal PhD thesis from 1960 (published in 1976) proposed a theory of FDI as an international extension of the industrial organization (IO) paradigm. Thereby, Hymer moved beyond prevailing explanations of international capital flows based on neoclassical financial and trade theory from the standpoint of perfectly competitive markets: firms extend a dominant market position in home markets with a dominant position in international markets. In perfectly competitive markets there would be little FDI, and cross-border exchange would mainly take place through licensing and exports. But in cases with deviations from competitive markets FDI would be common (Calvet 1981; Dunning and Rugman 1985).

In line with Hymer's original thinking, Knickerbocker (1973) introduced the notion of 'follow-the-leader' behaviour to describe situations in which firms imitate each other to minimize the threat of foreign cost advantages. Empirical evidence showed that firms matched strategic investments of competitors in oligopolistic industries even though return on these investments was uncertain (Flowers 1976). On a similar basis, Graham (1978) found that firms in oligopolistic industries retaliate investments by establishing subsidiaries in each other's markets on an 'exchange-of-threat' basis. These early approaches explicitly account for the mutual interdependence of firms in oligopolistic industries. In this view, firm internationalization and market entry decisions are not primarily driven by efficiency- or resource-based benefits. On the contrary, firms might estimate the risk of losing out to a competitor and this competitor consequently gaining an upper hand as a larger risk than that of potential financial losses.

However, this highly dynamic original stream of FDI theory has not been developed much beyond the early economic explanations of the 1970s, which looked at the national oligopolistic structure in internationalizing firms' home markets. This can in part be explained by a significant shift in research attention towards the firm level from the 1970s onwards, with the increasing prominence of transaction cost economics (Hennart 1982; Williamson 1975), the important advancement of internalization theory (Buckley and Casson 1976), the resource-based perspective (Barney 1991; Wernerfelt 1984) and the knowledge-based view of the firm (Grant 1996; Kogut and Zander 1993). This stream of literature focuses mainly on FDI as a way of generating efficiency in cross-border transactions

(Buckley and Casson 1998; Hennart 1982; Williamson 1975), and later also as a way to effectively leverage and build capabilities and transfer knowledge across borders (Kogut and Zander 1993). What is common to most of this literature is a focus on the characteristics of the entering firm, either its efforts to minimize transaction costs, expand market sales, or to grow its resources and capabilities.

Dunning's (1979) eclectic OLI (Ownership, Location, Internalization) framework with its numerous subsequent extensions to account for technological and political developments as well as institutional change (Cantwell et al. 2010; Dunning 1995, 2000; Dunning and Lundan 2008) essentially tried to integrate resource, efficiency and locational factors in an all-encompassing framework. Thereby, FDI is determined by the relationship between ownership-specific resources and capabilities, location factors and internalization factors.

In these more recent FDI theories, firm internationalization decisions are explained as a function of structural efficiency under a particular set of external and internal circumstances. However, oligopolistic industry structures do not figure prominently among those structures. Moreover, strategic aspects are downplayed (Calvet 1981; Li et al. 2005; Tallman 1991, 1992).

The changing nature of competition towards more global arenas (Carr and Collis 2011; Scherer and Ross 2009), however, increases the need to re-specify strategic industry level drivers of FDI. Thus, we combine dominant resource- and efficiency-based reasoning with the early FDI literature focusing on oligopolistic competition in the home market, and expand this view, applying a global perspective. We note that this does not replace efficiency- and resource-based explanations, but complements them.

A Model of Foreign Market Entry

Foreign market entry strategy is seen as a multidimensional construct, which entails three interdependent decisions of 'where', 'when' and 'how' (Buckley and Casson 1998; Estrin 2004; Hennart and Park 1994). Figure 6.1 captures our analytical framework of foreign market entry strategy.

First, the framework addresses the key questions of market selection, namely 'where' to invest, and closely related, 'why' to enter a specific market. The dominant literature mostly examines the motives of FDI as resource-, market-, efficiency- and strategic asset-seeking (Dunning and Lundan 2008). Other scholars have put increasing emphasis on the benefits to be gained from international activities by leveraging learning

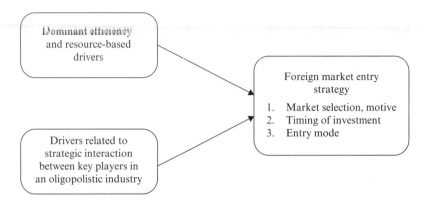

Source: Authors' own illustration.

Figure 6.1   Analytical framework of market entry strategy

and knowledge developed at foreign locations on a worldwide basis
(Birkinshaw 1997; Birkinshaw and Hood 1998; Dunning and Narula
2004). According to dominant frameworks, strategic market entry decisions link the global strategy with the specific local context in that
companies analyse the local environment of host countries and identify
potentially profitable business opportunities to exploit or enhance a firm's
ownership advantages abroad (Dunning 1992; Estrin 2004). In our framework, we complement this perspective with strategic motivations resulting
from the oligopolistic nature of the industry such as entry to follow, curb
or restrain competitors. To describe the nature of such strategic interaction in oligopolistic competition we draw on game theory metaphors.
'Global chess' builds on game-theoretic insights from strategic management literature. Game theory provides 'a systematic way to understand the
behaviour of players in situations where their fortunes are interdependent'
(Brandenburger and Nalebuff 1995, p. 57). Game-theoretic metaphors in
strategic management rely upon the simple analogy between games such
as chess (see, for example, Bartlett and Ghoshal 1993) and other situations in which players make decisions that affect each other – as opposed
to the emphasis given to mathematical perfection and rigorous model-
ling in economics (Ghemawat 1997). From this perspective, investments
are made to gain specific positions vis-à-vis competitors. MNCs may
acquire assets and positions in given locations, not due to the properties of
those assets as such, but because they provide them with pawns in future
games. This behaviour can take on different forms. Global chess dynamics include the systematic carving up of markets on a global scale among
dominant firms in oligopolistic industries to divide revenues and cut the

costs of head-to-head competition. Closely related variants to global chess – that is the systematic idea that all strategic moves among global oligopolistic rivals are interdependent on a global scale – have been explicated in the early literature by the 'mutual forbearance' (Edwards 1955), or 'exchange-of-threat', hypothesis (Graham 1978). This reasoning entails that dominant firms in an industry hold assets in each other's markets to maintain a credible threat against the other players in case they become too aggressive in other locations (cf. Graham 1978). However, these early theories do not explicate the systemic aspect of mutual interdependence among the key players in an oligopolistic industry on a global level.

Second, timing reflects the dimension of 'when' to enter a market. It has stimulated considerable interest in research (Arnold and Quelch 1998; Lieberman and Montgomery 1988, 1998; Luo 1997). The dominant perspective views timing issues mostly related to 'early' entry to exploit the 'window of opportunity' (Luo 1997, p. 769). Specifically, economic gains may result from the ability to acquire, sustain and exploit firm-specific resources and assets at an early stage of market development (for instance, resource access advantages such as facilities, scarce materials and distribution systems). In this asset-based understanding, economic returns in absolute terms are weighed against timing's operational risks and uncertainties (Lasserre 2007; Luo 1997). Inherently, however, every contribution on 'first-mover advantages' (Lieberman and Montgomery 1988) in fact embraces the industry level competitive notion: 'being first' naturally implies relative order of entry in view of competitors. Still, the 'first-mover' argument can be strengthened significantly by emphasizing this aspect of oligopolistic strategic interaction.

First-movers are, from a strategic interaction perspective, motivated by deterring followers or restricting the possibilities for later entrants by controlling new markets and capturing critical parts of the value chain early on (for example, forcing competitors into prohibitively costly investments in new sales and distribution infrastructures). While first-movers may not always gain full control, they may still benefit in the larger competitive game as their first move may force competitors to prematurely undertake investment in the location in question (Miller and Folta 2002). As 'competition for the future is competition to create and dominate emerging opportunities' (Hamel and Prahalad 1994, p. 22), the first-mover type of strategic interaction means to develop an independent, proactive road map of opportunities 'to stake out competitive space' (Hamel and Prahalad 1994, p. 22).

Another timing concept from the oligopolistic competition literature is the classical 'follow-the-leader' hypothesis of early theorists (Knickerbocker 1973), which entails that FDI essentially is a result of defensive moves in oligopolistic industries. Risk-averse firms follow their main competitors to avoid distorting oligopolistic equilibrium. When one firm moves into a new market, for instance, other firms will have to consider the move (Yu and Ito 1988). However, this early notion refers to oligopolistic equilibrium in the home market and does not capture the notion of the systematic carving up of global markets in oligopolistic industries characterized by competition at a global level.

Furthermore, we expect firms in oligopolistic industries to imitate each other's actions, because the alternative may prove costly and dangerous (Lieberman and Asaba 2006). So-called 'herding' is the 'reckless' behaviour of firms in the same industry simultaneously pouring investments into a particular country regardless of expected profitability due to the early stage of market development in that location (Lung 2000).

Third, entry mode is the firm's choice between various alternatives of how to enter a foreign market (for a review see Morschett et al. 2010). Firms can choose between non-equity entry modes such as licensing or exporting and equity-based entry. In the latter case, they have the choice between acquisition and greenfield – wholly-owned or in the form of joint ventures (JVs). Entry mode choices are typically differentiated using transaction cost, internalization or resource-based, organizational capability perspectives. For example, the choice of greenfield versus acquisition is about balancing a firm's own resources with those needed and those available on the market (Estrin 2004). Some studies incorporate additional explanatory variables to reflect global strategic considerations (Harzing 2002; Kim and Hwang 1992); conducted at firm-level, however, they do not explicitly address industry level characteristics.

From an oligopolistic competition perspective, entry modes differ in their potential to build competitive strength and affect rivals' international operations. In this view, entry mode choice is not only a matter of firm level efficiency- and resource-based parameters (for instance greenfield versus acquisition as a question of balancing a firm's own resources with those needed and those available on the market), but reflects a situation in which players make decisions that affect each other. Applying this perspective, entry strategy entails 'more than selecting between prototypical organizational forms' (Estrin 2004, p. 18), but can be understood as a strategic means to establish a robust competitive position while at the same time keeping competitors from doing so.

METHODS

We use an abductive research strategy. The abductive inquiry takes place through an iterative refinement of theoretical concepts and frameworks in light of empirical observations (Dubois and Gadde 2002). Abductive research is especially useful in more explorative types of research, where theory needs to be developed and refined to provide plausible hypotheses or propositions that can subsequently be subject to more stringent deductive analysis (Yu 1994). Contrary to pure inductive reasoning, abduction starts with predefined (theoretical) conceptions and categories and the purpose of empirical inquiry essentially is to render these more or less plausible (Yu 1994).

Case Selection

A longitudinal case study is used to obtain rich, qualitative data that can explain the complexity and dynamics at all levels (Marschan-Piekkari 2004). The following considerations based on previous literature informed the case selection to obtain an appropriate research context (Eisenhardt and Graebner 2007; Piekkari 2011). First, the industry context of the case should be characterized by competition on a global scale and an oligopolistic industry structure so that competitor behaviour is 'observable'. The global brewery industry is oligopolistically structured and characterized by immense growth pressure: while the top five brewers accounted for less than 20 per cent of global sales volumes in the mid 1990s, this share had increased to 46.6 per cent ten years later (*Business Week* 2006). Second, the case company should be in a relatively mature stage of internationalization with a number of foreign subsidiaries and an established strategy of market entry. Third, the company should pursue an investment strategy in emerging markets as competitive dynamics and oligopolistic strategic interaction are amplified in the immature and developing markets of emerging economies (Arnold and Quelch 1998; Hoskisson et al. 2000). We follow Wright et al. (2005) in that we find the particular context of emerging markets to be especially useful for developing and testing theories.

Carlsberg's entry into the emerging market of India meets all these criteria. Carlsberg is a publicly listed company and among Denmark's largest multinational corporations. As of 2010, Carlsberg's annual sales amounted to US$10.7 billion (DKK 60 billion), with approximately 41 000 employees worldwide and 137 million hectolitres (hl) of beer sold in more than 150 markets (Carlsberg Annual Report 2010). Carlsberg's brand portfolio encompasses 500 strong international and regional brands, including its namesake premium pilsner, Tuborg, Baltika and Grimbergen, as well as an extensive range of local brands. During the late 1990s and 2000s, Carlsberg embarked on a significant international expansion strategy with sales from outside its home region accounting for the dominant share of total sales. Carlsberg also followed an explicit strategy of engaging in

emerging markets. Carlsberg holds a strong record of successfully expanding into and strengthening its positioning in emerging markets such as
Russia and China.

Data Collection and Analysis

The major part of the empirical fieldwork was conducted in 2007 with
a follow-up informal interview conducted five years later with the same
responsible actors in the Asia Business Development Team in 2012.
Retrospective and real-time data were collected to capture process dynamics. To mitigate the risk of retrospective sense-making and impression
management, we used triangulation to contrast and compare the data
from our interviews with company reports, internal written documents
(such as strategy papers, board proposals, status updates and presenta-
tions prepared at headquarters as well as feasibility studies, beer market
reports or location analyses compiled locally in India) and organizational
charts (Huber and Power 1985; Leonard-Barton 1990). We also compared
our findings with independent secondary data sources such as public
media and official industry reports (Langley 1999). Furthermore, we trian-
gulated internal data with external and independent information sources
such as commercial market and industry research institutes, state authorities (for instance, the Indian Ministry of Food Processing Industries),
annual reports and press releases of competitors, as well as a systematic
review of renowned English business newspapers in India.

Data analysis was intertwined with data collection and earlier research
(Coffey and Atkinson 1996). Interview transcripts were returned for
factual verification and key company informants were asked to comment
on the case analysis (Ghauri and Grønhaug 2005; Patton 1990).

THE CASE: CARLSBERG ENTERING THE INDIAN BEER MARKET

A Sip of Carlsberg and the Global Brewery Industry

Over a span of 160 years, the Danish beer company Carlsberg has grown
from its beginnings as a small local brewer to the world's fourth largest beer
producer in 2012 behind the world's clear number one AB InBev, number
two SABMiller, and Heineken as number three on a global basis. As of
2007, when Carlsberg entered India, the top group of global beer companies was made up of five players: InBev, SABMiller, Anheuser-Busch,
Heineken and Carlsberg. These global brewers dominate the industry and

the gap to smaller-scale rivals has widened due to rapid consolidation. As a result, the global brewery industry has become highly transparent. The big players' strategic moves as well as their merger and acquisition activities are closely monitored by competitors. Further consolidation is expected as the top players continue to seek wider and stronger global footprints; for example, sales from outside the traditional home markets of the top 20 brewers had increased from one-third to more than half from 2001 to 2007 and have increased every year since (SABMiller 2007).

In this global positioning game, emerging markets play a pivotal role. Between 2006 and 2011, the most significant overall volume growth came from Asia (about half) as well as Central and South America and Eastern Europe (19.5 per cent each) (Canadean 2006). Opposed to, at best, stagnating mature markets, the Asian market is expected to grow further by a 4.8 per cent compound annual rate from 2011 to 2016 (*The Wall Street Journal* 2012). Stagnating or even declining beer consumption in Europe as well as in the US has made it an imperative for the large players to enter emerging markets. As a result, investment in the beer industry has been pouring into emerging markets, speeding up the globalization process of the industry.

What is striking about Carlsberg's international expansion is that the company chose a regional strategy – investing in selected emerging markets only (such as Eastern Europe, Russia and Asia). A notable feature of Carlsberg's entry strategy in emerging markets is entry at an early stage ('being first') and through acquisition, ideally in a 'cheap approach', often in the form of JVs. Ideally, such deals are undertaken with targets that own strong local brands (for example Beer Lao as a 'national icon' in Lao PDR), that are number one or two in the country/region, and that would enable Carlsberg to acquire a controlling stake (for instance Hanoi Brewery in Vietnam). At the time of the Indian market entry in 2007, Carlsberg's emerging market efforts had already come a long way, with market-leader positions in many of the Eastern European markets and Asia. Carlsberg was the market-leader in a JV with local partners in Russia (100 per cent ownership of Baltika as of 2012), one of the fastest growing beer markets in the world, Nepal and Sri Lanka. In China, the world's largest beer market in terms of population and size, Carlsberg is mostly present in the Western parts of the country, where it holds over 50 per cent market share.

The Indian Beer Market

India has experienced unprecedented development as one of the fastest growing major economies in the world. India also has a demographic advantage, offering a young vibrant market with more than half of the population below 25 and more than 65 per cent below 35 years of age. India's consumer markets change fast, with increasing disposable incomes, the development of modern urban lifestyles and the emergence of a burgeoning middle class of circa 300 million consumers by 2015–16 (*The Economic Times* 2011).

In the ten years prior to Carlsberg's market entry in 2007, the Indian brewery industry had benefited greatly from these trends and had grown at a compound annual rate of 8.7 per cent between 1997 and 2006 (Just-drinks 2007). Despite this growth, total beer sales in India amounted to a mere 10.6 million hl in 2007 (*The Economic Times* 2007a) – only roughly twice the consumption of Denmark despite a population multiple of about 200, and far below other emerging markets such as China. Thus the market as of 2007 – when Carlsberg fiercely pushed its entry – was still far from reaching critical volumes. In addition, future growth was highly contingent upon deregulation. The main growth obstacles were high taxes on beer with legal and excise requirements varying widely from state to state and restricted or even state-controlled distribution (Ministry of Food Processing Industries 2006). There was a general distribution challenge with one outlet for almost 17 000 people in 2005 in India compared to an average ratio of one to 300 in Europe and one to 195 in China (Just-drinks 2007). Finally, production, distribution, sales and marketing were strictly regulated by the government. Licences to run breweries, for example, had to be obtained on an annual basis (*Berlingske Nyhedsmagazin* 2008). Direct advertising of alcoholic drinks was not permitted. Another operational hurdle was the shortage and low quality of local raw materials, for instance, water (Just-drinks 2007).

The most striking characteristic of the Indian beer market was its already high level of consolidation in 2007. United Breweries Ltd (UB), in which the former British company Scottish & Newcastle (S&N) – acquired by Heineken in 2008 – held a 37.5 per cent stake, was the largest domestic beer company in India with a market share of 47 per cent, while the global giant SABMiller was second with 36 per cent as of late 2007 (*The Economic Times* 2007f). These two players accounted for more than 80 per cent of the domestic beer consumption (*The Economic Times* 2008).

Carlsberg's Market Entry into India

Carlsberg's first strategic interest in India dated back to the early 1990s. Carlsberg employees repeatedly travelled to India in the mid 1990s when a share in Mohan Meakins (India's number three brewery group at that time) was up for sale, and Carlsberg evaluated bidding for the 51 per cent stake (*The Economic Times* 2006a). The first visible manifestation of Carlsberg scouting for opportunities was the signing of a Memorandum of Understanding (MoU) with the largest local brewer UB in 1996 (*The Hindu Business Line* 2004). However, the deal found an 'acrimonious end' due to irreconcilable differences between the parties as reported by Indian media and neither deal actually materialized (*The Hindu Business Line* 2004). Carlsberg decided to allocate resources towards China (Carlsberg Annual Reports 1996, 2000).

India reappeared on the radar screen in 2000 and Carlsberg signed another MoU with Mysore Breweries Ltd (MBL), a large local brewer with production sites in Bangalore and the state of Maharashtra (Just-drinks 2007). However, Carlsberg did not move fast enough to strike the deal, with SABMiller acquiring MBL shortly before Carlsberg was ready in June 2001 (SABMiller 2005). Shaw Wallace Group (India's second largest brewer in the early 2000s) was the next potential target that Carlsberg negotiated with. Yet again, SABMiller moved faster (SABMiller 2005). At that time, Carlsberg's business development activities in Asia were handled by the regional unit, Carlsberg Asia Pte. Ltd based in Singapore, which had been established only a few years earlier in 2000. Entrepreneurial spirit and local execution power, while critical for expansion into India, were weak as the regional unit suffered from its structure as a malfunctioning 50:50 JV with Chang Beverages Pte. Ltd (Chang Beverages) in Thailand (Carlsberg Annual Report 2003). Carlsberg eventually terminated the JV in 2003 (Carlsberg Annual Report 2004). This went hand in hand with the closure of Carlsberg's regional business unit, which resulted in moving responsibility for Asia back to headquarters (Carlsberg Annual Report 2003).

In sum, the real problem during the first phase was not Carlsberg's strategy, but its inability to implement it because of a lack of deal-making capabilities and its slow decision-making speed. Back at headquarters, business development activities regarding India were not seriously reconsidered until almost two years later in 2005, because attention and resources were initially directed towards building a solid base in China, which had become its first priority. Only after having largely finalized the consolidation of western China by the end of 2005 did Carlsberg start looking at India again.

First rumours stating that Carlsberg was interested in a local brewery and was again scouting potential acquisition targets in India arose in mid 2005. Reportedly, Carlsberg was interested in starting wholesale trading of its namesake brand, and in a second step was looking at underutilized breweries in Goa and Aurangabad, as well as idle capacity in Rajasthan and Andhra Pradesh (*The Economic Times* 2005b). A third entry option that was discussed was setting up a greenfield production site. Very shortly after these first rumours, Carlsberg was said to have plans for setting up a 100 per cent Indian subsidiary to import and sell beer (*The Economic Times* 2005a). In August 2006, Carlsberg was in talks for a possible acquisition of Himneel Breweries located in Hamachal Pradesh with installed annual capacity of 150 000 hl (*The Economic Times* 2006b). Earlier that month, rumours were spreading that Carlsberg wanted to explore setting up greenfield projects in India in a JV with the Khetan Group, a leading business conglomerate of Indian origin in Nepal, with whom Carlsberg already worked in Nepal (*The Economic Times* 2006a). Their Nepalese JV Gorkha Brewery Pvt. Ltd (Gorkha Brewery), in which Carlsberg owned a majority stake, controlled over 70 per cent of the local beer market (*The Economic Times* 2006a). It was speculated whether Carlsberg had already obtained approval for a 100 per cent greenfield FDI through the JV, so that the project would not require any further clearance by the authorities (*The Economic Times* 2006a). At that point it was not clear how Carlsberg would structure its entry as the pitch for acquiring Himneel Breweries had reportedly not been made in the name of Gorkha Brewery, but on behalf of an entity called South Asia Breweries (SoAB). So, it was heavily speculated whether SoAB could be a separate JV, in which Carlsberg was involved. Carlsberg seemed to not have reached any conclusion on its India strategy. As Surendra Silwar, operation director and official spokesperson of Gorkha Brewery commented: 'We have a tie-up with Carlsberg for Nepal, but it has nothing to do with the Indian market. Carlsberg is trying to come up in India and we are simply sharing information with them on the market' (*The Economic Times* 2006b).

In October 2006, Carlsberg entered an agreement to acquire Himneel Breweries located in Himachal Pradesh, near the capital New Delhi, for about US$9 million. The transaction was formally effectuated by Carlsberg's subsidiary South Asia Breweries. It was unclear, however, whether Carlsberg was entering solo or with a partner. What was known was that Carlsberg had obtained a greenfield licence in Alwar, Rajasthan together with its Nepalese JV partner, the Khetan Group (*The Economic Times* 2006c).

It was not until the end of that year that Carlsberg announced that SoAB had been officially registered with the Indian authorities (*Børsen* 2006). The new entity had its head office in New Delhi. Carlsberg directly controlled a 45 per cent stake, while the Industrialization Fund for Developing Countries (IFU)[1] held 10 per cent, and the remaining 45 per cent was in the hands of a group of investors led by Carlsberg's partner in Sri Lanka, The Lion Brewery Ceylon Ltd (*Business Standard* 2008).

This was a time of an extremely high concentration of foreign entries,

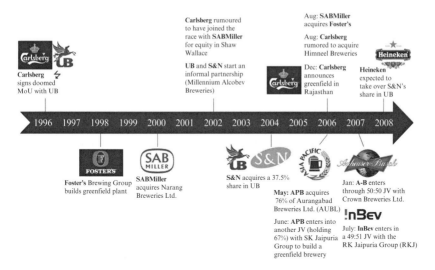

Source: Authors' own illustration.

Figure 6.2 Foreign market entries into the Indian beer market on a timeline 1996–2008

since mid 2006. As of early 2006, SABMiller had been the only one out of the top five global players that had established a strong foothold through its numerous acquisitions in the early 2000s (*The Hindu Business Line* 2005). The other four members of the top five had not yet entered India (Anheuser-Busch, Heineken, InBev and Carlsberg). However, all of them did so within only 14 months, following Heineken's initial move in May 2006, when its Singapore-based Asian arm Asia-Pacific Breweries (APB) made its highly anticipated move into the Indian market (see Figure 6.2).

APB acquired a 76 per cent stake in Aurangabad Breweries Ltd (AUBL), which owned two breweries in Maharashtra and Goa, for US$18 million (Asia-Pacific Breweries 2006a). In June, APB was ready to make its next move by entering into a JV partnership (holding 67 per cent) with Jaipuria Beverages and Food Industries Private Limited ('Jaipuria'), which is associated with the Jaipuria Group, one of the largest manufacturers of soft drinks in India (Asia-Pacific Breweries 2006b). The JV with an initial investment estimated at US$15 million would build a greenfield brewery with an initial brewing capacity of 250 000 hl near Hyderabad, the capital of Andhra Pradesh, expected to be operational by the end of 2007 (Asia-Pacific Breweries 2006b). In January 2007, Anheuser-Busch entered in a 50:50 JV with Crown Breweries Ltd (*The Hindu Business Line* 2007). Only six months later, InBev formed a JV with Ravi Jaipuria-promoted RKJ Group (RKJ), India's biggest bottler for Pepsi. Initially, InBev would hold a 49 per cent stake in the venture with an option to increase it at a later stage, while RKJ Group would hold 51 per cent (*Hindustan Times* 2007). InBev hoped to benefit from RKJ's strong distribution network. The plan was to start launching InBev products at the end of 2007, reaching nation-wide availability by 2008 (*Hindustan Times* 2007).

Carlsberg missed the opportunity of being the first foreign player to establish a presence in India because its first attempts to enter in the mid 1990s failed. Carlsberg basically sat on the sideline when, at the turn of the century, the Indian beer market suddenly went from almost zero international players to foreign companies occupying 80 per cent of the market. The first international company to enter was Foster's Brewing Group in 1998, building a greenfield plant in Aurangabad (*The Economic Times* 2007b). At the end of 2006, Foster's had a market share of only about 2–3 per cent in India. Nonetheless, in August 2006 SABMiller paid US$120 million to assume ownership of Foster's Indian assets, including the Foster's brand in India (SABMiller 2006). In total, SABMiller had had the most significant impact on early consolidation. Following a spurt of acquisitions starting in 2000, SABMiller had been able to set an extensive footprint throughout the country with an estimated total investment of US$600 million until 2007 (*The Economic Times* 2007b). SABMiller increased its market share significantly from 28 per cent in 2005 to 36 per cent by 2007 (*The Economic Times* 2005b, 2007d). A significant opportunity to participate in the consolidation at an early stage was present when India's domestic brewer UB (with a dominant market share of 47 per cent as of 2007) was on the lookout for a partner in the early 2000s (Just-drinks 2007). Carlsberg, however, dismissed this opportunity because of its previous negative encounters during the failed partnership attempts with UB in the mid 1990s. British competitor S&N and UB formally set up a JV in 2002 and S&N acquired a 37.5 per cent stake in UB for US$171 million in 2004 (*The Guardian* 2004). Thus, the Indian market had been consolidated by the two foreign players SABMiller and S&N. Or, as a member of Carlsberg's business development team for Asia summarized: 'There was no other apparent dominant player left, whom the international brewers could work with, and seen from the standpoint of S&N and SABMiller, they have done fantastic platform work' (Carlsberg 2007).

Contrary to Carlsberg's earlier failed attempts and a seeming lack of execution power in the Asian unit located in Singapore, the newly established organization SoAB could hardly be criticized for a lack of hands-on execution power (see Figure 6.3).

Since its establishment at the end of 2006, initially with a view of build-

Source: Authors' own illustration.

Figure 6.3 Carlsberg's entry into India in three phases from the mid 1990s to 2005 onwards

ing a greenfield brewery in Rajasthan, SoAB had until the end of 2007 realized four large investment projects with an ambition to further expand the business. In May 2007, Carlsberg was in talks with the Maharashtra Industrial Development Corporation (MIDC) to obtain yet another greenfield brewery licence, most likely in Aurangabad (*The Economic Times* 2007b). At the same time, the few still independent domestic brewers saw their valuations skyrocketing given the immense wave of entries by the big foreign players. It was estimated that domestic brewers had doubled their sell-out valuations in the course of the previous two years. A brewery, for example, with an annual capacity of about 150 000 hl, and no brand assets, had increased its value to approximately US$18 million in May 2007 compared to half the price only 18 months earlier (*The Economic Times* 2007b). Nevertheless, in September Carlsberg decided to further accelerate activities in India by acquiring a 60 per cent share in an existing plant, Parag Breweries Ltd, in West Bengal (*The Economic Times* 2007d). The newly formed 60:40 JV was Carlsberg's second acquisition of shares in a domestic brewer in just 12 months, after buying Himneel in October 2006. At the same time, Carlsberg was already in the process of building two greenfield breweries, one in Rajasthan and the other in Maharashtra, each at a cost of approximately US$20 million (*The Economic Times* 2007d). In total, these activities effectuated by SoAB in less than a year since its establishment would yield a total annual production capacity of over a million hectolitres (see Table 6.1).

Furthermore, SoAB was said to have filed for yet another licence for a greenfield site with the governmental authorities in Andhra Pradesh (*The Economic Times* 2007d). Carlsberg had a vision to extend activities to develop a network of six to eight greenfield projects in the next five years. An important milestone from a sales and marketing perspective was the launch of its flagship brand Carlsberg in September 2007 (*The Economic Times* 2007c). As of 2012, Carlsberg stood as a significant player in India,

Table 6.1   Carlsberg's investments into India as of 2007–08

	Rajasthan	Himachal Pradesh	Maharashtra	West Bengal
Entry mode	Greenfield in Alwar	Acquisition Himneel Breweries	Greenfield in Aurangabad	Acquisition Parag Breweries
Project characteristics	First project, operational Q1 2008	European standard production facility, operational 2007	'Clone' of Rajasthan, operational Q2 2008	Establishment of JV entity (60:40), operational end 2007
Investment	US$20 million	US$9 million	US$20 million	US$8 million
Total investment		US$57 million		
Capacity	450 000 hl	150 000 hl	450 000 hl	150 000 hl
Total capacity		1.2 million hl		

Source: Authors' own compilation.

although its competitor Heineken obtained S&N's stake in its Indian operations after splitting the assets acquired in the joint acquisition of the British competitor. Still, through its strategy Carlsberg had established itself in India, obtained a strong foothold in the premium segment, and has since set up several new greenfield production sites (with its fifth brewery becoming operational in 2011).

DISCUSSION

Market Selection

According to dominant literature on FDI motives, Carlsberg's strategic decision to invest in India is based on the identification of India as a profitable business opportunity based on the host country's local environment and its fit with Carlsberg's global strategy (Dunning 1992; Estrin 2004). Carlsberg's emerging market strategy rests on the very premise of establishing a position in future growth markets, or in other words is guided by market-seeking motives. On the one hand, the forecasted positive economic development and future beer market growth in India suggest that from a long-term strategic perspective it makes sense for Carlsberg to enter. On the other hand, even as of 2007, the beer market in India was at an extremely early stage, with beer consumption at negligible levels and growth rates still heavily impeded by numerous operational hurdles, most notably deregulation remaining elusive and highly uncertain. Thus, the decision to enter remains ambiguous – even more so considering the vast range of alternative investment opportunities for Carlsberg in other emerging markets, such as other regions in Asia or Eastern Europe, where it already had a position that could easily be leveraged further. Thus, from a market-seeking perspective, it is hard to justify India over other available investment opportunities involving much less risk and more immediate profitability.

The industry level characteristics of brewing as a global oligopoly suggest an analysis from a globally integrated perspective on foreign markets, which explicates the risk of being outperformed by competitors as a significant driver. The oligopolistic nature of the global brewery industry has led to considerable action-reaction or 'eat-or-be-eaten' behaviour among the top players. With consolidation going on and growth pressure increasing, players that do not grow at least as fast as rivals risk being marginalized and eventually overtaken. This competitive risk arises from one rival getting an insurmountable upper hand in a key growth market. If one or two of the large brewers achieve extraordinary growth benefiting from a strong position in one (or more) rapidly growing market(s), other players risk falling behind. This extends the analysis of market selection beyond the immediate battlefield, that is, the host country India. Not many beer markets remain untapped on a worldwide basis. Most large markets that have more or less recently appeared on the global map as emerging economies (for instance, Poland, Brazil, China, Russia or Vietnam) have already been occupied by the large international brewers. As India stands as 'the last potentially big beer market with consumption vaulting at robust double digits' (*The Economic Times* 2007e), all major players are trying to gain a foothold in India to minimize the competitive risk of falling behind. Carlsberg is one of the smaller players among the 'big five'. This makes it particularly important to ensure continued growth in order not to become marginalized under the constant threat of consolidation. As a consequence, Carlsberg faces a relatively higher competitive risk than its larger competitors. Seen as a function of competitive risk when *not* participating in future beer market growth in India, Carlsberg's entry is a logical – if not necessary – step to stay on top in the 'global chess game' that characterizes this 'eat-or-be-eaten' industry. India's sheer size and immense future growth potential implies that one must be present to ensure that competitors do not gain too much too quickly.

As to Carlsberg's market selection, both perspectives, market-seeking and global chess, yield compelling reasons for why Carlsberg entered India. The dominant market-seeking motive, however, does not necessarily predict it. The argument remains ambiguous, especially since other options that are less risky and promise more immediate earnings suggest an alternative allocation for Carlsberg's scarce resources. The oligopolistic strategic interaction perspective explicates the Indian market as one of the 'last battlefields' in the global brewery industry. As such, it is not an option to wait until the market reaches critical volumes, because of the risk of being outpaced by competitors with the consequence that the market is consolidated or 'closed off' for significant entry (such as Carlsberg experienced in Latin America). This global chess logic explains Carlsberg's strategic interest in India as early as in the 1990s in a pioneering approach, and even more so its forceful entry as of 2006–07, head-on with its main competitors, and many years before the market would reach critical volume.

Timing

Carlsberg attempted, but failed, to enter the Indian market in a pioneering first-mover approach in phase 1 during the mid 1990s. Carlsberg's original intention was to pre-empt competition to benefit from 'first-mover advantages'. This can be understood in terms of the dominant efficiency- and resource-based reasoning, such as exploiting 'windows of opportunity' at early stages of market development (Luo 1997) or taking advantage of still immature market conditions such as distribution, or an institutional context that allows less costly and fast entry into the marketplace, especially in emerging markets (Arnold and Quelch 1998; Hoskisson et al. 2000). Another key reasoning behind moving into a market first is to block competitors instead of having to fight off market share later.

Carlsberg's renewed interest after 2005 in phase 2 displays strong elements of a 'follow-the-leader' type of investment. At that time, SABMiller had already established a strong position as number two in the Indian market. Also, S&N, the global number six at that time, had gained a foothold in India by buying into the biggest domestic brewer UB.

By 2005, none of the other four key global players in the top five group had yet entered, but a move by Heineken was highly anticipated and followed in May 2006. Carlsberg had been rumoured to have scouted opportunities since mid 2005, and officially announced the establishment of a local subsidiary by late 2006. As early as January 2007, Anheuser-Busch moved into India and was followed by InBev in July 2007. Heineken's entry triggered a massive wave of entry or 'herding' of investments by global brewers moving into India. By mid 2007, all four of the remaining top five had entered the market within only 14 months of Heineken's initial move.

The previous analysis of the 'great Indian beer rush' (*Business Week* 2007), that is, the massive wave of entry within only 14 months, from 2006 to 2007, builds on the efficiency- and resource-based first-mover advantage argument and emphasizes industry level characteristics and oligopolistic strategic interaction as an explicit moderator of timing strategy. Competitors' behaviour is critical to timing – either reacting to strategic moves in line with the early follow-the-leader or herding concept, or anticipating next moves in the global chess game.

Entry Mode

Carlsberg's entry mode choices, each seen as a singular entity, are based on efficiency- or resource-based decision criteria; for instance, gaining control of idle production capacities and thus fast ramp up, or access to licence, land and raw material in greenfield investments. Despite offering great insight into the individual entry mode decision, the analysis remains limited in explaining Carlsberg's combined approach, mixing multiple types of entry via a locally established JV with Asian partners, and thus breaking with its dominant strategic logic of entering through acquisitions or JVs with a 'route to control', that is, obtaining the majority stake.

Exploring the implications that industry level factors such as oligopolistic strategic interaction have on this strategic decision offers a more comprehensive analysis. From an industry level perspective, an acquisition by one player reduces the number of available options for rivals. Carlsberg's original intention, for instance, was to go after 'the king' in the Indian market and obtain a strong position at once through the attempted acquisition of UB, the local number one, in 1996. This was no longer an option after its British competitor S&N had acquired a 37.5 per cent share in 2004.[2] The string of acquisitions effected by SABMiller since its foray into India in 2000 further impeded Carlsberg from implementing its acquisition strategy. After 2005, when all four remaining players of the 'big five' subsequently entered the game, the demand side for acquisitions saw a sharp rise. As a logical consequence, by 2007 sell-out valuations of domestic brewers were skyrocketing. Entry in a 'cheap approach' through acquisitions – as is the dominant logic in Carlsberg's emerging market strategy – was no longer feasible due to the scarcity of available targets and the high price premium. In oligopolistic industries firms pay a premium for valuable strategic positions. This is particularly striking in the global brewery industry, where acquisitions have become the 'name of the game', provided that beer remains a local product embedded in local culture and consumer tastes. Thus, it is necessary for the foreign entrant to gain access to strong local brands.

Given the scarcity of local partners to work with after 2005, Carlsberg structured its entry in a variety of entry modes (for example, hybrids like the partial acquisition of Parag Breweries, which had obtained the necessary licence to build a greenfield site). While constantly on the lookout for attractive acquisition deals (picking up attractive targets in an opportunistic manner), Carlsberg used greenfields in a complementary fashion. This allowed high flexibility in Carlsberg's next competitive moves and at the same time made the company less predictable for competitors, as summarized by a Carlsberg employee:

> So, we move in quietly, but quite fast and massive without them [competitors] knowing. That is, both in West China and in India, essential for coming from nowhere to a market position. You shoot up and play a dominant role. (. . .) If you want to come from point A to point B, the best way is to do it fast and discrete. It is just like an army coming from all different places. (Carlsberg 2007)

As Carlsberg was part of the massive wave of entries in 2006–07, a decisive factor in structuring its entry was to reduce its immediate visibility in the highly transparent industry. Industry observers, and competitors alike, were confused about the way Carlsberg initially structured its entry. It was speculated whether Carlsberg would enter solo or with a partner and who was actually behind filing for a greenfield licence or acquiring domestic brewer Himneel. The ownership structure and Carlsberg's venture into India was still not transparent until the end of 2006, when the new JV SoAB was officially registered with Indian authorities. This strategic choice enabled Carlsberg to arise in India in a discrete but fast manner, with greenfield licences already obtained and no further clearance required after official registration of the Indian JV. It seems that the high industry transparency in the global brewery industry was a main driver behind this strategic rationale and provides a compelling argument for entering via the locally established JV beyond dominant efficiency- or resource-based reasoning (for example, access to local market knowledge, lower cost and shared risk). Once competition realized that Carlsberg was actually behind SoAB, they were already in the process of building two greenfield sites.

Key aspects of Carlsberg's entry mode package was fast and discrete entry via the JV SoAB in parallel work streams and a variety of entry modes that made Carlsberg less predictable for competitors.

Summary

While dominant investment motives, transaction cost economics and resource-based reasoning remain key to market entry strategy, we find that industry level characteristics and oligopolistic strategic interaction among

Table 6.2   Contrasting perspectives: Carlsberg's market entry into India

Entry strategy dimension	Efficiency- and resource-based perspective at firm level	Oligopolistic strategic interaction perspective at industry level
Market selection, motive	• Market-seeking: India's market attractiveness? Long-term? • 'Strategic fit' between Carlsberg's strategy and local Indian context?	• India's role in the global positioning game (global chess) • Strategic move to mitigate the competitive risk of falling behind • Competitive risk estimated higher than financial and operational risk
Timing	• Economic returns from first-mover advantages no longer available • Failed attempts of 'cheap' early entry in mid 1990s ruling out asset-based, economic efficiency gains ('window of opportunity')	• Driven by rivals' past and anticipated moves (follow-the-leader, herding) • Forcefully pushing entry as of 2006–07 due to high entry concentration: all remaining top players enter head-on within 14 months
Entry mode	• Balancing resources with market • Key decision criteria: costs, access to resources, control • Necessary conditions at individual investment level (e.g. reasonable price proposition, acceptable governance structure and so on)	• Entry mode package via local JV SoAB to build competitive platform: (1) Fast and discrete entry (2) Parallel work streams in a variety of entry modes (less predictable)

Source: Authors' own compilation.

key players in global oligopolistic industries also impacted Carlsberg's strategic decisions in their entry into India (see Table 6.2).

A refined conceptual model summarizes these findings, accounting for how industry level characteristics and oligopolistic strategic interaction among global key players influence foreign market entry strategy (see Figure 6.4). The model entails two main propositions, which are outlined in the following.

First, we suggest a moderating effect of industry level characteristics and strategic interaction in global oligopolistic industries on the dominant drivers of firms' internationalization behaviour. This is to say that neither

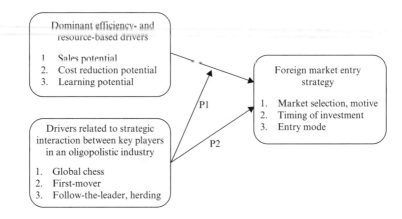

Figure 6.4   Refined conceptual model of foreign market entry strategy

of the perspectives offers a complete picture in itself when it comes to global oligopolistic industries, but that they complement each other. The future growth potential of the Indian market, for instance, is a necessary condition for entry into India, but not a sufficient reason to do so as of 2006–07, especially not at the expense of possible alternative investments in emerging markets that would yield returns much earlier. The fact that Carlsberg pushed its entry so forcefully in 2006–07 is hardly understood in terms of market-seeking investment (even in the long term) or efficiency- and resource-based reasoning in itself. At the time of entry, the Indian market was of a negligible absolute size, and was not expected to reach critical volumes within the next 10–20 years. Industry level characteristics and oligopolistic strategic interaction on a global scale enrich the analysis of timing. Carlsberg pushed its entry so forcefully in 2006–07 to prevent falling behind given the massive entry concentration during that time (follow-the-leader, herding). Thus, the industry level perspective extends dominant efficiency- and resourced-based first-mover advantage reasoning as being first to market was no longer an option as of 2006–07. To summarize, we suggest the following:

Proposition 1:   Drivers related to strategic interaction between key players in an oligopolistic industry have a moderating effect on the dominant efficiency- and resource-based drivers of firms' foreign market entry strategy.

Second, the model also entails a direct effect of industry level characteristics and strategic interaction on firms' foreign market entry strategy.

This refers to situations in which sales, cost reduction or learning potential drivers of entry strategy cannot explain firms' market selection, timing or entry mode decisions. This has important implications, for instance, for the definition of assets. MNCs in oligopolistic industries seem to have a different relation to economic assets from efficiency- or resource-based theory suggests. Specifically, strategic market positions are considered an asset. As a result, the definition of assets in global oligopolistic industries is broader. In such situations, it is the need to gain control of strategic positions that drives firms' internationalization behaviour. As for Carlsberg, for example, the threat of competitors' relative gain in the important Indian market and the cut-throat global positioning game among the top leading global brewers are important drivers of Carlsberg's market selection. Whereas the market is forecast to grow, it still has a neg-ligible absolute size, only modest mid-term potential for growth coming from the extremely low base, and thus little opportunity of conversion to profit within a reasonable timeframe. The high operational risk given the uncertainty of deregulation of the market would normally imply a 'no go' for MNCs (Arnold and Quelch 1998). The industry level perspec-tive of global chess emphasizes the role that the market plays beyond the immediate battlefield of India, but as part of the ongoing race among the competitors to carve up the global beer market. Rather than modest mid-term growth potential constrained by the immense operational hurdles and extremely high uncertainty as to market deregulation, the industry dynamics explain Carlsberg's decision to push an entry into India: the competitive risk associated with falling behind on a global scale was esti-mated to be higher than the financial and operational risks. Based on the above, we propose:

Proposition 2: Drivers related to strategic interaction between key players in an oligopolistic industry have a direct effect on firms' foreign market entry strategy.

CONCLUSION

The objective of this chapter was to examine the question of how industry level characteristics and strategic interaction among key players in global oligopolistic industries such as the global brewery industry impact foreign market entry strategy. To achieve this, we bridged the two research streams of early oligopolistic theories, which we took into the global context, and dominant efficiency- and resource-based perspectives. They seem largely disconnected as they have been researched separately at different times, and oligopolistic theories have faded from sight in more contemporary research, which is mostly conducted at firm level (Oligopolistic theory does not enjoy the same applicability or prominence. This and the fact that it is behavioural and dynamic in nature might explain why arguments have not been systemized and researched in the same way. Having combined both streams in the discussion of our case study, we derived a model that integrates industry level characteristics with the dominant perspective on FDI. The increasing emergence of oligopolistic industries on a global level makes this research particularly relevant. The global brewery industry is a prime example.

There are several limitations to our study and we outline a number of possibilities for future theoretical and empirical refinement below. First, insights from the field of global strategic management could inform future research and practice in terms of useful tools for competitor and industry analysis (see for example Chen 1996; Porter 1980, 1986) or multimarket competition (Baum and Korn 1996; Chen 1996; Karnani and Wernerfelt 1985; Porter 1980). Bringing the two research domains of strategic management and international business closer together offers promising future research avenues; for instance, the systematic integration of game-theoretic constructs. Second, future research could investigate other industry level characteristics and the wider industry context to extend the notion of oligopolistic strategic interaction, which is only one such characteristic (for example, Porter 1986). This current limitation and possibility for further research also extends to potential retaliations from local incumbent firms (for example, Buckley and Casson 1998). Third, this chapter does not address the fine line between competition and collaboration that often exists in oligopolistic industries with tendencies of collusive behaviour or collaborative strategic interaction in the form of 'co-opetition' (Brandenburger and Nalebuff 1995, 1998). Finally, much more rigorous empirical testing, for instance multiple case studies or panel data analysis, is needed to scrutinize our suggestions. To this end, we hope that this chapter inspires fresh approaches to examining effects of industry level characteristics on firms' foreign market entry strategies.

NOTES

1. IFU offers capital and advice to joint venture enterprises in developing countries.
2. With the joint acquisition of S&N by the consortium consisting of Heineken and Carlsberg in 2008, S&N's Indian operations became part of Heineken's global business.

REFERENCES

Agarwal, S. and S.N. Ramaswami (1992), 'Choice of foreign market entry mode: impact of ownership, location and internalization factors', *Journal of International Business Studies*, **23** (1), 1–27.

Arnold, D.J. and J.A. Quelch (1998), 'New strategies in emerging markets', *Sloan Management Review*, **40** (1), 7–20.

Asia-Pacific Breweries (2006a), 'Press release', 2 May.

Asia-Pacific Breweries (2006b), 'Press release', 30 June.

Barney, J. (1991), 'Firm resources and sustained competitive advantage', *Journal of Management*, **17** (1), 99–120.

Bartlett, C.A. and S. Ghoshal (1993), *Transnational Management Text, Cases, and Readings in Cross-border Management*, 3rd ed., Homewood, IL: Irwin.

Baum, J.A.C. and H.J. Korn (1996), 'Competitive dynamics of interfirm rivalry', *The Academy of Management Journal*, **39** (2), 255–91.

Berlingske Nyhedsmagazin (2008), 'Carlsberg i den store indiske ølkrig', *Berlingske Nyhedsmagazin*, 24 January.

Birkinshaw, J. (1997), 'Entrepreneurship in multinational corporations: the characteristics of subsidiary initiatives', *Strategic Management Journal*, **18** (3), 207–29.

Birkinshaw, J. and N. Hood (1998), 'Multinational subsidiary evolution: capability and charter change in foreign-owned subsidiary companies', *Academy of Management Review*, **23** (4), 773–95.

Børsen (2006), 'Carlsberg søsætter indisk offensiv', *Børsen*, 8 December.

Brandenburger, A.M. and B.J. Nalebuff (1995), 'The right game: use game theory to shape strategy', *Harvard Business Review*, 73 (**4**), 57–71.

Brandenburger, A.M. and B. Nalebuff (1998), *Co-opetition*, New York: Currency Doubleday.

Buckley, P.J. and M.C. Casson (1976), *The Future of the Multinational Enterprise*, New York: Holmes and Meier.

Buckley, P.J. and M.C. Casson (1998), 'Analyzing foreign market entry strategies: extending the internalization approach', *Journal of International Business Studies*, **29** (3), 539–61.

Business Standard (2008), 'Carlsberg to open 2 more breweries', *Business Standard*, 8 April.

Business Week (2006), 'Europe's brewers go global for growth', *Business Week*, 8 September.

Business Week (2007), 'The great Indian beer rush', *Business Week*, 23 April.

Calvet, A.L. (1981), 'A synthesis of foreign direct investment theories and theories of the multinational firm', *Journal of International Business Studies*, **12** (1), 43–59.

Canadean (2006), *Global Beer Trends*, Basingstoke, UK: Canadean.

Cantwell, J., J.H. Dunning and S.M. Lundan (2010), 'An evolutionary approach to understanding international business activity: the co-evolution of MNEs and the institutional environment', *Journal of International Business Studies*, **41** (4), 567–86.

Carlsberg (various years), *Annual Reports*, Copenhagen: Carlsberg.

Carlsberg (2007), Interview with Carlsberg employee in Copenhagen, October.

Carr, C. and D. Collis (2011), 'Should you have a global strategy?' *MIT Sloan Management Review*, **53** (1), 21–4.

Chen, M.-J. (1996), 'Competitor analysis and interfirm rivalry: toward a theoreti-
   cal integration', *The Academy of Management Review*, 21 (1), 100–34.
Coffey, A. and P. Atkinson (1996), *Making Sense of Qualitative Data:
   Complementary Research Strategies*, Thousand Oaks, CA: Sage.
Dubois, A. and L.-E.Gadde (2002), 'Systematic combining: an abductive approach
   to case research', *Journal of Business Research*, 55 (7), 553–60.
Dunning, J.H. (1979), 'Explaining changing pattern of international production:
   in defense of the eclectic theory', *Oxford Bulletin of Economics and Statistics*, 41
   (4), 269–95.
Dunning, J.H. (1992), *Multinational Enterprises and the Global Economy*,
   Wokingham: Addison-Wesley.
Dunning, J.H. (1995), 'Reappraising the eclectic paradigm in an age of alliance
   capitalism', *Journal of International Business Studies*, 26 (3), 461–91.
Dunning, J.H. (2000), 'Globalization and the theory of MNE activity', in N. Hood
   and S. Young (eds), *Globalization of Multinational Enterprise Activity and
   Economic Development*, Basingstoke: Macmillan, pp. 21–43.
Dunning, J.H. and S.M. Lundan (2008), *Multinational Enterprises and the Global
   Economy*, 2nd ed., Cheltenham, UK and Northampton, MA, USA: Edward
   Elgar.
Dunning, J.H. and R. Narula (2004), *Multinationals and Industrial Competitiveness
   a New Agenda*, Cheltenham, UK and Northampton, MA, USA: Edward Elgar.
Dunning, J.H. and A.M. Rugman (1985), 'The influence of Hymer's dissertation
   on the theory of foreign direct investment', *American Economic Review*, 75 (2),
   228.
Edwards, C.D. (1955), 'Conglomerate bigness as a source of power', in Bureau,
   Universities-National (ed.), *Business Concentration and Price Policy*, Princeton,
   NJ: Princeton University Press, pp. 329–58.
Eisenhardt, K.M. and M.E. Graebner (2007), 'Theory building from cases:
   opportunities and challenges', *The Academy of Management Review*, 50 (1),
   25–32.
Estrin, S. (2004), *Investment Strategies in Emerging Markets*, Cheltenham, UK and
   Northampton, MA, USA: Edward Elgar.
Flowers, E.B. (1976), 'Oligopolistic reactions in European and Canadian direct
   investment in the United States', *Journal of International Business Studies*, 7 (2),
   43–55.
Ghauri, P.N. and K. Grønhaug (2005), *Research Methods in Business Studies: a
   Practical Guide*, 3rd ed., Harlow: Financial Times/Prentice Hall.
Ghemawat, P. (1997), *Games Businesses Play: Cases and Models*, Cambridge, MA:
   MIT Press.
Graham, E.M. (1978), 'Transatlantic investment by multinational firms: a rivalis-
   tic phenomenon?', *Journal of Post Keynesian Economics*, 1 (1), 82–99.
Graham, E.M. (1992), 'The theory of the firm', in Peter J. Buckley (ed.), *New
   Directions in International Business*, Aldershot, UK and Brookfield, VT, USA:
   Edward Elgar, pp. 72–80.
Grant, R.M. (1996), 'Toward a knowledge-based theory of the firm', *Strategic
   Management Journal*, 17, 109–22.
Hamel, G. and C.K. Prahalad (1994), *Competing for the Future: Breakthrough
   Strategies for Seizing Control of your Industry and Creating the Markets of
   Tomorrow*, Boston, MA: Harvard Business School Press.
Harzing, A.-W. (2002), 'Acquisitions versus greenfield investments: international

strategy and management of entry modes', *Strategic Management Journal*, **23** (3), 211–27.

Hennart, J.-F. (1982), *A Theory of Multinational Enterprise*, Ann Arbor: University of Michigan Press.

Hennart, J.-F. and Y.-R. Park (1994), 'Location, governance, and strategic determinants of Japanese manufacturing investment in the United States', *Strategic Management Journal*, **15** (6), 419–36.

Hindustan Times (2007), 'InBev brews joint venture with RKJ Group', *Hindustan Times*, 18 May.

Hoskisson, R.E., L. Eden, C.M. Lau and M. Wright (2000), 'Strategy in emerging economies', *Academy of Management Journal*, **43** (3), 249–67.

Huber, G.P. and D.J. Power (1985), 'Retrospective reports of strategic-level managers: guidelines for increasing their accuracy', *Strategic Management Journal*, **6** (2), 171–80.

Hymer, S.H. (1976), 'The international operations of national firms: a study of direct foreign investment', MIT Monographs in Economics 14, Cambridge, MA: MIT Press.

Johanson, J. and J.-E. Vahlne (2009), 'The Uppsala internationalization process model revisited: from liability of foreignness to liability of outsidership', *Journal of International Business Studies*, **40** (9), 1411–31.

Just-drinks (2007), *The Beer Market in India – Forecasts to 2011*, Just-drinks, March.

Karnani, A. and B. Wernerfelt (1985), 'Multiple point competition', *Strategic Management Journal*, **6** (1), 87–96.

Kim, W.C. and P. Hwang (1992), 'Global strategy and multinationals' entry mode choice', *Journal of International Business Studies*, **23** (1), 29–53.

Knickerbocker, F.T. (1973), *Oligopolistic Reaction and Multinational Enterprise*, Boston, MA: Harvard Business School Press.

Kogut, B. and U. Zander (1993), 'Knowledge of the firm and the evolutionary theory of the multinational corporation', *Journal of International Business Studies*, **24** (4), 625–45.

Langley, A. (1999), 'Strategies for theorizing from process data', *Academy of Management Review*, **24** (4), 691–710.

Lasserre, P. (2007), *Global Strategic Management*, 2nd ed., New York: Palgrave Macmillan.

Leonard-Barton, D. (1990), 'A dual methodology for case studies: synergistic use of a longitudinal single site with replicated multiple sites', *Organization Science*, **1** (3), 248–66.

Li, S., S.B. Tallman and M.P. Ferreira (2005), 'Developing the eclectic paradigm as a model of global strategy: an application to the impact of the Sep. 11 terrorist attacks on MNE performance levels', *Journal of International Management*, **11** (4), 479–96.

Lieberman, M.B. and S. Asaba (2006), 'Why do firms imitate each other?', *Academy of Management Review*, **31** (2), 366–85.

Lieberman, M.B. and D.B. Montgomery (1988), 'First-mover advantages', *Strategic Management Journal*, **9** (S1), 41–58.

Lieberman, M.B. and D.B. Montgomery (1998), 'First-mover (dis)advantages: retrospective and link with the resource-based view', *Strategic Management Journal*, **19** (12), 1111.

Lung, Y. (2000), 'Is the rise of emerging countries as automobile producers an irreversible phenomenon', in J. Humphrey, Y. Lecler and M.S. Salerno (eds),

Global Strategies and Local Realities; the Auto Industry in Emerging Markets, Basingstoke: Palgrave Macmillan, pp. 16–41.

Luo, Y. (1997), 'Pioneering in China: risks and benefits', *Long Range Planning*, **30** (5), 768–76.

Marschan-Piekkari, R. (2004), *Handbook of Qualitative Research Methods for International Business*, Cheltenham, UK and Northampton, MA, USA: Edward Elgar.

Miller, K.D. and T.B. Folta (2002), 'Option value and entry timing', *Strategic Management Journal*, **23** (7), 655.

Ministry of Food Processing Industries (2006), *Model Policy for Alcoholic Beverages and Alcohol*, February, India: Ministry of Food Processing Industries.

Morschett, D., H. Schramm-Klein and B. Swoboda (2010), 'Decades of research on market entry modes: what do we really know about external antecedents of entry mode choice?', *Journal of International Management*, **16** (1), 60–77.

Patton, M.Q. (1990), *Qualitative Evaluation and Research Methods*, 2nd ed., Newbury Park, CA: Sage.

Piekkari, R. (2011), *Rethinking the Case Study in International Business and Management Research*, Cheltenham, UK and Northampton, MA, USA: Edward Elgar.

Porter, M.E. (1980), *Competitive Strategy: Techniques for Analyzing Industries and Competitors*, New York: Free Press.

Porter, M.E. (1986), *Competition in Global Industries*, Boston, MA: Harvard Business School Press.

Puck, J.F., D. Holtbrügge and A.T. Mohr (2009), 'Beyond entry mode choice: explaining the conversion of joint ventures into wholly owned subsidiaries in the People's Republic of China', *Journal of International Business Studies*, **40** (3), 388–404.

Rescher, N. (1978), *Peirce's Philosophy of Science: Critical Studies in His Theory of Induction and Scientific Method*, Notre Dame, IL: University of Notre Dame Press.

SABMiller (2005), 'Press release', 27 May.

SABMiller (2006), 'Press release', 4 August.

SABMiller (2007), *Annual Report*, London: SABMiller.

Scherer, F.M. and D. Ross (2009), 'Industrial market structure and economic performance', University of Illinois at Urbana-Champaign's Academy for Entrepreneurial Leadership Historical Research Reference in Entrepreneurship.

Sharma, V.M. and M.K. Erramilli (2004), 'Resource-based explanation of entry mode choice', *Journal of Marketing Theory and Practice*, **12** (1), 1–18.

Tallman, S.B. (1991), 'Strategic management models and resource-based strategies among MNEs in a host market', *Strategic Management Journal*, **12**, 69–82.

Tallman, S.B. (1992), 'A strategic management perspective on host country structure of multinational enterprises', *Journal of Management*, **18** (3), 455.

The Economic Times (2005a), 'Carlsberg plans 100% India subsidiary to import, sell beer', *The Economic Times*, 12 May.

The Economic Times (2005b), 'Carlsberg to add froth, eyes local breweries', *The Economic Times*, 5 May.

The Economic Times (2006a), 'Carlsberg brewing India foray plan', *The Economic Times*, 7 August.

The Economic Times (2006b), 'Carlsberg, Khetan in talks to buy HP brewery', *The Economic Times*, 12 August.

The Economic Times (2006c), 'Carlsberg blows India bugle with Himneel buy', *The Economic Times*, 6 October.

The Economic Times (2007a), 'Beer consumption in India grows by 90%', *The Economic Times*, 10 October.

The Economic Times (2007b), 'Carlsberg, A-B won't say cheers to buys', *The Economic Times*, 11 May.

The Economic Times (2007c), 'Carlsberg all-malt beer launched', *The Economic Times*, 25 September.

The Economic Times (2007d), 'Carlsberg to buy 60% in Parag for Rs 32 crore', *The Economic Times*, 14 September.

The Economic Times (2007e), 'Carlsberg to enter India with Palone', *The Economic Times*, 13 June.

The Economic Times (2007f), 'UB may let Carlsberg guzzle SandN', *The Economic Times*, 5 September.

The Economic Times (2008), 'InBev's JV with Jaipuria faces delay on quality issues', *The Economic Times*, 25 February.

The Economic Times (2011), 'India's middle class population to touch 267 million in 5 yrs', *The Economic Times*, 6 February.

The Guardian (2004), 'SandN gains joint control of India's biggest brewer', *The Guardian*, 20 December.

The Hindu Business Line (2004), 'InBev, SandN vie for UB stake', *The Hindu Business Line*, 8 December.

The Hindu Business Line (2005), 'SABMiller brews $125-m fresh investments in India', *The Hindu Business Line*, 15 June.

The Hindu Business Line (2007), 'Budweiser to be made in India', *The Hindu Business Line*, 24 February.

The Wall Street Journal (2012), 'Carlsberg needs Russian beer revolution', *The Wall Street Journal*, 21 February.

Wernerfelt, B. (1984), 'A resource-based view of the firm', *Strategic Management Journal*, **5** (2), 171–80.

Williamson, O.E. (1975), *Markets and Hierarchies Analysis and Antitrust Implications: a Study in the Economics of Internal Organization*, New York: Free Press.

Wright, M., I. Filatotchev, R.E. Hoskisson and M.W. Peng (2005), 'Strategy research in emerging economies: challenging the conventional wisdom', *Journal of Management Studies*, **42** (1), 1–33.

Yu, C.H. (1994), 'Abduction? Deduction? Induction? Is there a logic of exploratory data analysis?', *Annual Meeting of American Educational Research Association*, New Orleans, Louisiana.

Yu, C.-M.J. and K. Ito (1988), 'Oligopolistic reaction and foreign direct investment: the case of the U.S. tire and textiles industries', *Journal of International Business Studies*, **19** (3), 449–60.

PART IV

Cross-border M&A integration and subsidiary development

7. Subsidiary strategic responsibilities and autonomy in Carlsberg

Jens Gammelgaard and Bersant Hobdari

INTRODUCTION

The configuration of value-adding activities by multinational corporations (MNCs) is one of the primary research themes in international business research (Griffith et al. 2008). Among the most important aspects of these activities are the degree of autonomy and the strategic responsibilities allocated to subsidiaries.

In this chapter, we analyse the strategic development of MNC subsidiaries in the brewery sector by taking a longitudinal view of some of the foreign breweries acquired by the Danish MNC brewer Carlsberg over time. In particular, we focus on changes in subsidiary autonomy and in the charters of the subsidiaries in terms of the value chain activities delegated to them. 'Autonomy' is defined as decision-making rights at the sub-unit level. It reflects the ability of these units to make decisions on issues that are handled at a higher level in comparable organizations (Brooke 1984, p.9). 'Strategic responsibilities' are defined as subsidiaries mandates detailing the value chain activities delegated to the unit and the resources the subsidiary can use for those activities.

Surveys of the roles played by subsidiaries in MNCs highlight significant variability in terms of the value chain activities they handle (White and Poynter 1984; Birkinshaw and Morrison 1995). For example, some subsidiaries handle all value chain activities on a small scale, whereas others (such as sales or manufacturing units) specialize in only a few value chain activities but on a larger scale (White and Poynter 1984). Furthermore, some subsidiaries only operate within the host country, while others achieve global mandates (Birkinshaw and Morrison 1995). Finally, some subsidiaries enjoy high autonomy and operate without interference from headquarters, whereas others have limited autonomy (Young and Tavares 2004). Although the evidence implies substantial heterogeneity, the extant literature seems to lack a framework for analysing how subsidiary mandates are formed at the time of their acquisition or establishment, and how those mandates evolve over time.

In the next section we review the arguments presented in the literature on subsidiary autonomy and strategic responsibilities. Our theoretical propositions are then illustrated through a detailed look at the Danish brewer Carlsberg, its internationalization process and its overall strategy in terms of its subsidiaries. This is based on a close examination of Carlsberg's strategy for six of its subsidiaries. These subsidiaries have been carefully selected because they reflect the diversity of mandates within a single multinational. In the concluding section we summarize and discuss our findings.

LITERATURE REVIEW

Subsidiary autonomy is an important element of MNC strategy, as it is associated with positive effects on performance (Tran et al. 2010). Autonomy seems to matter more in cases where it is utilized in the subsidiary's collaboration with external partners (Gammelgaard et al. 2012). Furthermore, subsidiary autonomy has been associated with inter-unit power in the MNC, especially as it seems to enhance the amount of attention headquarters pay to the autonomous units (Ambos and Birkinshaw 2010).

In this chapter, we relate autonomy to the decision-making processes of the MNC. In this regard, subsidiary autonomy reflects the fact that strategic and operational decisions are not necessarily made exclusively by headquarters but, in most cases, are made by subsidiaries, or are the result of a bargaining process that leads to either a joint decision or a decision made by one partner after consulting the other (Taggart 1999; Dörrenbächer and Gammelgaard 2006). This implies that MNCs are typically organized as internal networks in which different forms of relationship are established among organizational units (Ghoshal and Bartlett 2005). Following Malnight (1996), autonomy is consequently a reflection of the network-based organization, where coordination takes place in an environment of shared decision-making. However, much of the literature on subsidiary autonomy does not adequately consider the fact that subsidiaries function within a hierarchy, which means that their level of autonomy is formally decided by headquarters and is not 'chosen' by the subsidiary. In an MNC hierarchy, autonomous subsidiaries have a high level of 'influence', but they do not possess formal or coercive power (Surlemont 1998). Nevertheless, influential subsidiaries affect headquarters' strategies regarding firm boundaries, resource allocation within the organization and intra-organizational integration (Verbeke and Kenworthy 2008).

A related point of analysis is delegation by headquarters of strategic responsibilities in the form of value chain mandates to their subsidiaries (Galunic and Eisenhardt 1996; Dörrenbächer and Gammelgaard 2010). In other words, headquarters can choose to allocate or reallocate value chain activities to the MNC's divisions or subsidiaries. In this respect, Yamin and Ghauri (2010) stress that MNC structures revolve around the disintegration of the value chain, while Mudambi (2008) finds that greater location flexibility is a central aspect of moves to break the value chain into a series of specific parts. Mudambi (2008) also emphasizes that, in some MNCs, the linkages among the disintegrated value chain activities are crucial to the competitive advantage of the MNC and it is, therefore, essential to keep the value chain activities in-house in wholly owned subsidiaries. In other cases, the MNC benefits from outsourcing value chain activities (Mudambi 2008). In both cases, the network idea is strongly emphasized.

The issue becomes whether the subsidiary primarily focuses on engagements with internal partners, such as headquarters of other subsidiaries, or on external relationships with customers, suppliers, competitors and agencies (Wang et al. 2009). In either case, subsidiaries are likely to increasingly perform narrowly specialized value chain functions. The development of information and communication technologies (ICTs) has, to a large extent, supported this trend towards subsidiary specialization. As a result, some subsidiaries provide goods and/or services for all parts of the MNC or, at least, for large parts of it. Alternatively, subsidiaries can provide services to specific parts of the MNC's global markets (Holm and Pedersen 2000). Such subsidiaries are likely to operate within more narrowly defined areas of specialization (Birkinshaw and Morrison 1995). One such example is found in White and Poynter's (1984) description of a particular subsidiary – a rationalized manufacturer – that produces a designated set of component parts while leaving sales activities to other corporate units.

An MNC is an organic organization, and upgrades or downgrades of subsidiary autonomy and strategic responsibilities occur regularly. In fact, an MNC can be viewed as an internal market in which subsidiaries compete for the attention and resources of headquarters (Cerrato 2006), and work to gain more autonomy or greater strategic responsibilities. In this competitive process, subsidiaries benefit from their possession of specialized resources (Mahoney and Pandian 1992). In fact, subsidiaries are likely to lose mandates when they lack such resources (Egelhoff et al. 1998). Furthermore, the subsidiary's external relationships and, in general, the market prospects associated with the subsidiary's location are helpful for the development of specialized resources, which in turn leads to autonomy and strategic responsibility (Luo 2003). At the same time, the subsidiary's internal relationships and its closeness to the MNC's head quarters further strengthen the subsidiary's position (Astley and Sachdeva 1984; Ghoshal and Bartlett 2005). A combination of these factors is likely to create situations of resource dependency, which increase the bargaining power of the subsidiary, leading to more autonomy and strategic responsibility (Bouquet and Birkinshaw 2008). This process is summarized by Forsgren et al. (2005), who find that well-functioning internal and external relationships, as well as an asymmetric distribution of dependency in favor of the subsidiary, enhance subsidiary influence.

In summary, we would expect to find significant heterogeneity in levels of subsidiary autonomy and strategic responsibility both across and within multinationals. Headquarters units are likely to engage in different combinations of interventions, which result in different development paths for subsidiaries. These differences may be driven by the entry form and ownership strategies of the MNC, as both of these elements allow for the emergence of differences in levels of autonomy and strategic responsibilities across subsidiaries of the same multinational. The context in which subsidiaries are established can result in differences in entry modes, such as greenfield or acquisition, or differences in ownership, such as partial versus full ownership. A third aspect is the significance of the acquired firm's market positions, where strong players are assumed to have more power in their negotiations with headquarters.

We therefore forecast significant differentiation in how subsidiaries develop in terms of autonomy and strategic responsibility following a takeover. The acquirer can adopt different entrance strategies and intervene in numerous ways, and the subsidiaries can hold varying levels of power. We therefore expect some subsidiaries to develop strategic responsibility and autonomy, while other subsidiaries are likely to lose strategic responsibility and autonomy. However, we wish to add a nuance to this notion by investigating whether these two lines of development occur simultaneously, so that subsidiaries win and lose mandates at the same time.

METHODOLOGY

Our empirical strategy, which focuses on developments in subsidiary mandates within one multinational, the Danish brewer Carlsberg, provides an ideal setting to investigate these claims. Our data are derived from archival sources, company reports and articles in the financial press. The data are used to flesh out the arguments made in academic sources, and provide interesting nuanced accounts of events within the company and the personalities involved. Furthermore, we adopt a longitudinal design to map the events that can be assessed as developments in value chain responsibilities and autonomy.

We focus on six acquisitions. These cases have been selected based on the size of investment (under the assumption that larger investments increase the likelihood of autonomy and strategic autonomy). Furthermore, all of the analysed acquisitions were made in Europe (including Russia), a prerequisite included in order to reduce the effect of cultural diversity. Furthermore, as the European market was under pressure at the time of this study, negative developments were expected.

CARLSBERG: THE COMPANY

Carlsberg is a Danish brewery that was founded in 1847 by Carl Jacobsen. Today, Carlsberg is one of the world's leading brewers with activities in more than 150 countries in which it markets more than 500 brands. Carlsberg's global reach has resulted in a high degree of internationalization, as expressed by the fact that foreign sales account for 92.6 percent of total sales (Carlsberg Annual Report 2011). Many minor markets are reached through export and licensing agreements (Carlsberg Annual Report 2010). Only 29 subsidiaries are listed in the annual report as having significant operations. These subsidiaries employ most of Carlsberg's 41 000 employees.

The Carlsberg Group produces 10 895 million liters of beer annually (Pedersen, Madsen and Lund-Thomsen, Chapter 1, this volume) and its net revenue was US$10 695 million in 2010 (Datamonitor 2011). Carlsberg's most important brand is Carlsberg, which is also its most recognized and fastest growing beer brand on a global basis (Annual Report 2008). Other well-known brands on an international scale are Tuborg, Baltika and Kronenbourg 1664. The company has a strong market presence in Denmark, Norway, Finland, France, Russia, the UK, Laos, Nepal, Cambodia, Malaysia and Vietnam. It has a weaker presence in the Americas (Datamonitor 2011). The company lacks operational scale when compared to its main competitors – Anheuser-Busch InBev, Heineken and SABMiller – in terms of volumes, investments in foreign acquisitions and growth in turnover (Pedersen, Madsen and Lund-Thomsen, Chapter 1, this volume).

Carlsberg A/S, the parent company, is owned by 20 000 institutional and private investors around the world, and it is listed on the NASDAQ OMX Nordic Exchange Copenhagen. The largest shareholder is the Carlsberg

Foundation, which was established by Carlsberg's founder, J.C. Jacobsen. The foundation acts as an active, long term shareholder and it supports scientific research in society. In 1876, Jacobsen stated that the foundation 'must forever own a minimum of 51 percent of the shares of Carlsberg A/S' (*Berlingske Tidende* 2000b). This stipulation has led to a relatively low-risk profile in terms of international investments (Geppert et al. forthcoming). For example, before 1997, Carlsberg rarely took majority stakes in companies – in 1996, Carlsberg held majority ownership in only eight of its 27 breweries (Iversen and Arnold 2008). In 2000, Carlsberg missed an opportunity to fully acquire Kronenbourg, as Carlsberg's ownership structure prevented the deal (Iversen and Arnold 2008).

The Carlsberg Foundation opened up for international expansion in 1999 by relinquishing the requirement that it must hold at least 51 percent of Carlsberg A/S. The wording was altered to require that the Foundation must hold a 'significant interest' in subsidiaries owned by Carlsberg A/S. In 2007, this requirement was further reduced to 25 percent (Iversen and Arnold 2008). The company rule stated that the Foundation must still own 51 percent, but that activities could be delegated to one or more subsidiaries in which the Foundation did not hold a majority of the voting rights (*Berlingske Tidende* 2000b).

A major reorganization took place in 2001 when Carlsberg divested the Danish amusement park Tivoli and the porcelain factory Royal Scandinavia. At that time, Carlsberg entered into a 60:40 joint venture with Norwegian Orkla, which led to a more international focus (*Ritzaus Bureau* 2001). As a consequence, Carlsberg immediately changed its investment profile, which meant that it was free to establish international collaborations or merger deals. These changes affected Carlsberg's internationalization path.

CARLSBERG'S INTERNATIONALIZATION PROCESS

Although Carlsberg started to export to the British market in the nineteenth century, its internationalization adventure did not really take off until after World War II. At that time, Carlsberg and its associated brewer Tuborg intensified their marketing campaigns abroad, which led to a tripling of exports between 1958 and 1972. In this period, the two companies also started to establish breweries around Europe and in Asia. An early investment outside Denmark was made in Malawi (Carlsberg Annual Reports 1987, 1988), although this investment led to a few licensee agreements rather than significant internationalization in Africa (*Børsen* 2010c).

Generally speaking, this period was characterized by a rather cautious investment strategy focused on licensee arrangements and exports. In 1967, Tuborg established Izmir in Turkey in cooperation with a Turkish partner (Carlsberg Annual Reports 1987, 1988). A few years later, in 1969, Tuborg entered into a licensee agreement with the biggest brewery in Iran, Shamce, and a new brewery was established in 1970. Another brewery was established outside Nicosia, Cyprus, in 1969. That same year, Carlsberg established a brewery through a licensee agreement with Brazilian CIBEB. However, due to quality problems, harsh competition and decreased sales, Carlsberg soon took over ownership of the Brazilian brewery, but the Danish company was unable to achieve sufficient turnaround and the brewery was divested in 1973.

Greenfield establishments continued, such as the establishment of the Malaysian unit in 1982 and Carlsberg Brewery Hong Kong in 1981 (Glamann 1997). Other Asian investments include the 1991 investment in Hite Brewery, Korea's largest brewery. Carlsberg launched operations in Vietnam in 1993 through two joint ventures with Hue Brewery and SEAB (Meyer and Tran 2006). More recently, Carlsberg has acquired Chinese companies. The first entrance in eastern China failed due to harsh competition on prices and expensive target prices. As a result, Carlsberg focused on breweries in western China. It now holds a controlling interest in Xinjang Wusu Beer and Dali Beer, and a minority interest in several other breweries (*Carlsberg Information til Aktionærer* 2006). Carlsberg also has four plants in India through a joint venture with South Asia Breweries (*RB-Børsen* 2008a; see also Hoenen and Hansen, Chapter 6, this volume).

Not every attempt by Carlsberg to take over foreign companies has been successful. For example, in 1972 Carlsberg attempted to acquire Swedish Pripps, which at that time held the majority of the shares in another Danish brewer – Ceres. As Carlsberg had substantial exports to Sweden, the two companies competed on both markets. However, even though the two companies negotiated, Pripps was taken over by the Swedish government. The resulting intensification in competition was resolved when Carlsberg entered into a licensee agreement with Pripps, Carlsberg took over Ceres and Pripps stopped exporting to Denmark (Sandberg 2010). Pripps was later acquired by Orkla and was eventually taken over by Carlsberg in 2004.

Carlsberg has also made major investments in the German market. In 1988, Carlsberg acquired 83 percent of Hannen Brauerei GmbH in a follow-up to a 1977 licensee agreement with German Reemtsa group, which included Hannen Brauerei. When the licensee agreement came to an end, Carlsberg took over Hannen. One reason for doing so was the

brewery's location near the Belgian border, which opened up sales opportunities in that market. Carlsberg also acquired Holsten-Brauerei in 2004
and Göttsche Getränke in 2006.

Other investments in the European markets included the 1991 acquisition of a controlling interest in Unicer, the largest brewer in Portugal
(Carlsberg Annual Report 2001). Subsequently Carlsberg sold its stake in
Spanish Union Cervecera, which had been experiencing losses for several
years. In 1970, the company entered into a partnership with the British beer
maker Watney in order to build a larger brewery in Northampton. Later,
owing to some restructuring in the industry, the Danish brewery obtained
100 percent control of this business (Business Insights Essentials 2012).
Furthermore, Carlsberg formed a strategic alliance with Allied-Lyons in
Britain. The new firm – a 50:50 joint venture known as Carlsberg-Tetley
P.L.C. – took an 18 percent market share. In Italy, Carlsberg acquired
Poretti in 1982. It acquired 50 percent of the shares in the Finnish brewing
operation Oy Sinebrychoff AB in 1988 and the remainder in 2000. That
same year, Carlsberg acquired Feldschlösschen Getränke in Switzerland.
In 1996, Carlsberg acquired 31.6 percent of Polish Okocim and it took
full ownership in 2004. In 2002, Carlsberg gained 11 percent of the
Croatian market by acquiring an 80 percent stake in Panonska Pivovara,
which manages three leading brands: Pan, Tuborg and Kaj (Niederhut-
Bollmann and Theuvsen 2008).

The latest major investment was the takeover of Scottish & Newcastle
(S&N; the former alliance partner in BBH). This was a joint acquisition
with Heineken. At the time of the takeover, S&N was considered to be a
leading European brewery with operations in 15 countries. S&N's assets
were divided between Carlsberg and Heineken, so that Carlsberg gained
100 percent ownership of BBH and S&N's French (Kronenbourg), Greek
(Mythos), Chinese and Vietnamese operations, whereas Heineken gained
control of S&N's UK, Irish, Portuguese, Finnish, Belgian, US and Indian
operations. The takeover gave Carlsberg leading positions in the East
European, Russian, French and Greek markets, which were expected to
counter the declining beer consumption in the mature West European
markets. Through the full control of BBH, Carlsberg controlled a range
of subsidiaries.

This historical overview illustrates a change in Carlsberg's preferred
entry mode from greenfield establishments towards acquisitions. However,
it was also an overall low-risk investment profile as some of these acquisitions were partial. Furthermore, reorganizations by spinoffs and intervention appear to be an established strategy. The ways in which these
elements affected subsidiaries' strategic responsibilities and autonomy are
investigated in the next section.

SUBSIDIARY STRATEGIC RESPONSIBILITIES AND AUTONOMY

Takeovers of breweries and their immediate launch into new roles as subsidiaries clearly illustrate Carlsberg's views on the strategic development of its subsidiaries. Carlsberg views efficiency in its production processes and distribution as key to its success. In numerous cases, this overall strategy has affected the acquired subsidiaries and their development. One example is found in the acquisition of Norwegian Ringness and Swedish Pripps, where old production plants were closed and production moved to new plants (Carlsberg 2001). Another case is the acquisition of Finnish Sinebrychoff, where production and administration improved after Carlsberg took full ownership. For example, new types of packaging were introduced in 2005 (Carlsberg Annual Report 2005). Many of the East European cases show similar developments, as is the case with Derbes in Kazakhstan, where major upgrades in production quality, national sales, distribution and management were evident (Carlsberg Annual Report 2002). In fact, the upgrading of Derbes' bottling line turned the brewery into one of the most modern in Europe. A new pilot plant was installed at Unicer-Bebidas in Portugal. Costs were reduced in the Turkish subsidiary by laying off workers in order to counteract the low sales of the local Skol brand. In Hong Kong, 27 managers were fired or replaced during an 18-month period due to strategic refocusing. Carlsberg also tends to restructure value chain activities, often leading to a centralization of functions. This was the case with the Finnish subsidiary and for the Italian division (Carlsberg Annual Report 2002). The implementation of joint purchasing is also common in terms of Carlsberg's post-acquisition restructuring activities.

These insights point to a general tendency in the brewery sector, where acquisitions often lead to loss of decision-making rights for the subsidiary and the removal of value chain activities. This general trend is confirmed in a case study of Heineken (Dieng et al. 2009). However, an investigation of Carlsberg's individual subsidiaries reveals that some subsidiaries are able to develop their strategic responsibilities and increase their level of autonomy over time. This phenomenon is reinforced by Carlsberg's strategy of leaving 'room to maneuver' at the local sites. This approach is embodied in the 'GloCal' strategy, implemented in the organizational matrix structure, which is characterized by front-end localization and back-end centralization (Carlsberg Annual Report 2011). As stated in Carlsberg's 2011 Annual Report, this entails 'working closely together at a GLObal level while allowing loCAL brands and initiatives to flourish'. By implementing such a matrix structure, the company aims to meet the

challenges of its industry, which include considerable variations in local
markets and customs, as well as significant pressure for efficiency and
standard solutions arising from other major international competitors
(Datamonitor 2011). An outcome of this strategy is evident in Carlsberg's
marketing expenditure, the majority of which is devoted to local brands
and directed towards emerging markets (Carlsberg Annual Report 2011).
However, even some of the global strategies recognized the need for
subsidiary autonomy and strategic responsibility. For example, central
coordination of procurement is located in Switzerland, accounting in
Poland and research and development (R&D) in France (Datamonitor
2011). Therefore, Carlsberg appears confident that it can derive value by
streamlining and centralizing across borders, while it still seems to recognize that substantial value is created locally in each individual market.

At this point, we can conclude that Carlsberg is motivated by an
efficiency-seeking strategy when acquiring foreign breweries and that it
creates value through such acquisitions. On the other hand, the GloCal
strategy points towards simultaneous upgrades in strategic responsibilities
and autonomy. This mixture of different processes is investigated in the
different cases.

OKOCIM

In 1996, Carlsberg acquired a 31.8 percent stake in the Polish brewery
Okocimskie Zaklady Piwowarskie S.A. (Okocim). At the time, Poland was
an interesting market for Carlsberg. It was a major, growing beer market
with 40 million inhabitants and a per capita annual demand of 40 liters.
Furthermore, in this transitional period, Polish citizens were experiencing
an increase in their purchasing power and shifting their consumption preferences from spirits to beer (Glamann 1997). Carlsberg made use of its revised
investment strategy and increased its ownership in the brewery to 50.1
percent in 2001 and to 100 percent in 2007 (Carlsberg Annual Report 2007).
Three minor breweries (Kaszelan, Bosman and Piast) were also acquired in
2001. In 2004, Okocim was delisted from the stock exchange and its name
was changed to Carlsberg Polska (Carlsberg Annual Report 2004).

The investment in Poland was initially problematic. Carlsberg's market
share fell from 8 percent to 5 percent. It took several years for the company
to increase this share to 17 percent, which it has achieved through additional acquisitions (*RB-Børsen* 2011c). Meyer and Tran (2006) attribute
this problem to the relatively low market share Carlsberg gained through
its acquisition when compared to the market shares held by Heineken
(via Zwyviec) of 33 percent or SAB (via Piwowarska) of 31.5 percent. As

a result, Carlsberg had a limited product portfolio compared to its main competitors.

Furthermore, at the time of the acquisition, Okocim was an inefficient brewery and Carlsberg spent €70 m to increase its efficiency, making major investments in production capacity and modernization, leading to a tripling of capacity (Carlsberg Annual Report 2006; *Reuters Finans* 2009). Later, associated breweries in Krakow and Chociw were closed (*Poland Business News* 2002) and production in Piast was reallocated to other plants (*Børsen* 2004c). In total, the number of production sites was reduced from four to three, the number of packaging sites from twelve to seven and the number of warehouses from twelve to six (Koudal and Engel 2007). The initial problems led to frequent changes in the subsidiary's management. For example, the subsidiary was unable to keep a sales manager employed for more than a year (*Berlingske Tidende* 2000a).

The situation improved with the replacement of the expatriate managers with local managers (*Berlingske Tidende* 2004b). This led to an improvement in managerial skills, which in turn led to the relocation of skilled managers from Carlsberg Polska to other subsidiaries, such as Tetley in the UK. Another example of strategic development was that the subsidiary gained an international market mandate – the Okocim brand was launched in the UK (*The Grocer* 2006), targeting the 600 000 Polish inhabitants in the country (*Marketing Week* 2007). The Okocim brand was also launched in India (*Business Today* 2007).

This case illustrates the subsidiary's loss of strategic responsibilities in the period immediately following the takeover, followed by the introduction of Carlsberg's best practices and control via expatriated subsidiary management. This development process is probably linked to Carlsberg's entry process, which was based on partial acquisitions of a brewery with low market power. However, the subsidiary developed a mandate and gained responsibility for international activities over time. The introduction of local management also ensured higher levels of autonomy. The subsidiary began to gain influence and build a more central position in the MNC network, as Polish managers were able to take on roles in other subsidiaries.

TETLEY

In terms of turnover, the 1997 acquisition of Tetley was the largest foreign takeover by a Danish company from 1994 to 1998 (Gammelgaard 2002). However, this acquisition was not the original strategic intent of Carlsberg's operation in the British market. For many years, the UK was

Carlsberg's dominant market in terms of exports (Iversen and Arnold 2000)

Carlsberg started to export to the UK in 1868. By 1939, 55 percent of all beer imported into the UK was from Carlsberg (*The Guardian* 2008). In 1970, Carlsberg entered the market via a joint venture with Watney, Man Truman, which was owned by Grand Metropolitan. This led to the opening of a brewery in Northampton in 1974. Grand Metropolitan left the alliance in 1975. In 1992, Carlsberg-Tetley was established as a 50:50 joint venture with Allied Lyons (*Børsen* 1997b, 1998a). Through this alliance, Carlsberg gained access to its partner's distribution network, which included 3500 pubs. After four years of disappointing results owing to a focus on discount brands, Allied Lyons sold its shares to Bass when the contract came to an end in 1996 (*Berlingske Tidende* 1997). Thereafter, a merger between Bass and Carlsberg was blocked by the Labour Party's new Minister of Industry, Margaret Beckett (*Børsen* 1998a). This move was a surprise for both companies, as the Ministry had approved the merger with S&N, which was similar in size, the previous year. The change in conditions for approval was primarily due to the change in the political regime from the Conservative Party to the Labour Party. However, as the merger was not completed, Bass took advantage of a clause in the original contract, which stated that it had the option to sell its shares back to Carlsberg for £110 m (*Børsen* 1997a). Carlsberg was left as the only major brewery in the UK without exclusive rights.

Carlsberg suddenly found itself 'alone' with a need to refocus its strategy in order to operate as a minor player in the industry. It held only 13 percent of the market (*Børsen* 2000). The company decided to implement a radical restructuring process. It divested or closed three of its five breweries in the UK, and was left with its original brewery in Northampton and Tetley's headquarters in Leeds (*Børsen* 1998a). Carlsberg invested around £40 m in increased capacity in these two breweries (Børsen 1998a; Carlsberg 1997). The restructuring also led to the layoff of 1500 of the 3700 employees in the UK (*Børsen* 1997b; *Jyllands Posten* 1998). Administration in Birmingham was relocated to Northampton. Despite these cutbacks, all brands were kept in the portfolio (*Børsen* 1997b).

In the period that followed, Carlsberg's earnings fell, although the restructuring reduced the negative effects of the blocked merger (*Børsen* 1998b). This 'success' was related to the pre-merger activities with Bass, which enabled Carlsberg to identify possible cost savings and to benchmark activities in the two corporations. Therefore, some of the anticipated merger synergies were achieved despite the merger's rejection (*Børsen* 1997a). The process continued with the renaming of Carlsberg Tetley to Carlsberg UK in 2004, although the Tetley brand was kept in the portfolio. In 2011, Carlsberg closed the original Tetley brewery in Leeds (Datamonitor 2008; *Børsen* 2011a) and relocated production of Tetley to Northampton. This move was based on a review of the supply chain, which indicated that two major Carlsberg breweries in the UK were not sustainable (ICM 2008), and on the recession's impact on demand, pub closures and higher duties (*The Guardian* 2008).

This case illustrates a subsidiary's dramatic loss of strategic responsibility. This should be understood in light of the initial importance of the British market, which should have led to high autonomy. The Tetley acquisition was significant in size. However, events external to the firm – mainly increasing governmental regulations and competitive reactions – led to a set of changes. The case also illustrates that the specialized resource in this market was access to distribution channels, which the subsidiary lacked in the end.

FELDSCHLÖSSCHEN

In 2000, Carlsberg acquired the Swiss brewer Feldschlösschen (Carlsberg 2000). The price was CHF 870 m. The target company had a 45 percent market share in Switzerland (Feldschlösschen brand: 24 percent; Cardinal: 11 percent) and employed 2600 people. It produced and marketed 2.4 million hl of beer at its four breweries, as well as 3.3 million hl of soft drinks and mineral water. In terms of exports, the company had found a niche – it sold 0.2 million hl of its non-alcoholic beer, Moussy, to the Middle East and North Africa. In the 1998–99 fiscal year, Feldschlösschen had CHF 1.02 bn in turnover and CHF 60 m in earnings. The company had seven production sites and 27 distribution centers. The company was diversified into beverage supplies for private customers, the wine business and soft drinks.

This acquisition introduced Carlsberg to the Swiss market, as Feldschlösschen did not have an international premium brand in its portfolio, even though this was a growing segment in the Swiss market. After the takeover, the sales, logistics and administrative functions were restructured. Significant investments were made to improve production efficiency (Carlsberg Annual Report 2001). Some of the breweries were integrated – for example, Rheinfelden North was integrated into Rheinfelden South (Carlsberg Annual Report 2002). In 2003, the soft drink establishment Eglisau Mineral Spring was spun off (Carlsberg Annual Report 2003) and wine activities were later divested (*Berlingske Tidende* 2004a). Over time, the number of employees was reduced from 2600 to 1600 (Business Insights Essentials 2012).

Initially, Carlsberg's chief executive officer (CEO), Flemming Lindeløv, saw this as a good investment. As he argued in a press release (Carlsberg 2000), the Swiss market was exclusive and centrally placed in Europe. However, what seemed to be a profitable investment soon turned problematic. First, the integration processes were delayed (*Børsen* 2001). Second, the Swiss beer market began to decline (Carlsberg Annual Report 2001). Despite this, in time Feldschlösschen was able to achieve income and profit equal to those of the most successful Carlsberg breweries (*Jyllands Posten* 2004).

The subsidiary's CEO, Thomas Amstutz, was appointed as subsidiary CEO of Kronenbourg in 2008 (*Ritzaus Bureau* 2008). His skill as a leader became clear when Feldschlösschen achieved a market share of 42 percent in 2008. This growth was based on cost-efficiency programs and market strategies for premium beers that had been adopted from Carlsberg. The company also initiated a new product – a beer labeled 'EVE' – which targeted women and gave Feldschlösschen a first-mover advantage on the Swiss market (*RB-Børsen* 2008b). Examples of losses of value chain activities were also present. The plant in Fribourg was closed in 2011 due to overcapacity in the Swiss breweries. The production was moved to the French Obernai brewery, which was a Kronenbourg subsidiary (*Ritzaus Bureau* 2010). In addition, Feldschlösschen's subsidiary in Dresden was sold to the German brewery Frankfurther Brauhaus (*RB-Børsen* 2011a). On the other hand, Switzerland was often used as a test market and as a producer of best practices, such as an information technology (IT)-based business standardization program. In addition, the experience with the Fribourg brewery was to benefit the MNC in subsequent closures (*Børsen Magasin* 2011).

In this case, headquarters exercised direct control at the operational level through personal monitoring. The group CEO regularly visits this subsidiary and other selected European subsidiaries on a yearly basis. During these visits, the subsidiary elaborates on its performance and initiatives, and the CEO visits a range of bars and stores to investigate how the brands are marketed, covering everything from the price of the beer to the brands that come out of the taps to how the products are placed in supermarkets (*Børsen Magasin* 2011).

At the time of the takeover, Feldschlösschen possessed many strategic responsibilities and was a subsidiary with substantial size and market power. In contrast to many of its other acquisitions, Carlsberg chose to make a full acquisition. However, due to efficiency processes, many of the subsidiary's mandates were removed. This process continues today, some 12 years after the takeover. However, the subsidiary still has the autonomy to develop and introduce new brands. Furthermore, the company still possesses valuable resources in terms of managerial expertise.

HOLSTEN

In 2004, Carlsberg acquired a majority shareholding in Holsten-Brauerei (Holsten), a brewery founded in 1879. Holsten had started exporting in 1952 and launched licensee production in the United Kingdom in 1976. At the time of the acquisition, the target firm was spread over four sites and had 1500 employees. Holsten was an international player with sales in 90 countries. The brewery had made a number of acquisitions in Germany, including Bavaria-St. Paulie-Brauerei in 1998 and König Pilsner in 2001 (Datamonitor 2004). Before the takeover, it held a market position as number two in northern Germany and number five in Germany as a whole.

The enterprise value of the acquisition was €1065 m, which included €542 m in net debt. Carlsberg entered into 'back-to-back' sale agreements to sell certain assets. These agreements covered brewing assets for a price of €469 m (Licht and König were sold to Bitburger) and water companies, such as Hansa-Mineral-Brunnen, which were sold to a third party for €159 m. The net price of the acquisition was therefore €437 m.

In terms of whether this was a reasonable acquisition, Carlsberg argued that Holsten held a key position in northern Germany (21.2 percent market share; 11.7 percent in Saxony).

Furthermore, Carlsberg saw potential benefits from exporting the Holsten brand to Russia and the UK. The company also believed synergies could be derived from transferring Carlsberg's best practices in production and procurement in the subsidiary, and from cross-selling the Carlsberg and Holsten brands. Most important, however, was the fact that the acquisition provided Carlsberg with access to Holsten's distribution network, which included 20 000 points of sale. In West European markets, control over distribution determines which brands will be offered in the shops. In many cases, these decisions are made by local distributors, which are not controlled by the breweries. Furthermore, it is time consuming and costly for breweries to build their distribution networks (*Børsen* 2004b). Some suggested that this distribution network was more important than the Holsten brewery itself given the brewery's low profitability (*Børsen* 2004b).

Market analysts viewed this takeover as risky and suggested that it was unlikely to enhance profits for several reasons. First, the divesture of König and Licher supported Bitburger, a competitor, by strengthening its premium brand profile. Second, Carlsberg kept the low-price brands, an area in which harsh competition could be expected. Third, the acquisition substantially reduced Carlsberg's liquidity reserves, thereby preventing the company from making additional investments in high-growth markets like

Eastern Europe and Asia. In general, market analysts assessed Holsten to be an expensive, low-profit firm (*Børsen* 2004n), and the reaction was a decrease in Carlsberg's share price (*Børsen* 2004b).

Nevertheless, cost efficiencies were achieved over time by, for example, reallocating production through the spinoff of the brewery in Monchengladbach and the transfer of 0.5 million hl of beer to Holsten (*Børsen* 2004a). Carlsberg also began production of Holsten beer at its Northampton production unit, which eliminated transportation costs, reduced lead times and allowed for faster responses to competitor promotions and changing customer demands (Carlsberg 2005).

In 2012, Carlsberg took over the Holsten brand in Russia, which was previously held by SABMiller. Holsten was the fourth-largest brand in the Russian super-premium segment (*Reuters Finans* 2012). At the same time, the *Financial Times Deutschland* stated that Carlsberg's CEO, Jørgen Buhl Rasmussen, was considering a spinoff of Holsten due to decreasing sales in the mature German market, which had led to a market share of less than 5 percent (*RB-Børsen*, 2011b).

Initially, Carlsberg's acquisition of Holsten held certain prospects, which could have led to a further strategic development of the subsidiary. However, the subsidiary lacked resources, which, when combined with the declining German market, meant that it lost mandates and autonomy. These developments should be viewed in the light of a takeover of a weak player in the market, and where financial reorganizations had to be made. This, in combination with market pressure, initiated a negative spiral in terms of subsidiary development.

KRONENBOURG

Kronenbourg, a French brewery, was 'indirectly' acquired by Carlsberg in 2008, when Carlsberg was involved in the S&N acquisition. Carlsberg and Heineken agreed that Kronenbourg would be transferred to Carlsberg. The company had been owned by Group Danone, but was taken over by S&N in 2000. At the time of its takeover by Carlsberg, Kronenbourg held a dominant position in the French market. It also had strong brands (such as 1664) and controlled important distribution networks. Furthermore, it was recognized for its innovative abilities and sophisticated approach to brewing (Protz 2004). However, due to decreasing sales on the French market, the general international financial crisis, and the increased regulation of the brewery sector, Carlsberg opted for a complete reorganization of the subsidiary. Consequently, 214 of the unit's 1400 employees were laid off, a range of minor brands were downgraded and the subsidiary's CEO was replaced with the Swiss CEO from Feldschlösschen (*Ritzaus Bureau* 2008). After three years of restructuring, however, the company was still struggling, despite expensive marketing campaigns (*Børsen* 2011b).

Nevertheless, the subsidiary gained a significant mandate, as the Carlsberg R&D center dedicated to beer and packaging – a €17 m investment – was located in the Obernai location. The Obernai plant already brewed and marketed several important brands, such as Kronenbourg 1664, Grimbergen, Kanterbrau and Carlsberg. Additional capacity was to be added through an investment of €11 m. This brought a geographical relocation of production – for example, some of the Feldschlösschen production was to be transferred to the French site, turning this site into a European cluster (*Just-drinks* 2012). There may have been several reasons for the decision to locate the R&D center in France. One reason may have been Jean-Yves Malpote, who had formerly served as subsidiary R&D CEO. After 2008, Malpote had served as vice president for Carlsberg R&D, which implies tight and personal connections with Carlsberg's top management. Another reason may have been the long tradition in brewing and R&D at this site. Finally, Kronenbourg 1664 was one of Carlsberg's strongest international brands and was distributed in more than 50 countries.

This case illustrates that a subsidiary can simultaneously win and lose mandates in different parts of the value chain. Furthermore, it highlights a relatively high level of autonomy, as evidenced by a statement from the Carlsberg CEO of Western Europe stressing that Kronenbourg employees were happy to fulfill the goals defined by Carlsberg as long as they could participate in the decision-making process (*Børsen* 2010b). Furthermore, after the acquisition the subsidiary controlled resources upon which both headquarters and other subsidiaries depended, such as R&D and capacity, which should also lead to higher levels of autonomy.

BALTIKA BREWERIES

The state-owned Baltika Brewery was formed in 1990 and it focused on quality beer from the beginning. In 1999, a modern factory was completed in St Petersburg, which was also the location of the company's headquarters. In 1992, Baltika became part of a joint venture with Orkla (named BBH – Baltic Beverages Holding), in which Carlsberg first held a 30 percent stake and then a 50 percent stake. In 2008, Carlsberg increased its share to 88.86 percent as an outcome of the acquisition of Scottish & Newcastle. Today, Baltika is the largest brewing company in the Russian Federation and in Eastern Europe. The subsidiary employs more than

9500 individuals. Baltika is also the most well-known brand in these regions and is sold in 98 percent of relevant stores in Russia (*Børsen* 2008). The brand was valued at US$ 2.3 bn in 2010 (Interbrand 2010). A substantial part of Carlsberg's revenue (approximately 25 percent) is generated by Baltika (Carlsberg Annual Report 2011).

Baltika controls ten subsidiaries and 12 production plants. An organization of this size is naturally well positioned in an MNC network, and Baltika collaborates with other Carlsberg subsidiaries to a high degree. For example, Baltika has an agreement to share marketing costs with the Finnish subsidiary Sinebrychoff Oy. It also has an agreement with Feldschlösschenin that the two subsidiaries buy consultancy services from each other. Furthermore, Baltika builds close institutional ties with a range of external partners. In this regard, the company emphasizes its connection with the government of St Petersburg. The fact that Baltika is visible in Russian industry is evidenced by the many awards it has received. In 2011, for example, it was named St Petersburg's best tax payer, and it received the 'Save Energy National Prize' from the Moscow government in 2010. Baltika deliberately changed its approach towards the Russian government to be more collaborative and proactive after the duty on alcohol was increased by 200 percent – an instance in which the company did not succeeded in its lobbying efforts (*Børsen* 2010a).

BBH's brand, production technologies and production capacity, and its close connections with the external environment place this subsidiary in a favorable position. Other organizational units depend on this subsidiary's resources. In particular, the external relationships represent a type of knowledge that is difficult for headquarters or other subsidiaries to capture on their own, such as the importance of managing personal relationships with outside stakeholders (Alcacer et al. 2010). The subsidiary's strategic importance is evident in the transfer of its best practices to other Carlsberg subsidiaries. As the CEO says: 'The rest of Carlsberg can learn from the drive that is in BBH and the rest of Eastern Europe' (Direkt 2007). Furthermore, the power the subsidiary gains from Carlsberg's investment in Baltika's 12 production plants increases the production capacity relative to other subsidiaries. In addition, the proportion of Carlsberg's total revenues derived from the Russian subsidiary has increased.

There have been several strategic developments. Since 2008, BBH has established licensee production in Japan, Uzbekistan, Australia, Kazakhstan, France, Italy and the Ukraine. Simultaneously, Baltika has launched exports to such countries as Lebanon, Vietnam, Norway, Chile, Malaysia, Guinea, Panama, Costa Rica, Congo, Syria, Mexico, Brazil, Bulgaria, Mali, Sierra Leone and Romania. In fact, the subsidiary has entered more than 60 markets since 2000. Product development has also taken place, including the introduction of new sizes of aluminum cans. However, the most significant indication is a greenfield investment to establish a modern brewery in Novosibirsk.

The level of autonomy in the subsidiary is naturally high for several reasons. First, the subsidiary holds a significant position on the Russian market. Second, high autonomy is driven by the fact that operational flexibility is needed to operate in the Russian market, given its diverse cultural aspects. Third, autonomous management is part of the tradition in Baltika, as the subsidiary has consistently emphasized decentralized decision-making among local managers (Alcacer et al. 2010). Fourth, autonomy is necessary because much of BBH's success is the result of connections with external partners, as is typical in weaker institutional settings. Despite the recession in the Russian market and increasing difficulties caused by additional regulations, the subsidiary has successfully grown and widened its products and market portfolios, and it has been able to make significant investments in capacity.

CONCLUSION

In this chapter we have looked at developments in subsidiary autonomy and strategic responsibilities in value chain activities. The extant literature emphasizes the importance of both dimensions in headquarter–subsidiary relations and stresses that the degree of either aspect is context dependent. We illustrate the forms and degrees of subsidiary autonomy and strategic responsibilities using the Danish brewery, Carlsberg, as a case study.

Carlsberg is an experienced international player in the brewery sector. It has developed a certain acquisition-integration strategy over the years, and this strategy influences the strategic development of the acquired subsidiaries and their level of autonomy. Typically, best practices are transferred from Carlsberg, mainly in the form of product and process technologies, and managerial skills. Plants are divested, some brands are spun off, and the Carlsberg or the Tuborg brand is added to the local product portfolio. However, over time, some subsidiaries gain new value chain mandates or they substantially increase their scale in terms of production capacities or the markets in which they operate.

However, Carlsberg seems to encompass stories of both failure and success, where Tetley and Holsten are examples of the former. Both breweries possessed significant market positions but suffered from negative market developments that they were unable to bypass. In both cases, the outcome was the removal of a range of strategic responsibilities. In contrast, in the Feldschlösschen, Okocim and Kronenbourg cases the subsidiaries managed to overcome such problems. After a period of mandate losses they appeared to be on positive developmental trends. However, an important finding is that this is a parallel process, as these subsidiaries simultaneously lost mandates in some value chain activities while they gained mandates in others. Finally, Baltika represents a special case. It successfully broadened its activities in a period characterized by a decline in the market resulting from the introduction of new regulations. The size of this subsidiary and the value of its brand put it in a central position where headquarters depended on its resources in terms of revenue and capacity. The subsidiary could therefore gain greater strategic responsibilities in all areas.

Through this analysis we contribute to research on subsidiary strategic development by demonstrating that subsidiaries undergo a simultaneously negative and positive process in some cases. Most research views subsidiaries as entrepreneurial units aiming for more strategic mandates. However, we see subsidiaries as more narrowly defined units in terms of value chain activities and autonomy that act as hybrids in which these mandates are constantly in play.

We recommend that future research investigates industry and geographical effects. The brewery sector in Western Europe is under pressure and, in some markets, subsidiaries operating in this business are struggling to survive. At the same time, some subsidiaries seem to be able to gain new strategic responsibilities and develop autonomy. To further examine the development path in terms of subsidiary strategic responsibility and autonomy, we recommend a qualitative research design in which managers are asked to reveal their considerations and motivations regarding specific events in the subsidiary's history. Given its focus on archival data, this chapter only presents a limited view of such processes. Furthermore, other breweries and other geographical regions can be investigated. Finally, entry modes in terms of greenfield subsidiaries can be analysed.

REFERENCES

Alcacer, J.R., R. Molander and R. Mabud (2010), 'Baltic Beverages Holding: competing in a globalized world', Harvard Business School Strategy Unit Case No. 710-471.

Ambos, T.C. and J. Birkinshaw (2010), 'Headquarters' attention and its effect on subsidiary performance', *Management International Review*, **50**, 449–69.

Astley, W.G. and P.S. Sachdeva (1984), 'Structural sources of intraorganizational power. A theoretical synthesis', *Academy of Management Review*, **9** (1), 104–13.

Berlingske Tidende (1997), 'BASS interesseret køber', *Berlingske Tidende*, 26 September.
Berlingske Tidende (2000a), 'Carlsberg vil vende polsk fiasko', *Berlingske Tidende*, 23 March.
Berlingske Tidende (2000b), 'Elefanten rører på sig', *Berlingske Tidende*, 11 November.
Berlingske Tidende (2004a), 'Bureaukratiet blev afskaffet', *Berlingske Tidende*, 5 March.
Berlingske Tidende (2004b), 'Polsk vinderkultur', *Berlingske Tidende*, 5 March.
Birkinshaw, J. and A.J. Morrison (1995), 'Configurations of strategy and structure in subsidiaries of multinational corporations', *Journal of International Business Studies*, **26** (4), 729–53.
Bouquet, C. and J. Birkinshaw (2008), 'Managing power in the multinational corporation: how low-power actors gain influence', *Journal of Management*, **34** (3), 477–508.
Brooke, M.Z. (1984), *Centralization and Autonomy. A Study in Organization Behaviour*, London and New York: Holt, Rinehart and Winston Brown.
Business Insights Essentials (2012), 'Carlsberg', accessed 30 October 2012 at http://bi.galegroup.com/essentials/article/GALE%7CI2501312365/bb974b9d5b884c6 34a9558f1ca97fe3f?u=cbs.
Business Today (2007), 'Ale and hearty', *Business Today*, 21 October.
Børsen (1997a), 'Historien om Carlsberg-Tetley', *Børsen*, 30 June.
Børsen (1997b), 'Drastisk spareplan fra Carlsberg', *Børsen*, 26 September.
Børsen (1998a), 'Carlsberg ser lys for enden af UK-tunnel', *Børsen*, 24 February.
Børsen (1998b), 'UK-overskud falder', *Børsen*, 1 December.
Børsen (2000), 'Bass-salg skaber nye Carlsberg-muligheder', *Børsen*, 16 June.
Børsen (2001), 'Kursløft til Carlsberg trods stagnation', *Børsen*, 14 May.
Børsen (2004a), 'Carlsbergs vækststrategi hæmmes', *Børsen*, 22 January.
Børsen (2004b), 'Usikkert om bryggeriernes vækstjagt vil lykkes', *Børsen* 2 February.
Børsen (2004c), 'Notespalte – Udland', *Børsen*, 18 August.
Børsen (2008), 'BørsenFakta – Baltika Breweries', *Børsen*, 19 November.
Børsen (2010a), 'Fyringer og nedskrivninger truer i Carlsberg', *Børsen*, 19 February.
Børsen (2010b), 'Carlsberg-chef sender ansatte ud af kontorerne', *Børsen*, 16 September.
Børsen (2010c), 'Carlsberg går ind i afrikansk ølkrig', *Børsen*, 12 December.
Børsen (2011a), 'Carlsberg sælger tysk bryggeri – taber millioner', *Børsen*, 3 January.
Børsen (2011b), 'Fransk hovedpine til Carlsberg', *Børsen*, 16 May.
Børsen Magasin (2011), 'Ølbossen inspicerer virkeligheden: Så starter dødsruten', *Børsen Magasin*, 28 September.
Carlsberg (1997), 'Three-year plan for a strong, independent Carlsberg-Tetley', press release, 25 September.
Carlsberg (2000), 'Carlsberg acquires largest Swiss brewery Feldschlösschen', press release, 3 November.
Carlsberg (2005), 'Carlsberg UK starts production of Holsten Pils', press release, 11 October.
Carlsberg (various years), *Annual Reports*, Copenhagen: Carlsberg.
Carlsberg Information til aktionærer (2006), 'Nyt', *Carlsberg Information til aktionærer*, 9 August.

Cerrato, D. (2006), 'The multinational enterprise as an internal market system', *International Business Review*, 15, 253–77.

Datamonitor (2004), *Alcoholic Drinks in Germany: Industry Profile*, London: Datamonitor

Datamonitor (2008), *MarketWatch: Global Round-up. Company Spotlight: Carlsberg*, London: Datamonitor.

Datamonitor (2011), *Carlsberg A/S: Company Profile*, London: Datamonitor.

Dieng, S., C. Dörrenbächer and J. Gammelgaard (2009), 'Subsidiary brands as a resource and the redistribution of decision-making authority following acquisitions', in C. Cooper and S. Finkelstein (eds), *Advances in Mergers and Acquisitions*, Bingley: Emerald, pp. 141–60.

Direkt (2007), 'Carlsberg/ny CEO: Vi skal lære af "drivet" i BBH og Østeuropa', 3 September.

Dörrenbächer, C. and J. Gammelgaard (2006), 'Subsidiary role development: the effect of micro-political headquarters-subsidiary negotiations on the product, market, and value-added scope of foreign owned subsidiaries', *Journal of International Management*, 12 (3), 266–83.

Dörrenbächer, C. and J. Gammelgaard (2010), 'Multinational corporations, inter-organizational networks and subsidiary charter removals', *Journal of World Business*, 45, 206–16.

Egelhoff, W.G., L. Gorman and S. McCormick (1998), 'Using technology as a path to subsidiary development', in J. Birkinshaw and N. Hood (eds), *Multinational Corporate Evolution and Subsidiary Development*, Houndmills: Macmillan Press, pp. 213–38.

Forsgren, M., U. Holm and J. Johanson (2005), *Managing the Embedded Multinational: A Business Network View*, Cheltenham, UK and Northampton, MA, USA: Edward Elgar.

Galunic, D.C. and K.M. Eisenhardt (1996), 'The evolution of intracorporate domains: divisional charter losses in high-technology multidivisonal corporations', *Organization Science*, 7 (3), 255–82.

Gammelgaard, J. (2002), 'Gaining competences in the multinational corporation through international acquisitions: an investigation of foreign Danish acquisitions 1994–1998', PhD dissertation, Copenhagen: Copenhagen Business School Press.

Gammelgaard, J., F. McDonald, A. Stephan, H. Tüselmann and C. Dörrenbächer (2012), 'The impact of increases in subsidiary autonomy and network relationships on performance', *International Business Review*, 21 (6), 1158–72.

Geppert. M., C. Dörrenbächer, J. Gammelgaard and I. Taplin (forthcoming), 'Managerial risk-taking in international acquisitions in the brewery industry: institutional and ownership influences compared', *British Journal of Management*.

Ghoshal, S. and C.A. Bartlett (2005), 'The multinational corporation as an inter-organizational network', in S. Ghoshal and D.E. Westney (eds), *Organization Theory and the Multinational Corporation*, Houndmills: Palgrave MacMillan, pp. 68–92.

Glamann, K. (1997), *Vores Øl: og Hele Verdens: Carlsberggruppen siden 1970*, Copenhagen: Gyldendal.

Griffith, D.A., S.T. Cavusgil and S. Xu (2008), 'Emerging themes in international business research', *Journal of International Business Studies*, 39 (7), 1220–35.

Holm, U. and T. Pedersen (2000), *The Emergence and Impact of MNC Centres of Excellence – A Subsidiary Perspective*, Houndmills: MacMillan Press.

ICM (2008), 'Carlsberg to shut Leeds brewery in 2011', The Institute of Commercial Management, accessed April 2009 at http://news.icm.ac.uk/retail/carlsberg-to-shut-leeds-brewery-in-2011/724/.

Interbrand (2010), *Best Russian Brands 2010: Creating and Managing Brand Value*, Moscow: Interbrand.

Iversen, M.J. and A. Arnold (2008), 'Carlsberg: regulation of the home market and international expansion', in S. Fellman, M. Iversen, H. Sjögren and L. Thue (eds), *Creating Nordic Capitalism: The Business History of a Competitive Periphery*, Houndmills: Palgrave Macmillan, pp. 365–91.

Just-drinks (2012), 'FRANCE: Carlsberg Kronenbourg to build EUR17m research centre', *Just-drinks*, 6 February.

Jyllands Posten (1998), 'Carlsberg øger I England', *Jyllands Posten*, 28 December.

Jyllands Posten (2004), 'Bryggeri: Feldschlösschen er Carlsbergs lille guldæg', *Jyllands Posten*, 4 August.

Koudal, P. and D. Engel (2007), 'Globalization and emerging markets', in H.L. Lee and C.-Y. Lee (eds), *Building Supply Chain Excellence in Emerging Economies*, New York: Springer, pp. 37–64.

Luo, Y. (2003), 'Market-seeking MNEs in an emerging market: how parent-subsidiary links shape overseas success', *Journal of International Business Studies*, **34** (3), 290–309.

Mahoney, J.T. and R. Pandian (1992), 'The resource-based view within the conversation of strategic management', *Strategic Management Journal*, **13**, 363–80.

Malnight, T.W. (1996), 'The transition from decentralized to network-based MNC structures: an evolutionary perspective', *Journal of International Business Studies*, **27** (1), 43–66.

Marketing Week (2007), 'Carlsberg brings in Polish pilsner brand on draught', *Marketing Week*, 28 June.

Meyer, K. and Y.T.T. Tran (2006), 'Market penetration and acquisition strategies for emerging economies', *Long Range Planning*, **39** (2), 177–97.

Mudambi, R. (2008), 'Location, control and innovation in knowledge-intensive industries', *Journal of Economic Geography*, **8**, 699–725.

Niederhut-Bollmann, C.N. and L. Theuvsen (2008), 'Strategic management in turbulent markets: the case of German and Croatian brewing industries', *Journal of East European Management Studies*, **1**, 63–88.

Poland Business News (2002), 'Poland-brewery-Carlsberg, Okocim', *Poland Business News*, 12 August.

Protz, R. (2004), 'Quality brewing from a big player', *All About Beer Magazine*, **24** (6).

RB-Børsen (2008a), 'Carlsberg indvier to indiske bryggerier', *RB-Børsen*, 10 April.

RB-Børsen (2008b), 'Carlsberg: Feldschlösschen har haft gavn af ejerskab', *RB-Børsen*, 16 June.

RB-Børsen (2011a), 'Carlsberg taber 130 mio. kr. på at sælge bryggeri', *RB-Børsen*, 3 January.

RB-Børsen (2011b), 'Carlsberg: Tyskerne drikker mindre øl', *RB-Børsen*, 3 May.

RB-Børsen (2011c), 'Carlsberg: Øger markedsandel i Polen', *RB-Børsen*, 19 October.

Reuters Finans (2009), 'Carlsberg udvider polsk bryggeri – nyhedsbrev', *Reuters Finans*, 29 April.

Reuters Finans (2012), 'Carlsberg sees German brand a boost in Russia', *Reuters Finans, 10 May.*

Ritzaus Bureau (2001), 'Strategien hos Carlsberg uændret efter Lindeløvs fratræden', *Ritzaus Bureau*, 21 August.

Ritzaus Bureau (2008), 'Carlsberg: Feldschlösschen-direktør til Kronenbourg', *Ritzaus Bureau*, 26 August.

Ritzaus Bureau (2010), 'Carlsberg: Lukker bryggeri og samler produktion i Schweiz', *Ritzaus Bureau*, 31 August.

Sandberg, P. (2010), 'The creation of big business in the Swedish brewing industry during the aftermath of the Second World War', *Scandinavian Economic History Review*, **58** (1), 43–59.

Surlemont, B. (1998), 'A typology of centres within multinational corporations: an empirical investigation', in J. Birkinshaw and N. Hood (eds), *Multinational Corporate Evolution and Subsidiary Development*, Houndmills: Macmillan Press, pp. 162–88.

Taggart, J. (1999), 'US MNC subsidiaries in the UK: characteristics and strategic role', in F. Burton, M. Chapman and A. Cross (eds), *International Business Organization*, Houndmills: MacMillan Press, pp. 29–46.

The Grocer (2006), 'Poland scores a hat-trick of lagers', *The Grocer*, 11 March.

The Guardian (2008), 'Tetley's Yorkshire brewery set to close', *The Guardian*, 5 November.

Tran, Y., V. Mahnke and B. Ambos (2010), 'The effect of quantity, quality and timing of headquarters-initiated knowledge flows on subsidiary performance', *Management International Review*, **50**, 493–511.

Verbeke, A. and T.P. Kenworthy (2008), 'Multidivisional *vs* metanational governance of the multinational enterprise', *Journal of International Business Studies*, **39** (6), 940–56.

Wang, J., X. Liu and X. Li (2009), 'A dual-role typology of multinational subsidiaries', *International Business Review*, **18**, 578–91.

White, R.E. and T.A. Poynter (1984), 'Strategies for foreign-owned subsidiaries in Canada', *Business Quarterly*, **49** (2), 59–69.

Yamin, M. and P.N. Ghauri (2010), 'A critical assessment of the business network perspective on HQ control in multinational companies', in U. Andersson and U. Holm (eds), *Managing the Contemporary Multinational: The Role of Headquarters*, Cheltenham, UK and Northampton, MA, USA: Edward Elgar, pp. 125–37.

Young, S. and A.T. Tavares (2004), 'Centralization and autonomy: back to the future', *International Business Review*, **13**, 215–37.

8. Post-acquisition resource redeployment and synergy creation: the case of Heineken's large acquisitions Scottish & Newcastle and FEMSA

Christoph Dörrenbächer and Andreas Zaby

INTRODUCTION

In a recent TV commercial, a Lilliputian, followed by a Protestant priest, an orthodox Jew, a nun, a neurotic (with his beloved duck), a football hooligan, a model and a horse, walk into a bar. As the commercial tells us, they all came to have a Heineken beer.[1] This commercial is precisely what Heineken is about: selling beer, and, in particular, selling its top brand Heineken to as many people as possible throughout the world.

It is quite a tradition at Heineken to see the whole world as a market. Immediately after Heineken's foundation in the second half of the 19th century the company started exporting beer to neighbouring European countries. From 1914 onwards licensed production took place in regions as diverse as Asia, America and the Caribbean. The first foreign direct investments were undertaken in the 1920s in Belgium and the Dutch East Indies (Jacobs and Maas 1991). Today, Heineken (in its own words) 'is a proud, independent global brewer committed to surprise and excite consumers everywhere', with its flagship brand 'Heineken', considered to be 'the first and only truly global beer brand, enjoyed in 178 countries around the world' (Heineken 2012a, p. 3).

This undeniable success has been achieved by the careful management of the founding family during Heineken's almost 150-year-long history, with Freddy Heineken, who ran the business from the mid 1950s until the 1990s, playing an important role. The main vehicle for Heineken's global coverage has been an extraordinarily large number of cross-border acquisitions (and partial shareholdings). Many small- and medium-sized acquisitions throughout the 1980s and 1990s preceded a few larger acquisitions in the early 2000s, as well as two very large acquisitions in 2008 (Scottish & Newcastle of the UK) and 2010 (FEMSA of Mexico).

From a theoretical perspective there are two basic rationales for acquiring other companies: (1) to grow in size and market share and (2) to access and make use of the strategic resources and competences of the target (with both reasons potentially applying at the same time) (Wernerfelt 1984). Growth in size and market share is clearly a strong explanation for the many international acquisitions Heineken, as well as other players in the global brewing industry, have undertaken in the past (Ebneth and Theuvsen 2007). After all, the brewing industry has recently been consolidating on a global scale (see the introductory chapter of this volume). To what extent, however, acquisitions in the brewing industry are spurred by the desire to access strategic resources and competences and make use of them is less clear. Taking Heineken as an example, this question is examined here.

A recent study investigating three small- and medium-size acquisitions of Heineken in Europe found that Heineken only very selectively made use of the resources and competences of the target company (Dieng et al. 2009). This finding, however, might be a natural outcome when a large and experienced multinational corporation (MNC) is taking over small local breweries. The question remains to what extent the very large acquisitions Heineken more recently undertook led to an extended use of newly accessed resources and competences.

In the remainder of the chapter we will first screen the acquisition-related literature in order to clarify what it means to access and to make use of newly acquired resources and competences. We will show that leveraging different types of synergies by recombining the resources of the acquirer and the target is the basis for creating value. We will also shed some light on the fact that post-acquisition value creation is a precarious process with many prerequisites.

Next, by looking into Heineken's internationalization history we will show that the company has a particularly large amount of experience with acquisitions. Comparing the more recent acquisition activity of Heineken with the activities of its main competitors we will further demonstrate that Heineken has comparatively strong experience in leveraging synergies due to the high number and large geographical spread of its past acquisitions.

Focusing on Heineken's two largest acquisitions (Scottish & Newcastle and FEMSA) we then empirically investigate what synergies Heineken, as one of the most experienced acquirers in the industry, expected to leverage. Based on the data available we will finally give a first account of how successful Heineken was in leveraging newly acquired resources from large acquisitions.

The chapter concludes by discussing how small and large acquisitions of Heineken differ in terms of leveraging resources and what the reasons are for our finding for the rather one-sided use of newly acquired resources.

ACQUISITIONS, SYNERGIES AND VALUE CREATION

International acquisitions are an important mode for firms to internationalize. Overall, there is empirical evidence that acquisition clearly outpaces greenfield investment as the principal mode of internationalization, at least when considering real economy indicators such as employment data (Wortmann 2008).

There are numerous reasons why firms grow abroad by acquisitions. Investigating both a large number of theoretical as well as empirical contributions, Gammelgaard (2002) discovered eight main motives and more than 20 subordinate motives for this method of growth. Studying the relative importance of these motives empirically from the 1970s until 2000, growth and market-related motives (such as gaining market share or getting access to new markets) have been very important throughout. Similarly, cost-related motives, most notably the wish to reduce costs of production and administration, have been found to strongly drive acquisitions at all times. Other reasons, such as risk diversification, the reduction of financial costs, empire building or undervaluation of the target, have been found to have rather low empirical importance. However, further reasons, so-called resource-related reasons, such as acquiring firms for the sake of gaining access to and making use of the resources and competences of the target, have been found to have significantly grown in importance over time and to equal market, growth and cost-related motives.

This leads to two basic types of acquisitions that can be considered important when looking at the current acquisition merry-go-round in the brewing industry, (1) outcome-based acquisitions: here desired outcomes, such as, for example, increase in size, market share and efficiency, are directly accessible through the acquisition; (2) resource-based acquisitions: here the focus is neither solely nor prima facie on outcomes but rather on the underlying resources and competences that create particular outcomes and that cannot be accessed without acquiring the company. Such resources can be particular technologies, brands, skills (capabilities), processes or routines (Wernerfelt 1984); such competences have been defined as superior managerial abilities to coordinate resources and capabilities (Gammelgaard 2002).

Newly acquired resources and competences unfold their value only when redeployed in a resource reconfiguration process following the acquisition (Hill et al. 2001). Thereby synergies need to be unleashed by combining existing resources with newly acquired resources, either in the acquiring company, the acquired company, or a third unit within the MNC (Capron et al. 2001). There are different types of synergies that can be developed (Chatterjee 1986):

(1) Cost-saving synergies occur when technology or superior managerial knowledge is redeployed from the acquirer to the target. In that case the acquiring company uses existing resources and competences at full capacity by combining them with highly specific complementary resources of the target. Such strategies are most likely to occur in industries '. . . where local firms possess specific, rare resources such as access to political elites or local brands, but are weak in terms of managerial and technological competences' (Estrin and Meyer 2011, p. 485). This situation is to be found quite often in the brewing industry, where small- and medium-sized (often family owned) firms possess unique access to distribution channels and own valuable local brands but miss superior managerial knowledge, for example in product management, general marketing expertise, or operations management. Cost-saving synergies are then derived through modernization processes that typically include the relocation of certain activities to the acquirer as well as the downsizing or closing of operations at the target.

(2) Revenue-generating synergies occur when resources of the acquiring and the acquired company are combined in order to generate more revenues. Such synergies might take the form of product enhancements (adding features to existing products, expanding service offerings), extended product lines, new products or new markets for certain products (Wiklund and Shepherd 2009). They can occur through resource transfers from the acquiring company to the target and vice versa. In the brewing industry, evidence of these synergies may then be, for instance, a transfer of global or speciality brands from the acquirer to the acquired company. Vice versa, it might take the form of local brands with potential beyond the local market being rolled out in some third countries or throughout the whole network of the acquirer. According to an empirical study by Capron and Hulland (2009, p. 51) that cuts across many industries, overall '. . . brands tend to be more redeployed from target to acquirer'.

Leveraging acquisition synergies, however, is a precarious process with some prerequisites. Following Larsson and Finkelstein (1999, p. 1), '. . .

synergy realization is a function of the similarity and complementarity of the two merging businesses (combination potential), the extent of interaction and co-ordination during the organizational integration process and the lack of employee resistance to the combined entity'. Vice versa, ill-fitting resources, a lack of integration effort and employee resistance are seen as basic reasons for the failure of acquisitions to realize synergies and in the same vein to increase the value of the acquiring company and its stakeholders (King et al. 2004). In addition, many studies have shown that the propensity to fail is increased if the target is overpriced; that is, excessive premiums are paid for expected synergies (for example, Eschen and Bresser 2005). Following Sirower (1997), about 70 per cent of acquisitions do not pay off in terms of value creation. In line with this finding, Ebneth and Theuvsen (2007, p. 401), in their study of large mergers and acquisitions (M&As) in the brewing industry, conclude that 'at least on average M&A in the brewing industry did not create value for the acquiring firms' stockholders'. This, however, indicates that some acquiring firms do better than others. Here Geppert et al. (forthcoming) showed that brewery companies from coordinated market economies with a family or foundation background incurred fewer risks with their large acquisitions and turned out be more successful than publicly-owned breweries from liberal market economies (which incurred high risks with their large acquisitions). The study also corroborates a number of other studies that see acquisition experience as important for successful acquisitions.

According to Hitt et al. (2001), acquisition experience, that is, learning from previous success and failure in acquisitions, materializes in a better selection of targets and in improved integration processes. Focusing on resource generation, acquisition experience leads to enhanced capabilities in detecting, acquiring, developing, accumulating, using and combining resources (Wiklund and Shepherd 2009). Acquisition experience is a historically contingent process that resides both within individuals' knowledge and in organizational routines (Prashantham and Floyd 2012). It is built through repeated practice (Eisenhardt and Martin 2000). Focusing on resource combination activities that are considered central to the value creation process, Wiklund and Shepherd (2009) argue that firms that have been engaged more often and more intensely in resource combination activities develop a stronger capability to discover and leverage synergies. According to Haleblian and Finkelstein (1999) this, in particular, is the case when the targets are from the same industry. Here previous acquisitions lead to an 'appropriate generalization of experience', as the new targets are similar to the previous ones (Haleblian and Finkelstein 1999, p. 49). This clearly applies to the brewing industry, as here most acquisitions are horizontal, that is, within the same industry.

This makes acquisition experience (in terms of numbers of acquisitions performed) a strong indicator for acquisition performance. Differences, however, remain with the size of the acquisition, as the complexity of tasks involved and the power distribution between the acquirer and the target is rather different in small and large acquisitions. Here inappropriate generalization errors might occur in particular when small acquisitions precede larger ones. Differences also remain with regard to the home country of the target, as almost all of the more recent acquisitions in the nationally consolidated brewery markets have been across borders. Here greater experience with foreign acquisitions has been found to pay off in terms of performance. As Collins et al. (2009) have found, learning through prior international acquisitions helps firms to deal with the many challenges involved in entering and competing in new international markets. Companies that in the past have acquired internationally '. . . not only learn[ed] about how to deal with different institutional environments but also about selecting acquisition targets, negotiating the acquisition deal and how to integrate the acquired firm in foreign countries' (Collins et al. 2009, p. 1333). In addition, they found that previous experience in the country of a target improved acquisition performance.

INTERNATIONALIZATION AND GROWTH HISTORY

Founded in 1864, Heineken more or less immediately began to export its beer to neighbouring European countries (especially to France) as well as to the Dutch East Indies (now Indonesia). These first steps abroad were followed by an initial expansion in a broad array of regions including Asia, North America and the Caribbean from 1914 onwards, mostly through licensed production. This created a springboard for a much stronger internationalization starting in the late 1920s. The first foreign brewery was acquired in Brussels in 1927 and a new one was built in Surabaja in the Dutch East Indies in 1929. Two years later forces were joined with soft drink producer Fraser and Naeve in Singapore to further expand into Asia. From 1933 onwards, following the lifting of prohibition, exports also went to the United States.

Further internationalizing occurred in Asia, North and South America and Africa in the following decades; Heineken initially made little effort to build up a strong foreign presence in Europe. Despite some success in exporting its premium brands to other European countries and the acquisition of interests in Belgium (1955, Albert Maltings) and Italy (1960, Group Mobiliare Industriale Cisalpina), Heineken only had a 3 per cent share of the overall, still nationally confined, European market in 1972 (Smit 1996, p. 166). In the following years Heineken undertook considerable efforts to internationalize in Europe, way ahead of its competitors. In 1972 the third largest French Brewery (ALBRA group) was taken over. This was followed by a large number of acquisitions in Southern Europe (Italy, Spain and Greece), Northern Europe (Ireland, Switzerland and Belgium) and, since the 1990s, in Central and Eastern Europe (Hungary, Bulgaria, Slovakia, Poland and Russia). Successful attempts to enter the two largest European markets – Germany and the UK – were made rather recently. In Germany, Heineken has been acquiring minority stakes in larger regional brewery groups since 2001 (for example, Schörghuber Gruppe in 2001, Karlsberg Gruppe in 2002) next to acquiring smaller breweries (for example, Hoepfener Bauerei in 2004, Würzburger Hofbräu in 2005). In the UK Heineken failed to acquire Bass in 2000 and only recently gained a noteworthy entry to the market by jointly taking over Scottish & Newcastle together with Carlsberg of Denmark in 2008 (see below).

Next to a widening internationalization in Europe, the last 20 years have also seen attempts to wipe out blind spots on the Heineken world map. Investments were made in China (1988/2004), Latin America (1983/2004/2010) and, more recently, in India (2008/2010). However, the internationalization in Europe was and still is very strong compared to the incumbent and the more recent internationalization elsewhere in the world; even in 2011 Heineken was still a home-region oriented MNC. According to a widely shared definition by Rugman and Verbeke (2004, p. 7), a company is home-region oriented if at least 50 per cent of its sales are in its home region. In 2011 Heineken earned 64.2 per cent of its revenues in its home region Europe, 23.5 per cent in the Americas, 13.0 per cent in Africa/Middle East and 1.3 per cent in the Asia Pacific (Heineken 2012a, the percentage discrepancy is due to head office eliminations). It is worth noting, however, that Heineken more recently, in particular due to some larger acquisitions after the millennium (Bravo International of Russia, BBAG/Brau Union of Austria with a strong presence in Central and Eastern Europe and FEMSA of Mexico), has strongly expanded its presence in emerging beer markets. At the end of 2010 (including the FEMSA acquisition), 68 per cent of Heineken's beer volume and 57 per cent of Heineken's earnings before interest and taxes (EBIT) was delivered from emerging markets (mostly from Eastern Europe, Latin America and Africa) (Heineken 2011, p. 6).

Overall, Heineken has grown quite big while internationalizing. Over the decades from 1960–2010 the volume of beer produced increased approximately by a factor of 40 (see Table 8.1). In 2010 it owned 140 breweries in 70 countries and employed some 65 000 employees.

Table 8.1   Heineken's production volume (mhl)

1960	1970	1980	1990	2000	2010
3.8	11.3	25.9	53.5	97.9	145.9

Source: Orbis company profile, Heineken N.V. accessed 9 October 2012, annual reports (various years).

ACQUISITION EXPERIENCE

As the previous section indicates, acquisitions have played a strong role in the growth and internationalization history of Heineken. Throughout the 1980s and 1990s Heineken acquired a large number of small- and medium-sized breweries (that is, breweries with an annual sales volume of up to two million hl) (Dieng et al. 2009, p. 149). This was followed by a few larger acquisitions in the early 2000s (breweries with an annual sales volume of up to 16 million hl) and two very large acquisitions: the 2008 takeover of Scottish & Newcastle of the UK (with an annual sales volume of 30 million hl) and the 2010 acquisition of FEMSA of Mexico (with an annual sales volume of 41 million hl) (see Table 8.2).

The previous section also reveals a distinct form of capturing foreign markets. If market structures do not allow for a 'big bang' market entry by one or two large acquisitions, Heineken follows a long-term strategy of acquiring first a platform from which the market is screened and then adds through further acquisitions, bit by bit until a strong market position is reached. This also includes joint ventures and partial (minority) acquisitions, with many subsequent increases in stakes to follow (see Table 8.2). Recently, this strategy can be observed in the regionally fragmented German market, in which family ownership often forecloses majority shareholdings. Up until 2007 Heineken has altogether acquired seven minority shareholdings, including the two somewhat larger regional brewery groups Schörghofer Gruppe and Karlsberg Gruppe. This strategy of incremental market capturing with its inherent overlaps creates a fertile ground for subsequent consolidation, a process that starts when sufficient activities are acquired and that leads to a full integration of the local firms into a regional Heineken subsidiary (such as, for example, Heineken France, or Heineken UK) in case full ownership status can be reached.

As theoretically outlined above, acquisition experience increases with the number and geographical spread of acquisitions performed in the past. Heineken has a long history of acquisitions, with acquiring foreign companies being the preferred mode of internationalization and growth, from at least the 1970s onwards. A comparison with the acquisitions activities

Table 8.2   Heineken's largest acquisitions until 2012 (by sales volume)

Company	Country	Year	First stake in per cent	Sales volume (in mhl) in year before acquisition
Femsa Cerveza	Mexico	2010	100.0	41.0
Scottish & Newcastle	UK	2008	100.0	29.7 (excl. BBH)
BBAG/Brau Union	Austria	2004	>50.0	16.0
Schörghofer Gruppe (Brau Holding International AG)	Germany	2001	49.9	10.5
Cruzcampo SA	Spain	2000	88.2	6.0
Karlsberg International Brand GmbH	Germany	2002	40.0	4.9
Bravo International	Russia	2002	100.0	2.9

Source: Zephyr database, accessed 9 October 2012.

Table 8.3   Takeover activities of large breweries 1997–2012 (numbers)

	Acquisitions (>50 per cent)	Minority stakes	Joint ventures	Increase resulting in majority stakes*	Increase in minority stakes (<50 per cent)
Heineken	39	10	7	22	2
AB InBev	34	11	3	19	2
Carlsberg	29	5	5	33	4
SABMiller	23	6	2	13	0

Notes: *Includes increases within majority stakes.

Source: Zephyr database, accessed 9 October 2012.

of other leading global breweries from 1997–2012 (see Table 8.3) further reveals that Heineken has been most active in fully or partially acquiring other companies or forming joint ventures.

Moreover, way ahead of its competitors AB InBev, Carlsberg and SABMiller, these activities involved a total of 37 countries located across all major regions of the world (Table 8.4). This leads to the conclusion that Heineken is among the most experienced acquirers in the industry, if not the most experienced of all.

Concerning the two largest acquisitions by Heineken (Scottish &

Table 8.4   Overall number and regional distribution of target countries

	Total number of target countries (deals*)	Target countries Europe	Target countries South America	Target countries North America	Target countries Africa	Target countries Asia Pacific
Heineken	37 (56)	16	5	1	8	7
AB InBev	23 (48)	15	4	2	0	2
Carlsberg	17 (39)	11	0	0	0	6
SABMiller	21 (29)	15	1	1	4	1

Notes: *Acquisitions, minority stakes and joint ventures only.

Source: Zephyr database, accessed 9 October 2012.

Newcastle and FEMSA, see Table 8.2), the following section will explore in detail what cost-saving and revenue-generating synergies were expected by Heineken and to what extent Heineken, as one of the most experienced acquirers, could leverage expected synergies.

SYNERGY CREATION THROUGH LARGE ACQUISITIONS: CASE EVIDENCE

In April 2012 Heineken's chief executive officer (CEO), Jean-Francois van Boxmeer, outlined some of the principles followed by the company in its frequent takeovers. According to van Boxmeer, Heineken's goal is to form 'one company' based on 'one culture'; that is, a 'culture of performance, belonging and sense of purpose'. He further stated that this culture was based on a set of values: 'passion for quality and respect for people and environment' that 'unite' the company. The CEO went on to stress that Heineken imposes control systems and centralizes certain tasks following its acquisitions. However, he also pointed out that Heineken attempts to absorb good practices that are observed at the acquired companies (van Boxmeer 2012).

As argued above, there is evidence that smaller takeovers by Heineken were hardly motivated by the wish to access particular resources, capabilities or, in the words of CEO van Boxmeer, 'good practices' (Dieng et al. 2009). However, as the size of the target companies acquired by Heineken has varied considerably, it can be hypothesized that small target companies may have less to offer in terms of transferable resources and

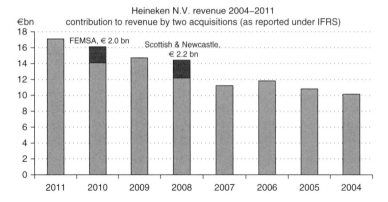

Source: Heineken (2008a, 2010a).

*Figure 8.1   Heineken N.V. contribution of the S&N and FEMSA
             acquisitions to revenue*

capabilities and that resource-seeking acquisition motives may be more prominent in significantly larger deals.

Among Heineken's many acquisitions, two transactions stand out concerning the size of the target companies. These are the 2008 acquisition of Scottish & Newcastle, which Heineken purchased as a joint buyer with Carlsberg, and the 2010 acquisition of the beer division of Fomento Económico Mexicano (FEMSA). Both acquisitions contributed to significant top-line growth for Heineken. As illustrated in Figure 8.1, the purchase of parts of Scottish & Newcastle in 2008 contributed about €2.2 bn to Heineken's revenue in 2008 on an eight-month basis (Heineken 2008a).[2] Similarly, the FEMSA transaction resulted in exceptional revenue growth. The reported revenue contribution in 2010 was €2.0 bn on an eight-month basis (Heineken 2010a).[3]

The following sections will provide a closer look at these two significant and similarly revenue-enhancing acquisitions by Heineken. In two separate short case studies the background of the transactions will be explained and a special focus will be provided on the motives underlying the takeovers. In particular, the cases will shed light on the specific types of synergies, that is, cost-saving or revenue-generating synergies, that were sought in each deal.

The Acquisition of Scottish & Newcastle

On 25 January 2008, following a lengthy takeover battle, Sunrise Acquisitions, a special purpose entity jointly owned by Carlsberg and

Heineken announced its bid to acquire the British brewing company Scottish & Newcastle, headquartered in Edinburgh, Scotland. After the bidder increased the bid price three times over the course of the negotiations (Bloomberg 2008), the final bid price in this all-cash consideration deal was 800 pence per share, valuing the equity of Scottish & Newcastle at about £7.8 bn on a fully diluted basis. This valuation represents an earnings multiple of 14.3x (EBITDA) (Heineken and Carlsberg 2008).

Scottish & Newcastle was, at the time of the acquisition, a brewing company that was listed on the London Stock Exchange with a longstanding tradition in Scotland and England and operations in a total of 15 countries. In 2008 three of the ten top-selling beer brands in Europe were owned by Scottish & Newcastle: Baltika, through BBH, which was a joint venture with Carlsberg, Foster's and Kronenbourg 1664. In addition to its beer brands, the company also owned other beverage brands, such as Strongbow for apple cider.

Prior to the transaction, Carlsberg and Heineken had agreed on how to split the assets of Scottish & Newcastle.[4] According to this agreement, Heineken acquired Scottish & Newcastle's operations in the UK, Ireland, Portugal, Finland, Belgium, the USA and India. All other operations, such as the BBH joint venture in Russia and other Eastern European countries, as well as the operations in France, Greece, China and Vietnam, went to Carlsberg. At the time of the acquisition, Heineken was the largest brewer in Europe with European revenue more than twice as high as Carlsberg, Europe's number two.

Scottish & Newcastle had strong market positions in the European countries that went to Heineken. Scottish & Newcastle was the market leader by volume in the UK (main brands: Foster's, John Smith's and Kronenbourg 1664, the latter under a continuing licence from Carlsberg's French operation after the takeover), number two in Portugal (main brand: Sagres), Finland (main brands: Lapin Kulta and Karjala) and Belgium (main brand: Maes) as well as number three in Ireland (main brand: Beamish). US operations were limited mainly to importing Newcastle Brown Ale, one of Scottish & Newcastle's UK brands. In India, Scottish & Newcastle owned 37.5 per cent of a joint venture with an Indian firm that brewed, among others, India's number one brand, Kingfisher.

The UK beer market had undergone considerable change in the decade before Scottish & Newcastle was acquired. First, changes imposed by the British antitrust authority limited the number of pubs that brewing companies were allowed to own. Up until the 1990s, Scottish & Newcastle and other UK brewers were the main owners of pubs in Britain. Subsequently, British brewers, including Scottish & Newcastle, sold off many of their pubs. However, in 2008 Scottish & Newcastle still had more than 2000 managed pubs in the UK. Second, consumer beer preferences also changed. Historically, the main types of beer sold in the UK were ale and, to a lesser extent, stout. However, in a process that had spanned several decades, the dominance of ale was replaced by lager beers. By the time of the takeover, lager accounted for about 75 per cent of the UK beer market, up from about 62 per cent ten years earlier. Third, several international players, such as InBev from Belgium, Carlsberg from Denmark and US brewers, such as Anheuser-Busch, entered the market. The new entrants primarily sold lager. As a result of these changes, overall competition in the UK beer market increased and margins deteriorated while Scottish & Newcastle changed its strategy to diversifying its product range from beer to other types of alcoholic and non-alcoholic beverages (*Financial Times* 2008a).

Despite rapid internationalization during the ten years prior to the acquisition (for example, the takeover of the French Brasseries Kronenbourg in 2000), the UK market was by far the most important single national market for Scottish & Newcastle (45 per cent of total sales in 2006). Scottish & Newcastle was the market leader in Britain and had consistently generated sales growth for the three years before 2008. Among the countries in Scottish & Newcastle's country portfolio acquired by Heineken, the UK represented by far the largest market. In 2007 Heineken only had a 1 per cent market share in Britain. Post acquisition, Heineken commanded a market share of approximately 30 per cent. With growth in the UK beer market stemming from increased lager sales, Heineken's global brands Heineken and Amstel were well positioned to benefit from the trend. Heineken's CEO, van Boxmeer, stated that the UK market was characterized by declining ale and stout and increasing lager sales, particularly in the premium lager segments to which the Heineken brand belongs (*Financial Times* 2008a).

Revenue-generating synergies

Thus, from Heineken's perspective, one of the key motives for the acquisition was to use Scottish & Newcastle as an 'outstanding platform for the growth of the Heineken brand' (Heineken 2008b), particularly in the UK market. This was driven by Scottish & Newcastle's distribution network, which was the largest in the UK market, and by its good control of sales channels, including the managed pubs. The capabilities were to be used to sell Heineken in the British market, which was experiencing attractive growth in this premium lager segment (Heineken 2008b).

Furthermore, Heineken saw value in the Strongbow brand. The UK cider market was growing significantly at approximately 19 per cent per annum. Scottish & Newcastle was the world market leader in cider and commanded a 43 per cent market share in the UK. Heineken planned on developing the international potential of older through the global Heineken network. In addition, a few of the acquired beer brands, such as Newcastle Brown Ale, Foster's and Belgian specialty brands, were also seen to hold internationalization potential. Heineken also hoped to be able to benefit from Scottish & Newcastle's know-how in running managed pub operations by leveraging this concept internationally. The primary goal of using national distribution systems as platforms for the global premium brand was also to be pursued for the other European markets that were acquired in the deal. The two non-European markets were either just minor import operations (US) or, in the case of India, a minority stake in a joint venture. Nevertheless, Heineken ascribed high growth potential to this emerging market where per capita beer consumption was less than one litre at the time of the takeover (Heineken and Carlsberg 2008).

Cost-saving synergies
In addition to revenue-generating synergies, Heineken also aimed at realizing cost-saving synergies. The company expected to reduce cost using its experience in running 'rigorous efficiency programmes' (Heineken and Carlsberg 2008). These cost reductions were to come mainly from the following activities:

- 'Reduce central overhead costs
- Centralize purchasing
- Combine administrative functions
- Integration of operations in UK, Ireland and USA
- Share best practices in logistics, distribution and production'. (Heineken 2008b, p. 30)

Heineken announced that it expected to realize cost synergies of €115m by the fourth year after the transaction. For comparison, expected revenue-generating synergies were announced to be only about €47 m by year four (Heineken 2008b). However, Heineken expected to realize more of the revenue-generation potential in the long term. At the announcement of the deal it was assumed that Scottish & Newcastle's headquarters would be closed as one of the cost-cutting measures following the closure of the transaction, sparking the involvement of government officials such as Scotland's First Minister (*Financial Times* 2008b). In fact, Heineken closed Scottish & Newcastle's headquarters at the prestigious St Andrew's Square location in downtown Edinburgh and consolidated brewery and pub management operations at an industrial location on the outskirts of the city. In April 2008 the shares of Scottish & Newcastle were delisted from the London Stock Exchange, and in 2009 the name of the company was changed to Heineken UK (*Scotsman* 2008; *Morning Advertiser* 2009).

In its presentation of the full year financial statement issued for 2008, the year in which the acquisition took place, Heineken announced that it was able to increase the sales of the Heineken brand in the UK by 24 per cent. The company further reported that sales of cider had increased and that market share had been added. In presenting its full year financial results for 2009, the first full year after the acquisition of Scottish & Newcastle, Heineken reported that the cost synergies realized were €184 m and were thus both higher and three years earlier than expected. The company stated that rigorous cost-cutting had taken place and announced the closure of two brewery sites in the UK and one brewery in Finland (Heineken 2009). In addition, it declared that the joint venture into which Heineken had entered in India was about to start production of the Heineken brand with the goal of selling this premium brand in the growing Indian market (Heineken 2010c).

The Acquisition of FEMSA

On 11 January 2010, Heineken announced that it would acquire the beer division of FEMSA, based in Monterrey, Mexico, after SABMiller had pulled out from the bidding citing that it would not enter into a value-destructive bidding war. As a result of the takeover of the world's 11th largest brewer in terms of volume, Heineken became the world's second largest brewing company in terms of revenues (Tartwijk 2009).

Heineken and FEMSA were not new to each other. As early as 2004, the two companies had signed an agreement under which Heineken would become the sole importer and marketer of FEMSA's beer brands in the US market. The deal proved to be rewarding for Heineken, as FEMSA's brands experienced significantly higher sales growth in the US than the Heineken brands. Furthermore, Heineken had been a minority share-holder of Kaiser, a Brazilian brewer that was majority owned by FEMSA since it had acquired Kaiser from the Canadian brewer Molson Coors in 2006 (FEMSA 2004).

At the time of FEMSA's takeover by Heineken, FEMSA's beer brand portfolio consisted of Dos Equis, Tecate, Sol, Carta Blanca, Bohemia and others. With a number two market position behind Grupo Modelo in the Mexican market, which was projected to be the number three market worldwide for beer consumption growth by 2015, behind China and Brazil, and with a market share of 8 per cent in the high-growth Brazilian market, the world's second largest beer profit pool behind the US, FEMSA was an attractive takeover target (Cleary 2010).

Heineken, which carried substantial debt from its partial acquisition of Scottish & Newcastle in 2008, was not in a position to offer a debt-financed cash offer. Thus, a dilutive all share deal was negotiated, under which Heineken issued shares that were partially deferred.[5]

The transaction valued FEMSA at a 12x earnings multiple. Comparable deals had been previously closed at 14x and 10.6x earnings multiples for the UK's Scottish & Newcastle and Colombia's Bavaria breweries, respectively (Cleary 2010).

Prior to the transaction, Heineken had been criticized by industry observers for being underrepresented in emerging markets with 80 per cent of revenues still coming from low-growth European markets. Analyst Gerard Rijk of ING, a Dutch bank, was quoted as saying that Heineken's 'positions in current and future global profit pools are small, nonexistent or worrying and need to be expanded' (Tartwijk 2009). At the same time, FEMSA was also under pressure for losing market share in its Mexican home market to the national champion Grupo Model, which was 50 per cent owned by AB InBev.

Cost-saving synergies

Heineken stated that realizing cost synergies was a key goal of the post-merger integration process. Cost synergies are expected to reach €150m per annum, starting in 2013. Heineken's 2011 end-of-year financial report demonstrated that cumulative cost synergies had been €94 m, that is, 63 per cent of the targeted amount, and that the company was on target for achieving its cost synergy goal in 2012, one year ahead of schedule (Heineken 2012b). According to Heineken investor materials, these savings were to be realized through cost savings in the following areas:

- Selling and distribution.
- Product procurement.
- Supply chain initiatives.
- Stock keeping unit rationalization.
- General administration.

The company points to its track record in delivering post-merger earnings enhancement through cost cutting based on implementing best practice in operations as exemplified by realized cost savings that exceeded expectations in the case of Scottish & Newcastle and other acquisitions (Heineken 2012a). In 2012 Heineken reported that the headcount in its Mexican operations had been reduced by 15 per cent (Heineken 2012c).

Revenue-generating synergies

Heineken has also communicated revenue-generating measures in the context of the FEMSA acquisition. First, Heineken aims at significantly increasing the sales volume of its lead Heineken brand in Mexico during post-merger integration. This is to be achieved by exploiting FEMSA's exclusivity arrangement with one of Mexico's largest and fastest growing convenience store chains, OXXO, with over 7000 outlets, and further national exclusive beer resellers. Under this exclusive contract, FEMSA will remain an exclusive supplier to OXXO until 2020. Heineken believes that it will be able to drive the premiumization of the Mexican market with the launch of the Heineken brand as no other international premium brand has been introduced. This type of revenue generation by introducing and growing the Heineken brand had already been successfully achieved in Vietnam, Argentina and Chile. The approach is aided by the fact that the Heineken brand is already known in Mexico through the global sponsorship of sporting events, particularly football (Heineken 2010b).

Revenue growth is also being realized through FEMSA's brands. The post-merger integration period is being used for applying Heineken's best practices across FEMSA's brands, especially in the following areas:

- Improving the return on marketing spending through optimized market segmentation, portfolio planning and distribution channel strategy.
- Driving premiumization of Mexican brands and leveraging the Mexican consumers' regional pride through regional brands such as Tecate in the north and Sol in the south.

These measures in the Mexican market are expected to boost revenues and to capture Mexico's projected overall annual beer consumption growth of 2.5 per cent through 2015 (Heineken 2010b).

In addition, revenues generated by FEMSA's brands are also expected to increase outside of Mexico. The vast majority of FEMSA's exports go to the US, the principal export brands being Dos Equis, Tecate and Sol. Heineken intends to bolster the strong growth the brands have experienced in the US market by building on successful marketing campaigns and leveraging the Mexican-American demographic development. Currently, 47 million Hispanics live in the US. This number is projected to triple by 2050. Heineken also plans to introduce FEMSA brands to other parts of the world, particularly Europe, by building on Mexican lifestyle appeal. This is to be achieved by replicating US marketing campaigns on an international scale. Previous experience has demonstrated that the four-year compound annual growth rate (CAGR) of volume growth of

FEMSA's brands in the US prior to the marketing agreement in 2004 (7.2 per cent) increased significantly under Heineken's marketing responsibility in the subsequent four years (CAGR: 10.8 per cent) (Heineken 2010b).

The Brazilian market represents another focus of the post-merger integration process. Heineken is using its management and marketing capabilities to turn around the troubled Kaiser brand and to position it for regional strength. It is, however, expected that revenue generation will be derived from a Heineken brand focus and an increasing premiumization. This is being communicated as the key initiative for the Brazilian market, which should be aided by Heineken's international sponsorship of the UEFA Champions League that has generated high brand awareness in Brazil. Overall, Heineken expects to benefit from the strong growth and high profitability level in the Brazilian market (Heineken 2010b).

CONCLUSION

While any type of inductive reasoning from a study based on merely two case examples should be avoided, the cases do highlight that Heineken's acquisition motives were similar, in that the company sought to realize similar types of synergies in its two largest acquisitions. Apart from attempting to capture national or regional overall market growth in the geographies in which a takeover target operates, a recurring theme is the realization of cost-reduction synergies by post-acquisition cost-cutting initiatives at the acquired companies. Revenue-generating synergies also weigh heavily as part of the rationale for the takeovers. However, in this context the main goal appears to be the utilization of the distribution networks and the channel access that the newly acquired companies have in place for driving the revenue of the global premium brand Heineken. Nevertheless, there is also evidence that in some cases Heineken will pursue the internationalization of acquired brands (for example, Dos Equis and Newcastle Brown Ale) or product categories (for example, cider beverages), particularly if they hold the potential for international premiumization.

It is this type of resource acquisition from the target to the buyer that appears to set the two large cases apart from smaller cases that were analysed before (Dieng et al. 2009). Nevertheless, in summary, the cases suggest that the transfer of resources and capabilities following Heineken's takeovers is primarily unidirectional, from Heineken to the acquired companies.

As indicated above, an empirical study of Capron and Hulland (2009, p. 51) across different industries concludes that overall brands tend to be more redeployed from target to acquirer, especially 'when the served markets were similar, a consumer products industry was involved and/or the target firm's resource strength was greater'. While the two former conditions hold true for the two large acquisitions studied here and the large number of smaller acquisitions studied in Dieng et al. (2009), it seems to be the overall resource strength of the inferior target firms that makes the difference. Neither Scottish & Newcastle nor FEMSA, nor the many small acquisitions, had a brand as strong and globally present as the Heineken brand.

It would be interesting to see whether the overall findings of this chapter can be generalized for the brewing industry. Given the strong acquisition experience of Heineken it seems unlikely that significant synergy potentials have remained undetected (at least if one assumes that Heineken's acquisition experience gained with the many small- and medium-sized acquisitions also pays off in large acquisitions). Moreover, the two large acquisition targets of Heineken are similar to what other top players in the industry have taken over in terms of resource strength. On the other hand, however, there is hardly any company in the brewing industry that is as strongly tied to its top brand as Heineken is. The Heineken brand is seen as the 'physical, emotional and financial heart' of the company; 'the jewel in the crown' (Heineken 2006, p. 12) that '[needs to be kept] healthy and growing' (Heineken 2007, p. 10). This more or less automatically awards acquired brands second-class status.

NOTES

1. http://www.youtube.com/watch?v=4msp9koKLrk, accessed 12 April 2008.
2. Since only the additional revenue from 1 May–31 December 2008 was recognized under international financial reporting standards (IFRS) accounting rules the pro-forma contribution on a full-year basis would have been even higher, amounting to a total of €3.1 bn. Thus, the pro-forma revenue recognition represents an increase of revenue of nearly 28 per cent compared to Heineken's 2007 consolidated revenue of about €11.2 bn (Heineken 2008a).
3. The pro-forma recognition was reported as €2.9 bn for the full year. Therefore, based on the pro-forma revenue recognition, the acquisition resulted in an increase of revenue of nearly 20 per cent compared to Heineken's 2009 consolidated revenue of €14.7 bn (Heineken 2010a).
4. The enterprise value of the Scottish & Newcastle assets acquired by Heineken was announced as amounting to €6.1 bn. Heineken financed the transaction mainly with new debt facilities from a consortium of nine major European and US banks (Heineken 2008b).
5. FEMSA's enterprise value totalled €5.25 bn, including assumed debt and pension obligations. As a result of the transaction, FEMSA held 20 per cent of the economic interest of the Heineken group while the Heineken family remained the controlling shareholder, and Heineken was able to maintain a Net Debt/EBITDA-ratio of 3.1 (Tartwijk 2009; Heineken 2010b).

REFERENCES

Bloomberg (2008), 'Carlsberg and Heineken agree to buy Scottish & Newcastle', 25 January, accessed 23 October 2012 at www.bloomberg.com/apps/news?pid= newsarchive&sid=anIDH9amUooc.

Boxmeer, van, J.F. (2012), 'Interview with Roger O. Crockett, Russell Reynolds Associates', accessed 22 October 2012 at www.russellreynolds.com/content/ heineken-ceo-jean-francois-van-boxmeer-global-growth.

Capron, L. and J. Hulland (1999), 'Redeployment of brands, sales forces, and general marketing management expertise following horizontal acquisitions: a resource-based view', *Journal of Marketing*, **63** (2), 41–54.

Capron L., W. Mitchell and A. Swaminathan (2001), 'Asset disvestiture following horizontal acquisitions. A dynamic view', *Strategic Management Journal*, **22** (9), 817–44.

Chatterjee, S. (1986), 'Types of synergy and economic value: the impact of acquisitions on merging and rival firms', *Strategic Management Journal*, **7**, 119–39.

Cleary, A. (2010), 'Heineken to buy Femsa beer unit in $7.7 billion deal', accessed 14 November 2011 at www.bloomberg.com/apps/news?pid=newsarchive&sid= aS6CwCsZV5Rs.

Collins, J.D., T. Holcomb, T. Certo, M.A. Hitt and R.H. Les (2009), 'Learning by doing: cross-border mergers and acquisitions', *Journal of Business Research*, **62** (2009), 1329–34.

Dieng, S., C. Dörrenbächer and J. Gammelgaard (2009), 'Subsidiary brands as a resource and the redistribution of decision making authority following acquisitions', in S. Finkelstein and C. Cooper (eds), *Advances in Mergers and Acquisitions*, Vol. 8, Bingley: Emerald Group Publishing Limited, pp. 141–60.

Ebneth, O. and L. Theuvsen (2007), 'Large mergers and acquisitions of European brewing groups – event study evidence on value creation', *Agribusiness*, **23** (3), 377–406.

Eisenhardt, K.M. and J.A. Martin (2000), 'Dynamic capabilities: what are they?', *Strategic Management Journal*, **21**, 1105–21.

Eschen, E. and R. Bresser (2005), 'Closing resource gaps: toward a resource-based theory of advantageous mergers and acquisitions', *European Management Review*, (2), 57–78.

Estrin, S. and K.E. Meyer (2011), 'Brownfield acquisitions. A reconceptualization and extension', *Management International Review*, **51**, 483–509.

FEMSA (2004), 'FEMSA and Heineken join forces in the U.S.A.', press release, accessed 14 November 2011 at http://ir.femsa.com/releasedetail. cfm?ReleaseID=188807.

Financial Times (2008a), 'Few crying into beers at decline of big six breweries', *Financial Times*, 26 January, p. 15.

Financial Times (2008b), 'Scots reject "tartan barrier" to stem takeovers', *Financial Times*, 28 January, p. 3.

Gammelgaard, J. (2002), 'Gaining competences in the MNC through acquisitions. An investigation of foreign Danish acquisitions 1994–1998', PhD Series 4, Copenhagen: CBS.

Geppert, M., C. Dörrenbächer, J. Gammelgaard and I. Taplin (forthcoming), 'Managerial risk-taking in international acquisitions in the brewery industry: institutional and ownership influences compared', *British Journal of Management*.

Haleblian, J. and S. Finkelstein (1999), 'The influence of organizational acquisition experience on acquisition performance: a behavioral learning perspective', *ASQ*, **44** (March), 29–56.

Heineken (2006), *Heineken Annual Report 2006*, Amsterdam: Heineken.

Heineken (2007), *Heineken Annual Report 2007*, Amsterdam: Heineken.

Heineken (2008a), *Notes to the Consolidated Financial Statements 2008 (Note 6)*, Amsterdam: Heineken.

Heineken (2008b), 'S&N acquisition', investor presentation, 25 January, accessed 25 October 2012 at www.heinekeninternational.com/content/live/Heineken%20 Investors%20Presentation%20Final.pdf.

Heineken (2009), 'Heineken: the world's premium beer brand and the world's most international brewer', investor presentation, 20 November, accessed 27 October 2012 at www.heinekeninternational.com/content/live/Heineken_ MS_11202009_for_handouts.pdf.

Heineken (2010a) *Notes to the Consolidated Financial Statements 2010 (Note 6)*, Amsterdam: Heineken.

Heineken (2010b), 'Transforming our future in the Americas', investor presentation, 11 January, accessed 27 October 2012 at www.heinekeninternational.com/ content/live/Files%202010/100108%20TH%20-%20IR%20presentation%20 -%20Final.pdf.

Heineken (2010c), 'Heineken N.V., full year results 2009', investor presentation, 23 February.

Heineken (2011), *Heineken Annual Report 2010*, Amsterdam: Heineken.

Heineken (2012a), *Heineken Annual Report 2011*, Amsterdam: Heineken.

Heineken (2012b), 'Heineken N.V., full-year results 2011 shaping the future', investor presentation, 15 February, accessed 24 October 2012 at www.heineken-international.com/content/live/Files%202012/Presentations/FY_2011_Final_ draft_V1.0_without_VT220224.pdf.

Heineken (2012c), 'Heineken N.V., what's brewing Heineken Americas', investor presentation, 23 March, accessed 24 October 2012 at www.heinekeninternational. com/content/live/Files%202012/Presentations/FY_2011_Final_draft_V1.0_with out_VT220224.pdf.

Heineken and Carlsberg (2008), 'Heineken N.V. and Carlsberg A/S, recommended cash offer for Scottish & Newcastle plc by Sunrise Acquisitions Limited', 25 January.

Hitt, M.A., D. King, H. Krishnan, M. Makri, M. Schijven, M. Shimizu and H. Zhu (2001), 'Mergers and acquisitions: overcoming pitfalls, building synergy, and creating value', *Business Horizons*, **52**, 523–9.

Jacobs, M.G.P.A. and W.H.G. Maas (1991), *Heineken 1949–1988*, Amsterdam: Heineken.

King, D.R., D.R. Dalton, C.M. Daily and J.G. Covin (2004), 'Meta-analyses of post-acquisition performance: indications of unidentified moderators', *Strategic Management Journal*, **25** (2), 187–200.

Larsson, R. and S. Finkelstein (1999), 'Integrating strategic, organizational, and human resource perspectives on mergers and acquisitions: a case survey of synergy realization', *Organization Science*, **10** (1), 1–26.

Morning Advertiser (2009), 'Scottish & Newcastle to become Heineken UK', *Morning Advertiser*, 28 September.

Prashantham, S. and S.W. Floyd (2012), 'Routine microprocesses and capability learning in international new ventures', *Journal of International Business Studies*, **43**, 544–62.

Rugman, A.M. and A. Verbeke (2004), 'A perspective on regional and global strategies of multinational enterprises', *Journal of International Business Studies*, **35** (1), 3–18.

Scotsman (2008), 'S&N sails into history as brewer taken over', *Scotsman*, 28 April.

Sirower, M.L. (1997), *The Synergy Trap: How Companies Lose the Acquisition Game*, New York: Free Press.

Smit, B. (1996), *Heineken, een leven in de brouwerij*, Nijmegen: SUN.

Tartwijk, M. v. (2009), 'Heineken's debt poses hurdle to a Femsa deal', *WSJ*, 26 October, accessed 14 November 2011 at http://online.wsj.com/article/SB100014 24052748703573604574491202399103112.html.

Wernerfelt, B. (1984), 'A resource based view of the firm', *Strategic Management Journal*, **14** (3), 4–12.

Wiklund, J. and D.A. Shepherd (2009), 'The effectiveness of alliances and acquisitions: the role of resource combination activities', *Entrepreneurship Theory and Practice*, January, 193–211.

Wortmann, M. (2008), *Komplex und Global. Strategien und Strukturen multinationaler Unternehmen*, Wiesbaden: VS-Verlag.

PART V

Leadership and internationalization

9. Leadership and preparedness to internationalize in the brewing industry: the case of Asahi Breweries of Japan

Christopher Williams, Seijiro Takeshita, Mélanie Gilles, Caroline Ruhe, Janne Smith, and Svenja Troll

INTRODUCTION

Japanese exports after World War II mainly consisted of industrial and durable goods such as ships, steel, electronics, precision equipment, machinery and automobiles. However, following the acute appreciation in the yen after the Plaza Accord in 1985, Japanese firms sought internationalization for two principal reasons: (1) to increase local production to counter the effects of the strengthening yen, and (2) to tap directly into growing foreign markets. In addition, changing demographics suggested dampening of market growth in Japan. Furthermore, deregulation encouraged overseas competitors to enter Japan and gain market share.

At the same time, opportunities in Asia were blooming. After the region overcame the Asian financial crises in the late 1990s, Japanese companies were in an ideal position to make their presence felt. They were close geographically and had a long history of doing business in the region. Increasingly, interest in Japanese food, as a part of a growing appreciation of Japanese culture, was also on the rise. Consumer goods companies – including food and beverage makers – started to internationalize in the mid 1990s, although they lagged well behind industrial and durable goods manufacturers.

Today, Asahi Breweries Ltd is one of the top ten breweries in the world. The company has international subsidiaries in North America, Europe and Asia, and it licenses its products in many countries around the world. The company was not always international. What looks like a success story today, could have been the story of bankruptcy in 1982. At that

time, Asahi was a pure Japanese player fighting for survival in the domestic market. By 1998, however, the company was a dominant player in the
Japanese market, and growing internationally.

By studying key events over three eras of leadership at Asahi Breweries
between 1982 and 1998, we provide new insight into the mechanisms that
trigger internationalization in brewing firms from developed markets that
have traditionally been domestically focused. We emphasize how successive leaders' actions in these three eras impacted Asahi as a company and,
more specifically, how leaders laid the foundation for Asahi to internationalize. The case data is drawn mainly from four secondary sources:
the company website, newspaper articles, academic articles and data
published annually by Toyo Keizai, Inc., listing Japanese overseas investment from 1987–2006 (Toyo Keizai 2006). Our approach is novel in that
it delves into the leadership and organizational changes that result in a
company's preparedness to internationalize. From a theoretical perspective, we argue that this is a particular ownership advantage of the firm
that connects internationalization theory (Andersen 1993; Dunning 1981,
1988, 2000; Johanson and Vahlne 1977, 2009; Johanson and Wiedersheim-
Paul 1975) with concepts from leadership theory (Avolio et al. 1999; Bass
et al. 2003; Higgs and Rowland 2005).

The first part of our chapter provides a brief theoretical background. We
then discuss the case context and company background, before detailing
the main events and actions occurring in the three leadership eras that had
a profound impact on Asahi's ability to internationalize. We then discuss
the case in light of key concepts from internationalization and leadership
theories to develop fresh insight into how domestically focused firms in the
brewing industry can build a foundation for internationalization.

THEORETICAL BACKGROUND

There are two theoretical strands that are highly relevant to the Asahi
case: internationalization theory and leadership theory. Our starting point
is to note that internationalization and leadership theories have traditionally been two separate fields of research. While there has been an emphasis
in the emerging international entrepreneurship field on the entrepreneurial
behavior that underpins internationalization moves by firms (Jones and
Coviello 2005), few have addressed the question of how different types of
leaders (or leadership strategies) are needed to enable a brewing company
to embark on a sustainable internationalization program. To our knowledge this question has not been addressed using internationalization or
leadership theories. The use of both of these theoretical perspectives is

especially important when we consider the Japanese context. Corporate governance in Japan is distinctive, largely because of the way leaders are trained over many years within their organizations and selected into leadership positions. Distinctive corporate governance within Japan may add constraints to how Japanese brewing firms internationalize.

Early stages theories of internationalization (Johanson and Wiedersheim-Paul 1975; Johanson and Vahlne 1977) depict firm internationalization as a long and gradual process. It was argued that simultaneous tensions for growth, long-term profitability and risk reduction made firms choose multi-stage internationalization strategies. During the different stages firms have time to learn progressively from foreign markets and gradually increase their commitment in terms of equity investment and financial risk. These theories imply that firms learn from their home market before expanding internationally. In this vein, firm internationalization has also been portrayed as an innovation (Andersen 1993).

Theories of internationalization stress how foreign direct investment (FDI) arises because of the need for firms to internalize transactions across national boundaries (Buckley and Casson 1976; Coase 1937). Dunning's eclectic OLI theory (Dunning 1981, 1988, 2000) brought together arguments relating to ownership ('O') and location ('L') advantages, and, in addition to these, internalization ('I') advantages. Dunning later differentiated between so-called Oa advantages, (asset-based advantages such as those arising from the company's technology and patents) and Ot advantages (that cover transaction ownership advantages: 'the capability of MNEs to internalize markets') (Dunning 1988, p. 3; Dunning 1988).

As a later extension to these theories of internationalization, Johanson and Vahlne (2009) developed a network approach in which they distinguish between liabilities of outsidership and liabilities of foreignness. This approach emphasized the role of networks and the firm's position relative to those networks in determining internationalization strategy. Each market is seen as a set of invisible networks of relationships between firms (Johanson and Vahlne 2009, p. 1411). To successfully internationalize, firms have to become part of market-specific networks by building trust and developing knowledge through relationships. If a company is not part of a network relevant to their operations, they will face a 'liability of outsidership' in the foreign market (Johanson and Vahlne 2009, p. 1411).

Leadership theory categorizes different types of leadership (Avolio et al. 1999; Bass et al. 2003; Higgs and Rowland 2005). A principal focus has been on the differences between two types, namely: (1) transformational leadership, and (2) transactional leadership. Both types of leadership are seen not just as the actions of the individual leaders but also in terms of how the individual leaders can engage, motivate and integrate their followers in decision-making processes (Avolio et al. 1999; Bass et al. 2003). Depending on a given firm's operating environment, different leadership traits might be preferable (Higgs and Rowland 2005; Senge 1997).

Transformational leadership is defined as the kind of adaptive leadership applied in groups or organizations confronted by changing or challenging environments. Transformational leaders motivate their followers to generate 'creative solutions to complex problems' (Bass et al. 2003, p. 207). By motivating their employees, they enhance their identification with the organization, and thereby potentially trigger higher performance (Bass and Avolio 1990). Three traits are associated with transformational leaders: (1) charisma/inspirational (ability to motivate followers), (2) intellectual stimulation (ability to encourage followers' 'out-of-the-box' thinking), and (3) individual consideration (ability to understand followers) (Avolio et al. 1999; Bass et al. 2003).

Transactional leadership is defined as the interactions (or transactions) between leaders and their employees (Bass and Avolio 1990). A transactional leader is characterized by setting clear performance targets for his or her followers. The leader also defines the consequences of underachievement. Two factors characterizing transactional leadership are: (1) contingent reward (the definition of clear performance targets and rewards), and (2) management-by-exception (monitoring and maintaining current performance levels).

Given that our case company is a Japanese brewing company, we need to consider characteristics of the Japanese national business system that will be highly salient to the key case events. We note that corporate governance in Japan traditionally has involved banks, rather than shareholders, providing the largest part of corporate finance through loans, and, in turn, monitoring company management (Yamamura and Streeck 2003). Banks were, and are, the center of corporate groupings, providing Japanese corporations with long-term 'silent' capital, enabling Japanese firms to concentrate on long-term growth (Takeshita 2007). If a business failed, it was up to the banks to decide whether to continue funding or to reconstruct, with bank management brought in to take over operations, virtually leaving autonomy to the banks (Takeshita 2007).

THE CASE CONTEXT

The Japanese Beer Industry in the 1980s and 1990s

The Japanese beer industry is a classical example of 'cluster' competition (Hayashi 1984), where similar types of company battle over limited market share backed by their conglomerates, or *zaibatsu*, which also tend to have similar corporate structures (Takeshita 2007). The outcome is usually severe competition that results in little innovation in a heavily regulated market (Takeshita 2007). Such competition has the characteristic of a cartel, and competition is usually based on service and product, and not on price (Yoshida 1993). Coordination among the competition becomes frequent, with actions taken based on game theory; an ideal environment for bureaucrats to govern (Takeshita 2007).

Four local brewers had dominated the Japanese market for decades: Kirin, Asahi, Sapporo and Suntory. These four companies had a 97 percent market share in 1990 (Craig 1996) and were still holding 89 percent of the Japanese market in 2010 (Euromonitor International 2011). The beer industry in Japan was highly regulated (Craig 1996). This regulation had a significant impact on the national players. Even though price competition was theoretically possible, the Japanese beer brewers kept their prices fixed. Consequently, Japanese beers were expensive. Traditionally, there had been a lack of product innovation. The brewers assumed that consumers only wanted a strong-tasting beer (Kokuryo and Asaba 1994). Thus, the four Japanese leaders only differentiated their brands in terms of product quality and packaging, advertising campaign and distribution channels. Hence, it was crucial to have a high quality product and a good brand reputation.

The Japanese distribution network was one of the most powerful barriers preventing new firms from competing in the Japanese market. Indeed, it was a multilevel, highly decentralized network with a high emphasis on relationships (Martin et al. 1998). This was one of the reasons why foreign firms were not actively operating in the Japanese market.

In the mid 1980s, multiple consumer trends emerged and were encouraging market changes. What truly sparked off hyper-competition in the Japanese beer market was the launch of Asahi Super Dry beer in 1987. The hyper-competition era was characterized by a range of product innovations attempting to satisfy changes in consumer demand. Between 1964 and 1984 the average number of new beers introduced was low: 0.76 new beers per year. In contrast, this average number increased to 7.56 per year between 1985 and 1993 (Craig 1996).

Between 1992 and 1994, the Japanese economy was hit by a massive economic crisis. The country also suffered from a significant appreciation of their currency. This urged Japanese consumers to become more price-sensitive; a shift in Japanese behavior (McLain et al. 1995; Reid 1994). These changing conditions had an impact on the beer industry.

Foreign beer sales were gaining market share. One of the key reasons for the spike in demand was the lower prices of foreign beers. On average, foreign beers were 20 percent to 40 percent cheaper than Japanese beers

(Craig 1996), whose prices were still fixed by the Japanese government and hampered by the yen's appreciation. Japanese customers were also more open towards foreign brands (McLain et al. 1995). Furthermore, the Japanese beer market was maturing and consumption decreased for the first time in 1993.

These new trends profoundly changed the rules of the beer industry and forced Japanese breweries to adapt their strategies. To answer these new challenges Kirin first set the pace by entering an alliance with Anheuser-Busch in 1994 (Craig 1996). The other Japanese brewers quickly followed Kirin's lead. Hence the beer industry, like many others in Japan, had started to expand into overseas markets, due mainly to: (1) a slowdown in domestic consumption, (2) increased competition in Japan from foreign entities, and (3) taking advantage of growth in the Asian region.

The Internationalization of Asahi Breweries

The birth of Asahi happened in 1949 through a division of Dai Nippon Brewery. The market shares at that time were Nippon Brewery (Sapporo): 38.7 percent, Asahi Brewery: 36.1 percent and Kirin: 25.3 percent. Asahi initially suffered from declining market share and attempted to counter this by being a comparatively innovative player. In 1958 it launched the first Japanese canned beer and the 'mini barrel' in 1977, targeting in-home draft beer consumption. None of the initiatives led to a sustained competitive advantage (Barney 1991) because competitors could immediately imitate any initiative taken. In the 1980s, Asahi's customers were disappointed with both the quality and taste of Asahi's beer. By 1985, Asahi's market share dropped to a record low of 9.6 percent, only slightly ahead of fourth place Sapporo (9.2 percent). On the other hand, Kirin became the market leader, holding 61.4 percent of market share in 1983 (Craig 1996).

However, with the successful launch of Super Dry in 1987, Asahi's overall Japanese market share more than doubled between 1986 and 1992 to around 23 percent in 1992. Nearly two decades later, Asahi Breweries could claim that it had the number one position in terms of beer sales for a 13th consecutive year (Asahi Breweries Ltd 2010). Even though beer markets were maturing and, in some areas, even declining, Asahi Breweries Ltd generated the main profits for Asahi Group Holding.

By the turn of the century, Asahi Group became a well-diversified company with investments in the soft drinks industry, food industry, and other business areas. However, it was the alcoholic beverages segment with Asahi Breweries Ltd which accounted for 62.8 percent of Asahi Group's net sales and 88.8 percent of net income (Asahi Breweries Ltd 2010).

Asahi's first move towards internationalization was actually to import

Source: Toyo Keizai (2006).

Figure 9.1 Increasing foreign investments

foreign alcoholic drinks (excluding beers) through licensing agreements (Gale Database 2011). For instance, Asahi formed a national joint venture in 1971 with Nikka Whiskey Distilling Company to import foreign scotch and whiskeys. Moreover, they reached a licensing agreement in 1982 with a German brewery to produce Löwenbräu Beer in Japan. In 1984 Asahi started collaborating with Schweppes to produce several soft drinks for the Japanese market (Gale Database 2011).

Asahi's first FDI was made in 1992 through the acquisition of a 20 percent stake in the Australian Foster's Brewing Group Ltd. In 1994, Asahi entered the Canadian market though a licensing agreement with Molson Breweries. They entered the US market in 1995 through an alliance with Miller Brewing Company and set up another licensing agreement in the UK in 1996 with Bass Breweries Ltd (Asahi Breweries Ltd 2011). Furthermore, Asahi progressively invested in the Chinese market, starting with purchases of equity stakes in three breweries in 1994. In 1997 they created a joint venture with the Chinese market leader, Tsingtao Breweries Co. (Gale Database 2011). Figure 9.1 shows growth in the total number of foreign transactions (foreign equity investments in joint ventures and wholly owned subsidiaries) from 1987–99.

THE MURAI ERA (1982–86)

In 1982 the Japanese beer market continued to show constant growth. The Japanese beer producers had not yet felt the need to introduce product changes nor had they deemed it necessary to internationalize. Unlike its competitors, however, Asahi's market share had been declining for more than 35 years. This poor performance could be attributed to: (1) deterioration in product quality, (2) a lack of between-division communication, and (3) a self-centered orientation. Asahi had not engaged in any significant international activities at this point.

To reestablish a competitive position, a change in corporate culture was inevitable (Craig 1996; Jameson 1988; Nakajo and Kono 1989). Asahi's employees, however, did not feel the need for change; there was a reluctance to change. In this era the company focused on survival rather than international expansion. In 1982, Asahi appointed Tsutomu Murai as their new chief executive officer (CEO). Murai was the fourth consecutive CEO to be called in from Sumitomo Bank, fifth in the history of Asahi since 1949.

Changing Corporate Culture

Murai's very first goal was to create a feeling of crisis within Asahi in order for employees to realize that change was necessary for survival (Nakajo and Kono 1989). Murai identified a lack of communication between the different departments of the company as a major obstacle. This resulted in inferior product quality and a lack of customer focus (Nakajo and Kono 1989). Under Murai, goals were set for developing consumer-oriented products matching new customer needs. Furthermore, a new corporate culture was established to facilitate innovation.

Murai instigated structural change within Asahi. To overcome problems of silos between the different departments, Murai took every opportunity to get into direct contact and socialize with his employees. He wanted to create an atmosphere of openness where employees felt comfortable with each other, with managers and with their CEO. In order to reduce the hierarchical structure within the company, Murai went out for drinks with his younger employees (Pascale and Rohlen 1983). Although socialization was common in Japanese organizations, it was less common for CEOs to go out for drinks with younger employees. Murai became known as a 'hands-on' leader, and one who understood how important his presence was (Nakajo and Kono 1989). He had a focus on quality and was keen to have case discussions with staff instead of relying solely on internal management reports.

Due to strong functional units and very weak coordination between units, no department took responsibility for mistakes. Internal conflicts prevented the company from moving forward (Kokuryo and Asaba 1994; Nakajo and Kono 1989). Murai believed that building relationships and fostering better communication between the departments were key factors for success. His vision was to increase the feeling among employees of identification with the company as a whole. He also wanted employees to be involved in the change process. Murai believed that middle managers were the key implementers of new strategies; they were the driving force of cultural and structural changes (Nakajo and Kono 1989).

Just like he had done before to save Mazda, Murai fundamentally changed the way people had been thinking at Asahi. According to Murai, the four Japanese beer companies had been 'resting on their oars' for far too long (Jameson 1988). Employees' attitudes were turned 180 degrees (Nakajo and Kono 1989) through manifesting a belief that was common in Japanese firms in other sectors at that time; that nothing is impossible (Jameson 1988). He was also described as a motivating and inspirational visionary.

Murai introduced two noteworthy initiatives: Total Quality Control (TQC) and the establishment of a Corporate Identity Committee (CIC) (Kokuryo and Asaba 1994). TQC was established for three main reasons: (1) spreading of the new corporate policy, (2), encouraging product quality improvement and (3) introducing quality control circles to ensure high quality beers are delivered to customers. The goal of the second initiative, the CIC, was to make Asahi more responsive to customer needs (Craig 1996). To achieve this, Asahi issued a survey to 5000 people in order to identify consumer preferences and their opinions on what constituted a 'good beer' (Nakajo and Kono 1989). The survey discovered that customers wanted a 'rich but smooth tasting beer' (Nakajo and Kono 1989, p. 31). Employees were trusted to be innovative. Marketing and manufacturing were finally able to integrate customer orientation and, above all, communicate more effectively. Moreover, they were able to combine their strengths in order to produce new sample beers (Craig 1996). This new attitude eventually led to Asahi's greatest success – the development and introduction of Super Dry in 1987 (Craig 1996; Jameson 1988).

Importance of the Murai Era to Asahi's Internationalization

After four years of presidency, Murai had set up a foundation for the transformation of Asahi. Murai took over the presidency right after Asahi had hit rock bottom. He introduced a new vision for the company, reconfigured and redefined Asahi's corporate culture, and to some extent the organizational structure. His leadership style can be described as transformational (Avolio et al. 1999), since it was visionary, inspiring and engaging.

Transformational leaders are not as common in Japan as in the West.

In Japan, senior managers tend to be career employees rather than operating in an externally competitive market for managerial labor; hence they are less motivated to maximize the wealth of shareholders (Geringer et al. 1998). These managers are elected by consensus, as the consensus representative of the group, and hence as the protector of vested rights and interests of that group, rather than as a top-down leader making rational decisions (Takeshita 2007). In this context, it has been very difficult for leaders in Japan to conduct corporate transformation (Takeshita 2007). However, when corporations have been on the brink of bankruptcy or liquidation, the barriers against making Western style transformations in Japan have reduced significantly.

Murai's leadership was the basis for overcoming employees' reluctance to change. Murai encouraged his employees to think 'out-of-the-box' and to explore entirely new product ideas. Employee empowerment in Japan tends to be bottom-up, giving workers the right to change rules and alter methods of working (Muto 2007). Murai therefore tapped into an implicit employer-employee relationship (Yoshida 1993), where employers and employees share views on long-term benefits (Abegglen and Stalk 1986). His focus was on introducing a new vision and implementing a new corporate culture, not on reaching specific performance targets. We note that his strategy neither had a significant effect on profits (Figure 9.2), nor on internationalization.

By 1986, despite the changes implemented by Murai, the company's market share was still below the 10 percent break-even market share point (Craig 1996). Murai needed someone to implement the changes and allow the company to become profitable again (Kokuryo and Asaba 1994). At this point he called in the vice president of Asahi's shareholder, Sumitomo Bank, to succeed him in the position of CEO: Hirotaro Higuchi.

Source: Reuters Ltd.

Figure 9.2   Improving operating profits

THE HIGUCHI ERA (1986–92)

At the age of 62, Hirotaro Higuchi had had a fast-track career, becoming the youngest vice president of Sumitomo Bank in history (Kokuryo and Asaba 1994). Higuchi had no previous experience in the beer industry (Conger and Nadler 2004). As such, he was able to bring an outside perspective into the company. Murai had mentored Higuchi and they knew each other well from their time at Sumitomo Bank. Higuchi continued the initiatives Murai put in place, most significantly the CIC initiative and the focus on customer needs and innovation. Higuchi was responsible for launching the product that was going to revolutionize the Japanese beer market: Asahi Super Dry. Research showed that 14.4 percent of Japanese preferred beer with their meal, as opposed to 11.0 percent who preferred their meal with sake, and 7.5 percent with whisky (Utsunomiya and Hashizume 2008). The Japanese had traditionally been eating fresh fish, and hence their sensitivity towards freshness was very high. However, use of oil and fat had doubled over the two decades from 1960 to 1980 in Japan, and Asahi estimated that the domestic market was ready for a light-tasting beer that was compatible with oily food (Nagai 2002).

At the point of Higuchi's succession, Asahi was still fighting for survival. His focus was therefore still on the Japanese market, not yet on internationalization. Higuchi was operations focused (Conger and Nadler 2004; Craig 1996; Kokuryo and Asaba 1994). He emphasized perfect implementation. At the same time, however, he was a man of fast decision-making, very much against the usual practices at Asahi (Kokuryo and Asaba 1994).

Building on Murai's work, Higuchi wanted to overcome the hierarchies prevalent at Asahi. He continued to improve the inter-departmental communication within Asahi (Craig 1996). Higuchi introduced a top-down management style, and focused on centralized decision-making (Conger and Nadler 2004; Craig 1996; Kokuryo and Asaba 1994). Important pieces of information were to be reported directly to him, as fast as possible (Kokuryo and Asaba 1994). He was especially open towards innovative ideas. To shorten communication cycles within the company, he made sure that proposals for new products reached top management directly (Craig 1996). It was this openness and employee empowerment that finally led to Asahi Super Dry.

Launching Asahi Super Dry

A draft beer, Asahi Draft, had been developed over previous years, and the product was ready for launching in 1986, just before Higuchi took office. He knew that in order to survive, Asahi had to win on two fronts: (1) product quality and (2) image. He started a freshness campaign, using rather unorthodox methods to underline the new emphasis on product quality. Higuchi ordered that all old stocks of Asahi Draft be recalled and destroyed – only fresh Asahi Draft was to be sold. This cost the company about ¥1.5 billion – about half of Asahi's 1985 profit (Craig 1996; Kokuryo and Asaba 1994; Nakajo and Kono 1989). In doing this, Higuchi took a huge risk. To place even more emphasis on the freshness and high quality of the new product he changed the company's sourcing strategy, using only high quality inputs from Germany (Kokuryo and Asaba 1994). The risks Higuchi took paid off: the new Asahi Draft showed a sales increase of 12 percent in the first year (Nakajo and Kono 1989).

Asahi was no longer fighting for immediate survival. With the new corporate culture slowly being embedded in the overall organization, Asahi's employees continuously aimed at developing new products to strengthen the company's market position. In 1987, the product development team approached Higuchi with a new product called Asahi Super Dry (Craig 1996). Originally Higuchi rejected the new product, fearing that launching a new product so shortly after Asahi Draft would cannibalize sales. The employees kept pushing the new product. After trying the new, lighter-tasting beer Higuchi realized the market potential and gave the launch his approval (Nakajo and Kono 1989; Craig 1996).

Asahi was the first brewer in Japan to realize changes in consumer demand and the first to introduce product innovation in a very long time. This gave Asahi a first-mover advantage (Craig 1996). Asahi Super Dry became a new top-seller (Nakajo and Kono) and the company's profits and market shares were on the increase.

Before the introduction of Asahi Super Dry, the Japanese beer industry was highly regulated and extremely stable. With the new product launch, the industry entered a 'shake-out' phase. The following years were soon to be known as the 'Japanese Beer Wars' (Craig 1996; Kokuryo and Asaba 1994): a phase of hyper-competition between the four big beer manufacturers. This hyper-competition was arguably one of the factors limiting Asahi's ambitions for international expansion. The company had to focus on securing their new, stronger position in their home market.

Even though Asahi Super Dry's success was originally thought to be a fad (*Financial Times* 1989; Kokuryo and Asaba 1994), the product remained successful. Asahi and the other Japanese beer manufacturers started a product launch race, at its peak in 1989, leading to 12 new product launches in the industry (Craig 1996). None of the new products came close to matching Asahi Super Dry's success. By 1990, Japanese beer producers realized that in order to remain profitable focus had to be shifted to cost-efficiency rather than new product introductions. The state of hyper-competition was slowing down (Craig 1996).

In 1992, Higuchi was ready to step down. He had built on Murai's efforts to transform the company. A new culture of consumer and quality focus had successfully been embedded in the company. Despite his central-ized decision-making role, he listened to what his employees had to say and engaged them in innovation processes.

Importance of Higuchi to Asahi's Internationalization

Asahi had undergone a phase of massive transformation. With Asahi Super Dry, Asahi had managed to launch the most successful beer product to date. The Japanese beer industry had been shaken up, with few key brands surviving and now dominating the market in a new evolving equilibrium. By 1992, when Higuchi stepped down, Asahi was the second largest brewery in Japan, with a slowly growing export business to over 30 countries (Gale Database 2011).

Between 1986 and 1992, Asahi's overall Japanese market share more than doubled, to around 23 percent in 1992. The company furthermore marked operating profits of around ¥15 billion in 1990 (Craig 1996). With a strong position in a stabilizing Japanese home market, Asahi could now turn its attention to foreign markets. Up until 1990, Asahi focused on the Japanese beer market through the production of local beer and the import of foreign beer. The company slowly started looking abroad for investments and additional exporting opportunities. Even though Asahi was exporting to more 30 countries, its organizational structure did not accommodate coordinated equity investments in overseas operations. In 1990, Asahi opened up an international sales office to manage its export business. The same year, it made the stake (mentioned above) in Australia's Foster's brand (Gale Database 2011).

THE SETO ERA (1992–99)

When Yuzo Seto took over as CEO of Asahi in 1992 he found the company in a far better state than his two predecessors had. Thanks to the success-ful launch of Asahi Super Dry, Asahi had a stable competitive position in the Japanese market, a leading product with potential foreign demand and already established relations with overseas players. Asahi enjoyed an operating profit of approximately ¥36 billion in 1992 (Craig 1996).

Seto was Higuchi's successor of choice, even though making him CEO was rather unusual for Asahi. Over the previous 21 years, Asahi had chosen their CEOs from Sumitomo Bank. The incumbent CEO wanted Seto because he had been vice president at Asahi for the past two years and had originally joined the company in 1953 (Tomioka 1996). Asahi had invested so much in human capital that Higuchi's successor should be an Asahi employee (Kyodo News International 1992). Higuchi had had the chance to mentor Seto and to prepare him for the challenges lying ahead (Conger and Nadler 2004).

When Seto took office, he addressed Asahi's employees with three statements: 'Stick to the basics', 'Think positively' and 'Always act with sincerity' (Tomioka 1996). These statements were very much in line with the new corporate culture introduced by Murai and implemented by Higuchi: focus on high quality and customer needs.

Navigating the Japanese Crisis

Seto led Asahi through a severe recession from 1992–94. Not only did Asahi make it through this recession without major losses, the company even managed to gain market leadership in Japan by 1998 (Gale Database 2011). Despite the challenges put upon Asahi through the Japanese financial crisis, the company still managed to slightly increase its operating profits from 1992–93 (Reuters 1994). This indicates that thanks to the transformation process initiated and implemented through Murai and Higuchi, Asahi was now stabilized and strong enough to survive and prosper, even in a hostile environment.

Seto decided to concentrate his attention on Asahi Super Dry. He reiterated the importance of improving the freshness of the beer (Tomita et al. 2008) and seized upon the Japanese inclination towards gratifying freshness. When quenching thirst, 22.6 percent of Japanese have a tendency to consume beer (1.1 percent for sake and 0.6 for percent whisky); 11.5 percent want to have beer under the hot sun (0.5 percent for sake, and 0.2 percent for whisky), and 16.3 percent when relieving stress and to refresh (4.1 percent for sake and 1.6 percent for whisky). This led Asahi to believe that the consumers were also yearning for a light, but refreshing, beer (Nagai 2002).

Seto decided to cut the time of shipment from the factory. In 1993 it took ten days for the beer to be shipped after it was bottled. In 1994 this was cut to five days. In 1997 he introduced TFM (Total Fresh Management), and made it possible to ship beer from the factory to a retailer in eight days (Tomita et al. 2008). In addition to the cut down in lead time of the factory, he abolished DCs (Distribution Centers), and shipped directly from the factory to the wholesalers and retailers. He also introduced an automatic warehousing system and automatic picking system, realizing FIFO (First-In-First-Out). All in all, he managed to cut down on distribution by two days (Tomita et al.). Super Dry's OPM (operating profit margin) had been around 2 percent, but jumped to around 5 percent in 1992. After the introduction of TFM in 1994, OPM reached 7 percent (Tomita et al. 2008).

Importance of Seto to Asahi's Internationalization

Asahi had already engaged in foreign imports and had leveraged established relationships to engage in exporting. The company had started exporting their best-selling product, Asahi Super Dry, to respond to global demand. A year into Seto's mandate, Asahi started significantly expanding foreign operations. Seto emphasized that international expansion, especially in the US and China, was of strategic importance. The US and China were at this point in time the two biggest markets for beer consumption (Tomioka 1996). Furthermore, these were the two markets on which Asahi's Japanese competitors focused their internationalization efforts (Craig 1996).

In order to gain access to the US market, Asahi established a licensing agreement with the Canadian Molson Brewery in 1994. The deal required Molson to manufacture Asahi Super Dry for distribution in all of North America (*New York Times* 1998). Building on this relationship, in 1995, Asahi then set up a marketing and distribution alliance with the Miller Brewing Company (Asahi Breweries Ltd 2011). Through this alliance, the company had achieved their goal of entering the US market. A year later, the company had become the 34th largest import brand in the US (*New York Times* 1998).

Asahi entered the Chinese market in 1994 by acquiring equity stakes in Chinese breweries as part of three joint ventures. Asahi was the first Japanese brewer to enter China. Compared to their international competition, Japanese brewers were late entrants (Kanabayashi 1997). The company entered into a joint venture with Tsingtao Breweries in 1997. This was very much in line with Seto's target of expanding Asahi's presence in Asia (Tomioka 1996). In addition to its licensing agreement in Canada, its alliance in the US and its equity stakes in Australia and China, the company also set up a licensing agreement in the UK with a former exporting partner during Seto's time in office.

Figure 9.3 shows the three leadership eras under scrutiny in this study.

DISCUSSION

Asahi's internationalization was made possible first and foremost as a result of Super Dry's success. This success had its origins in the redesigning

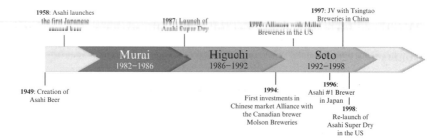

Source: Authors' own illustration.

Figure 9.3   Three eras of leadership

of the company's organizational systems and culture in the home country (Murai), leveraging these systems to create a product that could be used to 'spearhead' internationalization (Higuchi), and then perpetuating and enhancing the growth momentum through selected and differentiated internationalization moves (Seto). Ultimately, the successful launch of Asahi Super Dry in 1987 enabled Asahi to be in a position to internationalize, and to keep up with Kirin's positioning in international markets. Table 9.1 summarizes the leadership eras in which this took place.

Role of Japanese Corporate Governance

The way these leaders approached the specific problems and challenges confronting them raises a question relating to the role played by the unique system of Japanese corporate governance (Yamamura and Streeck 2003), in particular, Sumitomo Bank's involvement. Its long-term supply of 'silent' capital enabled the company to focus on long-term growth (Takeshita 2007). Without this facility, Asahi would not have been able to make the changes it did during the Murai and Higuchi eras, and for their success to be 'handed over' to Seto. This was particularly the case during Higuchi's era, where large capital expenditure (at a time when Asahi's balance sheet looked very weak) was conducted to increase market share.

Asahi is an example of where the Japanese style of governance and banking was effective. In spite of Asahi's dire financial condition, Sumitomo conglomerate and Sumitomo Bank provided adequate finance to fund Asahi's large capital expenditure. We would not have seen the birth and expansion of Asahi Super Dry had it not been for this funding.

Asahi did not have a deliberate internationalization strategy. Seto sought opportunities arising in the company's trading (import/export) network. Under Seto, Asahi engaged in more extensive international

Table 9.1 *Leadership phases and Asahi's readiness for internationalization*

	Murai (1982–86)	Higuchi (1986–92)	Seto (1992–98)
International activities	Few selected exports	Increasing exports	FDI in selected markets using different ownership structures
What?	1. A new vision and re-designing the company's foundation in the home market 2. Increased important licensing with German and US brewers (1982/1984)	1. Genesis of new product with global appeal 2. Centralization for fast decision-making, combined with more openness to encourage innovation	1. Differentiated internationalization based on new spearhead product 2. Focus on distribution and product freshness
Why?	Company cannot internationalize if facing bankruptcy in home market or does not understand foreign competitors	Company cannot internationalize without a product to spearhead the expansion; an innovative orientation is needed to generate new product ideas	Given that the spearhead product was a success in the home country, it was necessary to avoid risk of losing appeal
Key leadership traits	Transformational leadership – set a new vision, created a feeling of crisis, created structural change, engaged employees	Elements of transformational and transactional leadership – continuing the vision set by Murai, overcoming hierarchies that prevent innovation	Transactional leadership – facilitated and developed capabilities put in place by predecessors
Leader's legacy	Saved company from bankruptcy	Left the company as the second largest beer brewer in Japan	Established a strong international position

Source: Authors' own compilation.

agreements with existing trading partners. Despite these internationalization efforts, Asahi's international operations only generated 1 percent of
its sales revenue in 1997 (Reuters 1997). Nevertheless, international performance gradually improved over the subsequent 15 years. For the June
2012 interim, Asahi's overseas business reached ¥74.7 billion out of a total
¥710.3 billion in sales (Asahi Breweries Ltd 2012), exceeding 10 percent
of the total sales of the group. According to Asahi's long-term plan it
expected to boost sales from ¥1.5 trillion (US$18.8 billion, at ¥79.78/$
as of 22 October 2012) at the end of December 2012 to ¥2.0–2.5 trillion
(US$25.0–31.3 billion at ¥79.78/$ as of 22 October 2012) by December
2015 through substantially expanding overseas sales to 30 percent of total
sales (Asahi Breweries Ltd 2009). This equates to quadrupling the overseas
business to ¥400 billion between 2010 and 2015 (Nikkei 2010).

Theoretical Reflection

A limitation of internationalization theory is that it assumes that at the
point of internationalization the firm has corporate systems and a culture
in place that are supportive of – and conducive to – an international
expansion. The Asahi case shows how a company may need to learn from
– and indeed, challenge – past assumptions in its own domestic market
and institutional environment as a prerequisite to internationalizing.
Moreover, potential foreign demand for the firm's product is crucial. For
much of the 1980s, Asahi was a company struggling for survival in its
home market. Before internationalizing, Asahi first had to undergo a corporate transformation. Classic internationalization theories do not specify
when a company should start internationalizing from this 'preparedness'
perspective. Asahi provides evidence that preparedness to internationalize
is determined by the mentalities and actions of leaders present in different
capability development stages. This downplays the role of experience and
networks in foreign markets, and highlights the internal corporate environment in the home country and how this environment may need to be
transformed in order to generate new product innovations that then are
used to spearhead internationalization.

Murai can be described as a transformational leader. He was involved
in creating the case for change, creating structural change and engaging
others in the change process. However, his focus was on introducing a
new vision and implementing a new corporate culture, not on reaching
specific performance targets. The CEO in office at the early thrust of the
internationalization, Seto, was more of a transactional leader. Between
1992 and 1997 Asahi started international operations in six new countries.
When Seto stepped down in 1998, Asahi's internationalization strategy

had not been all that successful. In 1997 its international sales still only marked 1 percent of its overall sales (Reuters 1997). This raises a question of whether a more transformational leader is better suited for a company that remains at this departure point to internationalization.

Nevertheless, Murai, Higuchi and Seto acted in accordance with Higgs and Rowland's (2005) model. It was Murai's visionary turnaround and Higuchi's precise implementation that laid the foundation for Seto to take the company international. This suggests that different leaders are appropriate at different evolutionary stages of a company in the run-up to it internationalizing. It also suggests that internationalization patterns (timing, locations, entry and ownership modes) of a company are a function of the business conditions and the mentalities and actions of leaders many years before the company actually starts to embark on FDI.

We believe future research needs to dig more deeply into the subtle nuances between different types of ownership advantages (Dunning 1981, 1988) as they relate to the construct of preparedness to internationalize. The current case suggests that one angle to this is the ownership advantages embodied in products that are used as a platform to internationalize. These can be seen as asset ownership advantages (Oa) in Dunning's (1988) terms. Whether this advantage accrues from innovative technology, a country of origin effect, or some other source, these spearhead products are clearly needed in the early stages of international market-seeking where a company has previously been domestically focused. Another angle to this preparedness-to-internationalize construct relates to the leadership qualities that steer the company towards a new global vision and reality. Such transformational qualities may be seen in terms of a transaction ownership advantage (Ot) in Dunning's (1988) terms. Not to be confused with transactional leadership, these advantages relate to how benefits arise through hierarchical governance of the multinational enterprise (MNE). Future research could investigate how – as suggested by the current case – Ot advantages of domestic transformation are a precursor to Oa advantages of innovative products that subsequently have international appeal.

CONCLUSION

In 1982 Asahi had its back against the wall. The company was facing bankruptcy. It appointed a transformational leader, Murai, who introduced his vision to Asahi, laying the foundation for a turnaround. His successor, Higuchi, implemented Murai's vision and continued the transformation in Asahi, resulting in the launch of Asahi Super Dry. When

Seto took over the company in 1992, Asahi had a stable competitive position in the home market, a product with potential foreign demand and established relations with overseas trading partners. In the aftermath of the Japanese financial crisis, Seto continued to engage in significant international expansion.

The principal driver for the internationalization of Asahi was the introduction and success of Asahi Super Dry. The case highlights how there is a lack of appreciation in popular internationalization theories of the role that successive leaders play in laying out the organizational foundations in the home country by which a spearheading product can be developed and sustained to build a platform for increasing commitments in foreign markets. The case of Asahi suggests that transformational and transactional leaders are necessary at different times to take a brewing company to a stage where it is ready to internationalize.

REFERENCES

Abegglen, J.C. and G. Stalk Jr. (1986), 'The Japanese corporation as competitor', *California Management Review*, **28** (3), 9–27.

Andersen, O. (1993), 'On the internationalization process of firms: a critical analysis', *Journal of International Business Studies*, **24** (2), 209–31.

Asahi Breweries Ltd (2009), 長期ビジョン*2015*&中期経営計画*2012* (2015 Long-Term Vision and 2012 Mid-Term Vision), Tokyo: Asahi Breweries Ltd.

Asahi Breweries Ltd (2010), *Annual Report*, accessed November 2011 at www.asahigroup-holdings.com/en/ir/annual_report/index.html.

Asahi Breweries Ltd (2011), 'Corporate website – history', accessed November 2011 at www.asahigroup-holdings.com/en/company/history/index.html.

Asahi Breweries Ltd (2012) *2012*年第*2*四半期決算と通期事業方針 (2012 2Q Earnings and Full Year Outlook), Tokyo: Asahi Breweries Ltd.

Avolio, B.J., B.M. Bass and D.I. Jung (1999), 'Re-examining the components of transformational and transactional leadership using the multifactor leadership', *Journal of Occupational and Organizational Psychology*, **72**, 441–62.

Barney, J. (1991), 'Firm resources and sustained competitive advantage', *Journal of Management*, **17** (1), 99–120.

Bass, B.M. and B.J. Avolio (1990), *Transformational Leadership Development: Manual for Multifactor Leadership Questionnaire*, Palo Alto, CA: Consulting Psychologist Press.

Bass, B.M., B.J. Avolio, D.I. Jung and Y. Berson (2003), 'Predicting unit performance by assessing transformational and transactional leadership', *Journal of Applied Psychology*, **88** (2), 207–18.

Buckley, P.J. and M. Casson (1976), *The Future of the Multinational Enterprise*, London: Macmillan.

Coase, R.J. (1937), 'The nature of the firm', *Economica*, **4** (16), 386–405.

Conger, J.A. and D.A. Nadler (2004), 'When CEOs step up to fail', *MIT Sloan Management Review*, **45** (3), 50–56.

Craig, T. (1996), 'The Japanese beer wars: initiating and responding to hypercompetition in new product development', *Organization Science*, **7** (3), 302–21.

Dunning, J. (1981), *International Production and the Multinational Enterprise*, London: Allen and Unwin.

Dunning, J. (1988), 'The eclectic paradigm of international production: a restatement and some possible extensions', *Journal of International Business Studies*, **19** (1), 1–31.

Dunning, J. (2000), 'The eclectic paradigm as an envelope for economic and business theories of MNE activity', *International Business Review*, **9** (2), 163–90.

Euromonitor International (2011), *Beer in Japan*, 2 March, accessed via Global Market Information Database, 13 November 2011.

Financial Times (1989), 'Survey of Japanese industry: a taste for new products – beer industry', *Financial Times*, 4 December, accessed via Factiva.

Gale Database (2011), *Asahi Breweries Ltd*, accessed via Gale Database, 13 November 2011.

Geringer, J.M., C.A. Frayne and D. Olsen (1998), 'Rewarding growth or profit? Top management team compensation and governance in Japanese MNEs', *Journal of International Management*, **4** (4), 289–309.

Hayashi, Shuji (1984), *Keiei to Bunka*, Tokyo: Chuo-Koron sha.

Higgs, M. and D. Rowland (2005), 'All changes great and small: exploring approaches to change and its leadership', *Journal of Change Management*, **4** (2), 121–51.

Jameson, S. (1988), 'Team spirit: the case of Asahi Breweries illustrates how bank rescues of struggling firms help the Japanese economy. But there is no guarantee of success', *Los Angeles Times*, 8 December.

Johanson, J. and J.E. Vahlne (1977), 'The internationalization process of the firm – a model of knowledge development and increasing foreign market commitments', *Journal of International Business Studies*, **8** (1), 23–32.

Johanson, J. and J.E. Vahlne (2009), 'The Uppsala internationalization process model revised: from liability of foreignness to liability of outsidership', *Journal of International Business Studies*, **40**, 1411–31.

Johansson, J. and F. Wiedersheim-Paul (1975), 'The internationalization of the firm: four Swedish cases', *Journal of Management Studies*, **12** (3), 305–22.

Jones, M.V. and N.E. Coviello (2005), 'Internationalisation: conceptualising an entrepreneurial process of behavior in time', *Journal of International Business Studies*, **36**, 284–303.

Kanabayashi, M. (1997), 'Top Japan breweries expand quickly to tap China's beer market', *The Asian Wall Street Journal*, 27 March.

Kokuryo, J. and S. Asaba (1994), 'Asahi Breweries Ltd', *Harvard Business Review*, Case 9-389-114.

Kyodo News International (1992), 'Asahi breaks habit in picking new president', 28 July, accessed via Factiva.

Martin, D., C. Howard and P. Herbig (1998), 'The Japanese distribution system', *European Business Review*, **98** (2), 109–21.

McLain, T.E., M.D. Schultz and J. Kawai (1995), 'Japan – why more foreign firms are succeeding in Japan', *East Asian Executive Reports*, **17**, 7–7.

Muto, Y. (2007), 人材戦略のキーワード 第20回：エンパワーメント (Keyword for Human Resource Strategies, No. 20: Empowerment), Strategy and Technology of Management, Yasuaki Muto homepage, electronic version, accessed 12 October 2012 at http://muto-web.jp/rensai/keyword020.html.

Nagai, T. (2002), ビール15年戦争 すべてはドライから始まった (15-Year Beer War – All Started With Dry), Nihon Keizai Shinbun Sha, pp. 41–4.

Nakajo, T. and T. Kono (1989), 'Success through culture change in a Japanese brewery', *Long Range Planning*, **22** (6), 29–37.

New York Times (1998), 'The company that makes Japan's best-selling beer seeks inroads into the U.S. market', *New York Times*, 20 April, p. 8.

Nikkei (2010), 'アサヒ、5年で海外売上高4倍に 中国最大手に出資' ['Asahi to quadruple overseas sales in 5 years, investing in largest Chinese firm'], *Nihon Keizai Shinbun*, electronic version, 24 September 24, accessed 18 September 2012 at http://www.nikkei.com/.

Pascale, R. and T.P. Rohlen (1983), 'The Mazda turnaround', *Journal of Japanese Studies*, **9** (2), 220–63.

Reid, T.R. (1994), 'Japan's brewing price war – retail revolution sends imported beer to the bargain basement', *The Washington Post*, 17 August.

Reuters (1994), 'Asahi Brew 1994 parent current up 45.9 pct', Reuters Ltd, accessed via Factiva.

Reuters (1997), 'Asahi sees Japan market share bubbling', 4 June, accessed via Factiva.

Senge, P.M. (1997), 'Communities of leaders and learners', *Harvard Business Review*, **75** (5), 30–31.

Takeshita, S. (2007), 'The transformation of the Japanese business system; structural, institutional and organizational determinants of change and continuity', dissertation, University of London.

Tomioka, K. (1996), 'The secret behind Asahi's growth – interview with Yuzo Seto', *Japan 21st*, November, pp. 12–13.

Tomita, J., Y. Takai and N. Jinmae (2008), 'アサヒビールの競争力の源泉' (Asahi Brewery's Source of Competitiveness), MMRC Discussion Paper No. 221, University of Tokyo.

Toyo Keizai (2006), *Kaigai Shinshutsu Kigyou Souran* (Japanese Investments Overseas 2006), Tokyo, Japan: Toyo Keizai Inc.

Utsunomiya, H. and K. Hashizume (2008), *Investigation of Consumers' Motives for Their Choice of Sake, Beer, and Whisky*, Hiroshima: National Research Institute for Brewing.

Yamamura, K. and W. Streeck (2003), *The End of Diversity? Prospects for German and Japanese Capitalism*, Ithaca, NY: Cornell University Press.

Yoshida, K. (1993), *Nihongata keiei system no kozai*. Tokyo: Toyo Keizai Shinposha.

10. The demise of Anheuser-Busch: arrogance, hubris and strategic weakness in the face of intense internationalization

Ian M. Taplin, Jens Gammelgaard, Christoph Dörrenbächer and Mike Geppert

INTRODUCTION[1]

Anheuser-Busch (A-B) began operations in 1852 in St Louis, Missouri (as the Bavarian Brewery) and has held the position of industry leader in the US since 1957. It has been run, but not controlled, by the Busch family since its founding. Despite wielding considerable influence and being able to appoint family members to the chief executive officer (CEO) position, the Busch family nonetheless owned only 4 per cent of the company's stock and in that respect ultimately lacked authority and the requisite control that could have allowed them to counter the moves that subsequently undermined their 'rule'. By the time the company was taken over in 2008, following a year of on-and-off negotiations, it was ultimately the A-B board that finally agreed to an offer of $70 a share from In-Bev SA/NV and it was submitted for shareholder approval which subsequently came at the end of the year. The acquisition cost In-Bev $53 bn (€33 bn) and gave them prime position in the world's most profitable beer market but also marked the end of A-B's 150 years of independence. The events that precipitated this takeover surprised many, but for others it was the inevitable nail in the coffin of inefficiency, arrogance and the failure to react to an emerging global marketplace when domestic beer sales were declining.

A-B's demise is simultaneously a tale of obsession about domestic market share by key family members, profligacy and an unwillingness to embrace internationalization until it was too late and even then done haphazardly and without strategic focus. It is the story of how a family-run business retained oversight often through sheer force of individual personality yet refused to acknowledge the impact of other key players in the global brewing industry. This proved increasingly problematic as the market for beer internationally was changing dramatically. An almost myopic view of globalization, plus mistrust of overseas brewers with whom tentative strategic alliances were forged, ultimately hindered the firm's ability to pursue internationalization strategies that were increasingly the norm for their competitors. Behind this America-centric culture at A-B, and framing the firm's operating philosophies, was a corporate arrogance by key Busch family members whose single-minded pursuit of domestic market share blinded them from the realities of an increasingly international brewing industry undergoing consolidation. The more they equivocated in their response to changing market conditions, the more vulnerable they became to a takeover.

In this chapter, we look at A-B's strategy and performance over the past 30 years, examining the acquisitions and diversification they embraced, the single-minded pursuit via expensive marketing of dominance over the US domestic beer market, and ultimately the larger than life role played by key family members and their almost feudal arrogance when it came to day-to-day decision-making. Increasingly, therefore, A-B must be seen as a company that was forged through the visions of family members who exercised authoritarian leadership but whose unwillingness to cede legitimacy to alternative viewpoints left it vulnerable to a changing marketplace that they were ill-equipped to navigate.

The events at A-B are part of a broader story of the global consolidation in the brewing industry, where firms are searching for ownership of strong international brands when domestic consumption is either declining or at least stable. This has assumed greater importance with opportunities in the two growing markets of China and Russia, long denied access to foreign brands, as well as in mature markets where prominent brands allow premium pricing (*Financial Times*, 24 July 2008). Since raw material and transportation costs have risen dramatically in previous years, premium pricing allows firms to absorb these costs without excessively damaging their profitability. Because local brands sell more cheaply it is difficult to raise prices in this segment to offset such increases.

The strength of A-B's two major beers, Bud Light and Budweiser (numbers one and three in the top beer brands ranked by sales volume in 2007), were seen by In-Bev as a lever to transfer their own domestic success to international markets. Their assessment of A-B was that the company's brand management was superior to their cost-efficiency, their operations often viewed as 'bloated' (*Wall Street Journal*, 12 June 2008). Because A-B had made substantial profits on beer sales, there had always been a disincentive to focus upon costs and expenses. This was combined with the company's renown for its largesse locally and an extravagance that was firmly entrenched in the operating culture. That extravagance meant that the marketing side of the firm was given considerable freedom and budgets to build an image-defining brand, one that could leverage A-B to a prominent position in the domestic US market. As one advertising agency executive noted, 'they wrote the book on sports marketing ... putting a Budweiser sign in every stadium in every town and devising local programs and promotions' (MacIntosh 2011, p. 61). Marketing and brewing operations were spared no expense under August Busch III (known generally as the Third) and it was this that In-Bev honed in on when they prepared their takeover plans.

In-Bev's reputation as a tough and efficient operator gave it the confidence to mount a bid since it believed there were opportunities for rationalization. It also gave In-Bev access to the US market in which hitherto it had little presence. For A-B it was the culmination of many unsuccessful diversification strategies and a late entry into international expansion that often left it paying more for acquisitions than experts felt was appropriate. It is also a testament to ongoing struggles for control within the firm and tensions between the Third and his son, August Busch IV, who took over as CEO in 2006.

For the past 20–30 years, A-B had relentlessly pursued a strategy designed to increase its domestic market share, which by 2002 had reached 52 per cent. This was driven by an obsession by the Third to become the dominant brewer in the US and it often subordinated all other concerns. Since he took over in the 1970s, the Third had almost single-mindedly pursued this goal, sparing no expense in ever more costly marketing campaigns. He believed that the more dominant A-B became domestically, the more it could be insulated against whatever might be happening internationally – not that he was ever really that aware of international beer trends. The further away from St Louis executives were, the less input they had into routine decision-making and corporate strategy. In fact, overseas positions were often used to park managers who were deemed insignificant and therefore whatever insights they might have had about global brewing went unheeded. The Busch family was so dependent upon the US market for sales that it largely ignored what was happening internationally. Since the US was the largest and most highly profitable beer market, A-B's managers felt confident concentrating their efforts domestically, and with the Third's indifference to overseas expansion, it was almost inevitable that complacency became entrenched.

Whenever there was threat from domestic competition, A-B's response was to flex its marketing muscle, demanding high standards from its advertising agencies but also rewarding them lucratively. Having built strong relationships with its distributors, and having rewarded them handsomely, the goal was typically to move more beer into the mouths of consumers. The reliance upon marketing to get it out of difficulties had worked in the 1970s and even the 1980s but in subsequent decades the marketplace for beer was changing to such an extent that such strategies were no longer so effective. Not only were sales falling as consumers shifted to wine and liquor plus craft beers, but imports were also increasing. On top of that the marketers found it increasingly difficult, as MacIntosh notes, 'to invent beer occasions that provided excuses for people to drink' (2001, p. 105). With fewer and fewer opportunities for growth domestically, overseas expansion would be the obvious route. Yet the intransigence on the part of the Third to seriously develop an international strategy during the 1980s meant that efforts in this area would be too little and probably too late.

A-B had entered into a series of joint ventures and strategic alliances as part of an overseas expansion strategy in the mid 1980s and this trend continued as it aggressively pursued acquisitions in China. In the 1980s it also pursued vertical integration by acquiring container manufacturing facilities; as well as investing in industries deemed complementary to beer – wine coolers and soft drinks, snacks and entertainment. Success in these industries varied and some were subsequently divested. The Third's logic here was that such industries were probably related (people eat snacks whilst drinking beer) so there should be marketing synergies.

HISTORY

In 1982 A-B acquired bread and snacks maker Campbell Taggert for $560 m ($110 m more than the firm's market value at the time) in the belief that it could use their existing distribution and marketing networks to sell pretzels and cookies efficiently, thus recouping the premium they paid for the company (*Financial Times*, 10 June 2006). This was part of A-B's strategy to find synergies from complementary activities and remained a core value during the 1980s and 1990s. According to Annual Reports of this time period, the stated core competencies included a commitment to product quality, comprehensive marketing, a solid wholesale distribution system, and the synergies that come from complementary investments in key industries (baking, container manufacturing and entertainment). Throughout this time period, despite significant losses in several of these sectors, it continued to believe that the skills and capabilities derived from beer making could be easily applied to the related industries and thus operating efficiencies could be maintained.

Alongside Campbell Taggert was a continued investment throughout the 1980s in Metal Container Corporation (the fastest growing container and lid manufacturer in the US, which enabled A-B to benefit from increased sales in the soft drinks industries), Eagle Snacks, Inc. and Busch Entertainment (theme parks). These were a crucial part of A-B's long-term diversification strategy, with each seen as an integral part of building the A-B brand across a range of activities. According to the 1987 Annual Report (p. 2), 'this vertical integration and diversification strategy resulted in increased knowledge of the economics of those businesses, assured quality, and control of both packaging and raw materials costs'.

Whilst A-B has retained its profitable amusement parks business, it sold the St Louis Cardinals baseball team and the Eagle Snack division in 1996, the latter proving to be perennially unprofitable and damaging to overall earnings (*Wall Street Journal*, 25 August 1996). Seventeen years of red ink for Eagle Snacks resulted in little initial interest in the company when it went up for sale, and a significant mark down in the selling price left A-B with a $206 m write-off and the acknowledgment of how difficult it is even for firms with a marketing powerhouse to expand operations to other industries. What were assumed to be synergies (distributing and marketing salty snacks and bread along the same channels as beer) proved wrong, as distributors saw the moves as diversions that diluted their focus (*Business Week*, 3 April 1996). It turns out that beer and snacks go to different areas of supermarkets and convenience stores and are ordered by different officials, making distribution more complicated than A-B anticipated. Furthermore, the margins on snacks are much lower than beer since people are not prepared to pay high mark-ups for the former, whilst the latter continued to be a 'money minting machine' for A-B (MacIntosh 2011, p. 113).

With sales of wine coolers slowing during the late 1980s, together with an increase in the adult population, A-B focused upon reaching this growing population and invested heavily in plant modernization to expand brewing capacity. However, during this time period A-B and other brewers faced pressures from the anti-drinking lobby (neo-Prohibitionists) and attempts by the federal government to increase taxes on alcohol. This resulted in the diversion of resources to fund lobbying efforts to fight the growing stigmatization of beer drinking[2] and is symptomatic of the conservative social and political climate purveyors of alcoholic beverages continue in some ways to face in the US. As a result of these external pressures, A-B devoted much time and energy to promoting the positive aspects of beer drinking. In the 1991 Annual Report, for example, it argued that 'beer is an enjoyable and healthful American tradition' and provided it is consumed responsibly and in moderation A-B should have a right to brew beer. The same tone continued in subsequent reports for the next decade.

Growth of beer volume and sales was constant through the late 1980s, with market share climbing from 26 per cent in 1979 to 39.9 per cent in 1987 and 43.7 per cent in 1990. This, however, changed in the 1990s as the domestic beer market changed, with competition from imports and alternative alcoholic beverages increasing, plus increased regulations added to operational costs.

REGULATORY ENVIRONMENT AND PRICE WARS

In 1991 the excise tax on beer doubled, and with the normal price increases that reflected increased production costs the result was a 10–12 per cent price increase at the retail level, which produced a 0.5 per cent reduction in sales volume (although industry wide the figure was a 2 per cent decline, so A-B fared relatively well). During the early 1990s, flat consumer demand had started to dent prices and market share, with growth in the latter stalling (from 44 per cent in 1991 to 45 per cent in 1995, then falling to 44 percent in 1996). In 1995 A-B's beer profits fell 5 per cent. Market share remained between 46 and 48 per cent, reaching a peak of 52 per cent in 2002. Since then market share has fallen back to the upper 40s.

In 2005, price wars with lower priced competitors, such as SABMiller's Miller Lite and Molson Coors, resulted in a reduction of wholesaler profits by 20 per cent, the reduction of the price of beer to levels that according to industry experts potentially damage brand equity, and finally, to two consecutive quarters of lower than expected earnings (*Financial Times*, 20 November 2005).

Increased market fragmentation along age and income lines forced brewers to develop niche products such as 'premium light beers' and foreign brands. A-B entered the spirits industry with a subsidiary, Long Tail Libations, that launched a flavoured spirit called Jekyll and Hyde. Beer's share of alcohol servings fell from 59.6 per cent to 58.1 per cent between 1998 and 2004 as consumers switched to wine and spirits (Adams Beverage Group 2007).

In 2006 A-B faced significant price competition from its major domestic competitor SABMiller, whilst also experiencing pressure from an increase in wine and spirits consumption in the US. Together with an increase in 'craft beers'[3] and foreign imports such as Heineken, these events have had a significant impact on A-B. It responded by acquiring domestic regional brewer Rolling Rock in 2006 plus several craft brewers, although in the latter case allowed them to retain their craft brewing name and image to allay fears of a decline in quality. The idea was to capitalize upon A-B's distribution system to promote and sell such beers without their status as craft brewers being diminished.

An overview of the basic financial performance of A-B during the past two decades is contained in Table 10.1.

OPERATIONAL STRATEGY

Alongside its marketing prowess, A-B under the Third placed emphasis upon production, making quality a central part of its operating strategy. It invested in plant modernization alongside new product development, designed to keep product lines fresh and appealing and meet increased consumer demand. For example, the introduction of Michelob Dry in 1988, using a unique DryBrew™ method of brewing, was designed to bolster the super-premium category as the industry's first dry beer (Annual Report 1988, p. 12). In addition, new breweries came online during the later 1980s and early 1990s as part of a planned capacity expansion programme. The entry of Bud Draft into national distribution in 1990 allowed A-B to solidify the 'dry' category and provide 'consumers with a whole new direction in beer taste' (Annual Report 1990, p. 14). This innovation required investments in newer brewing processes but, when coupled with an aggressive marketing campaign, proved to be a successful new product with consumers.

In 1992 A-B had initiated a total quality process that was designed to enhance individual job performance by employees, which resulted in productivity improvements whilst retaining a commitment to quality. This led to an expense reduction of $720 m since 1980 (Annual Report 1992, p. 11). It also continued to maintain strong, often personal, and even family relationships with its distributors. Approximately 900 independent wholesalers distribute A-B products and both parties indicate the strength of open communication sharing as key to their operating success. Yet numerous Busch relatives, including half brothers and their wives, owned distributors, sustaining a further dimension to the family aura of the company as well as providing lucrative opportunities for such individuals. On top of minority shareholding a picture increasingly emerges of a company very much beholden to the interest and opinions of family members (see MacIntosh 2011 for further details). The consequence of this was the persistence of a culture of conformity, with critical shareholder groups outside of this minority effectively silenced. The strength of A-B in its home town and the strong institutional legacy of de facto if not de jure family control reinforced this situation.[4]

Table 10.1 Net income and earnings per share: 1986–2006

	1986	1987	1988	1989	1990	1991	1992	1993*	1994	1995
Net income (millions of $)	518.0	614.7	715.9	767.2	842.4	939.8	994.2	594.5 (980.6)	1032.1	642.3
Earnings per share	1.69	2.04	2.45	2.68	2.95	3.25	3.20	2.17 (3.55)	3.88	1.24

Cont.	1996	1997	1998	1999	2000	2001	2002	2003	2004	2005	2006
Net income (millions of $)	1189.9	1169.2	1233.3			1705	1933.8	2075.9	2118.7	1744.4	1965.2
Earnings per share	2.34	2.34	2.53			1.89	2.23	2.51	2.65	2.24	2.55

Notes: * Pre-tax restructuring charges; amounts exclusive of such charges indicated in parenthesis.

Source: Annual reports.

In 1995 A-B retrenched and closed the Tampa, Florida brewery and reduced its wholesaler inventory levels – actions claimed to be in the interests of efficiency and freshness of products, but also indicative of heightened market competition around costs. In making these moves A-B recognized that the domestic marketplace was changing and rationalization of production was drastically needed.

Market share declined to 48.8 per cent in 2005 following increased competition from other domestic brands and imports. Combined with an increase in raw materials and energy costs this reduced margins, and the result was a significant drop in operating income and lower earnings per share over the previous year (see Table 10.1). The company responded by cutting bonuses, freezing salaries and changing health care obligations. Employment levels were reduced by 4.1 per cent. The eras of company largesse were beginning to fade. Productivity increases followed and the price of beer fell, which allowed A-B to remain competitive in a fiercely cost-driven marketplace. Nonetheless, market share fell to 48.4 per cent by 2006.

In 2006 A-B experimented with a further localization strategy called 'you choose it, we'll brew it', allowing local breweries to customize their beer and solicit input on styles from local consumers. Preferred types would subsequently be brewed in larger batches for that area (Annual Report 2006). In this respect they were trying to address a flat domestic market with localized production strategies designed to woo adherents to craft beer. This also came at a time when wine and spirits sales were rising in the US, potentially eroding the market for beer consumption.

By 2008 A-B continued to struggle to reduce costs throughout its manufacturing and distribution system and implemented further modernization in its brewing operations. Increased cost competition in the domestic market, slower sales and the growth of wine and spirit sales all cut into A-B's domestic market. Its entertainment segment (theme parks) remained successful though. Following an earlier realization that anticipated synergies from diversification were not occurring and that continued losses were unsustainable, in the mid 1990s A-B had switched from an interest in snack food and bakeries to an aggressive policy of international expansion in beer – its core product. Finally it recognized that its past strategies in this area were insufficient to compensate for changes in the domestic market. But, unlike other major global brewers, it lacked both the experience internationally and was arriving late on the scene. Furthermore, few were convinced that the Third really believed in international expansion as he seemed hesitant to commit resources to acquisitions, often preferring joint ventures. Even then, many of the decisions were questionable from both a financial and strategic point of view.

INTERNATIONALIZATION

As domestic market growth waned, A-B used strategies of joint ventures and strategic alliances to gain market entry overseas. The period 1999–2006 is one in which international sales assumed greater significance in A-B's balance sheet; growth of 20 per cent annually since 1999 resulted in such sales accounting for 32 per cent of net income in 2006. A-B identified overseas markets, originally Japan, the UK, Mexico and Europe and then China and now more recently Russia (the world's fifth largest beer market), as the key regions targeted for growth.

Budweiser has been distributed in Japan since 1981 and through the 1990s was the leading international beer brand in that country. In 1993 a joint venture between A-B and Japan's Kirin Brewery (operating as Budweiser Japan Company Ltd) was formed to control marketing, sales and distribution of Budweiser in Japan. In Korea a licensing agreement with Oriental Brewing Company Ltd allowed Budweiser to establish a share in excess of 70 per cent of the international beer brands in that country (Annual Report 1993, p. 16).

Budweiser was introduced to the UK in 1984 and has continued to gain market share as one of the fastest growing premium lagers in the market. Budweiser began to be brewed in Ireland in 1986 under licensing agreements with Guinness-Ireland and by 1990 achieved a sales growth of 52 per cent. In 1990 Anheuser-Busch European Trade Ltd was formed to develop sales, distribution and marketing of A-B beer brands in Europe and to take advantage of the elimination of trade barriers and moves towards market-based economies (Annual Report 1990, p. 17).

In 1991 Busch and O'Douls were introduced in the Canadian market and sales have grown. In the 1992 Annual Report (p. 14) there is a clear statement on the importance of growth opportunities in the world beer market and the need for A-B to aggressively pursue the dual objectives of building Budweiser's worldwide presence and establishing a significant international business operation through equity investments and joint ventures.

In 1993 A-B invested \$16.4 m for a 5 per cent stake in Tsingtao, China's largest brewing company. Also in 1993, A-B acquired a 17.7 per cent interest in Mexico's leading brewer, Grupo Modelo SA, for \$477 m; this built upon a 1989 agreement between the two brewers that established an export distribution of Budweiser in Mexico. In May 1997 A-B doubled that stake to 37 per cent with an additional \$550 m investment, and then two months later in June announced its intention to exercise the remaining option to increase ownership to 50.2 per cent. According to several *Wall Street Journal* articles this was in part motivated by a desire to reduce its reliance upon the mature US beer market and also to capitalize upon the growing success in the US of Modelo's best-selling brand, Corona. This complemented sales increases in Latin America and the Caribbean, although A-B by 1999 still only had a 2 per cent share of sales in these regions (*International Herald Tribune*, 24 June 1999). In most cases A-B sought minority stakeholding in established brewers in these regions, hoping to capitalize on their growing beer markets. In January 2006 Grupo Modelo's CEO, Carlos Fernandez, was appointed to A-B's board.

In 2002 A-B increased its stake in Tsingtao to 9.9 per cent and although the company did not provide sales figures for China at that time it says it that it reached operating profit there in 2001 (*Wall Street Journal*, 30 June 2003).

In 1995 A-B acquired an 80 per cent stake in Wuhan brewery in China but had to invest substantially ($170 m by 2003) in equipment modifications to attain the requisite operational efficiency. Then in 2004 A-B entered a bidding war with SABMiller over a hostile bid for Harbin Brewery, China's fourth largest brewer. Seen by many as an effort by A-B to counter SABMiller's expansion in China's fast growing beer market (*Financial Times*, 6 May 2004), it surprised Tsingtao's chairman Li Guirong who thought that it would undermine Tsingtao's strategic partnership with A-B (*Financial Times*, 17 May 2004) and breached exclusivity agreements. Instead it led Tsingtao to reaffirm its own strategy of consolidation in the Chinese beer market (acquisition of 48 breweries allowed it to raise its sales from 2 per cent to 12.8 per cent between 1996 and 2003) as it imposed its own operating efficiencies and economies of scale on many money losing ventures.

A-B's winning bid of $720 m was viewed by some in the business press as excessive (about $200 m more than the company was worth)[5] and a year later the company had still not conclusively decided what to do with the acquisition or how it related to their relationship with Tsingtao (*Financial Times*, 29 June 2005). A-B stated that it had no intention of combining Harbin and Tsingtao's operations, with the result that margins would probably get even thinner. Its early attempts at marketing Budweiser to wealthy Chinese consumers would have little relevance to the Harbin acquisition since the market is different. Even with Budweiser it faced problems, since premium beer is only 5 per cent of total consumption and the majority of beer is essentially a commodity product. As Heracleous (2001, p. 40) argued about the entry into the Chinese market by resource rich Western brewers in the 1990s, brand advertising successfully created awareness of the product but not the desire or the ability to pay for it. Or as Lawrence (2000) stated, in quoting Tsingtao's chairman, Western brewers brought the best equipment and the best technology and made a

high quality product, but then had to sell it at a high price to get the high
returns. This proved not to be the case, as in recent years Chinese consum
ers have shown a propensity to prefer local beers and are very price sensitive. Until Harbin can attain operating efficiencies to lower its production
costs it will also be at a price disadvantage in the domestic Chinese market.

A-B SUFFERS ITS OWN TAKEOVER

With the 2008 In-Bev takeover of A-B, the largest all-cash deal in history,
A-B's earlier profligacy and strategies that were often inappropriate or too
late came to an end. In-Bev had initially offered $65 a share, confident that
it could get the necessary financing for such a deal and attain the requisite
cost savings to repay the loans. In-Bev's CEO Carolos Brito also realized
that such an offer would probably be rejected by A-B even though the
company had seen its share price decline and thus become vulnerable to
a takeover. However, it would make the board realize that the company
could be worth more if sold than through operating profits and this would
certainly stimulate interest by the newer investors in the company. Since
A-B's shareholders were no longer predominantly small time, once local
investors, but now institutional investors and hedge funds, the short-term
financial benefits to such a takeover amongst this group would be readily
apparent. Brito recognized this as a lever to sway the board in favour of
a takeover even if A-B's family members were opposed to such a deal.
He was prepared to wait and then evaluate the counter offer proposed by
A-B. When this came at $70 a share and he was able to secure financing
from a broad array of banks,[6] the deal was complete.

Initially it appeared that August Busch III was hostile to the takeover
since he told beer distributors at an April 2008 meeting in Chicago that a
takeover would not happen 'on my watch' (*Wall Street Journal*, 12 June
2008). Eventually however, he gave it his support and this eliminated any
nascent opposition within the senior management staff and amongst the
board.

Although he had been replaced as CEO in 2006 by his son, August
Busch IV, it was apparent to most people that he still exercised considerable control as chairman of the board. When the latter took over he
inherited a company lacking a coherent global strategy since the Third had
been too preoccupied with beating Miller in the domestic marketplace to
systematically think about internationalization. Whilst the Fourth recognized that A-B's only real chance of growth would be overseas, he was still
opposed in many of his initial overseas forays by his father, who continued
to view him as a combination of wayward son and inexperienced strategic

manager. Nonetheless, the Fourth initiated frantic discussions to purchase the remaining shares of Grupo Modelo SA that would have made A-B too expensive for In-Bev to acquire.

At this time Modelo suspected that A-B's play was defensive and motivated by its own desire to remain independent. Although behind the scenes discussions were intensely secretive, involving bankers and lawyers from major institutions (particularly Goldman and Citigroup), word soon leaked out. Secretly, the Fourth had finally secured Modelo's tentative compliance with the plan only by offering Carlos Fernandez the position of CEO of the new combined company, to be still headquartered in St Louis. Done mainly to secure the support of Modelo's voting trust, which in turn is controlled by a family patriarch, 90-year-old Antonio Fernandez, this was clearly too much for the Third (and to be frank many others on the board) who could not countenance this venerable American brewer and family dynasty being run by a Mexican. When this proposal was shelved (*Wall Street Journal*, 13 June 2008), executives at Modelo felt betrayed and considered making their own overtures to In-Bev. By then, however, In-Bev's final offer was too much for A-B's board to ignore in the interests of maximizing shareholder interests.

Resistance by family members, plus others in the St Louis area where A-B is headquartered, proved short-lived because A-B's defences were ultimately quite weak. But it was also apparent that many on the board lacked confidence in the Fourth's ability to run the company. Because of his inexperience and earlier wayward behaviour he was still viewed by many as a playboy rather than a CEO. They felt he did not really understand the business and were not confident he could stamp his authority and vision (if he had one) on the company. Finally, in an effort to increase the transparency of corporate governance – a belated response to the Third's autocratic rule – the board felt they had to be unambiguously clear in representing shareholder interests. Since In-Bev was valuing the company so highly it would have been churlish of them to ignore the offer and conceivably a violation of their fiduciary responsibilities to not accept it.

Writing in the *Wall Street Journal* (17 June 2008), Andrew Sorkin noted 'There's no staggered board and shareholders can act by written consent – meaning they can oust the board at any time. But that's not the real point. The Buschs have done a lousy job of managing the company and shareholders have suffered.' At the end of the day, a family run company was victim to shareholder value concerns and was incapable of finding an alternative scenario to postpone what many saw as inevitable. Its failure to invest significantly overseas – a legacy of August Busch III – and growing domestic competition from craft beers and wines, plus a flattened domestic market, all resulted in a lacklustre stock price which made the company a takeover target. Furthermore, its powerful US domestic presence, and the brand that it has built, has proved expensive in marketing terms ($500 m in advertising plus $300 m in sponsorship), although it reflects a strategy of 'outspending' the major competitors that undoubtedly will be cut by In-Bev.

CONCLUSION

As the dominant player in a mature market, where competition is price-based and cost-driven and where consolidation has apparently allowed major competitors (SABMiller) to realize economies of scale and drive down their own cost structures, A-B was in an almost frenzied state of rationalization to cope with the changing marketplace. A-B's ventures overseas led to an increase in sales and a growth of market share but it did not always demonstrate fiscal wisdom in some of its acquisitions, especially in China. Paying above market value for some firms led the business press to view its expansion strategies with scepticism – as if it were driven reactively to deprive its major competitors from acquiring market share rather than as part of a proactive plan to build market presence in emerging markets. Memories of its disastrous forays into snack foods and soft drinks in the 1980s, when synergies were deemed abundant and inevitable by the company, also came back to haunt the company in its last few years as an independent operator.

While A-B remained an operationally efficient company, willing to continuously upgrade manufacturing capabilities to squeeze ever greater scale efficiencies, relative to its competitors it often seemed adrift and wavered when it came to executing strategy. It recognized that further consolidation both domestically and in international markets was inevitable, but also recognized that its brand was under constant threat from similarly resource rich competitors. At the end of the day it failed to get the most from its major asset, which is its brand and taking it overseas, despite investing heavily in marketing. By relying too heavily upon the domestic market and with it an obsession over gaining market share in the US, it failed to recognize the growth potential of overseas markets until it was too late. Only 5 per cent of A-B's beer is sold internationally. As one investment banker said, 'Budweiser has always been much better known than drunk around the world. With In-Bev's takeover Bud could easily become their big global brand' (*Financial Times*, 24 July 2008).

All of the above was further compounded by the way the company had been run as a virtual fiefdom of the Third. In many respects this is a classic example of how a minority shareholder group can silence critical voices and lead to a stalled if not circumvented internationalization strategy. Why so many shareholders who should have known better chose to remain silent is an interesting question that is difficult to answer. The force of personality and family history is uppermost in this situation – one marked by minority family interests that remain powerful arbiters of the corporate culture. It was in fact the Third's obsession with domestic market share that drove strategic thinking through the 1980s and 1990s; his profligacy when it came to operating and marketing expenses was accompanied by an almost prophetic belief that profits would continue to be high in beer sales and fund such excesses. His indifference and disdain for global markets meant that when internationalization came to the US A-B was woefully unprepared to deal with it. Half-hearted responses were costly and reactive and suggested to many that the company was not run as efficiently as it could be. In-Bev was astute enough to recognize this and saw potential cost savings that would make the takeover viable financially.

When the takeover was finalized, it became clear that the Third had thrown his support behind it, endorsing the view of A-B's board that their responsibility was to accept the offer. There were too many people who saw an opportunity to make money out of the takeover and A-B's current management had few if any alternative strategies that were convincing to the board and the new cohort of investors to whom they were answerable. Thus ended the reign of the Busch family in A-B, a somewhat inauspicious departure from a firm over which it had exercised a larger than life influence.

Perhaps the final telling moment in the conclusion of the takeover came when Brito flew to St Louis to meet the senior managers at the company's headquarters. It was a Tuesday, the day after the merger had been announced. True to past form, the company had booked a suite of rooms for him at the Ritz Carlton, St Louis's most prestigious and expensive hotel, plus arranged for a town car to transport him to the headquarters. Upon arrival however, and told of the arrangement, Brito informed them that he had already booked a room at the local Holiday Inn chain and he took a ride from the airport with the head of marketing, Dave Peacock. The cost savings were already beginning to take hold and a new culture born!

THE A-B CASE FROM AN INTERNATIONAL BUSINESS THEORETICAL PERSPECTIVE

In the reminder of the chapter we will make use of selected international business theories in order to analytically frame and substantiate our account of the A-B case. In particular we aim to generalize our historical narrative of how A-B lost power over time, could not withstand competitors' attacks and finally was taken over by In-Bev. We will elaborate on concepts of interfirm rivalry (Chen 1996), liability of foreignness (Johanson and Vahlne 2009) and the internationalization-diversification dichotomy (Stopford and Wells 1972).

According to Chen (1996), the likelihood of a firm (in this case A-B) reacting to a competitor's strategic attack depends on the degree of market commonality and resource similarity between the two firms. Market commonality is the 'degree of presence that a competitor manifests in markets it overlaps with the focal firm' (Chen 1996, p. 106), and the strategic importance of these particular markets. Consequently, the strategic attacks from SABMiller and Heineken in the US forced A-B to make counter-attacks as A-B was directly hit on its bottom line in its most strategically important market. However, even though A-B had investments in China for example, the company was nonetheless unable to react to attacks from other global players in this market, due to the reduced strategic importance of this market and its domestic market preoccupation. However, if A-B had been a global player it would probably have reacted with investments in China in ways similar to that of its competitors. Second, the way a company reacts to an attack depends on its resource endowments (Chen 1996). A-B possessed capabilities in domestic marketing rather than in global operations, and continued to commit investments in the former. Consequently, A-B never became a global player able to coordinate strategic attacks and retaliation across multiple geographical markets in ways characteristic of a true global player (Chen and Stucker 1997). In fact, A-B did not possess any of the criteria as outlined by Chen and Stucker (1997) of companies that engage in cross-border competitive engagements. Such multinational corporations (MNCs) are global rather than multi-domestic, management has an international experience, wholly owned subsidiaries are the typical establishment form, and the organization manages intra-organizational knowledge flows where the latter are based on low cultural differences among headquarters and subsidiaries and low diversity among markets.

This leads to a second issue, which is the lack of international engagement that would constrain A-B's ability to operate efficiently in international markets. The work of Johanson and Vahlne (2009) provides a theoretical underpinning on how companies efficiently can operate in an international environment. They distinguish between the *liability of foreignness*, which is the additional cost of internationalization caused by a lack of institutional market knowledge in terms of rules and regulations, norms and values, and cognitive structures (Zaheer 1995), and the *liability of outsidership*, which is a lack of business-market knowledge in terms of the market, its players and their mutual relationships (Eriksson et al. 1997). To reduce *liability of foreignness* MNCs need to form networks, which in turn lead to 'relations-specific knowledge'. This can be gained through joint venture partnerships, in which trust-based relationships occur that display accepted social behaviours from both partners. Otherwise discrepancies are likely to occur (Kumar and Nti 1998). In the A-B case many of these discrepancies occurred. In addition, to overcome liability of outsidership, MNCs can increase the number of network relationships, especially to third-party partners. However, this requires an intensive focus on international activities, which was not the case at A-B.

One may therefore hypothesize an inadequate ability in the case of A-B to gain insights about how a specific foreign market operates and the different roles of the various actors. This became an entrance barrier for utilizing its two types of expertise, which seems to be locally embedded in national US market characteristics in terms of: (1) marketing campaigns towards US customers based on their cultural preferences for beer, and (2) lobbying behaviours managing the changing attitudes of society towards beer and alcohol. Furthermore, A-B never reached the point where subsidiaries gained global mandates and became influential in the organization (Birkinshaw and Morrison 1995; Andersson et al. 2002), reaching a level of autonomy in their strategies where they could operate more freely, which in many cases has been documented to improve performance (Birkinshaw et al. 2005; Gammelgaard et al. 2012). Instead, subsidiaries became a parking place for expatriate managers, with these managers focusing on control rather than the strategic development of such entities (Harzing 2001).

Finally, it is worth comparing the A-B case with the classic Stopford and Wells (1972) model of firm internationalization. They predict two routes of internationalization, either an initial focus on product diversification that is subsequently utilized in an increasing number of foreign markets, or the opposite situation where a single product is marketed internationally and the resulting regional or global presence is used to start diversification. In both cases, organizational matrix structures are developed to organize the relationships between various products and markets. In the A-B case, however, upon completion of diversification into a number of industries, they started to divest several of these activities instead of focusing on international growth. Having reached the stage of a less diversified company, A-B then started to internationalize, which currently has been framed as a global focusing strategy (Meyer 2009). However, internationalization took place at a speed and degree which was assessed by market analysis to be too risky, and not aligned to managerial and capital resources (Geppert et al. 2012). At the end, this then resulted in the takeover by In-Bev.

NOTES

1. This chapter is based upon multiple secondary sources, including annual reports, electronic databases (Zephyr) and newspaper articles from the financial press, that were systematically retrieved from Lexis-Nexis and the HWWA (Hamburg Institute of International Economics) press archive. This generated a dense and overlapping data basis that provided interesting nuanced accounts of events within A-B and the personalities involved, while minimizing typical problems associated with the use of secondary data, such as source bias, measurement error, mismatch with the research aim and low reliability (Emory and Cooper 1991). The chapter embarks on a longitudinal case study approach that in particular is able to bridge the gap between company specific historical narratives and reductionist, theory driven statistical research (Burgelman 2011).

2. For example, the 1987 Annual Report lists succinctly A-B's strategies for dealing with these sorts of issues when it states: 'First, the company recognizes that it must make positive, effective efforts to solve any problems associated with its business or the misuse of its products. And second, through the Industry and Government Affairs Department, A-B has developed a full array of political tools enabling it to effectively counter misguided legislative efforts' (Annual Report 1987, p.10). Whilst the company does not break down costs such as these, press coverage suggests that they are not an insignificant amount of money.

3. See Caroll and Swaminathan (2000) for a discussion of how organizational space permits the growth of specialist firms (microbreweries) in niches not occupied by generalist firms (large brewers).

4. See Ahrend (1972) for a discussion of how minority shareholder groups effectively silence the majority by being aggressive and assertive.

5. For example, analysts quoted in the *Economist*, 4 June 2004, called the bid 'irrational' and 'more about ego than common sense' and that there were no obvious synergies. The Chinese market is fiercely competitive, with 400 brewers and razor thin profit margins of about 0.5 per cent. The bid represented 50 times Harbin's 2003 earnings and 35 times its forecast 2004 profits.

6. Because of the unfolding financial crisis there was concern that it would be difficult to secure commitments for the large amount of capital needed. However, In-Bev spread the risk very widely with banks in Europe and the US and was able to move quickly enough before the fallout of the banking crisis finally occurred. See MacIntosh (2011) for further details on the financing details of the takeover.

REFERENCES

Adams Beverage Group (2007), Wine and Spirits Marketing, Norwalk, CT.

Ahrend, H. (1972), *Civil Disobedience*, New York: Harcourt Press.

Andersson, U., M. Forsgren and U. Holm (2002), 'The strategic impact of external networks: subsidiary performance and competence development in the multinational corporation', *Strategic Management Journal*, 23 (11), 979–96.

Birkinshaw, J., N. Hood and S. Young (2005), 'Subsidiary entrepreneurship, internal and external competitive forces, and subsidiary performance', *International Business Review*, 14 (2), 227–48.

Birkinshaw, J. and A.J. Morrison (1995), 'Configurations of strategy and structure in subsidiaries of multinational corporations', *Journal of International Business Studies*, 26 (4), 729–53.

Burgelman, R.A. (2011), 'Bridging history and reductionism: a key role for longitudinal qualitative research', *Journal of International Business Studies*, **2**, 591–601.

Caroll, G. and A. Swaminathan (2000), 'Why the microbrewery movement? Organizational dynamics and resource partioning in the US brewing industry', *American Journal of Sociology*, **106** (3), 715–62.

Chen, M. (1996), 'Competitor analysis and interfirm rivalry: toward a theoretical integration', *Academy of Management Review*, **21** (1), 100–34.

Chen, M. and K. Stucker (1997), 'Multinational management and multimarket rivalry: toward a theoretical development of global competition', *Academy of Management Proceedings*, **97**, 2–6.

Emory, C.W. and D.R. Cooper (1991), *Business Research Methods*, Irwin: Homewood.

Eriksson, K., J. Johanson, A. Majkgård and D.D. Sharma (1997), 'Experiential knowledge and cost in the internationalization process', *Journal of International Business Studies*, **28** (2), 337–60.

Gammelgaard, J., F. McDonald, A. Stephan, H. Tüselmann and C. Dörrenbächer (2012), 'The impact of increases in subsidiary autonomy and network relationships on performance', *International Business Review*, **21**, 1158–72.

Geppert, M., C. Dörrenbächer, J. Gammelgaard and I.M. Taplin (2012), 'Managerial risk-taking in international acquisitions in the brewery industry: institutional and ownership influences compared', *British Journal of Management*, 1–16.

Harzing, A. (2001), 'Of bears, bumble-bees, and spiders: the role of expatriates in controlling foreign subsidiaries', *Journal of World Business*, **36** (4), 366–79.

Heracleous, L. (2001), 'When local beer beat global: the Chinese beer industry', *Business Strategy Review*, **12** (3), 40.

Johanson, J. and J.-E. Vahlne (2009), 'The Uppsala internationalization process model revisited: from liability of foreignness to liability of outsidership', *Journal of International Business Studies*, **40** (9), 1411–31.

Kumar, R. and K.O. Nti (1998), 'Differential learning and interaction in alliance dynamics: a process and outcome discrepancy model', *Organization Science*, **9**, 356–67.

Lawrence, S.V. (2000), 'Beer making: a thirst for success', *Far Eastern Economic Review*, 28 December.

MacIntosh, J. (2011), *Dethroning the King*, New York: Wiley.

Meyer, K.E. (2009), 'Globalfocusing: corporate strategies under pressure', *Strategic Change*, **18**, 195–207.

Stopford, J. M. and L.T. Wells (1972), *Managing the Multinational Enterprise. Organization of the Firm and Ownership of Subsidiaries*, New York: Basic Books.

Zaheer, S. (1995), 'Overcoming the liability of foreignness', *Academy of Management Journal*, **38**, 341–63.

Primary Sources

Anheuser-Busch Companies, Inc.
Annual Reports 1987, 1988, 1989, 1990, 1991, 1992, 1993, 1994, 1995, 1997, 1998, 1999, 2002, 2003, 2004, 2005, 2006.

PART VI

Boundless customer interfaces:
social media and tourism

11. The use of social media in the beer brewing industry

Nicolai Pogrebnyakov

INTRODUCTION

Social media offer breweries an opportunity to engage with and learn more about their customers in detail on an unprecedented scale. Insights gained through social media are useful in downstream activities such as marketing, potentially leading to lower operating costs for these activities. Upstream activities such as new product development can also benefit from new ideas harnessed from social media. Furthermore, these benefits may be reaped by large multinational companies and small local producers alike. Needless to say, the term itself is also very fashionable today. However, before getting carried away by the hype, let us ask: what exactly is social media and how and in what circumstances can breweries enjoy these benefits?

Social media have been understood as software platforms and corresponding websites that allow the publication of user-generated content and establishing connections among users to share this content (Kaplan and Haenlein 2010; Kietzmann et al. 2011). User-generated content includes various types of media: text, photos, videos and music. Examples of social media technologies according to this definition are microblogs (Twitter), social networks (Facebook, LinkedIn, Xing) and media sharing sites (YouTube, Flickr), among others. This distinguishes social media from, for example, predominantly one-way content publication platforms such as blogs (e.g., WordPress, Blogger).

Companies can use social media in a wide variety of activities, both downstream and upstream, including branding, sales, customer support and product development and improvement (Culnan et al. 2010). In product improvement, for example, companies can monitor customer comments on Twitter or Facebook and look for ideas for potential improvements (Wilson et al. 2011). A more proactive stance would be to solicit customer input during the development of a new product and incorporate this feedback in the design of the new product (Wilson et al. 2011).

The release of a new product can also be announced on social media with a campaign that would build up customers' expectations.

Importantly, many social media initiatives require smaller advertising expenditure than campaigns in 'traditional' media such as TV, radio and print (Armelini and Villanueva 2011). And the differences between these types of media are not limited to cost. The objectives of the use of the two are different as well. In traditional media the strategy is typically to build brand awareness and knowledge of the product. Social media focus on sparking a conversation about a product, engaging with customers and facilitating sharing (Weinberg and Pehlivan 2011). Indeed, connecting with other users is one of the main goals of using social media in the first place, and companies should strive to strengthen existing, or build new, relationships between users as part of their social media campaigns (Piskorski 2011).

A finer distinction is between social and digital online strategies. First, many companies maintain a corporate website that is independent of any social media platform. Such websites may have some rudimentary functions found on social media platforms, for example the ability to 'tweet' or 'like' a page, which are typically implemented through functionality provided by the social media platforms themselves (plug-ins). However, there are important differences between maintaining a standalone website and a page on a social media platform, which is a significant reason why many companies maintain a presence across several social media platforms in addition to a corporate website. For example, users often cannot interact among each other on these websites. Where such interaction is supported, it is often a secondary activity to the site's content, for example, users commenting on the site's articles or newsfeed (recall that social media are built on the premise of user-generated content). This makes it unlikely that a standalone corporate website becomes a sustained destination for repeat visitors. On the other hand, social media pages facilitate co-creation of content and make it easy to share and follow updates of this content. A larger point concerns the fact that corporate websites do not facilitate the creation of new connections with like-minded people, since they do not maintain a 'network' of users.

The second aspect of the distinction between social and digital strategies concerns advertising. Many companies use advertising on websites other than social media to reach their audience, an effort that may complement or substitute a social media strategy. Such advertising includes graphic banners, as well as text snippets. Despite their location on the internet, though, their purpose is largely similar to ads in 'traditional' media: broadcast advertising (Piskorski 2011), albeit with easier purchasing capability. It is easier to click on a banner and be taken to an internet store, for example, than to type the address seen on TV into the computer, which is often a few feet away. Thanks to these differences, social media is not seen as a displacement for 'traditional' media, at least currently (Armelini and Villanueva 2011). It is rather a complement with a growing share of customers' attention due to changes in media consumption.

There are several benefits specific to social media that companies can derive from the use of these platforms. These benefits arise from applying social media to solving a particular business problem or facilitating a business process (DiMauro and Zawel 2012). One advantage of using social media is the fact that users reveal rich information about their identity to these platforms, such as their age, gender, occupation and location (Kietzmann et al. 2011). This in principle can be used to better target advertising. With the proliferation of social media 'plug-ins', or snippets of code on non-social media sites (for example, Twitter's 'Tweet' button and 'Sign in with Facebook' functionality), social media sites accumulate even more information about the interests and preferences of their users. Another potential benefit is engaging customers in communication about a product or company (Kietzmann et al. 2011). In the movie industry, for example, more communication about a movie in social media was found to be related to higher revenue. Moreover, this effect held independent of advertising expenditures that went into these social media activities. Of course, this communication can be negative as well as positive, as companies do not control what is being said on social media (Kaplan and Haenlein 2010; Armelini and Villanueva 2011; Kietzmann et al. 2011). In case of negative commentary, companies have been advised not to try to 'whitewash' their image as these efforts are typically recognized and can backfire (Kietzmann et al. 2011). Users can also participate in the creation of content that benefits the company (Culnan et al. 2010). Proper incentives can help engage customers to help other customers, thereby facilitating customer service, and propose designs or functionality for new products, which aids in new product development.

Overall, the existence of a social media strategy has been indicated by more profitable firms to a larger degree than by lower performing firms (National Center for the Middle Market 2012).

Enterprise uses of social media can be further categorized into internal and external, or customer-facing uses (Culnan et al. 2010). Many social media uses mentioned above, such as new product development and customer support, can be deployed internally. Engaging employees in internal use of social media allows companies to experiment more freely without the fear that competitors find out about their upcoming products, or without the fear of public failure; for example, if a new product development process on a social networking site does not attract quality submissions (Wilson et al. 2011). At the same time, social media can be a valuable tool for communicating among companies in a supply network (Petrick and Pogrebnyakov 2008). In this case, these tools, although transcending company boundaries, are used internally within the supply network and not made visible to the public.

This chapter focuses specifically on external uses of social media. Company spending on advertising in social media is expected to grow from $3.8 billion in 2011 to $9.8 billion in 2016 (PRNewswire 2012). This corresponds to a forecasted increase from 7.4 per cent of advertising budgets in 2012 to 19.5 per cent in 2017, again confirming the rising prominence – but not complete replacement – of social media compared to 'traditional' media (SimplyZesty 2012).

Accordingly, the research question pursued in this chapter is: what is the extent of social media usage by breweries today? This question will be answered based on the case of a specific social media platform, Facebook, and for breweries based in the US.

THE USE OF SOCIAL MEDIA BY BREWERIES

Uses of Social Media by Large Multinational Breweries

As in other segments, companies in the brewing industry have a variety of marketing tools at their disposal. These include print advertising, web advertising, radio/TV advertising, outdoor advertising and advertising through social media. Benefits to breweries from using social media are to a large extent similar to those enjoyed by companies at large as described above. In line with the growth of spending on social media by companies in general, the beer brewing industry is increasingly engaging itself with these platforms. For example, Heineken International expected to dedicate 15 per cent of its marketing budget to social media as of 2012 (Rotunno 2012). This growing spending is a reflection of the importance of social media, particularly for younger people who spend a significant amount of their time online, second only to watching TV (Rotunno 2012).

Large multinational breweries have deployed a wide variety of social media implementations. One of the most popular strategies is to attract users to the pages companies set up on social media sites. Heineken, for example, boasted 9.6 million 'likes' of its main Facebook page as of November 2012, which makes it the company with the largest fan base in the industry on that site. Cultivating such a following typically requires regular updates of the page (users may 'like' these updates, which will show in their activity list, potentially making their friends in turn 'like' these updates, and so on).

AB InBev's Anheuser Busch used the location-based social network Foursquare to connect people with others in their vicinity who would like to socialize at a bar over a beer. To that end it also developed a mobile application that displays a map with bars offering Budweiser, Anheuser Busch's flagship brand, and discounts for beer. In another instance, Anheuser Busch recruited participants on social networks Facebook and Renren (China) for its worldwide reality show 'The Big Time'. The reality show connected selected participants with stars in sports (motor racing, soccer and basketball) as well as the fashion business, who then coached and mentored them.

In another example, Heineken set up a 'social Christmas tree' in Singapore in 2011. The 11-metre-tall 'tree' consisted of 48 TV screens. Users of the company's dedicated Facebook page could post greetings with text, music and video that would be displayed on the 'tree'. The last two examples suggest that it is possible to combine online social media initiatives with offline activities, and such combinations (as indeed purely social media activities) do not have to be directly related to beer consumption. Rather, the point is to engage with the customers, leverage their connections and possibly give them an opportunity to create new connections.

At the same time, the beer brewing industry is to a large degree a local industry. Companies often cater to customers in a specific and limited geographic area. And even for multinational companies operating in several markets, the additional dimension of the use of social media is the potential need to tailor their social content to these markets. For example, Heineken maintains separate Twitter accounts for many countries it is present in, including the USA, Italy, Malaysia, Singapore and New Zealand. In addition to the need to create content in local languages, these separate accounts can better react to local events such as music festivals or movie premieres sponsored by the company.

However, location matters for small breweries too, which often distribute their products close to the production facility. For example, in the US 89 per cent of companies are microbreweries or breweries at restaurants or pubs (US Brewers Association 2012). While these smaller companies may not have the millions of followers enjoyed by large multinational companies, social media present the opportunity to connect with a local audience. Specific usages are described below for each platform.

Thus beer breweries can employ a variety of social media platforms. Since this research is done on Facebook, it will be reviewed in detail in this chapter. The use of other platforms by breweries is reviewed as well.

Facebook

Facebook offers companies a variety of tools for marketing themselves. Unlike traditional advertising methods, which are typically unidirectional and offer limited insights into the target audience, Facebook includes a wide variety of tools for reaching out to diverse audiences and metrics that help track the response and the engagement from these audiences.

One of the first steps for companies on Facebook is to create a Facebook page. This includes a description of the company along with its contact information. It also includes what is known as the timeline, which are the company's posts on its webpage organized by time. The company can publish updates and posts on its timeline. Depending on the user's settings, these updates can also show on his or her own timeline. If the company periodically posts updates on its page, users will regularly see these updates on their timelines, which increases the exposure of the page.

Users can interact with a page in a variety of ways. They can, for example, 'like' a page. If a user does so, this is reflected on his or her own timeline which is visible to the friends of the user. Thus users' friends also become aware of the page. Given that an average Facebook user has 229 friends (Goo 2012), this increases the exposure of the company's page. Additionally, users can see which of their friends, if any, have 'liked' the page.

Another way to interact with a page is to visit the physical location of the business and indicate so on Facebook by clicking the 'check in' button. This measure can be seen as a very approximate indication of visitors to the company location. Of course, not all visitors will have internet access at the time of their visit and those who do would not necessarily want to publicize the visit by clicking 'check in'. And this number may differ between industries (people may have different interests in visiting a barber shop and a bar) and by company promotions targeted at increasing this specific metric. However, studying this measure in the context of a single industry, especially in the context of services tied to a specific location, may yield useful insights into customer interaction with the company's Facebook page (Heine 2011; Facebook 2012).

Customers can also talk about the page. This includes mentions of the page by the user in his or her posts, posting to the page's timeline, tagging pictures with the company's page or visiting the physical location (Finn 2011). Facebook displays the number of such interactions with the page for the past seven days. 'Were here' shows the number of visitors to the physical location of the brewery, and 'talking about' indicates the number of times the page has been discussed.

How can these tools be used by breweries and to what effect? Here are some common ways to use these tools.

Increase exposure through page 'likes'

A brewery can post a sign on its property inviting customers to 'like' it on Facebook. As described above, likes lead to increased exposure of the page which, crucially, is done by the customers themselves.

Advertise by posting updates

As noted above, companies can post updates on their timelines. In the case of breweries, these can be updates about new products or upcoming events. Smaller breweries, many of which frequently produce new brews and flavours of beer, can especially gain from posting updates about them: their loyal customers would find out about the new product and by 'liking' it can expose it to their friends. Further, since many breweries are located at bars or restaurants, they can post updates about upcoming events (such as concerts) to attract customers and potentially increase sales. Such events are 'pushed' to users who have 'liked' the brewery's Facebook page – they will show up on users' Facebook walls. This is in contrast with the need to 'pull' information posted on breweries' websites: customers would need to take the specific action of visiting the website and looking for any events there.

Increase engagement by 'educating' customers

Breweries can use their Facebook presence to provide more detailed information about their product's supply related information. A popular example is to suggest food pairings with specific brews. For example, New Belgium Brewing Company offers an application on its Facebook page that allows the sharing of recipes inspired by New Belgium brews. Facebook allows for easy sharing and commenting on such recipes, and tracking subsequent commenting activity. This is again different from a website, which would typically offer only limited sharing and commenting functionality, and make it hard to track future activity.

Increase engagement through games, contests and so on

'Liking' a page requires a relatively small effort from the user. Breweries can engage users in a deeper way by requiring some action on the part of the user. This can be done, for example, by creating a company-specific game on Facebook or holding contests. For example, Carib Beer produced a game that coincided with an annual offline boat race which it sponsored. In the game players accumulated points by racing in a virtual boat and evading obstacles. Carib maintained a scoreboard and when the game was closed it distributed beer to the top 50 winners as well as arranging a photo shoot with beer promoters, which it called the 'Carib Girls'. There was also an opportunity to vote for a 'People's Choice' boat in the offline race. The boat that won that vote received a year's supply of beer.

Another way to increase engagement is to advocate for local causes. This may include calling for donations that the company would then match, or organizing a campaign for a particular issue. Again, smaller breweries are well positioned to use this approach, being well aware of local issues. For example, Brooklyn Brewery launched the 'Save the G Train' campaign in March 2012 to prevent the closure of a subway line extension in Brooklyn, New York. It invited users to submit a song about the line, and the winner or winners would visit a music festival in Sweden, with the costs paid for by the company. Another advocacy example is again New Belgium, which developed a Facebook application in collaboration with a magazine. One dollar from each download was donated to local animal protection organizations.

Most of these events (posts, updates, applications) can be 'liked' and commented on by users as well, which again increases exposure.

Other Social Platforms

Of course, Facebook is not the only social platform that companies, including breweries, use. Many companies maintain a diverse portfolio of social media, including a Twitter, Foursquare and Untappd presence. Foursquare is a location-based service that allows users to register their presence ('check in') at a physical location. This can be, for example, a bar or a restaurant. Knowing that a particular person checked in at specific premises allows companies to offer promotions to that person for products or services at that location. Thus it is useful for both large companies and small local breweries. An important sales channel for large breweries is distributors: these breweries may refund any discounts that beer distributors offer on their beer. Small companies can also use this functionality. For example, Sprecher Brewery awarded a pair of tickets to a local beer and food festival to the Foursquare 'mayor' of Sprecher. A 'mayor' on that platform is the customer who visited the premises the most over the preceding 60 days. This incentivizes customers to spend time on the premises.

Untappd is a social platform developed specifically for the brewing industry. It combines geo-location and company presence features. Thus users can post updates about a particular brew they are consuming at a particular bar or restaurant, and include their opinion of that brew. This offers companies vast opportunities to connect customers to each other (an important part of social media appeal for users) and with the company, as well as to promote and solicit customer opinions on new brews.

FACEBOOK USE BY SMALL AND MEDIUM-SIZED US BREWERIES

Building on the social media concepts discussed above, this section will present the results of research that investigated the use of Facebook by small- and medium-sized breweries in the US.

The domestic US beer brewing industry can be largely classified into large and 'craft' breweries (Pontinen 2010). Large breweries are companies, typically multinational ones, such as MillerCoors (a joint venture between SABMiller and Molson Coors) and Anheuser-Busch InBev. They maintain a presence in most geographic areas of the country and run nationwide advertising campaigns. By contrast, craft breweries are typically small companies that cater to local customers. These breweries can be standalone, in which case they often supply to local restaurants and bars; or they are actually co-located with a restaurant or a bar. There are exceptions, of course: Boston Beer Company with its Sam Adams brand maintains a close to nationwide presence, yet it is still considered a craft brewery due to lower volumes and the seasonality and wide assortment of its brews.

Methodology

A complete list of US breweries was obtained for this research from the US Brewers Association. Companies in this list were looked up on Facebook to determine whether they maintain a page there. For companies that did have a page, the number of 'likes' of their page, the number of instances of 'were here' and the number of times the page was talked about in the past seven days were recorded. The population of the city where the brewery is located, obtained from the 2010 US census, was recorded as well, irrespectively of whether the brewery had a Facebook presence or not.

Of the total of 3940 existing and planned brewery locations 2408 unique existing breweries were identified.[1] Of those, 879, or 36.5 per cent, had a Facebook page. Some of these breweries were in fact part of a chain company, but maintained a separate Facebook page for each location. This again highlights the importance of tailoring a brewery's social media presence to the needs of a local community, even if the parent company is large. Further, given that just over one-third of all US breweries have a Facebook presence, there is clearly room for growth in the presence of breweries on this social platform.

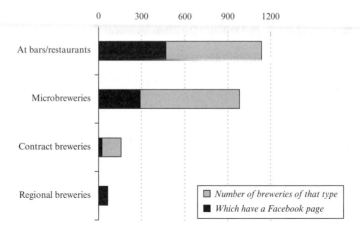

Source: Brewers Association.

Figure 11.1   The number of US breweries by type

Results

The US Brewers Association classifies breweries into several types, all of which were included in the analysis. Microbreweries are defined by the Brewers Association as breweries producing less than 17 600 hectolitres of beer per year, of which at least 75 per cent is sold off-site. Regional breweries are breweries producing between 17 600 and 7 040 000 hectolitres per year. Contract breweries are companies that subcontract another brewery, which carries out brewing and packaging, while concentrating on marketing, sales and distribution itself (US Brewers Association 2012). The number of breweries by type is shown in Figure 11.1.

Overall, only 35.7 per cent of US breweries maintain a Facebook page. The largest group is breweries co-located with bars or restaurants, 41 per cent of which have a Facebook page. Microbreweries is the second largest group, and 29 per cent of them have a Facebook page. Contract manufacturers and larger regional breweries are smaller in number, and 86 per cent of regional breweries have a Facebook page. Because of the importance of reaching out to potential customers, specifically around the physical location of the bar or microbrewery, which has been implemented by larger regional breweries, there is ample room for growth in terms of Facebook presence for co-located beer manufacturers and microbreweries.

Table 11.1 shows the median values of the three metrics for the breweries' pages, and Figure 11.2 shows the distribution of these metrics.

*Table 11.1 Descriptive statistics of the three metrics for US brewing
company Facebook pages*

	Minimum	Maximum	Median	Standard deviation
'Likes'	1	70 644	964	13 475.14
'Were here'	1	63 009	1 740	5 823.98
'Talking about'	1	4 858	56	372.1

Source: Facebook.

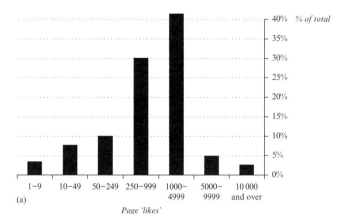
(a)

Page 'likes'

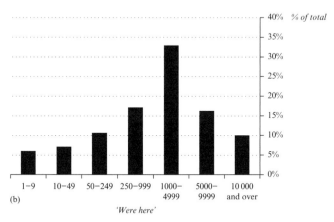
(b)

'Were here'

Source: Facebook.

*Figure 11.2 Numbers of: (a) 'likes', (b) instances of 'were here'
and (c) instances of 'talking about' breweries' pages, as
percentage of the total for each metric*

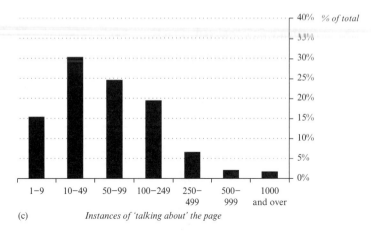

(c)   *Instances of 'talking about' the page*

Figure 11.2   (continued)

Interestingly, the median number of instances of 'were here' is much larger than that of page 'likes'. This suggests that more customers prefer to announce an activity in the offline world, such as visiting the brewery or pub, to their Facebook friends, than take a rather abstract action of 'liking' a page. The median number of instances of 'talking about' is far smaller than for the other two metrics, but that is to be expected since that metric shows activity in the past seven days.

Most Facebook pages of breweries (41.5 per cent) have between 1000 and 4999 'likes', indicating a fair degree of popularity. Pages that have fewer than 50 'likes', a low number (about 10 per cent of total), either have been recently launched or are not well maintained and promoted. Clearly, for this industry having more than 10 000 page 'likes' is indicative of high popularity: only 22 company pages (2.5 per cent) have over 10 000 'likes'.[2] The distribution of this measure is highly concentrated: 70 per cent of brewery pages have between 250 and 4999 'likes'.

The pattern is different for instances of 'were here': approximately one-third of pages (and, consequently, business locations) have values for those between 1000 and 4999. At the same time, over one-quarter of pages have more than 5000 instances of 'were here'. Thus this measure is more uniformly distributed than the number of 'likes'. Further, the number of people visiting the location is on average greater than the number of people 'liking' it (the median page received 1740 instances of 'were here' while only 964 'likes'). Again, this may suggest that customers prefer to take a specific action (that is, indicate they were at the brewery location by clicking 'check in') rather than 'like' a page, which in most cases is a rather abstract action. At the same time, 13 per cent of pages

Table 11.2   *Correlation coefficients of brewery page 'likes', instances of 'were here' and 'talking about' the brewery, and the population (the number of residents) of the city where the brewery is located*

	'Were here'	Instances of 'talking about'	Population
Page 'likes'	0.365**	0.164**	0.078*
'Were here'		0.537**	0.177**
Instances of 'talking about'			0.050

Notes:
* $p < 0.05$
** $p < 0.01$

have fewer than 50 instances of 'were here', which suggests rather low popularity.

In the case of 'talking about's, about half of the pages have between 10 and 99 'talking about's. Recall that this metric reflects activity in the past seven days, and it is important to sustain a constant customer conversation or 'buzz' around the company's page.

The next step of the analysis was to correlate these numbers between each other as well as with the population of the city the brewery was located in. The correlation results are shown in Table 11.2.

The coefficients of correlations of all three Facebook page measures between each other are statistically significant. This suggests that the higher popularity of the brewery's Facebook page expressed as the number of 'likes' is related to a higher number of physical visitors to the brewery location ('were here') as well as to a higher number of discussions about this page (the number of instances of 'talking about' the page). This may indicate that breweries that pursue a social media strategy see this strategy paying off at least in terms of visitors to their location.

Another interesting result surfaces while examining the relationship between Facebook page measures and the population of the city where the brewery is located. The number of 'likes' and instances of 'were here' are significantly correlated with city population. This is to be expected: higher population overall presents more opportunities to the brewery in terms of potential clients. (Of course, the actual number of clients depends on the demographic profile and consumption preferences of the population, among others.) However the correlation coefficient between population and the number of instances of 'talking about' the page, while positive, is not statistically significant. This suggests that breweries may generate significant 'buzz' around their page even if they are located in a small town. (Of course, the reverse also holds: big town breweries may struggle with conversations about themselves.) By having or generating conversations about themselves breweries can market themselves more effectively, which is one of the important benefits of social media. Since most small breweries operate in a limited geographic area, they can spread the word in this manner to neighbouring towns or, if they are located at a tourist destination, market themselves to visitors.

Figure 11.3 shows the location of US breweries and the number of 'likes' of its Facebook page, if one was found for the company. The map is overlaid with population density. The map clearly shows clusters of brewery locations: along the coast in the Northeast; around the Great Lakes; southern Texas cities: Houston, San Antonio and Austin; Denver, Colorado area; Oregon coast; and San Francisco and Los Angeles areas in California. Interestingly, some highly populated areas do not have significant numbers of breweries. Southern states in particular have relatively few breweries, except for Florida and the above-mentioned southern Texas cities. Those breweries that are there mostly do not have a Facebook page. These two observations can be explained in several ways. First, there simply might not be as strong a beer drinking culture in these areas (The Beer Institute 2012). Second, most breweries included in this research are craft breweries, it is they who are absent and large labels may be consumed instead. In other words, beer consumption patterns in these areas overwhelmingly favour large labels and not craft beer. The fact that breweries in southern states tend not to have a Facebook page on the one hand may point to a weak beer consumption culture, and on the other lends further support to the link between a brewery's Facebook strategy and interest in craft beer among the local population. This may indicate an opportunity for craft breweries to establish a presence in southern states and to launch a corresponding social media strategy.

A further look at the map confirms that breweries with the largest number of page 'likes' tend to be in urban areas. Great Lakes Brewing Company, a regional brewer with over 70 000 'likes', the highest number in the sample, is located in Cleveland, Ohio. Three microbreweries (as opposed to large breweries or breweries located at bars and restaurants) in the sample have over 10 000 'likes': Switchback Brewing Company of Burlington, Vermont (over 10 000 'likes'); Cigar City Brewing, located in Tampa, Florida (over 14 000 'likes'); and Broken Tooth Brewing Company of Anchorage, Alaska (over 18 000 'likes').

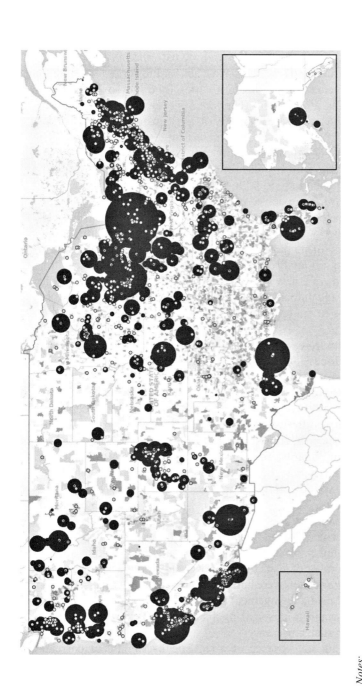

Notes:
Blue circles represent breweries with a Facebook page and the circle size indicates the number of 'likes' for that page (dark grey in black and white).
Yellow circles represent breweries without a Facebook page (white in black and white).
Background shows population density: lower density in yellow (light grey in black and white), higher density in green (dark grey in black and white).
This image can be viewed in colour at https://sites.google.com/site/nppubs/breweriesfacebook.

Sources: Brewers Association; Facebook; US Census Bureau.

Figure 11.3   Locations of US breweries and the number of 'likes' of their Facebook pages, overlaid with population density

CONCLUSION

This chapter has analysed the use of social media, especially Facebook, by US breweries. It reviewed several approaches for breweries to maintain their Facebook presence along with a motivation for doing so. It has been noted that Facebook, along with other social media, can be a powerful tool to engage with customers, learn more about them and market to them (Harris and Dennis 2011).

It has also been shown that, simply put, location matters. Many breweries, even chains with a presence in multiple locations, establish Facebook pages for each individual location. The rationale for doing so is clear from the examples reviewed earlier in this chapter. First, much of Facebook activity is location-based: the number of instances of physical presence at the brewery ('were here') is on average higher than simply the number of 'likes' of its page. Second, it is easier to engage customers in conversations about breweries that are located in the area: for example, impressions of a new beer flavour from a local brewery. Third, some breweries engage in local advocacy and charitable causes, and it is easier for customers to relate to such causes if they are occurring in the vicinity.

The results of this research suggest that even small-town breweries can have vigorous discussions around their brand on Facebook and thus engage potential customers.

The median values and distribution of Facebook page metrics in this research can give breweries guidance on the boundaries of acceptable values on these metrics. Breweries can use these numbers in measuring outcomes of their social media strategies and answering the question 'How do we measure against the competition?' For breweries outside of the US these metrics may be different. However the numbers here can still be used as an indication of the relative importance of different metrics.

Another interesting result is the statistically significant correlation between the engagement of users with the brewery Facebook page (expressed as the number of 'likes' as well as instances of 'talking about' the page) and the number of visits to the brewery location itself (measured in the number of instances of 'were here'). This indicates interplay between the brewery's social media engagement and visits to its physical location. Breweries with no significant social media presence may use this as a rationale to develop such a presence.

On the other hand, the absence of a statistically significant correlation between the population of the city the brewery is located in and the number of instances of 'talking about' the page was also an intriguing result. It might be expected that larger populations would generate more active conversations around the page. However it may present an incentive for breweries to market themselves to neighbouring localities or to visitors, especially if the brewery is located near a tourist destination.

While this research reviewed breweries in the US, its findings are relevant for the broader context as well. One group of breweries for which this research has implications specifically is multinational brewing companies. This chapter already noted the need to tailor social media strategies for individual countries. One reason is language specificity and the need to develop content in the local language, which is an important prerequisite for engaging customers with the brewery's social media presence. Further, many breweries sponsor local events such as soccer championships and music festivals, partly in response to limits imposed on explicit advertising. Because of the importance of relating social media presence to a specific geographic location, establishing not only country specific but also possibly region and even in some cases city specific social media pages might be an advantage. Multinational companies are well positioned to establish such multi-country presence and spread best practices in this regard across their subsidiaries. Interestingly, however, breweries with the greatest number of 'likes' in the US in this research are craft breweries, rather than large multinational ones with headquarters in the US. By contrast, Heineken developed an impressive Facebook base. This suggests that there exists scope for improvement for multinationals, at least US-based ones.

For small breweries in countries with low levels of computer use and internet access, adopting social media practices may be more challenging. Even though many countries with low computer use rates have higher mobile phone use instead, these phones are typically 'feature phones' that do not offer an internet experience as rich as that offered by smartphones. From the user's perspective, interacting with social media is meaningfully possible on a phone with a large screen, an internet browser and at least EDGE-rate internet access speed, features that are not commonplace in mobile phones and networks in many developing countries.

Further, while Facebook is a global platform, which as of March 2013 included more than one in seven people in the world as its members, in some countries it is not the predominant social platform. In some countries it is not even accessible: for example, access to it is blocked outright in China. Thus breweries in some countries, as well as multinational breweries, have to consider other social platforms, which may not offer a similar functionality in terms of interacting with the company page or the physical location of the brewery.

NOTES

1. The numbers in this chapter were current as of August 2012, the time the research was conducted, unless indicated otherwise.
2. This chapter does not discuss the actions the company undertakes to obtain these 'likes'. These actions may include posting content on Facebook that is widely shared among users ('goes viral' in the jargon), offline activities such as posters at bars, and so on. As the discussion in the section 'The use of social media by breweries' indicates, there is a wide variety of online and offline activities a company may deploy to attract users to its Facebook page and increase the number of 'likes'.

REFERENCES

Armelini, G. and J. Villanueva (2011), 'Adding social media to the marketing mix', *IESE-Insight Magazine*, **3** (4), 29–36.

Culnan, M.J., P.J. McHugh and J.I. Zubillaga (2010), 'How large US companies can use Twitter and other social media to gain business value', *MIS Quarterly Executive*, **9** (4), 243–59.

DiMauro, V. and A. Zawel (2012), 'Social media for strategy-focused organizations', *Balanced Scorecard Report*, **14** (1), 1–4.

Facebook (2012), 'Facebook API reference: checkin', accessed November 2012 at http://developers.facebook.com/docs/reference/api/checkin/.

Finn, G. (2011), 'Demystifying Facebook's "people are talking about this" metric', accessed November 2012 at http://searchengineland.com/demystifying-facebooks-people-are-talking-about-this-metric-96104.

Goo, S.K. (2012), 'Facebook: a profile of its "friends"', Pew Internet & American Life Project.

Harris, L. and C. Dennis (2011), 'Engaging customers on Facebook: challengers for e-tailers', *Journal of Consumer Behavior*, **10** (1), 338–46.

Heine, C. (2011), 'Facebook's "were here" feature exposes mobile buzz', accessed November 2012 at www.clickz.com/clickz/news/2111462/facebooks-feature-exposes-mobile-buzz.

Kaplan, A.M. and M. Haenlein (2010), 'Users of the world, unite! The challenges and opportunities of social media', *Business Horizons*, **53** (1), 59–68.

Kietzmann, J.H., K. Hermkens, I.P. McCarthy and B.S. Silvestre (2011), 'Social media? Get serious! Understanding the functional building blocks of social media', *Business Horizons*, **54** (3), 241–51.

National Center For The Middle Market (2012), *Blueprint for Growth: Middle Market Growth Champions Reveal a Framework for Success*, Columbus: Ohio State University.

Petrick, I.J. and N. Pogrebnyakov (2008), 'Innovation in distributed networks and supporting knowledge flows', in A. Dwivedi and T. Butcher (eds), *Supply Chain Management and Knowledge Management: Integrating Critical Perspectives in Theory and Practice*, Basingstoke, UK: Palgrave Macmillan, pp. 3–19.

Piskorski, M.J. (2011), 'Social strategies that work', *Harvard Business Review*, **89** (11), 116–22.

Pontinen, J. (2010), 'The US beer brewing industry', Unpublished MBA thesis, University of Minnesota – Duluth.

PR Newswire (2012), 'BIA/Kelsey forecasts U.S. social media ad spending to reach $9.8 billion by 2016', accessed November 2012 at www.prnewswire.com/news-releases/biakelsey-forecasts-us-social-media-ad-spending-to-reach-98-billion-by-2016-151489335.html.

Rotunno, T. (2012), 'Building a beer brand, one "like" at a time', accessed November 2012 at www.cnbc.com/id/47505112/Building_a_Beer_Brand_One_Like_at_a_Time.

SimplyZesty (2012), 'Social media ad spend to hit 19.5 per cent of total marketing budget in five years', accessed November 2012 at www.simplyzesty.com/social-media/social-media-ad-spend-to-hit-19-5-of-total-marketing-budget-in-five-years.

The Beer Institute (2012), 'Shipment of malt beverages and per capita consumption by state, 2003–2009', accessed November 2012 at http://beerinstitute.org/BeerInstitute/files/ccLibraryFiles/Filename/000000001059/State per cent20data per cent20per per cent20capita per cent20consumption per cent202003 per cent20to per cent202009.pdf.

US Brewers Association (2012), 'Market segments', accessed November 2012 at www.brewersassociation.org/pages/business-tools/craft-brewing-statistics/market-segments.

Weinberg, B.D. and E. Pehlivan (2011), 'Social spending: managing the social media mix', *Business Horizons*, **54** (3), 275–82.

Wilson, H.J., P.J. Guinan, S. Parise and B.D. Weinberg (2011), 'What's your social media strategy?', *Harvard Business Review*, **89** (7–8), 23–5.

12. Sun, alcohol and sex: enacting beer tourism

Ana María Munar

Most forms of contemporary tourism are inextricably linked to the consumption of alcohol, sometimes in prodigious amounts. (Moore 1995, p. 301)

INTRODUCTION

Tourism is often linked to ideas of escapism and release from everyday duties and obligations. Modern societies are characterized by highly complex systems of social and cultural control, and citizens of these societies find forms of liberation in travel (Jafari 1987). Tourism destinations act as magnetic spaces of leisure and relaxation that can be visualized as the realm of 'touristhood' – a theatrical arena in which individuals adopt different masks and conduct themselves according to expectations and norms that differ from those that rule their everyday lives. The consumption and enjoyment of alcoholic drinks constitutes a relevant element of the scenery of touristhood. In touristic spaces the beer product is socially transformed and constructed; tourists enact beer tourism through drinking practices and rituals performed at the destination.

Alcohol, and in this case beer consumption, is constitutive of socio-cultural traditions in many national cultures (such as those in Northern Europe). National and local beer cultures are however being transformed and re-shaped in tourism destinations. This study examines the interrelation of beer cultures, more specifically German beer culture, and tourism. It analyses how beer culture, combined with touristhood, produces extreme and novel forms of consumption, transforming both tourism practices and the world of beer. Researchers have indicated how the legitimacy of firms depends upon the environment's institutional characteristics, the organization's characteristics and the process of legitimation by which the environment builds its perception of the organization (Kostova and Zaheer 1999). By examining beer drinking behaviour in a tourism setting, this study suggests that the legitimacy of beer firms is increasingly

310

affected by how beer is consumed and not just by the characteristics of production or of the internal organization of the breweries.

The intangible and perishable nature of the tourism product makes tourism consumption dependent on fantasies of what the tourism experience would be like. Imagination about drinking experiences linked to aesthetic, sexual and sensual fantasies are at the core of beer tourism. Tourists get attracted to places due to a sense of anticipation of intense pleasures (Urry 2002). These pleasures are characterized by being out of the ordinary, either by taking place in an activity at a different scale (not only drinking but binge drinking) or involving different senses (having a beer garden experience wearing swim clothes on a hot summer night). Urry also suggests that the tourism encounter with the local place is dominated by a greater sensitivity to visual elements. Tourists see places through different lenses than the residents. Also, tourists experience and dream of embodied experiences where senses are stimulated (Munar and Ooi 2012). Other scholars, such as Larsen et al. (2007), show the importance of the social element in tourism. For example, enjoying being with others (family, partners, locals or other tourists) is a key motivation to travel to sun and beach destinations (Prebesen et al. 2011). Moreover, pleasures related to the tourism experience take place not only in the destination, but also at pre-trip and post-trip stages by sharing the excitement of anticipation and remembering shared moments (Haldrup and Larsen 2010). The way in which beer is consumed and enjoyed also has a strong social component. Some tourists dream of drinking and having fun with others.

As this chapter will show, fantasies of the tourism experience include the promises of pleasures related to enjoying extreme forms of alcohol consumption in safely controlled and familiar environments. While Jafari (1987) and Urry (2002) suggest that the attractiveness of tourism lies in the power of novelty, other scholars, such as Prentice (2004), have reflected on the attraction of the familiar. Tourists often find their experiences richer when they confirm their expectations and see familiar aspects of the attractions they visit (Jackson 2005). The authentic in most cases presupposes getting to know the local culture and interacting with the residents of the destination. This also includes the purchasing and consumption of local products such as gastronomic delicacies or alcoholic beverages. However, in some cases this immersion in the local environment is not perceived as necessary or even desirable by the tourists. As indicated by Aramberri (2001), tourists may want 'the host to get lost'.

It is not usually the primary aim for beer tourists travelling to Spain for a German tourism experience to get to know Spanish culture and traditions. They want to enjoy traditional German beer in Spanish beach scenery. This lack of interest in the local culture is not a novel

phenomenon. The view of mass tourists as consumers that are satisfied by having superficial experiences of other peoples and other places
has been prevailing for decades (MacCannell 1999). But to what extent
does the lack of local awareness constitute a superficial and unauthentic
experience? In the specific form of beer tourism examined in this chapter,
the reality lies between these two different academic positions. Tourism
experiences are often a complex mixture of the familiar and the novel, and
tourists often display versatile behaviour (Ooi 2002). Mature destinations
melt and blend national traditions. This study shows that touristic places,
often criticized as 'touristic ghettos' or described as 'tourist bubbles'
(Jacobsen 2003), can be highly complex and hybrid cultural systems that
invite out-of-the-ordinary forms of entertainment, escapism and sojourn.
Tourists often lack the local knowledge to be able to differentiate between
what may be original, restored or totally artificial aspects of the destination. This artificiality may not even matter for the quality of the experience. As Prentice (2004) suggests, tourists may just as well prefer to be
'fooled' into the 'authentic' experience. Drinking beer and enacting beer
tourism play an important role in the creation of these 'artificial' destination environments.

By focusing on Bierstrasse on Majorca, this study shows the critical
importance of performance, place and the drinking environment for the
understanding of beer consumption. Its main objective is to present a
critical reflection on how the beer product is enacted and transformed
through tourism. First, the chapter explores the literature of alcohol
consumption and tourism. Second, by analysing the powerful aesthetics
and poetics of extreme touristic alcohol consumption, it challenges predominant discourses of authenticity and explores the consequences that
beer tourism may have for the destination and for the individual tourist.
It discusses how unethical behaviour related to beer drinking practices
in tourism environments may impact the legitimacy of the beer industry.
Insights of this study highlight the intensity of the experience of beer
tourism (an experience rooted in alcohol consumption and hybrid staged
national cultures) and reflect upon its attractiveness as an exercise of social
joint affirmation, masculinity and pleasure.

TOURISM BEER CULTURES

Alcohol consumption and tourism has been the theme of many different
studies throughout the years. Tourist drinking behaviour is often examined in four ways. First, tourists use drinking habits and choices of alcohol
as identity and socialization tools. Alcohol consumption can be seen as a

lifestyle marker, and increasingly independent and highly reflexive tourists may demand high quality brands or locally produced beverages at the destination. Second, alcohol consumption-related tourism experiences may be perceived as more or less authentic. Novel forms of special-interest tourism such as wine tourism in La Rioja or beer tourism in Bavaria are often described as being closer to the 'real' culture of the host community. Third, alternative forms of tourism can bring opportunities to the destinations in the form of the development of alcohol-related provision facilities and attractions, for example through the creation of routes, festivals and educational activities (Quadri-Felitti and Fiore 2012). Finally, tourist alcohol consumption is seen as an abnormal activity that reflects extreme forms of behaviour. This latest perspective combines both a sociological tradition that looks at alcohol consumption as a social problem to be dealt with (Hanson 1995 cited in Gee 2012; Gee and Jackson 2012) and a stream of research in tourism studies that examines disruptive and problematic forms of tourist behaviour (for example, studies in binge drinking and child prostitution) (Andrews et al. 2007). Unethical behaviour and negative stereotypes related to heavy drinking may impact on the legitimacy of firms and the tourism industry.

Lifestyle, Socialization and Identity

In countries where the population has traditionally consumed beer, such as Germany, Belgium and Denmark, the choice of brand and the way in which beer is consumed act as lifestyle markers. There is also a connection between specific forms of alcohol consumption and national identities (Edelheim and Edelheim 2011). German tourists bring their lifestyle and drinking practices to the destination. The encounter between tourists and residents can result in the adoption of tourists' behavioural and consumption habits by the local population. In tourism studies this phenomenon has been labelled 'the demonstration effect' (de Kadt 1979) and is the topic of a vast array of different studies (Fisher 2004). Changes in drinking cultures have been a substantial indicator of the impact tourism development has had on host communities. In his study of alcohol use in a Greek tourist town, Moore (1995) shows how the patterns of drinking by the locals have been altered by their exposure to tourists' preferences. For example, in the case of the Greek destination of Arachova this exposure resulted in an increasing beer culture that eventually supplanted the traditional drinking regime based on locally produced wine and ouzo-like liqueur (Moore 1995). There may also be changes in drinking behaviour among genders. According to Moore (1995), the bars and discos that opened to cater for tourists allowed the local women to drink and interact with men more freely.

While acting as tourists may seem attractive to local populations, it is also possible to find host communities that develop antagonistic behaviour towards tourists. Residents of mature Mediterranean destinations, such as Majorca, often manifest anti-touristic attitudes and opinions (Aguiló Pérez and Rosselló Nadal 2004). The cross-cultural meeting can also foster a sense of identity, a discovery of the satisfaction of being local as opposed to sharing the culture of the 'foreigners'. In the case of the Greek destination mentioned above, the increase in beer consumption resulted in locally produced alcoholic beverages such as wine becoming a sign of local identity for the residents (Moore 1995).

Food and drink are culturally rooted and central elements of social activities and public life. Leisure time is often related to drinking traditions (Pettigrew and Charters 2010). In many Western societies alcohol consumption is used as a symbolic marker of the shift from work to leisure time (for example, the Friday evening beer tradition in Danish workplaces marks the beginning of the weekend) or from 'duty' time to free, private time (such as drinking when arriving home after a long day at work). The beer gardens in Germany or public houses (pubs) in the United Kingdom are public leisure spaces but, most importantly, they are a frame of reference for the set of practices that constitute a beer culture – rituals, traditions, social interactions, symbols and specific aesthetics. Larsen (1997) presents pubs as places that shape a public sphere centred on beer, where people can connect with each other and escape from the pressures of work and an increasingly individualized lifestyle (Beck and Beck-Gernsheim 2002). Studies have also suggested that in venues such as bars and pubs the social interaction is in some cases more important than the actual alcohol consumption (Pettigrew and Charters 2010).

Tourism time is social time. Alcohol consumption helps individuals to communicate desired images to specific and generalized others (Pettigrew and Charters 2010). Without the pressure of everyday duties tourists can indulge in drinking as a social activity. Social rituals differ from habits due to the strong social compulsion associated with them, in that participants are made to feel obligated to join in the rituals and are penalized if they do not carry them out. An example of a ritual in drinking cultures is the buying of rounds in Britain. Drinking rituals can also act as rites of passage into manhood (or adulthood). What to drink and how to drink become strong symbolic practices which convey social messages to friends, partners and significant others.

Social practices create a sense of community and are vehicles to express shared values, meanings and interests, but these practices can be used to block access to other social groups (Habermas 1989). Drinking rituals and traditions act as mechanisms of social inclusion and exclusion. This division can reflect gender differences – public leisure spaces for heavy drinking were often dominated by men – and also the traditional visitor–host divide in tourism (Larsen 1997; Moore 1995). Drinking cultures represent wider societal values. These values structure the institutional environments in which breweries operate.

A study of the Majorcan tourist resort Magaluf (Andrews et al. 2007) shows a link between heavy drinking and a general magnification of sexual sensibilities. Sexual and pornographic images and other references to sexual intercourse are abundantly displayed in tourist venues and souvenir shops. In the case of Magaluf, drinking rituals appear to be closely related to sexual gratification:

> One feature of hotel entertainment, for example, is a game involving male contestants having sangria poured down their throats until they can swallow no more, a challenge to kiss as many people in the audience as possible within 45 seconds, and then a demand that they show constraint by gurgling water whilst in the process of singing a nursery rhyme. (Andrews et al. 2007, p. 257)

Authenticity and Gender

Tourist areas characterized by extreme alcohol consumption and outrageous tourist behaviour, such as that exhibited on Sunny Beach or in Magaluf, can make these destinations comparable to social ghettos ruled by different cultural norms which are kept isolated from the host communities. Jacobsen (2003) indicates how tourism destinations in the Mediterranean often adopt the structure of a 'tourist bubble'. The staging and isolation of tourism is also suggested in MacCannell's theory of staged authenticity. He uses Erving Goffman's theory of social structural change (1999, pp. 92–6) to explain how tourists increasingly 'act out reality'. This conceptualization of tourism as 'theatre' and 'role playing' is also present in Jafari's (1987) idea of the destination as a stage. According to MacCannell, tourism consumption is essentially performative. This performance includes a front (the staged show for the sake of tourists) and the back (where the residents' intimate and real lives unfold). The front is a fake or pseudo representation of the 'true' reality of place and culture (the back). However, experiences perceived as fake by residents or cultural experts may still constitute an authentic experience for the tourists.

Tourists do not only pursue objective authenticity such as that disclosed in cultural canons, but invest time and money searching for a symbolic authentic experience (Wang 2000) as anticipated in their imagination. Extreme forms of alcohol consumption can be despised by residents and still be perceived as individually and existentially authentic by tourists. Some of these extreme forms of touristic behaviour are often related to feelings of liminality, a state of mind that leads people to behave differently away from home by, for example, being more adventurous or adopting uncharacteristic or 'anti-self' attitudes.

A review of studies in the field of beer tourism indicates a strong link between identity, gender and beer consumption (Duarte Alonso 2011; Gee 2012; Larsen 1997). Some tourist attractions have been developed to cater for gender-specific desires, for example the sexual needs of male tourists in sex tourism regions (Wearing et al. 2010). Gee and Jackson (2012), in their interesting study of the New Zealand beer Speight's advertising campaigns, show how beer consumption appears to be one of the last bastions where masculine identity and a confirmation of male power and brotherhood are embodied and encouraged. A similar observation has also been made in sport studies (Jackson and McKenzie 2007 cited in Gee and Jackson 2012) and by Pettigrew and Charters (2010) that the use of promotional girls hired to wear uniforms branding imported beer and to mingle with the drinkers was now a common sight in Hong Kong venues. Edelheim and Edelheim's (2011) study of female travelogs in Australia indicates that drinking cultures during travel are often constructed in a gendered way and that there are differences between masculine and feminine discourses. Besides gender, age, educational level and marital status can also have an impact on tourists' drinking habits (Jingxue et al. 2005). Alcohol consumption is a symbolic act that not only encourages stronger social ties but helps to communicate our status in a specific social setting (Gee and Jackson 2012).

Developing the Tourism Destination

Alcohol consumption is a means to revitalize or foster the economic development of touristic areas (Pechlaner et al. 2009). This is mostly obvious in the case of wine tourism, where whole regional policies have been developed in order to cater for the increasing demand for wine consumption and wine-related activities among tourists (examples of this include La Rioja in Spain or the Barolo region in Italy). Although more seldom, beer tourism development is becoming increasingly relevant (Duarte Alonso 2011). Tourism organizations in Bavaria, Germany, have actively pursued the strengthening of the collaboration between tourism and the beer industry, aiming to transform beer services into attractive aspects of the destination (Pechlaner et al. 2009). These cases are examples of the touristification and staging of traditionally non-touristic agricultural and industrial settings – the back stage is moving up front. Duarte Alonso's

(2011) study of beer tourism development in Alabama, USA, explores how microbrewing and beer tourism are opportunities to enhance visitors' travel experiences. Tourists perceive craft beer culture as being unique and authentic in opposition to commercialized, mass-produced beer. Other scholars have also suggested a relationship between the growth of micro-breweries and a renewed taste for craft beer and a stronger feeling of community and identity in the host communities (Duarte Alonso 2011; Larsen 1997). In the case of Majorca, the feeling of identity in the local communities is related to the extensive development of wine tourism that has taken place on the island during the last two decades. The development of this new tourist product has been led by entrepreneurs who, while pursuing financial success and an increased number of visitors, have also engaged in what Ateljevic and Doorme (2003, p. 139) call 'the active reaffirmation of the local'.

Outrageous Tourism and Legitimacy

Scholars have also analysed tourists' alcohol consumption as a symptom of irresponsible touristic behaviour. Often this 'bad' behaviour is seen as a consequence of forms of mass tourism, while alternative tourism is said to represent a more sustainable type of travel. Many scholars have focused on ethical alternatives to the supposedly damaging practices of mass tourism; Wheeller (2003, p. 230) indicates a 'spate of articles and books advocating the ethics of the new tourism and urging the tourist to behave correctly'. Charter tourism is often related to alimentary and alcoholic excess, an image that is cultivated by tour operators (Andrews et al. 2007). Also, easy access to abundant and cheap alcohol is an important aspect of destination decision-making (Edelheim and Edelheim 2011). Visual explorative studies of drinking destinations show alcohol-related behaviour resulting in exaggerated camaraderie, sexuality and house-party like familiarity (Stringer and McAllister 2012). In the Spanish media these forms of tourism have been described as *drunken tourism*. Drunken tourism is often associated with erotic or sexual experiences (Andrews et al. 2007). The association of the exotic and the erotic in tourism helps reproduce and enhance specific gender stereotypes (Aitchison and Reeves 1998). Tourism marketing is often found to portray women as sex objects and a line of research adopting feminist or critical theory perspectives has suggested a dominance of a masculine bias in tourism experiences (Wearing et al. 2010).

Drunken tourism is portrayed as an outrageous form of tourism in international media and academic research. The connection between immoderate and unethical touristic behaviour and beer brands may result in negative legitimacy for these specific brands. According to Kostova and Zaheer (1999), multinational enterprises doing business abroad have to face a liability of 'foreignness' due to the use of stereotypes and different standards of judging foreign versus domestic firms. In specific national markets there is a tendency to use stereotypical judgments based on the legitimacy or illegitimacy of certain types of organizations (for example, the ways in which North American fast food chains such as McDonalds and Kentucky Fried Chicken were targeted by anti-globalization activists in Europe in the 1990s). The loss of legitimacy of one or several firms in a specific field could result in an external spillover of illegitimacy for the whole industry.

BIERSTRASSE

Bierstrasse is located on the Spanish island of Majorca. Majorca, situated in the Mediterranean Sea, is a mature holiday destination area visited by people from many countries and social strata. From the 1960s onwards, Majorca embraced what is commonly known as 'the sun and sand tourism model' (Knowles and Curtis 1999). In 2012, Majorca received more than 12 million tourists, over 9.9 million being international arrivals and over 3.6 million coming from Germany; 99.6 per cent of German tourists are leisure and holiday travellers (Conselleria de Turisme i Sports 2011). The vast growth of the tourism industry in the Balearic Islands was made possible not only by hundreds of Spanish entrepreneurs, but also by relationships with foreign tour operators who carried out the promotion and sales necessary to capture the European market (Amer i Fernàndez 2006). Holiday packages supplied by tour operators have been the typical option for Majorca's international holidaymakers. Some of the most important tour operators are major players in the German travel market, such as TUI.

The origin of the area is also related to the birth and development of some of the most important Spanish hospitality firms (such as Sol Meliá and Barceló), which began their entrepreneurial activity there. But after the golden period of the first decades, Palma Beach experienced an increasing decay during the 1990s. The competitive model of charter travellers and sun and sand tourism was being increasingly challenged by the emergence of new destinations like Thailand or Bulgaria and by the offering of new tourism products such as spa and wellness tourism. At the millennium, however, the destination of Majorca saw a change in its competitive strategy. The island has since seen a considerable increase in independent tourists. This is partly owing to the expansion of scheduled air services to the island. The airline Air Berlin, for example, established a hub in the airport of Palma de Majorca, expanding the availability of direct flights between German cities and the island.

Moreover, Majorca has experienced diversification among accommodation suppliers, an increased variety of tourism products (including spa and wellness centres and golf) and an expansion of second home ownership. It has however proven to be difficult to change the product offering of Palma Beach. Transformations in the tourism market have resulted in an increased awareness by the destination management organizations as well as the local entrepreneurs and during the first decade of the millennium the Balearic government and local authorities developed several initiatives to restore and improve the quality of this destination.

Palma Beach is one of the oldest tourism destinations on the island. This area in particular, traditionally a place characterized by its fishing harbours, large beach and small houses where the local population of Palma and the nearby village of Lluchmajor spent their summer holidays, experienced a fast tourism development in the late 1960s and 1970s. Large hotels were built at the seafront and restaurants, bars and other types of services were established to cater to the needs of a rapidly growing tourist population. Palma Beach is a large destination and in 2010 it had over eight million overnight stays, while the tourism expenditure for the same period was €524 563 805 (Palma Beach Hotels' Association 2010).

Bierstrasse is an iconic destination located at the centre of the bay. It was created and developed by Mallorquin entrepreneurs during the 1970s. Bierstrasse comprises both a single street and a larger geographical area that stretches for 1 km along the seaside. I have chosen to use the concept of 'destination' for the whole area of the Bierstrasse and the concept of 'tourist attraction' for its most important venues and sites. The destination has four main attractions and several touristic and spatial markers. The attractions are Schinkestrasse, which includes the Bierkönig, a large and very popular beer venue, the surroundings and facilities of a large open-air discotheque 'Mega Park' (popularly known as 'The Abbey' because its aesthetic resembles that of a Gothic church), the iconic beer street and the beach promenade where the 'balnearios' (open-air bars situated on the beach) are located. The Bierstrasse area comprises the space between balnearios five and seven; the most iconic and symbolic of the balnearios being the one at the centre of the area: 'Balneario Six'. The number, pronounced as 'sex' in German, gives this balneario a very specific connotation (see Figure 12.1). Balneario 'six' is also the name of a controversial German TV documentary which describes extreme forms of tourist behaviour in the Bierstrasse area.

Source: Author's own photo.

Figure 12.1   Balneario Six on Palma Beach

STUDY METHODS

This chapter examines beer tourism and how this phenomenon transforms tourism practices and the world of beer. A case study approach was
considered appropriate to undertake this task. Case studies are used to
investigate complex contemporary phenomena where the organizational
or sociocultural context is relevant (Veal 2006; Yin 2003). Case studies
allow for gaining insights into specific and complex social phenomena.
Limitations of case studies include a lower level of generalization when
compared to other methodological approaches. This study does not aim to
provide a general or global overview of beer tourism but to present a rich
and detailed analysis of the complexities of a sociocultural phenomenon
in a specific tourism setting. This case analysis is used as a springboard
to critically reflect upon the theories that structure the knowledge field of
drinking/alcohol tourism.

Based on the literature review and the researcher's knowledge of the
topic, several different destinations were identified as drinking destinations. Some examples in Europe include Sunny Beach in Bulgaria,
Magaluf in Majorca, Playa del Inglés in Gran Canaria and Lloret de Mar
and Calella in Catalonia. Bierstrasse in Majorca shares many similarities
with these destinations, such as attracting young holidaymakers, being

located on the seaside and offering drunken circuits. Bierstrasse was considered to be an appropriate case for this study because its history, aesthetics and drinking culture are traditionally linked to beer consumption.

The methods used for the examination of the case were fieldwork and observation. Extreme drinking, vandalism and rowdy behaviour may be considered as tourism activities that lie on the margins of conventional, accepted morality. In these types of situations observation is likely to provide more information than traditional interviews or focus groups (Veal 2006, p. 178). People are unlikely to reveal to researchers their extreme forms of behaviour; however, choosing observation as a key method poses questions about the ethical use of the data and the right to privacy of those observed. All the audiovisual material was recorded in public venues and to avoid identification no personal data on the tourists has been included. Furthermore, to gain broader knowledge on the management of the destination the researchers conducted an in-depth interview with Immaculada de Benito, a crucial planner of the area. In the spring of 2012, de Benito was the manager of the Mallorca Hotel Business Federation. This organization represents 26 hotel associations and a total of 859 hotel firms. She was previously the manager of the Palma Beach Hotel Association and was responsible for the regional governmental initiative to develop the destination. Other forms of empirical data were gathered using a documentary analysis of the destination management organization's reports.

To identify differences between low and high season patterns at the destination the fieldwork took place during two periods of time, at the beginning of April – the low season – and at the end of July and beginning of August, the period with the highest tourist demand on the destination. The observation consisted of repeat visits to the Bierstrasse area, visual data collection in the form of photographs and videos and brief interviews with eight service providers. These interviews consisted of short questions to gain insights into the issues of host–guest relationships, alcohol offering and tourists' drinking behaviour. The researcher approached the service providers at their workplaces and the interviews were not recorded in order to allow for a feeling of familiarity. The majority of these interviews were conducted in Spanish. Service providers on Bierstrasse included, among others, waitresses, hotel receptionists, taxi drivers and public relations workers. The lack of recording may be seen as a limitation to the reliability of these data, but the comments and answers were immediately written down after the interviews had taken place. The researcher collected visual data of the spatial and functional use of the attractions and different sites at the destination. These included photos of venues, alcohol providers, tourism provision (hotels, shops and so on), recreational spaces, signs and tourists. Short videos were recorded to document the level of noise in the area and specific behavioural patterns of drinking tourists, such as loud singing/shouting, and to gain a general overview of the atmosphere at the most important attractions.

ENACTING BEER TOURISM

The Server and the Served: Staged Nationalism and Performed Masculinity

To enter Bierstrasse is like entering a stage. MacCannell (1999) mentions that tourism attractions are characterized by the dialectics of authenticity. These dialectics are represented by attractions having a front and a back stage, the front being where tourists are catered for and the back where the locals have their lives and display their 'real' sociocultural traditions. On Bierstrasse the front is the overall, dominant reality and the back is absent. In the spatial area of the destination, residual elements of 'the back' can be seen in only a few traditional Spanish summer houses – lonely representations of another era that are now trapped between large hotels and drinking venues – and in the few spaces reserved for the service providers. Beer culture and German beer brands provide the theme for staging the experience. The attractions of the destination use breweries as sponsors and their logos and signs are ubiquitous in the area. There are beer names on the signs of bars and leisure venues and the design of the furniture and facilitating goods resemble those used in traditional beer gardens in Germany. Drinking venues are characterized as having 'open-kitchen' facilities and there are only minor physical divisions between the environment of the workers and that of the tourists. Beer tourism servers are immersed and perform on-stage. Servers dress and look like customers in casual summer clothing (such as T-shirts and shorts) or disco outfits (for example, public relations workers wearing short 'sexy' dresses). It is often difficult to differentiate between the servers and the served.

The mimetism between server and served is also present in the form of communication. Workers at the drinking venues will often approach new customers in German instead of Spanish. It was also observed that German was in most cases their mother tongue, while some had a poor basic knowledge of the local languages (Spanish or Catalan), and if the tourist did not speak German most preferred to communicate in English.

Language is a cultural marker and the use of German in the service provision indicates that beer tourism personnel are culturally closer to the tourists than to the host community. It is a German drinking experience staged and played by 'German-like' servers. Language dominance draws a cultural border around the 'tourist-bubble' (Jacobsen 2003). This dominance is also prevalent on menus, displays giving information of beer offerings at restaurants, and signs on discotheques, nightclubs and souvenir shops. De Benito characterizes Bierstrasse as:

> a type of outdoor leisure model [. . .] based on beer consumption, but not only that type of consumption, and food. It is German food and drinks. It reproduces the German model of leisure [. . .] They like to sing and dance outdoors and this German model has prevailed [. . .] Locals go there as spectators, because there is a language barrier. The waiters speak in German, the menus are in German [. . .] also the music is not the music repertoire that is used in the Spanish discotheques.

Staged Nationalism

As suggested by Prentice (2004), familiarity is an important element of the tourism experience. Communication and signage as well as the design of the beer venues on Bierstrasse are developed to provide German tourists with a feeling of being at home away from home (see Figure 12.2). The use of German beer culture also extends to the music and food offered at the venues. German popular music is mixed with the latest summer hits. Sausages and other forms of traditional German food are offered on menus and photographic displays and are combined with a few well-known Spanish gastronomic dishes such as paella, but there are no Mallorquin

Source: Author's own photo.

Figure 12.2   Signage at Bierstrasse

specialities offered in the area. German flags hang at the entrances of drinking establishments, sometimes alone and sometimes combined with Spanish or European flags. Drinking venues have large TV screens displaying sports events broadcasted by German TV channels. In the summer months thousands of German tourists gather in the Bierstrasse area to see their national football team competing in the European or World Championships. At the time of the observation, the venues were broadcasting the performances of German athletes in the London Olympics.

The beer tourism of Bierstrasse is very different from the cases of Bavaria or Alabama introduced in the literature review (Pechlaner et al. 2009; Duarte Alonso 2011). It does not enhance feelings of community or identity among the residents and it is not linked to the touristification of beer production settings. On the contrary, its 'raison d'être' is to promote feelings of community and identity among the visitors. By combining drinking, leisure and sport the destination provides the scene to celebrate German nationalism. De Benito mentions that the model of tourism developed in the 1960s that lies at the origin of Bierstrasse did not aim to provide experiences of otherness or authentic local cultures, but was established to imitate tourists' national cultures by, for example, replicating beer gardens in Palma Beach or British pubs in Magaluf (see Figure 12.2). However, beer tourists in Majorca are not only seduced by the familiar (as suggested by Prentice 2004), drinking tourists seek novelty, excitement and a different experience from their daily lives at home. They obtain these not by approaching the world of the residents, as suggested by Jafari (1987) or MacCannell (1999), but by experiencing their own cultural background being transformed in a theatrical and excessive way thanks to touristification.

In beer tourism the dialectics of authenticity are not to be found in the destination but between the destination and the rest of the island. The dialectical relationship of host–guest culture is instead a staged consensus; the bubble is an immersing experience in which both the served and the servers are embedded. The host and the guest look alike, the difference being the leisure–work divide, while the 'real host' – that is the Majorcan local community – is absent in the staging of the experience. The host in this type of destination is an 'abstract' host and it is present in two forms: in the form of ownership – the entrepreneurs owning the venues on Bierstrasse are Spanish (personal communication, Immaculada de Benito), and in the form of the environmental and sociocultural background of the island. The 'back' is mostly to be found elsewhere on the island (for example, in some neighbourhoods in the city of Palma, traditional service providers or in small mountain villages). The local community and culture is absent in the spatial and aesthetic organization of the beer tourism destination. The front represents a stage, and the show that is being performed every summer night is the enactment of beer drinking tourism. The locals, as de Benito mentions, become 'spectators' in their own home.

Performed Masculinity

There is a clear exception to the mimetism between servers and served and the distinction is gender and sex based. As Moore (1995) suggests in his study of alcohol consumption, in beer tourism there is also a relationship between drinking practices and gender and sex. While waiters, public relations workers and other service providers mingle with the crowd, the go-go/dancing girls dressed in 'sexy' underwear are displayed on top of big beer barrels (see Figure 12.3). This specific display sets the stage for one of the social practices of beer tourism. Groups of young male tourists, often only dressed in swim clothes, drink and sing around these barrels (see Figure 12.3). The dancers will change barrel after a while and tourists will take turns climbing on top of the barrel to be photographed by the rest of their peers while touching or hugging the dancer. The abovementioned practice is linked to a historical male dominance of public leisure spaces for heavy drinking (Larsen 1997).

Source: Author's own photo.

Figure 12.3   Male tourists and go-go girls in the Bierkönig

The tourists' act of hugging half-naked young women appears as an exer-cise of masculinity and 'manhood', resembling the imaginary and fantasies of the last bastions of masculinity described by Gee and Jackson (2012) in their study of Australian beer, or the use of beer promotion girls in Hong Kong venues (Pettigrew and Charters 2010). Beer tourists do not only 'enact' masculinity, they memorialize it. Beer tourists' photographing of masculinity is a social act. Tourists stand and pose for an audience. Beer tourism entails 'out of the ordinary' social performances of masculinity and heterosexuality. Sex and alcohol consumption are closely related in the aesthetics of the destination. Souvenir shops offer T-shirts and beach towels with slogans such as 'Majorca triathlon: eating, drinking, fucking' that may be offensive for the residents. Similar to the findings of Andrews et al. (2007), the relevance of sex for the Bierstrasse experience is obvious in the display of pornographic images and sexual references in the inven-tories of souvenir shops (such as lighters depicting penises). Prostitution is often mentioned as one of the problems of the area by de Benito, and close to the main attractions there are a large number of night clubs offering striptease or other sexual performances. While tourist females can be seen in the beer venues, they are a minority. There are no male dancers address-ing heterosexual women and the venues do not include gay or lesbian performances either. Beer tourism is an exercise of staged masculinity. The activities observed in the Bierstrasse venues have a clear masculine bias (Wearing et al. 2010) which may help to reproduce and enhance specific gender stereotypes and forms of tourism that present women as sex objects and keep attractions as a male-dominated ghetto.

Group Drinking, Ritualization and Joint Affirmation

Another important ritual of beer tourism cultures is related to group drinking practices. Larsen (1997) suggests how drinking spaces are frames of reference for the making of rituals, traditions, symbols and specific aesthetics. On Bierstrasse, group drinking is a central touristic ritual. This form of alcohol consumption is characterized by groups of tourists sharing the same drink and drinking from a single large mug or bucket. Group drinking is an extreme form of alcohol consumption and often entails excessive/binge drinking. It transforms traditional drinking habits of beer consumption and drastically changes the scale and aesthetics of traditional German beer gardens. In a touristified environment taken-for-granted societal values are suspended and exchanged for a novel set of rules. Tourists on Bierstrasse go through a touristic socialization and education. They learn to codify and make sense of new norms and rituals of alcohol consumption.

Source: Author's own photo.

Figure 12.4   Group drinking in Mega Park

The alcoholic offering, pricing and service provision of the Bierstrasse area is adapted to this extreme form of drinking. The supply of alcoholic beverages in the area is characterized by a mix of traditional German beer, which is still the dominant alcoholic drink, with a large majority of German beer brands available such as Krombacher, Veltins and Oberbayern, international cocktails (mojitos, cosmopolitans and so on) and specific offers that cater to group drinking tourists. The latest offering, which can be seen in Figure 12.4, is one of the destination's most popular products.

While group drinking provides tourists with large amounts of alcohol at low prices, this could also have been achieved by consuming alcohol on an individual basis. What makes group drinking especially relevant in the context of tourism practices is that it entails an exercise of joint affirmation, social enjoyment and trust. Tourists sit close to each other or in circles and, using long colourful drinking straws, drink from a common jug or plastic bucket. The long drinking straws are displayed as decorative elements in the venues, used and played with by the tourists (for example, using them to make funny hats) and are a symbolic element of this specific drinking culture. Similar to the culture of buying 'rounds' in the British pubs, group drinking shows how beer tourism creates a stage where people connect with each other and where modern and post-modern individualistic lifestyles (Beck and Beck-Gernsheim 2002) are replaced by communality and social interaction. The success of the Bierstrasse is that it provides a public sphere where this exercise of joint affirmation and escapism can take place. Drinking tourism performativity is authentic, not as an objective cultural authenticity related to the local environment, but as a symbolic authentic experience (Wang 2000) nurtured by tourists' fantasies and imaginations. It is an experience that involves all senses, and is not only to be gazed upon (Urry 2002), but enacted and embodied.

Group drinking has a dark side and is a problematic form of tourist behaviour. Tourists drinking on Bierstrasse are often despised by the local residents. This type of extreme alcohol consumption often results in health problems for the tourists and there are several medical centres providing services 24 hours a day alongside the drinking venues. Local authorities complain about the expenses and inconveniences related to heavy drinking and the destination is actively involved in public campaigns to encourage responsible drinking behaviour (personal communication, Imma de Benito, 2012). An example of how authorities try to embellish tourist drinking behaviour can be seen in Figure 12.5. The campaign tries to discourage tourists from group drinking and leaving garbage on the beach.

Vandalism and rowdy behaviour are also observed in the area. Music

Source: Author's own photo.

Figure 12.5   Campaign to prevent group drinking on the beach

is not allowed in open-air facilities after 12 midnight; however, during the fieldwork service providers such as hotel receptionists complained that they experienced loud behaviour and music until 4–5 a.m. Heavy drinking is also closely related to novel forms of extreme tourist behaviour such as 'balconing' – tourists trying to jump between hotel balconies or from the balconies to the swimming pool – which has resulted in the death of several tourists in Majorca. While beer tourism brings tourists to the destination and has proven to be a highly resilient and successful form of tourism, it is not desired or endorsed by regional authorities. The success of drinking tourism is seen as a problem that has a negative impact on the tourism demands of families or seniors in the area. According to Imma de Benito, excessive drinking behaviour in the destination:

> is really deplorable. This is people that drink for the sake of drinking. There are even competitions on the Internet on how much one can drink. However, it is also true that there are venues that promote this with very cheap prices and offer very cheap alcohol [. . .] This results in 'balconing' which is an effect of heavy drinking. They destroy the rooms of the hotels, throw the furniture in the rooms out the windows [. . .] Furthermore they share it on social media and as a result the image of the destination really suffers, and it is very difficult to come out of this situation.

The culture and aesthetics of the world of German beer drinking activities are the central elements in the culture of heavy drinking and outrageous tourist behaviour at this Spanish destination. German breweries such as Krombacher, Veltins or Oberbayern provide the visual imagery of drunken tourism. German beer brands are representatives of outrageous drunken tourism in Majorca, thereby fuelling a potentially negative external spillover effect for the whole beer industry. It is often seen that global crises relating to the legitimacy of multinational firms explode due to a critical incident (Kostova and Zaheer 1999). The death of a tourist due to balconing or heavy drinking on Bierstrasse could become a critical incident for the beer industry. The increased use of social media by tourists may further expand the possibilities of such a legitimacy crisis.

Extreme drinking practices and rituals become strong symbolic practices which convey social messages to friends and nurture the expectations and dreams of other tourists. The theatrical display of German drinking culture provides tourists with a familiar environment, but it also establishes a visual divide between 'them' and 'us' (the local population versus the tourists). Besides the contact with a few service providers, no interaction between the host population and the groups of drinking tourists was noted. Some Spanish service providers, such as hotel receptionists and taxi drivers, show feelings of alienation and divide in their description of the work environment of beer tourism. A taxi driver, while looking at the public relations workers and tourists interacting outside the attraction of Mega Park, commented on his work: 'I am here waiting . . . [shaking his head in antipathy] They are just Germans . . . Germans.'

CONCLUSION

The motivation behind this study was to critically explore the relationship between beer consumption and tourism. Through the lens provided by the Bierstrasse case, this chapter shows that beer cultures have the potential to be at the centre of the making of a highly resilient and attractive tourist destination, but also to foster a kind of problematic tourism with negative consequences for local communities. For more than four decades, Bierstrasse has staged tourism experiences for different generations of German tourists. It has become an iconic destination made from the fantasies, imaginations and wishes surrounding beer tourism.

Beer consumption is transformed and magnified by tourism. Tourism as an activity that promises out-of-the-ordinary experiences reshapes beer cultures into extreme staged beer-related performances. The beer drinking venues resemble large theatrical arenas; the tourists on the stage perform drinking scenes and games that follow rituals and scripts of social performance. These scenes are broadcast for physical and virtual audiences. The local residents are both spectators of these extreme drinking shows and administrators that benefit economically while still trying to maintain some kind of control over and monitoring of a 'wild' form of tourist behaviour. Beer tourism is a very intense form of experience, one that immerses the tourist in a state of release and liberation of the constraints often imposed by modern societies, but it is also a form of escapism and egocentric practice which is grounded in a lack of personal accountability and an irresponsible attitude towards the local culture and the well-being of the residents.

This study shows that alcoholic products come alive and get their value and meaning not only from the functional or aesthetic features related to beer production (or the single beer product), but increasingly through the enacting and embodiment of drinking cultures. It is through the social interactions, the sensual and embodied activities of leisure spaces and the drinking rituals that the beer product becomes alive and realizes its value potential, not just as a simple alcoholic drink but as a catalyst for socialization, staged masculinity, nationalism and sensuality.

As seen in the analysis of this case, unethical behaviour at the Bierstrasse venues is often perceived as being representative of a specific nationality, in this case German. Negative stories of unrestrained, violent or unethical behaviour among beer tourists combined with a dominance of German beer products offered on Bierstrasse may have a negative impact on the legitimacy and reputation that German breweries have in the Spanish market and nurture negative stereotypes for the industry. German breweries should consider the illegitimacy that results from their participation in Bierstrasse's extreme consumption practices and become increasingly concerned not only about how beer is produced and sold, but about how it is consumed and enacted.

REFERENCES

Aguiló Pérez, E. and J. Rosselló Nadal (2004), 'Host community perceptions: a cluster analysis', *Annals of Tourism Research*, **32** (4), 925–41.

Aitchison, C. and C. Reeves (1998), 'Gendered (bed)spaces: the culture and commerce of women only tourism', in C. Aitchison and F. Jordan (eds), *Gender, Space and Identity: Leisure, Culture and Commerce*, Eastbourne: Leisure Studies Association, pp. 47–68.

Amer i Fernàndez, J. (2006), *Turisme i política: L'empresariat hoteler de mallorca*, Palma: Edicions Documenta Balear.

Andrews, H., L. Roberts and T. Selwyn (2007), 'Hospitality and eroticism', *International Journal of Culture, Tourism and Hospitality Research*, **1** (3), 247–62.

Aramberri, J. (2001), 'The host should get lost: paradigms in the tourism theory', *Annals of Tourism Research*, **28** (3), 738–61.

Ateljevic, I. and S. Doorne (2003), 'Unpacking the local: a cultural analysis of tourism entrepreneurship in Murter, Croatia', *Tourism Geographies*, **5** (2), 123–50.

Beck, U. and E. Beck-Gernsheim (2002), *Individualization*, London and Thousand Oaks, CA: Sage.

Conselleria de Turisme i Sports (2011), *El turisme a les illes balears. anuari de turisme, 2011*, accessed 10 December 2012 at www.caib.es/sacmicrofront/archivopub.do?ctrl=MCRST865ZI128370&id=128370.

de Kadt, E. (1979), 'Social planning for tourism in the developing countries', *Annals of Tourism Research*, **6** (1), 36–48.

Duarte Alonso, A. (2011), 'Opportunities and challenges in the development of micro-brewing and beer tourism: a preliminary study from Alabama', *Tourism Planning & Development*, **8** (4), 415–31.

Edelheim, J.R. and S.M. Edelheim (2011), 'Sober on the holiday – is it un-Australian?', *Annals of Leisure Research*, **14** (1), 22–42. doi:10.1080/11745398. 2011.575044.

Fisher, D. (2004), 'The demonstration effect revisited', *Annals of Tourism Research*, **31** (2), 428–46.

Gee, S.J.S. (2012), 'Leisure corporations, beer brand culture, and the crisis of masculinity: the Speight's "Southern man" advertising campaign', *Leisure Studies*, **31** (1), 83–102.

Gee, S. and S.J. Jackson (2012), 'Leisure corporations, beer brand culture, and the crisis of masculinity: the Speight's "Southern man" advertising campaign', *Leisure Studies*, **31** (1), 83–102.

Habermas, J. (1989), *Theory of Communicative Action 2*, Boston, MA: Beacon Press.

Haldrup, M. and J. Larsen (2010), *Tourism, Performance and the Everyday: Consuming the Orient*, London: Routledge.

Jackson, R. (2005), 'Converging cultures: converging gazes', in D. Crouch, R. Jackson and F. Thompson (eds), *The Media and the Tourist Imagination: Converging Cultures*, New York: Routledge, pp. 183–97.

Jacobsen, J.K.S. (2003), 'The tourist bubble and the Europeanisation of holiday travel', *Journal of Tourism and Cultural Change*, **1** (1), 71–87.

Jafari, J. (1987), 'Tourism models: the sociocultural aspects', *Tourism Management*, **8** (2), 151–9.

Jingxue, J.Y., A.C. Liping, M.M. Alastair and S. Linton (2005), 'An analysis of wine festival attendees' motivations: a synergy of wine, travel and special events?', *Journal of Vacation Marketing*, **11** (41), 41–58.

Knowles, T. and S. Curtis (1999), 'The market viability of European mass tourist destinations. A post-stagnation life-cycle analysis', *International Journal of Tourism Research*, **1** (2), 87–96.

Kostova, T. and S. Zaheer (1999), 'Organizational legitimacy under conditions of complexity: the case of the multinational enterprise', *Academy of Management Review*, **24** (1), 64–81.

Larsen, C.K. (1997), 'Relax and have a homebrew: beer, the public sphere, and (re)invented traditions', *Food and Foodways: Explorations in the History and Culture of Human Nourishment*, **7** (4), 265–88.

Larsen, J., J. Urry and K.W. Axhausen (2007), 'Networks and tourism: mobile social life', *Annals of Tourism Research*, **34** (1), 244–62.

MacCannell, D. (1999), *The Tourist: A New Theory of the Leisure Class*, Berkeley: University of California Press.

Moore, R.S. (1995), 'Gender and alcohol use in a Greek tourist town', *Annals of Tourism Research*, **22** (2), 300–13.

Munar, A.M. and C.S. Ooi (2012), 'The truth of the crowds: social media and the heritage experience', in L. Smith, E. Waterton and S. Watson (eds), *The Cultural Moment in Tourism*, London: Routledge, pp. 255–73.

Ooi, C.S. (2002), *Cultural Tourism and Tourism Cultures: The Business of Mediating Experiences in Copenhagen and Singapore*, Copenhagen: Copenhagen Business School Press.

Palma Beach Hotels' Association (2010), 'Impacto económico del turismo de la Playa de Palma'.

Pechlaner, H., F. Raich and E. Fischer (2009), 'The role of tourism organizations in location management: the case of beer tourism in Bavaria', *Tourism Review*, **64** (2), 28–40.

Pettigrew, S. and S. Charters (2010), 'Alcohol consumption motivations and behaviours in Hong Kong', *Asia Pacific Journal of Marketing and Logistics*, **22** (2), 210–21.

Prebesen, N., K. Skallerud and J.S. Chen (2011), 'Tourist motivation with sun and sand destinations: satisfaction and the wom-effect', *Journal of Travel and Tourism Marketing*, **27** (8), 858–73.

Prentice, R. (2004), 'Tourist familiarity and imagery', *Annals of Tourism Research*, **31** (4), 923–45.

Quadri-Felitti, D. and A.M. Fiore (2012), 'Experience economy constructs as a framework for understanding wine tourism', *Journal of Vacation Marketing*, **18** (3), 3–15.

Stringer, B. and J. McAllister (2012), 'Fluorescent heart of Magaluf', accessed 10 December 2012 at upcommons.upc.edu/revistes/bitstream/2099/12248/1/C_195_3.pdf, pp. 1–9.

Urry, J. (2002), *The Tourist Gaze*, 2nd ed., London: Sage.

Veal, A.J. (2006), *Research Methods for Leisure and Tourism: A Practical Guide*, 3rd ed., New York: Prentice Hall.

Wang, N. (2000), *Tourism and Modernity: A Sociological Analysis*, Oxford: Elsevier.

Wearing, S., D. Stevenson and T. Young (2010), *Tourist Cultures: Identity, Place and the Traveller*, London: Sage.

Wheeller, B. (2003), 'Alternative tourism – a deceptive ploy', in C. Cooper (ed.), *Classic Reviews in Tourism*, Clevedon: Channel View, pp. 227–34.

Yin, R.K. (2003), *Case Study Research: Design and Methods*, 3rd ed., Thousand Oaks, CA: Sage Publications.

Index